artibus et historiae

an art anthology

IN THIS ISSUE SPECIAL ARTICLES IN HONOR OF
RACHEL WISCHNITZER

IRSA

nr 17 (IX)
vienna
1988

EDITORIAL BOARD:

A-1030 WIEN, KRUMMGASSE 3/18, AUSTRIA, Tel. 0043/222/827197

PUBLISHER:

IRSA VERLAG GMBH

A-1130 WIEN, AUHOFSTR. 112/5, AUSTRIA

PRINTER:

RAUCHDRUCK Ges.m.b.H. & Co. KG

A-6040 INNSBRUCK, KUGELFANGWEG 15

LAYOUT:

MARIA BOGNA GRABSKA

N
7415
A78
1988

DISTRIBUTION AND SUBSCRIPTIONS:

IRSA VERLAG GMBH

A-1130 WIEN, AUHOFSTR. 112/5, AUSTRIA

DISTRIBUTOR FOR ITALY:

LIBRERIA COMMISSIONARIA SANSONI (LICOSA) S.p.A.

50121 FIRENZE, VIA LAMARMORA, 45

ISBN 3-900731-06-3

Editor-in-Chief:

JÓZEF GRABSKI

Advisory Committee:

artibus et historiae nr 17, 1988

IN THIS ISSUE SPECIAL ARTICLES IN HONOR OF RACHEL WISCHNITZER

Contents:

———————— * ————————

Preface

Rachel Wischnitzer's career is extraordinary for its length and she herself for the breadth of her interests. Her first publication, an article on synagogue architecture, appeared in 1913; her latest, on Picasso's *Guernica*, was published in this journal in 1985. In the years between, she has written original studies on manuscript illuminations, printed books, iconography and contemporary art, and has authored innumerable reviews of exhibitions and published works. She has been an art historian, architectural historian, an editor and critic, and a museum curator. Rachel Wischnitzer is also a witness to the art culture and intellectual life of a world that has largely disappeared.

The present collection of essays was gathered to honor her lifetime of achievement and to reflect the varied subjects of her writings. One of her major interests, the ancient synagogue paintings of Dura Europos, discovered in 1932, is the focus of Joseph Gutmann's essay, which examines their possible influence on later art. Gabriel Sed-Rajna notes Rachel Wischnitzer's prescient insight positing the existence of a Jewish biblical cycle like the Dura frescoes that was published a year before their discoverey, and then elaborates on the correctness of that vision. That Jewish models were the basis of some images in medieval Christian art has been the subject of many studies; that of Ursula Schubert concentrates on the representation of the Table of the Showbread.

Another aspect of Rachel Wischnitzer's scholarship is her identification of sources for the imagery found in Jewish art, a reflection of her lifelong effort to place Jewish art in the context of world art. One instance of this interest was her identification of the models for the engravings of the Amsterdam Haggadah printed in 1695. Kurt Schubert's contribution to this volume, in effect, carries this line of inquiry forward in time by investigating the Haggadah as a model for later manuscripts. Colin Eisler's discussion of the Christian uses of subjects drawn from the Hebrew Bible emphasizes the symbolic value attached to models.

As Joseph Gutmann writes in the "Introduction", Rachel Wischnitzer was, in her youth, one of the few women who trained as an architect. Her knowledge of this field became the basis for her studies of synagogue architecture, an interest reflected in Ralf Busch's essay on Constantin Uhde. Philip Fehl's article on the Vienna Stadttempel reaches beyond architectural history. The author appears as witness and participant in the pre-war world of European Jewry, a role assumed also by Moshe Barasch.

Rachel Wischnitzer pioneered in presenting to the public unknown material on Jewish art, both older and modern. Vivian Mann's essay continues that endeavor, while Ziva Meisels' discussion of Jankel Adler reflects Professor Wischnitzer's long involvement with contemporary art, dating to the 1920's.

No single volume could match the scope of Rachel Wischnitzer's career and interests. However, these essays suggest one common point, that her work is a basis, a point of reference, for all later scholarship in the field of Jewish art.

Vivian B. Mann
Józef Grabski

Introduction: Rachel Wischnitzer

Rachel Wischnitzer is truly a legend in her own time. She has many distinctions to her name: She was one of the first women to become an architect; she was the first female scholar to lay the foundation of a new discipline — Jewish art — at a time when no one considered it a legitimate field of study; she was the first woman to teach Jewish art history on the university level. In addition, she has the distinction of being a centenarian who is still a productive scholar. Her name and the discipline of Jewish art history are intricately interconnected. Wischnitzer never "saw Jewish art objects as mere parochial material to describe and be proud of, but as part of the history of world art."[1] She wisely stated: "I have always regarded Jewish art as part of the general creative process modeled inexorably by the times and the artist's personality..."[2]

Born on April 15, 1885, in Minsk, Russia, to an assimilated middle-class Jewish family, she is a product of two major cultures, that of pre-World War II Europe and that of the post-World War II United States. Within her memory live the rich cultural Jewish worlds and their unforgettable Jewish monuments of both Eastern and Western Europe, all so ruthlessly destroyed by the Nazi hordes. Such world-renowned personalities as the artists Marc Chagall, Eleazar Lissitzky and Issachar Ryback, the poet Saul Tchernikovsky, the writers Samuel Agnon and Isaac Peretz, and the statesman Zalman Shazar were her friends and associates.

Wischnitzer went to high school in Warsaw and studied art and philosophy at the universities of Heidelberg and Munich. She attended the Académie Royale des Beaux-Arts, École Supérieure d'Architecture, at Brussels, earning diplomas in architecture from the École Speciale d'Architecture and the Alliance Française in Paris in 1907. She was one of the first art historians to study illuminated Hebrew manuscripts at the British Museum in London and the Bodleian Library at Oxford. With the encouragement of Adolf Goldschmidt, the noted art historian, she intended to establish photo archives of illuminated Hebrew manuscripts at the Berlin Staats- und Universitätsbibliothek, a plan which unfortunately never materialized. 1921 found her and her husband, the well-known Jewish historian Mark Wischnitzer, in Berlin. Here, from 1922 to 1924, she was art editor of the beautiful magazines *Rimon* (Pomegranate), in Hebrew, and, its counterpart, *Milgroim*, in Yiddish. She gathered around her a distinguished body of artists and writers and published articles in those magazines on ancient, medieval and modern art, as well as poetry and literature. "We wanted", she wrote, "to reach out to the Jewish groups in America and the growing Jewish community in Palestine."[3] The eighteenth-century paintings of the now-destroyed Russian synagogue of Mogilev, copied by Lissitzky, were reproduced in the magazines and are probably the only records we have of that significant monument. From 1927 on, she was associated with the Berlin Jewish Museum, and from 1935 to 1938 she assisted Franz Landsberger, the director, with the Don Isaac Abrabanel show and the Akiba Eger Memorial Exhibition. At the 1936 display of *Unsere Ahnen* (Our Ancestors), which featured eighteenth-nineteenth-century portraits, she guided the notorious Nazi Adolf Eichmann through the exhibit. 1935 also saw the publication of her first book, a pioneering work entitled *Gestalten und Symbole der jüdischen Kunst*. With the forced closing of the Berlin Jewish Museum in 1938, she and her family emigrated to Paris. Here she arranged the *Vente Leisrael Exposition* for the *Keren Kaymet Leisrael*, which took place in the Palmarium of the Jardin d'Acclimatation. The show was a cross section of the work of Jewish artists residing in Paris at that time. At the Sorbonne, she enrolled in a course given by Comte Robert du Mesnil du Buisson on the recently discovered synagogue of Dura-Europos — a sensational archaeological find of a painted synagogue, dated 244/45 A.D. — situated in a remote Roman military outpost in Syria. Coming to the United States in 1940, she continued her studies on the Dura Synagogue under the direction of Karl Lehmann, a distinguished art historian of Greek and Roman art, at the Institute of Fine Arts of New York University. She earned a Master's degree in 1944; her thesis,

"The Messianic Theme in the Paintings of the Dura Synagogue", was published in 1948 by the University of Chicago Press. In 1956, at age 71, she undertook to teach art history at Stern College for Women of Yeshiva University in New York, and received a doctorate *honoris causa* upon her retirement in 1968.

Although she never practiced architecture, she wrote two basic works on synagogue architecture. In the introduction to *Synagogue Architecture in the United States: History and Interpretation* (1955), she rightly asserted: "this is the first comprehensive attempt at explaining American synagogue architecture in terms of form and function against the background of the history of ideas." In 1964 she published *The Architecture of the European Synagogue*.

Rachel Wischnitzer's bibliography, published in Volume 6 (1979) of the *Journal of Jewish Art*, a volume dedicated to her, numbers 344 items.[4] To this must be added her latest study on Picasso's *Guernica*, which appeared in *Artibus et Historiae* in 1985. Her articles have been published in such noted journals as *Art Bulletin*, *Gazette des Beaux-Arts*, *Eretz-Israel* and the *Journal of the Society of Architectural Historians*. Not only has she written on illuminated Hebrew manuscripts, synagogue architecture and Jewish ceremonial art, but on Rembrandt van Rijn, Benozzo Gozzoli and modern art, as well. May she long continue to grace us with her insights and productivity!

Joseph Gutmann

---

[1] B. Narkiss, "Editor's Note," *Journal of Jewish Art*, 6, 1979, p. 5.
[2] S. Schnur, "Is there a Jewish Style in Art?," *Reform Judaism*, March, 1981, p. 4. Cf. also R. Banner, "An Art Historian's Long Lived Career," *Newsday*, April, 17, 1985, p. 17.

[3] R. Wischnitzer, "From my Archives," *Journal of Jewish Art*, 6, 1979, p. 7.
[4] R. Weinstein, "Rachel Wischnitzer: A Bibliography," *Journal of Jewish Art*, 6, 1979, pp. 158-65.

VIVIAN B. MANN

"New" Examples of Jewish Ceremonial Art from Medieval Ashkenaz

For Rachel Wischnitzer

Among Rachel Wischnitzer's outstanding contributions to the field of Jewish art were her early and persistent efforts to publish articles on Hebrew manuscripts, Jewish ceremonial art, painting and graphics by Jewish artists, and synagogue architecture. Her 1913 article on the old synagogue in Lutzk, which appeared in the Russian periodical *Novy Voskhod*, was the first of these publications and was followed by hundreds of others in German, Hebrew, Yiddish, and English.[1] Professor Wischnitzer's aim was to make the material of Jewish art known, at a time when few recognized the existence of the subject, and most thought the Second Commandment had precluded the creation of any art by Jews.[2] So prolific were her efforts and so wide ranging her interests, that historians of Jewish art today are constantly confronted by the need to consult Dr. Wischnitzer's writings and to take her opinions into account.[3] The present study is offered in the spirit of her earliest pioneering efforts at establishing a corpus of Jewish art, and is an attempt to enlarge the known body of Jewish ceremonial art dating to medieval Ashkenaz, the Jewish community of Northern France and the Rhineland and areas under its influence.[4]

Recent archaeological excavations along the shores of the Mediterranean have led to the recovery of numerous ancient synagogues of the classical and early medieval periods.[5] Occasionally, ceremonial objects are found within their precincts, such as the spectacular discovery of the gable of a third-century Torah ark in the synagogue of Nabratein, in the Galilee.[6] However, a gap of several centuries separates these early works from the High Middle Ages, when a continuous history of Jewish ceremonial art might be said to begin.

Our knowledge of medieval Judaica derives from several sources: literary references, depictions in illuminated Hebrew manuscripts, and a small body of extant works. Taken together, this evidence indicates that the twelfth to fourteenth centuries constitute a creative period in the history of Judaica during which specifically Jewish types of objects appeared and others were taken from surrounding cultures and adapted for Jewish use.

Among the extant works whose forms seem to have been used exclusively by Jews is the Hanukkah lamp consisting of eight lights in a row, which first appears in the twelfth-thirteenth century.[7] The earliest examples are of stone and of the so-called bench type that is intended to sit on a flat surface. Slightly later are the wall-hung bronze lamps whose backplates are architectural in form and reflect the style of contemporaneous Gothic buildings and their sculptural decoration [Fig. 1]. Both the bench-type and the wall-hung examples mark the beginning of an association of architectural motifs with the Hanukkah lamp that continues into the modern era.[8]

Another type specifically associated with Jewish usage is the ring whose bezel is in the form of a small gabled building inscribed *mazel tov*, Hebrew for good luck and the wish commonly expressed at weddings.[9] Integral to the first part of

1) «Hannukkah Lamp», Germany, 14th century, bronze (New York, Congregation Emanu-el of the City of New York).

2) «Wedding Ring», Germany, first half of the 14th century, silver (from Fritz, *Goldschmiedekunst der Gotik*).

a Jewish wedding, the *erusin* or betrothal, is the groom's placement of a ring on a finger of the bride's right hand as a token of her consecration to him. Marriage, in Jewish lore, is often equated with the establishment of a household which would explain the shape of these rings.[10] The earliest securely

dated example was excavated in 1826 in Weissenfels, now in Halle, along with other jewelry datable to the first half of the fourteenth century [Fig. 2].[11] The same date may be ascribed to the ring, making it the first in a continuous series and the forerunner of modern examples. Another fourteenth-century wedding ring represents a unique adaptation of architectural forms; its bezel is formed as a turreted castle.[12] The ring is mentioned in the 1598 inventory of the Munich Kunstkammer, probably because of its unusual shape.[13] Although the more typical Weissenfels ring was first published twenty years after its discovery,[14] it has never appeared in discussions on the history of Jewish ceremonial art.

Documentary evidence attests to the existence of a third uniquely Jewish ceremonial object by the twelfth century. Maimonides (c. 1136-1204) mentions removable silver or gold *rimmonim*, finials for the staves of a Torah scroll, but the earliest extant pair dates some three hundred years later.[15] Now in the Cathedral treasury of Palma de Majorca, these *rimmonim* from a Sicilian synagogue are multi-tiered towers embellished with architectural details and Hebrew inscriptions [Fig. 3]. This tower form became traditional for Torah finials made in both Sephardi and Ashkenazi Europe or in areas under their influence,[16] and contrasts sharply with the pomegranate shape customary in the Middle East that is the root of the finials' name. One of the earliest Ashkenzi references to ornaments for Torah staves appears in a *responsum* (a rabbinic discussion of a legal issue) of Rabbi Meir of Rothenberg (ca. 1215-1293).[17] Although the reference clearly states that the ornaments were gilt, the term used to refer to them, *tzippui* or plating, is ambiguous as to their form.

Other medieval Jewish ceremonial objects are adaptations of Christian and secular forms whose functions were similar to those required by the celebration of Judaism. A twelfth-century *responsum* mentions that Rabbi Ephraim of Regensburg (1110-1175) used a glass container (called a *hadas*) to hold the spices for *havdalah*, the ceremony marking the close of Sabbaths and festivals and their separation from the workaday week.[18] Later, the spice container was made of metal and shaped as a tower, and was, therefore, similar to censers and other ecclesiastical vessels.[19] Sixteenth-century records from the Frankfurt silversmiths' guild underscore the formal relationship between the Jewish spice containers and the Christian censer by listing the object as a *Hedes oder Rauch-fass*.[20] The earliest Ashkenazi tower-form containers date to the fifteenth-sixteenth centuries. An example in The Jewish Museum, New York, though dated ca. 1550, is of Gothic form and presumably based on older models [Fig. 4].[21] This work reflects the strong sense of traditionalism in Jewish art that is but part of a broader cultural attitude, the significant and sacred character of custom.[22]

3) «Torah Finials», Spain or Sicily, 15th century, silver (Palma de Majorca, Cathedral).

4) «Spice Container», Frankfurt (?), ca. 1550, silver (New York, The Jewish Museum, JM 23-52).

15

5) «Festival Prayer Book», Germany, ca. 1300 (from Metzger, *Jewish Life in the Middle Ages*).

sanctification. *Kiddush* is a ceremony which occurs often in Jewish life, at the onset of Sabbaths and festivals, during holidays and at their close for *havdalah*, and at life-cycle events like circumcision and marriage. As is true of the regulations regarding Sabbath lamps mentioned above, the rabbinic laws governing *kiddush* are more concerned with the function of the vessel as a holder for wine and its cleanliness, than with its form.[29] As a result, the beakers and goblets used for *kiddush* may vary widely in appearance as a glance at depictions of the ceremony in illuminated Hebrew manuscripts readily shows.[30] There are representations of footed goblets, some with covers, as well as beakers and cups of different materials. Despite the ubiquity of the *kiddush* ceremony in Jewish life and the frequency of its representation, no actual examples of medieval *kiddush* cups have ever been discussed in the literature on Jewish ceremonial art. However, there are two sets of beakers dated to the fourteenth century which can be associated with Jewish ownership and which must have been used for ritual purposes.

The star-shaped hanging lamp is another example of adaptive use. Jews mark the onset of Sabbaths and festivals by kindling lights in the home. Talmudic law is concerned with the nature of the oil and wick to be used, but is indifferent to the form of the lamps themselves.[23] From the many manuscript illuminations depicting Jewish homes and synagogues, it is apparent that during the High Middle Ages Ashkenazi Jews, like their Gentile contemporaries, used star-shaped hanging lamps attached to a fixed shaft [Fig. 5].[24] However, because of the association of this form with Jewish religious ceremony, it became known, by the sixteenth century at the latest, as a *Judenstern*, or Jewish star.[25] The form remained traditional among Jews for centuries after it had fallen out of disuse by the general population, even though some Jews adopted more modern types of illumination.[26] Several extant medieval examples dating from the twelfth to the sixteenth centuries are thought to have belonged to Jews.[27]

Two other popular medieval forms were also used by Jews for ritual observance, but have never appeared in the literature on Jewish art. The first is the aquamanile in the form of a lion. An example in the Walters Art Gallery, Baltimore, is inscribed with the Hebrew blessing recited upon washing the hands before eating bread [Fig. 6] and was probably used in a home. Two other published examples stem from synagogues and must have been used to wash before the recitation of prayers.[28.] The lion aquamanile was an elegant solution to basic requirements of Jewish ceremony. Equally basic is the need for a drinking vessel to hold wine used at *kiddush*, literally,

6) «Aquamanile», Germany, 14-15th century, bronze (Baltimore, Walters Art Gallery, 53.25).

The first set was discovered in a Gothic house at Kutna Hora, the imperial mining town of the Luxembourg dynasty, and is now in the Germanisches National Museum, Nuremberg [Fig. 7].[31] It consists of five nested beakers which range in size from 8.2 to 9.2 cm in height. The largest cup is distinguished by its heavier weight and the two gilt bands which run around the circumference. From the point of view of style and comparison with other faceted forms, the cups may be dated to the first half of the fourteenth century. A more precise dating is offered by the imperial coats of arms of Austria, Poland, and Bohemia, found at the bottom of three of the cups [Fig. 8]. They identify the original owner of the set as Rixa Elizabeth (1288-1335), daughter of King Przemysl II of Poland. Rixa Elizabeth was first married to Wenzel II of Bohemia and later to Rudolf II of Austria, and died in 1335, which establish a *terminus ante quem* for the beakers. In the same year, the connection between the royal houses of Bohemia and Poland, both of whose arms appear on the cups, was severed, confirming the date. The last two coats of arms have not been identified. One with three Jews' hats (*Judenhutte*) is similar to the coat of arms on a fourteenth-century double cup now in the Cloisters collection of the Metropolitan Museum of Art.[32] Since both Jews and non-Jews used Jews' hats on personal and corporate shields of the fourteenth century, this detail does not confirm Jewish ownership or patronage of the beakers, though it does suggest the beakers may have been a gift from a Jew.[33] But the fifth coat of arms does confirm eventual Jewish ownership. It shows a rampant wolf facing left above which someone crudely inscribed the Hebrew word *ze'ev* (wolf), an unthinkable addition unless the beakers, which were originally made for Rixa Elizabeth, had become the property of a Jew whose name was probably Ze'ev or Wolfe.[34] The use of nested beakers as Jewish ceremonial objects is attested to by manuscript illuminations, for example, a page in the Yahuda Haggadah from Southern Germany, ca. 1450.[35] It is also interesting that a similar series of heraldic shields appears in a German holiday prayerbook, or *mahzor,* that dates to the same period [Fig. 5].

The second group of medieval beakers that belonged to Jews was found in the Lingenfeld treasure trove, a group of objects discovered in Lingenfeld, west of Speyer, in 1969 and first published in 1975 [Fig. 9].[36] The trove consisted of 2,369 coins and six silver vessels including three faceted beakers, a silver *Nuppenbecher*, and a double cup, plus rings and broken clothing ornaments. Since all the coins date before 1355, it has been suggested that the trove belonged to a Jew who buried it in 1349, the year of major persecutions of the Jews of Speyer. Two of the faceted beakers are ten-sided, and one is octagonal in cross section. Given their fine workmanship and precious material, we may presume that the Lingenfeld

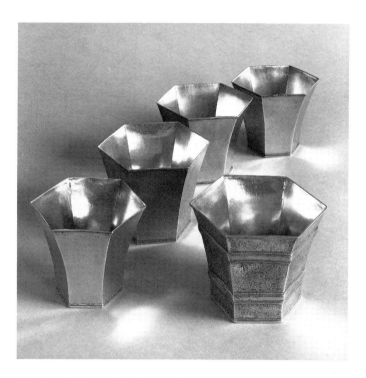

7) «Set of Nested Beakers», Germany, first half of the 14th century, silver (Nuremberg, Germanisches Nationalmuseum Nürnberg, no. HG 11628 a-e).

8) «Interiors of Nested Beakers», Germany first half of the 14th century (from Schiedlausky, ''Ein gotischer Becherschatz'').

9) «Beaker», Germany, first half of the 14th century, silver (Speyer, Historisches Museum der Pfalz).

beakers, like those from Kutna Hora, were used for ceremonial purposes.[37]

Other treasure troves, as well as church treasures, have yielded another type of drinking vessel which should be included in the corpus of medieval Ashkenzi ceremonial art. This is the double cup known in German as the *Doppelkopf or Doppelscheuer*. As the original names indicate, this vessel is comprised of two footed spherical goblets, one of which serves as a cover when the vessel is not in use. The earliest example is the cup of St. Godehard (d. 1038), in Hildesheim, which was created for his canonization in 1131.[38] It lacks the handle attached to the bottom half that became typical by the thirteenth century. The latest examples date to the seventeenth century.

The most interesting double cup from the perspective of Jewish ceremonial art is also one of the most lavish of all extant medieval ones.[39] Now in the Graflich Erbachsche Samm-lungen, the cup, dated to the second quarter of the fifteenth century, is of jasper mounted in gilt silver; the whole forms an ensemble that is 37 centimeters high [Fig. 10].[40] Presently, the

cup and its original leather case bear the arms of Dietrich Schenk zu Erbach who served as archbishop of Mainz from 1434-59, but these are later additions. Beneath the archbishop's arms on the case is an engraved medallion enclosing a running deer framed by a Hebrew inscription indicating the name of the first owner, ''Isaac, son of the noble Rabbi Zakhariah, blessed be the memory of the righteous'' [Fig. 12a].[41] This combination of symbol and circular inscription resembles the design of carved Jewish seals, although no known medieval examples with deer exist.[42] The remainder of the tooled decoration on the case consists of birds in foliage [Fig. 11]. On the cup, the archbishop's arms were carved on the reverse of a medallion originally featuring a battle between a lion and a horned animal [Fig. 12 b, c].[43]

The Erbach cup is closely related in form, size and materials to a double cup formerly in the collection of Karl von Roth-schild.[44] Yet the inscription on the Rothschild cup clearly indicates Christian ownership. It reads roughly: ''Help me Maria, with your child help me, who enjoys this will quench his thirst and prolong his life''.[45] These nearly identical works are differentiated only by their inscriptions. Their usage within Jewish and Christian tradition remains to be explored.

Three other, earlier double cups may be associated with Jewish patronage or ownership. The first is that from the Lingenfeld treasure trove discussed above [Fig. 13]. It is simpler in form and materials than the Erbach cup and resembles other fourteenth-century cups from Southern Germany, the Upper and Middle Rhineland, the Bodensee, Swabia, and Switzerland. In form and style, the Lingenfeld cup is closest to a double cup in the Historisches Museum, Basel, dated to the 1330's, and is presumed to have come from the same workshop.[46] Both cups bear medallions with family coats of arms; the one on the Basel cup belonged to the Von Froberg family who died out in 1367, providing *a terminus ante quem* for its dating; the shield on the Lingenfeld cup, which is partly enamelled, has not been identified although it resembles known heraldic devices.[47] However, the Basel double cup bears a second, partly enamelled roundel, whose center is a deer running left that is remarkably close to the drawing of the original Erbach leather case [cf. Figs. 12 and 14].[48] In place of the Hebrew inscription on the latter, there is a series of four petalled flowers, a motif that appears prominently on one of the Lingenfeld beakers.[49]

Both the Basel and Lingenfeld double cups must have belonged to members of the nobility because of their coats of arms. However, the combination of medallions on the Basel cup suggests that it may have been a gift from a Jew associated with the Von Froberg family at court, just as the Nuremberg beakers were probably given by a Jew to Rixa Elizabeth.[50] The double cup now in the Metropolitan Museum may represent a

10) «Double Cup and Case», Germany, second quarter of the 15th century, silver, jasper, leather.

similar gift, since it, too, is decorated with both Christian and Jewish elements.[51] The inscription mentions the Three Kings, Caspar, Melchior and Waltazar, patron saints of Cologne, but the cup bears two medallions with coats of arms that incorporate three Jews' hats in a centrifugal arrangement similar to the device on one of the Nuremberg beakers. In sum, there exist one double cup made for a Jew (Erbach), one eventually owned by a Jew (Lingenfeld), and two apparent gifts from Jews to nobles (Basel and New York). For what purpose were they used?

The custom of ceremonial drinking was widespread in the classical and pagan Germanic word and was gradually assimilated into Christian usage.[52] Germanic toasts to the goddess Minne were reinterpreted and dedicated to saints and even to Jesus and Mary. Among the saints who were the objects of ceremonial toasts were the Three Kings, mentioned

11) «Case of the Erbach Double Cup», Germany, second quarter of the 15th century, leather, detail (from Gall, *Leder im Europäischen Kunsthandwerk*).

12) Details of the «Erbach Double Cup and Case»: a) original coat on case, b) medallion with coat of arms, Dietrich Schenk zu Erbach, c) original decoration of medallion (reverse of b) (from Feigel, ''Das Geheimnis um den Schenkenbecher von Erbach?'').

13) «Double Cup», Konstanz (?), first half of the 14th century, silver (from Fritz, *Goldschmiedekunst der Gotik*).

14) «Double Cup», Konstanz (?), first half of the 14th century, silver, detail (Basel, Historisches Museum, 1894.264).

15) «Yahuda Haggadah», Germany, early 15th century.

16) «Watercolor», Lucerne, ca. 1460 (from Fritz, *Goldschmiedekunst der Gotik*).

in the inscription on the Metropolitan Museum cup. Toasts or *minnetrinken* were offered on saints' feast days and also on other occasions like the onset of journeys and bridal feasts. It was believed that *minnetrinken* made men virile and women beautiful. Double cups were often used for *minnetrinken*, and the appearance of its mature form with handle by the thirteenth century coincides with a rise in popularity of the toasts.[53] The double cup was thus intimately connected to ritual, and was often presented as a wedding gift and used for display purposes.[54]

That Jews owned double cups and employed them for ceremonial uses is amply demonstrated by numerous depictions in medieval Ashkenzi *haggadot*, the service books used on Passover. The cups are either held by the head of the household or placed on the *seder* table, as on several folios of

the Yahuda Haggadah, dated ca. 1450 [Fig. 15].[55] An interesting watercolor of ca. 1460 shows Jews pulverizing silver drinking vessels [Fig. 16]; the figure at left is placing a double cup in the large pot before him. Can one assign a specific Jewish ceremonial purpose to these double cups which would account for their frequent appearance in medieval German *haggadot*? The analogy of later inscribed eighteenth-century double cups of barrel form suggests two possibilities: the cups were used at circumcisions or at weddings. However, the widespread German custom of using double cups as wedding presents (since the form symbolizes the union of two into one)[56] favors an interpretation of these medieval examples as wedding gifts.[57] Further, the appearance of the double-cup form in the twelfth century and its dissemination in the thirteenth century coincides with a major transformation of the

Jewish wedding ceremony that necessitated the use of two cups.

In the Talmudic period and for centuries thereafter, the ceremony of betrothal (erusin), which involved the drinking of wine, occurred twelve months prior to the nissuin, or marriage, at which seven blessings are recited and more wine is drunk. For various reasons, one of which was the influence of Christian weddings, the Ashkenazi Jews of France and Germany began to combine the two ceremonies in the twelfth century.[58] When this change occurred, the rabbis became concerned with the number of cups to be used at the combined ceremony. Rabbi Jacob ben Asher (ca. 1270-1340), who migrated from Germany to Spain, ruled that two cups were needed and his opinion was accepted in later medieval codes.[59] According to Rabbi Jacob ben Moses Moellin of Mainz (ca. 1360-1427), head of the Jewish communities of Germany, Austria and Bohemia in the period under discussion, two cups were used at weddings.[60] Later, Rabbi Moses Isserles of Cracow (1525-72), who emended the Shulkhan Arukh (Code of Jewish Law) for use by Ashkenazim, required the use of two cups during the Grace after Meals following a wedding stating, "This is an old custom in these lands" (i. e., Ashkenazi Europe).[61]

Concurrently with the fusion of the ceremonies of betrothal and marriage in medieval Askenaz, a second change took place in the Jewish marriage ceremony during the late eleventh and early twelfth centuries. As the result of Christian influence, it became, in its entirety, a public affair attended by officials of the community, family and friends.[62] Since these two developments, the fusion of two ceremonies requiring the drinking of wine and their public enactment, occurred at least

in part because of Christian influence, it is not all that surprising that Jews also adopted a distinctively Germanic medieval form, the double cup, a form associated with ritual toasts, bridal feasts and ceremonial display. The actual examples we discussed, made of silver and precious metals, were obviously owned only by wealthy Jews, just as their Christian counterparts were owned by the nobility and wealthy burghers. From the same class of patrons came the commissions for lavishly illuminated manuscripts, whose genre scenes of Passover rituals reflect their owners' homes and furnishings.

The remaining medieval works of apparent Jewish ownership are alms containers and secular objects. The most interesting of these is a Minnekästchen decorated with a zodiac cycle ordered according to the Jewish year that was probably presented as a New Year's gift by one Jew to another.[63] That so little remains of Jewish ceremonial art from the medieval period is not surprising given the recurrent persecutions and the fact that works in precious metals were ready sources of capital. Yet another factor affected the number and character of the extant works. Since Jewish law emphasizes the function of ceremonial objects over their form, Jewish ritual objects are often indistinguishable from works intended for Christian purposes and could easily be adapted for Gentile use, as was the Erbach double cup. Unless some sign remains of the work's original function or owner, the once Jewish ritual object becomes anonymous, losing its particularity. The recovery of more evidence concerning extant medieval works, as well as increased archaeological investigations, will undoubtedly further enlarge the corpus presented here.

The research for this paper was supported by a grant from the National Endowment for the Arts. I would also like to thank Dr. Christopher Rüger, director of the Rheinisches Landesmuseum, Bonn, who suggested the investigation of publications on fourteenth-century coin hoards; and Dr. Wolfgang Milde of the Herzog Anton-Ulrich Bibliothek, Wolfenbüttel, for providing offprints of work unavailable in the United States.

[1] On the occasion of her 95th birthday, a complete bibliography of Professor Wischnitzer's writings, including works on non-Jewish art and cultural topics, was published in the Journal of Jewish Art, VI, 1979, pp. 158-64. In 1985, her article "Picasso's Guernica. A Matter of Metaphor" was printed in this periodical, XII, 1985, pp. 153-72.

[2] The first work devoted to Jewish ceremonial art was an exhibition catalogue published in 1878. (Paris, Galeries du Trocadero, Collection de M. Strauss. Description des objects d'art religieux hébraïques exposés dans les galeries du Trocadero, à l'Exposition Universelle de 1878, Poissy, 1878). The first facsimile of a Hebrew manuscript appeared in 1898 (D. H. Müller, J. von Schlosser, Die Haggada von Sarajevo, Vienna, 1898); and the first journal devoted to Jewish art in 1901: Mitteilungen der Gesellschaft zur Erforschung Jüdischer Kunstdenkmäler zu Frankfurt a. M. (8 vols. in 7; Frankfurt: 1900-15). For a bibliography of Jewish art, see L. A. Mayer, Bibliography of Jewish Art, Jerusalem, 1967; W. L. Gross, "Catalogue of Catalogues. Bibliographical Survey of a Century of Temporary Exhibitions of Jewish Art", Journal of Jewish Art, VI, 1979, pp. 133-57; and the series "Current Publications" in Journal of Jewish Art, II-XIII, 1975-87.

[3] For examples, see C. Roth, "Majolica Passover Plates of the XVIth-XVIIIth Centuries", Eretz-Israel, VII, 1964, pp. 107-8; and V. B.

Mann, "The Rediscovery of a Known Work", *Journal of Jewish Art*, XII-XIII (1987), pp. 269-278.

[4] On the meaning of the term "Ashkenaz", see *Encyclopaedia Judaica*, Jerusalem, 1972, vol. III, cols. 719-22.

[5] For a recent survey, see L. I. Levine, ed., *Ancient Synagogues Revealed*, Jerusalem, 1981.

[6] E. M. Meyers, J. F. Strange, C. L. Meyers, "The Ark in Nabratein — A First Glance," *Biblical Archaeology*, XLIV, 1981, pp. 237-43, illustration p. 238.

[7] See B. Narkiss, "Un object de culte: la lampe de Hanuka," *Art et archéologie des Juifs en France médiévale*, ed. B. Blumenkranz, Toulouse, 1980, figs. 3 and 5. New research indicates that the Victoria and Albert lamp (and the two others form the same mold) are probably 19th-century copies of the lamp in the Cluny collection. (See forthcoming catalogue of the Judaica in the Victoria and Albert Museum by Michael Keen.)

[8] See Jerusalem, Israel Museum, *Architecture in the Hannukah Lamp*, exhibition catalogue, 1978, for comparative photos of lamps and buildings.

[9] Frankfurt, Historisches Museum Frankfurt am Main, *Synagoga Jüdischer Altertümer, Handschriften und Kulturgeräte*, exhibition catalogue, 1961, fig. 166, for numerous illustrations.

[10] For example, "When you are twenty years of age build thy house. Marry a wife...," from the ethical will of Joseph ibn Caspi (1297-1340), quoted in P. and H. Goodman, *The Jewish Marriage Anthology*, Philadelphia, 1965, p. 45. In a section on "Wedding Rings" in the same work, Israel Abrahams suggested that the building "on the ring always represents the Temple of Jerusalem or one of its more modern counterparts — a synagogue," but without providing any basis for this interpretation (*ibidem*, pp. 100-1). Gertrude Seidman views the house as a symbol of the wife in accord with Talmudic sayings ("Marriage Rings Jewish Style," *Connoisseur*, CCVI, 1981, p. 50).

[11] M. Sauerlandt, "Ein Schmuckfund aus Weissenfels von Anfang des 14. Jahrhunderts," *Cicerone*, XI, 1919, p. 520; J. M. Fritz, *Goldschmiedekunst der Gotik im Mitteleuropa*, Munich, 1982, no. 318. Interestingly, one of the pieces of jewelry is the fragment of a clasp with a representation of King David playing his harp. (Sauerlandt, *op. cit.*, p. 524).

[12] Cologne, Kölnischen Stadtmuseum, *Monumenta Judaica. 2000 Jahre Geschichte und Kultur der Juden am Rhein*, exhibition catalogue, 1964, no. E. 162.

[13] Y. Hackenbroch, *Renaissance Jewelry*, Munich, 1979, p. 50.

[14] Sauerlandt, *op. cit.*, p. 520.

[15] Maimonides, *Sefer Mishneh Torah*, Hilkhot Sefer Torah, X: 4.

[16] See S. Kayser, G. Schoenberger, *Jewish Ceremonial Art*, Philadelphia, 1955, pls. XIV-XVIII, for illustrations.

[17] Meir of Rothenberg, *She'alot u-Teshuvot*, Sedilkov, 1835, no. 879.

[18] Isaac ben Moses of Vienna, *She'alot u-Teshuvot 'Or Zaru'a*, Zitomir, 1862, II, no. 92.

[19] The adoption of a tower form may have taken place by the 13th century, if a work in the Victoria and Albert Museum was indeed used by Jews and is not a Christian reliquary. (For opposing views, see B. Narkiss, *op. cit.*, p. 193, fig. 6a, and S. Sabar, The Beginnings and Flourishing of *Ketubbah* Illustration in Italy: *A Study in Popular Imagery and Jewish Patronage During the Seventeenth and Eighteenth Centuries*, University of California, Los Angeles, unpublished doctoral dissertation, 1987, p. 122, n. 103.

[20] W. Scheffler, *Goldschmiede Hessens*, Berlin-New York, 1976, pp. 86, 106.

[21] Two other works without secure provenance may be spice boxes: one in the Floersheim Collection, Zurich, dated ca. 1500 and a 15th-century north Italian example in the Victoria and Albert Museum, London (M40-1951).

[22] I am indebted to Michael Signer for this observation. The operative force of tradition in the commissioning of Jewish ceremonial objects is underscored by a Frankfurt court case of 1556 in which a Jew, Joseph Goldschmidt, sued the silversmith Heinrich Heidelberger for failing to make a spice container similar to that owned by the plaintiff's father. A model drawing submitted as evidence shows a Gothic tower form. (W. K. Zülch, "Das Hedes. Ein rätselhaftes Werk der Frankfurter Goldschmiedekunst," *Alt-Frankfurt*, I-II, 1928-9, pp. 61-2.

[23] Mishnah, Shabbat 2: 1-4; also S. Ganzfried, *Code of Jewish Law*, translated by H. Golden, New York, 1963, ch. 75: 2-3.

[24] For a listing of some of these illustrations, see H. G. Meyer, "Eine Sabbatlampe im Erfurter Dom," *Studien zur Kunstgeschichte*, XVI, 1982, pp. 7-10. See also the *Index of Jewish Art*, Vol. II, New York-London-Paris, 1978: Hileq and Bileq Haggadah (Paris, Bibliothèque Nationale, ms. Hebr. 1933), fols. 4v, 5v and 20v; Second Nuremberg Haggadah (Jerusalem, Schocken Library, ms. 24087), Yahuda Haggadah (Jerusalem, Israel Museum, ms. 180/50), fols. 4r, 4v, 5r, 6r. See also M. Metzger, *La Haggada Enluminée*, Leiden, 1973, figs. 77, 96, 105, 107, 108, 278. For a history of hanging lamps, see J. Dudova, "Sabbat Lampen aus Messingguss", *Judaica Bohemia*, IX, 1973, pp. 73-7.

[25] See Scheffler, *op. cit.*, pp. 88, 106, for citations from the "Probierbuch der Frankfurter Goldschmiedezunft 1512-1576" (Frankfurt, Stadtarchiv, Ugb. C. 30D).

[26] Rabbi Solomon ben Abraham Adret of Barcelona (ca. 1235-ca. 1310) was asked if one could use wax candles to kindle the Sabbath lights (*Teshuvot Shealot*, Rome, 1470; reprinted Jerusalem, 1968, no. 416). He replied that it was permissible.

[27] Cologne, Kölnisches Stadtmuseum, *Judaica. Kölnisches Stadtmuseum*, by L. Franzheim, Cologne, 1980, no. 121; Paris, Petit Palais, *Israël à travers les âges*, exhibition catalogue, 1968, no. 405. The original purpose of the Erfurt lamp is still a matter of dispute (see note 24 above).

[28] O. von Falke, E. Meyer, *Bronzegeräte des Mittelalters. I. Band. Romanische Leuchter und Gefässe. Giessgefässe der Gotik*, Berlin, 1935, nos. 480 and 534.

[29] Babylonian Talmud, *Pesahim*, 108b; *Berakhot*, 51a.

[30] For examples, see T. and M. Metzger, *Jewish Life in the Middle Ages. Illuminated Hebrew Manuscripts of the Thirteenth to the Sixteenth Centuries*, New York, 1982, figs. 132-6, 151-2, 165, 334-7, 366, and 378.

[31] This discussion is based on the article by G. Schiedlausky, "Ein gotischer Becherschatz," *Pantheon*, XXXIII, 4, 1975, pp. 300-9.

[32] T. Husband, "Double Cup", in New York, Metropolitan Museum of Art, *Notable Acquisitions, 1982-83*, 1983, p. 20.

[33] Schiedlausky, *op. cit.*, p. 307. Also D. M. Friedenberg, *Medieval Jewish Seals from Europe*, Detroit, 1987, nos. 69, 70, 73, 76, 78, 83, and 86.

[34] Published documents yield only one Jew of the period who might have been the owner. Wolfin von Bamberg was active as a moneylender in Franconia during the 1340's. (Z. Avineri, *Germania Judaica*, Vol. II, Tübingen, 1968, p. 235).

[35] B. Narkiss, *Hebrew Illuminated Manuscripts*, Jerusalem, 1969, pl. 41; also *Encyclopaedia Judaica*, Vol. III, colorplate between cols. 300-1.

[36] H. Ehrend, *Der Münzschatz von Lingenfeld 1969*, Numis-

matische Gesellschaft Speyer e. V., 1975.

[37] Günter Stein in his discussion of the beakers, and of the double cup to be discussed below, categorically rejects the view that the vessels found at Lingenfeld were used for Jewish ceremonial purposes. (''Zu vier Gefässen des Lingefelder Münzschatzfundes,'' in Ehrend, *op. cit.*, pp. 56-7). He gives the following reasons concerning the beakers: 1) No other fourteenth-century Jewish cult objects like these are known (though he discusses the Kutna Hora set); 2) It is inconceivable that a Jew would profane a ceremonial object by filling it with coins that he wanted to hide since Jews bury cermonial objects that are no longer being used in the same manner in which a corpse is buried. As for the first objection, we do know from manuscript illuminations that similar beakers were used in home ceremonies. The Kutna Hora examples must have been employed for Jewish purposes, or else the owner would not have marred the appearance of the cups by adding a Hebrew inscription. In regard to Stein's second objection, he has taken regulations which apply only to a certain class of ceremonial objects, principally writings including the name of God and appurtenances for the Torah, *mezuzah* and *tefillin* (*tashmishei kedushah*), and applied them to all ceremonial objects. Other Jewish ritual objects are not considered to possess holiness *sui generis*, but only by virtue of their function (see, for example, the reference to Maimonides cited in note 15 above). Stein restated his views on the Lingenfeld beakers in ''Der Schatzfund von Lingenfeld,'' *Geschichte der Juden in Speyer. Beiträge der Speyerer Stadtgeschichte*, Heft 6, Speyer, 1981, p. 65.

[38] H. Kohlhausen, ''Der Doppelkopf: seine Bedeutung für das Deutsche Brauchtum des 13. bis 17. Jahrhunderts,'' *Zeitschrift für Kunstwissenschaft*, XIV, 1-2, 1960, pp. 25-6.

[39] Kohlhausen, *op. cit.*, p. 37. The other similarly expensive jasper double cup is the one formerly in the collection of Karl von Rothschild to be discussed below.

[40] A. Feigel, ''Das Geheimnis um den Schenkenbecher von Erbach,'' *Aus Dom und Diözese Mainz. Festgabe Prof. Georg Lenhart*, Mainz, 1939, p. 120.

[41] Feigel published the drawing of the original Hebrew inscription (Fig. 12) which became visible by 1939 due to the flaking of the paint used to depict the arms of the archbishop. Errors in transcription led to an erroneous translation which was repeated by later authors. (Feigel, *op. cit.*, p 122; J. M. Fritz, *op. cit.*, no. 641). The Hebrew should read: יצחק בן הנדיב רבי זכריה זצ״ל

[42] For examples of the period, see B. Bedos, ''Les sceaux,'' in *Art et archéologie des Juifs en France Médiévale*, ed. B. Blumenkranz, Toulouse, 1980, pp. 207-28; and D. M. Friedenberg, *op. cit.*, nos. 74 and 82.

[43] Feigel, in 1939, interpreted the scene as a battle between a unicorn and a lion, i. e., between Christianity and Judaism, which he describes as ''*christusfeindlich*'' (Feigel, *op. cit.*, pp. 123-4). However, the published drawing shows a beast with two horns and the exact significance of the scene is uncertain.

[44] Kohlhausen, *op. cit.*, pp. 37-8, figs. 11 and 12.

[45] *Ibidem*, p. 38.

[46] For an illustration of the Basel cup, see Fritz, *op. cit.*, no. 356. On the attribution of both cups to the same shop, see Stein, ''Zu vier Gefässen ...,'' p. 53 and no. 13a.

[47] Stein, *op. cit.*, pp. 53-4, and ''Der Schatzfund ...'' fig. 48 for an illustration.

[48] It is interesting that the name of the owner of the Erbach double cup does not fit his coat of arms, a deer which is usually associated with the name Hirsch or Zvi. Perhaps the symbol was inherited from a forbearer who may have been associated with the Lingenfeld double cup. This suggestion remains speculative, of course, until the discovery of supporting documentary evidence.

[49] Stein, *op. cit.*, no. 13a, fig. 2. The cup is also illustrated in Fritz, *Goldschmiedekunst der Gotik*, *op. cit.*, no. 374.

[50] Schiedlausky, *op. cit.*, p. 307.

[51] Timothy Husband's suggestion that the Three Kings inscription is merely an apotropaic device, and that the cup was commissioned by a very wealthy Jew for his own use, seems untenable given the state of Jewish-Christian relations during the Middle Ages (Husband, *op. cit.*, pp. 19-21).

[52] Kohlhausen, *op. cit.*, pp. 39-42, 47.

[53] Kohlhausen, *op. cit.*, p. 55.

[54] See H. M. von Erffa with D. F. Rittmeyer, ''Doppelbecher,'' *Reallexikon zur Deutschen Kunstgeschichte. IV Band*, Stuttgart, 1958, cols. 168-9, for documents recording the gift of double beakers as wedding presents.

[55] Other depictions are published in the *Index of Jewish Art*, New York, London, Paris, 1976-8: Vol. I, The Birds Head Haggadah, Upper Rhine, ca. 1300, (Jerusalem, Israel Museum, 180/57), fol. 5v, where it is mistakenly described as a spice box, and fols. 28r, 30r and 46v, where the figures hold the bottom half of a thirteenth-century type; Erna Michael Haggadah, Upper Rhine, ca. 1400 (Jerusalem, Israel Museum, 181/18), fols 4v, 6v, 7v, 10r, 40r, and 45r. Vol. II: Hileq and Bileq Haggadah, South Germany, 1450-1500, (Paris, Bibliothèque Nationale, Ms. hebr. 1933, fols. 4r, 5v, 19v (?) 20v and 23r; Second Nuremberg Haggadah, Upper Rhine, ca. 1450 (Jerusalem, Schocken Library, Ms. 24087), fols. 6v, 25r, 25v; Yahuda Haggadah (Jerusalem Israel Museum, Ms. 180/50), fols. 4r, 6r, 22r, 26r (?), see also Metzger, *op. cit.*, fig. 112.

[56] R. Pechstein, ''The 'Welcome' Cup. Renaissance Drinking Vessels by Nuremberg Goldsmiths,'' *Connoisseur*, CXCIX, 1978, p. 181.

[57] In 1939, Feigel reported the suggestion of Professor Kalt of Mainz that the Erbach cup was a Jewish wedding cup because a Jewish marriage involves drinking wine twice (Feigel, *op. cit.*, p. 122). That there was a definitive use for the cup in Jewish ceremony will be seen below. Thus there is no basis to Stein's objection to viewing the Lingenfeld double cup as a Jewish ritual object (Stein, *op. cit.*, pp. 56-7).

[58] On the development of the Jewish wedding ceremony, see *Encyclopaedia Judaica*, Vol. 11, 1031 ff. especially 1035; also Ze'ev W. Falk, *Jewish Matrimonial Law in the Middle Ages*, Oxford, 1966, pp. 35-6, 43-4, 64.

[59] Jacob ben Asher, *Arba'ah Turim*, Hilkhot Kiddushin, 62.

[60] Jacob ben Moses Moellin, *Sefer Maharil*, Jerusalem, 1969, p. 64.

[61] *Shulkhan Arukh*, Hilkhot Kiddushin, 62: 10.

[62] Falk, *op. cit.*, pp. 45, 82-4.

[63] V. B. Mann, ''A Sixteenth-Century Box in the New York Jewish Museum and its Transformation,'' *Journal of Jewish Art*, IX, 1982, pp. 54-60.

JOSEPH GUTMANN

The Dura Europos Synagogue Paintings and their Influence on Later Christian and Jewish Art*

The third-century Dura Europos synagogue paintings represent the earliest continuous narrative cycle of biblical images known in art. Not until the fifth century do we find similar complex and elaborate narrative cycles of biblical images in church art.

Since the Dura synagogue paintings are the earliest continuous surviving narrative biblical cycle, they have naturally raised the question of whether there exists a relationship between them and later biblical scenes found in medieval Jewish and Christian art. No systematic study has been devoted to this problem, but scholars have occasionally attempted to compare certain narrative scenes appearing in the Dura synagogue paintings with those found in later Christian and Jewish art.

One such comparison involves the Dura synagogue depiction of a nude figure standing in the water and holding a child [Fig. 1]. The figure has been identified as the Egyptian princess standing in the Nile, rescuing the child Moses. Since the nude princess in the waters is also found in several medieval Jewish and Christian miniatures dating from twelfth- to fourteenth-century Spain, some scholars have posited a direct connection between the Dura synagogue painting and the medieval Spanish illustrations. However, this need not be the case. The Dura synagogue painting appears to be closely related to such sources as the contemporary *Targumim* (Aramaic paraphrases of the Hebrew Bible), which clearly explain that the princess, suffering from leprosy, went down to bathe in the Nile and was miraculously cured of her affliction when she touched the basket containing the child Moses. The

medieval Spanish depictions usually reveal three or four nude figures in the water, but in only one miniature [Fig. 2] is a nude figure labelled "Tarmuth" (a name for the princess found in early sources like Josephus and repeated in later texts). The inscription on this miniature further explains that

"the daughter of Pharaoh [accompanied by] her maidens cleanses herself [in the Nile]."

Iconographically, the medieval illustrations do not show three clothed maidens awaiting the princess on shore, and the child is not held aloft by the princess, as is the case in the Dura synagogue painting. Furthermore, the Dura painting and the medieval Spanish miniatures appear to be influenced by different literary traditions.[1]

Scholarly attempts to link the rendition of the Sacrifice of Isaac in the Dura synagogue with depictions in Spanish art are equally unconvincing. The Leon Bible of 960, fol. 21v, for instance, shares with the Dura painting only the element of Isaac lying atop the faggots on the altar. In the Leon Bible scene Isaac and Abraham are shown facing the viewer rather than with their backs to the spectator as in the Dura synagogue version [Figs. 3-4]. Moreover, the ram at Dura is standing next to a tree, while in the Leon Bible it is entangled in the thicket, in keeping with the biblical narrative. Although the hand of God (rather than the angel) is revealed in both depictions, the Leon Bible has the hand bestowing the Christian benediction (the *benedictio latina*). In addition, Abraham uses a knife in Dura, while in the Leon Bible Abraham uses a sword (the more

1) «The Finding of Moses», Dura Europos Synagogue, west wall, Syria, ca. 245 A.D., Damascus National Museum.

common implement featured in Christian art). Furthermore, Abraham's grasping of Isaac's hair in the Leon miniature is a detail not found in the Dura painting.

Thus the tenth-century Leon Bible miniature appears to differ too greatly from the Dura synagogue painting to be considered dependent upon it.[2]

The analogies that have been drawn between some scenes in the eleventh-century Spanish Ripoll Bible and the Dura synagogue depictions do not prove a direct connection between them. The only similarity in the illustrations of Haman and Mordecai in the Dura painting and in the Ripoll Bible (Biblioteca Vaticana, MS lat. 5729, fol. 310v) is that Haman

is leading Mordecai's horse. There are, however, significant differences. In the Dura synagogue scene there are three figures with arms raised in a gesture of acclamation; in the Ripoll Bible we find four. Moreover, the four figures are behind the horse in the Ripoll Bible, rather than in front of the horse as at Dura. Furthermore, the Ripoll Bible figures are not presented frontally, as at Dura, and, in addition, their garments differ radically.[3] Close stylistic and iconographic parallels to the Haman and Mordecai scene of the Dura synagogue can be found in the roughly contemporary sculptural reliefs from Palmyra.[4]

On folio 82 of the Ripoll Bible the illustration of the Crossing

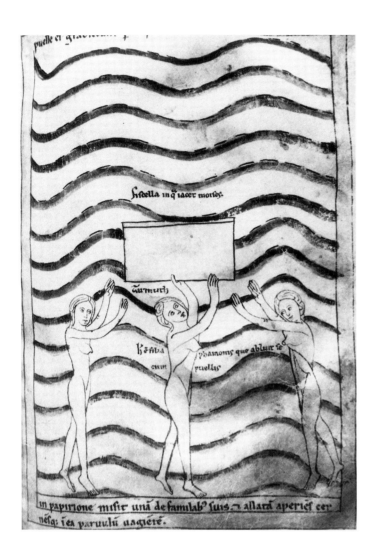

2) «The Finding of Moses», Pamplona Bible, Spain, ca. 1200, Harburg, Collection Prince Oettingen-Wallerstein, MS I, 2, lat. 4, fol. 49.

3) «The Sacrifice of Isaac», Dura Europos Synagogue, west wall, Syria, ca. 245 A.D., Damascus National Museum.

4) «The Sacrifice of Isaac», Leon Bible, Spain, 960, Léon, Colegiata de San Isidoro, Cod. 2, fol. 21v.

of the Red Sea [Fig. 5] bears an interesting iconographic similarity to the same theme in the Dura synagogue. In both instances we see the hand of God, armed Israelites and naked Egyptian bodies drowning in the water. However, there need not be a direct connection between these two renderings, since references to armed Israelites and naked Egyptians drowning can be found in both Jewish and Christian literary traditions.[5]

Narrative scenes in the Dura synagogue paintings have been linked not only with Spanish illustrations, but with Byzantine ones as well. Such depictions as that of Jacob blessing the sons of Joseph in the Dura synagogue have been compared

5) «The Exodus from Egypt», Ripoll Bible, Spain, first half of 11th century, Vatican City, Biblioteca Apostolica, MS lat. 5759, fol. 310v.

with Byzantine Octateuchs (for instance, Istanbul, Topkapi Saray Library, Cod. gr. 8, fol. 141), yet the similarities are rather superficial. In both renderings the four major persons described in the Bible are present, and the patriarch is seen reclining. However, the costumes in the two scenes differ. In the Dura synagogue painting Joseph is clad in a Persian trousered costume, whereas in the Octateuch he is shown wearing the draped robe. Furthermore, in the Dura painting Jacob is neither bearded nor has white hair, as in the Octateuch miniature. In addition, in the Dura scene neither Jacob nor Joseph are haloed, as they are in the Octateuch rendition. In the Octateuch all of the figures are shown in profile, while at Dura they are presented frontally. Moreover, in the Octateuch Jacob's hands are shown crossed, an antitype of Jacob's preference for his younger son Ephraim (interpreted by the Church Fathers as *Ecclesia*). The Dura depiction seems to have avoided the crossing of Jacob's hands — the prefiguration of the cross.[6] It seems, then, that the differences in the two scenes far outweigh the resemblances, and appear to rule out any direct connection between them.

Such is also the case in the comparison between the Destruction of the Temple of Dagon miniatures in the eleventh-century Book of Kings (Biblioteca Vaticana, MS gr. 333, fols. 9v-10) and the scene in the Dura synagogue. The Book of Kings miniatures follow the biblical narrative of the Septuagint and render the ark-box with cherubim, but in the Dura synagogue painting we see the Torah ark-chest — a purposeful substitution to indicate that the illustration is related to contemporary Palestinian liturgical synagogal practices and texts. Thus, while there may be some similarities in the depiction of the idols in the double arcade and in the exterior and interior views of the Dagon Temple, the reliance on different textual traditions, the rendering of different arks and the diverse costumes worn augur against claiming a direct relationship between the Dura painting and the Book of Kings miniatures.[7]

It should be stressed that the Dura synagogue and its cycle of paintings was buried as part of the Roman defense system against Sasanian attacks, which occurred around 256 A. D. During the short period of time preceding their burial it is unlikely that they exerted an influence on later Christian art. It has been suggested recently that models for the Dura synagogue paintings may have existed in a synagogue in a larger nearby center, such as Palmyra. It should be noted, however, that even if that were true, they could not have exerted an influence on Christian art, either, as Palmyra was sacked by Rome around 272 A. D.[8]

It seems evident from all the scenes discussed herein that no concrete and indisputable connection can be established between the illustrations in Christian and Jewish art and the paintings at the Dura synagogue.[9] The parallels cited by scholars are too problematic to be convincing.

* I am deeply indebted to Dr. Marilyn Gutmann for reading this paper and making many suggestions for its improvement.

[1] J. Gutmann, "Josephus' Jewish Antiquities in Twelfth-Century Art: Renovatio or Creatio?," *Zeitschrift für Kunstgeschichte*, 48, 1985, pp. 435-438; *idem*, "The Illustrated Midrash in the Dura Synagogue Paintings: A New Dimension for the Study of Judaism," *American Academy for Jewish Research Proceedings*, 50 (1983), p. 94. Cf. T. Gaster, "A Samaritan Poem about Moses," *The Joshua Bloch Memorial Volume* (ed. A. Berger, *et. al.*), New York, 1960, pp. 120, 125. Cf. also K. Schubert, *Bilder-Pentateuch von Moses dal Castellazzo, Venice, 1521*, Vienna, 1985, pp. 114-115, for another version of the nude princess and three of her handmaidens (on fol. 73). This scene appears to follow the similar depiction in the fourteenth-century *Kaufmann Haggadah*, fol. 10; Gutmann, "Josephus' Antiquities...," *op. cit.*, p. 437, n. 13.

[2] J. Gutmann, "The Sacrifice of Isaac: Variations on a Theme in Early Jewish and Christian Art," *Thiasos ton Mouson: Studien zu Antike und Christentum. Festschrift für Josef Fink zum 70. Geburtstag* (ed. D. Ahrens), Cologne, 1984, pp. 118-119; *idem*, "The Dura Europos Synagogue Paintings: The State of Research," *The Synagogue in Late Antiquity* (ed. L. I. Levine), Philadelphia, 1987, p. 69, no. 1.

[3] C. Walter, "Papal Imagery in the Medieval Lateran Palace," *Cahiers archéologiques*, 21, 1971, pp. 130-131.

[4] H. J. W. Drijvers, *The Religion of Palmyra*, Leiden, 1976, pls. LXVI and LXIX/1, pp. 25, 28.

[5] Gutmann, "Illustrated Midrash...," *op. cit.*, pp. 102-103; C. H. Kraeling, *The Synagogue* (The Excavations at Dura Europos, Final Report, 8/1), New Haven, 1956, pl. LIII, p. 83; L. Ginzberg, *The Legends of the Jews*, Philadelphia, 1947, VI, p. 55, no. 11 (*Eliyahu Rabbah* 1:2 mentions that God punishes the wicked while naked and *Esther Rabbah* 3:14 relates that "The Egyptians when they sank in the sea were also punished naked"). Cf. H. Kunz, *Materialien und Beobachtungen zur Darstellung der Lotgeschichte (Genesis 19, 12-26) von den Anfängen bis gegen 1500*, Munich, 1981, p. 109, who cites Christian sources which indicate that in the Middle Ages nakedness was an outer sign of sin and guilt. Since the Egyptians were a sinful people they are depicted naked and thus deprived of spiritual merit.

[6] K. Weitzmann, "The Question of the Influence of Jewish Pictorial Sources on Old Testament Illustration," *No Graven Images: Studies in Art and the Hebrew Bible* (ed. J. Gutmann), New York, 1971, pp. 77-78; cf. W. Stechow, "Jacob Blessing the Sons of Joseph from Early Christian Times to Rembrandt," *No Graven Images*, op. cit., p. 262, LXI, and R. Haussherr, *Rembrandts Jacobssegen. Überlegungen zur Deutung des Gemäldes in der Kasseler Galerie*, Opladen, 1976, pp. 30-32. D. Korol, *Die frühchristlichen Wandmalereien aus den Grabbauten in Cimitile/Nola*, Münster, 1987, pp. 109-129, re-examines this Dura synagogue painting and questions interpretations based on the assumption that Jacob is not crossing his hands.

[7] Weitzmann, *op. cit.*, pp. 312-315; J. Gutmann, "The Illustrated Jewish Manuscript in Antiquity: The Present State of the Question," *No Graven Images...*, *op. cit.*, p. 239, n. 19.

[8] Gutmann, "Dura Europos Synagogue...," *op. cit.*, pp. 66-69.

[9] The connections I cited between the Dura synagogue paintings and the Ashburnham Pentateuch miniatures (J. Gutmann, "The Jewish Origin of the Ashburnham Pentateuch Miniatures," *No Graven Images...*, *op. cit.*, pp. 329 ff.) should be corrected in the light of a new study by F. Rickert, *Studien zum Ashburnham Pentateuch*, Bonn, 1986. Rickert convincingly shows that the Ashburnham Pentateuch is a Christian liturgical manuscript and that "Die Beziehungen zu jüdischen Darstellungen besteht lediglich darin, dass auch diese aus dem antiken Formenvorrat schöpften," p. 85).

COLIN EISLER

Power to Europe's Chosen Peoples.
A New Maccabean Page for Louis XIV by Liévin Cruyl

From a Christian perspective, the first Testament was far more than merely prefatory to the second; in addition to creating a world and the sin requiring salvation by Christ, it provided his terrestrial ancestors. A massive prophetic framework, the Old Testament foretold all the triumphs, the tribulations and glories to come. Cementing their powers by an ancestry close to Christ's, Catholic and Protestant kings and queens often saw to it that they were perceived as in a direct line of succession to those of ancient Israel. Their coronation regalia and ceremony, palaces, cathedrals and chapels were frequently charged with overt and covert references to such ancient Judaic lineage. Descent from the ruling house of Israel functioned as passport to truly exalted status.

Christian republics too assumed an equal if not still more intimate association with the Children of Israel, needing and finding verification for their collective validity by professing communal status as the new Chosen People, intimately allied to Jews of yore in a way that often went far beyond the bounds of Catholic propriety. However, some Catholic nations and political movements exercised similar claims, especially those like France or Venice whose leaders' powers assumed some of those of the popes'.[1]

Strong links to ancient Israel were forged by those republics practicing the new art of capitalism, Venice and the Lowlands above all others. Both found support and solace in their self-engendered association with God's first people who were freed from the absolute, uncompromising prohibitions against wealth and profit as laid out in early Christian communism. When Savonarola had Florence under his brief leadership, he vowed to run that new republican theocracy along Venetian lines, reminding its citizens that they were indeed the Chosen People. Since then almost all devoutly Christian reformers or revolutionaries have sought to legitimize and strenghten their cause by seeing themselves as or like the true Children of God, new Jews for Jesus, indeed.

By far the most important building ever erected on earth, for Christian and Jew alike, will always be the First Temple. Constructed in Jerusalem between 965 and 928 B. C., this sanctuary is the only edifice where God is believed to have participated in quite such direct fashion. A miraculous snowfall may have laid out the groundplan for Santa Maria Maggiore and the Santa Casa might have been flown by angels from Nazareth to Loreto, but no other building could ever hope to occupy so central a role in Western faith, as none but the temple is credited by scripture with divine design.

God is often characterized in the Bible as a potter, a builder, a sculptor, as the divine architect of the universe, but never is the result of his creativity cast in terms of art rather than nature, in the geneses of artifice, with a single major exception. Only once, for Solomon's temple, in its proportions and furnishings, is he, albeit indirectly, the architect of architecture.

David received the building's plan from God but was, as a man of war, forbidden to realize it, so the design was transmitted to Solomon (I Chron. 28, 3, 11-12). Here, uniquely, the Builder becomes builder, metaphor meeting reality. Two precedent projects, each inseparable from the temple itself, pertain to the Creator as artistic creator. He incised the tablets of the law and may have provided the design of the ark of covenant, the box-like container for the tablets.

The need to enshrine the ark of the covenant provided the temple's *raison d'être*. Noah's ark of salvation is taken from a different Hebrew word (*tebah*) — meaning chest or box —

than that of the covenant (*aron habrit*), but in Christianity Noah's ark is seen as close to Moses', both prototypical of Ecclesia. There may well be a previous parallel Jewish tradition for viewing the first vessel — often shown as box-like in design — as a forerunner of the sanctuary.

For Jews, without the Solomonic temple's unique privileges of sacrifice, mystery and attendant priestly class, all subsequent places of, worship could never be more than communal centers for study or prayer. Only that building afforded a perpetual link between heaven and earth, as the sole divinely ordained sanctuary. For Catholics and many Protestant sects, any church, from the very greatest to the humblest parish chapel, is consecrated in the temple's name, image and function.

Solely by recreating the temple's actual appearance could the word and wish of God in humanly realizable form be fully apprehended. Visual documentation alone was crucial toward the absolute understanding of the physical expression of the divine. Never was the seen more important than in this single quest, the only known instance where the art of man, by recreating what had been devised for him by God, could extend the experimental dimension of divine wisdom into a spatial and visual as well as a verbal or aural area.

The origin and, in a profound way, even the motivation for post-Vitruvian Western architectural history may be found in Jews' and Christians' mutual compulsion to reconstruct the appearance of the first, second and third temples. Readings of the Bible, of Josephus, of the Talmud, of the medieval Jewish scholars like Rashi and Maimonides (so brilliantly studied by Rachel Wischnitzer, ''Maimonides' drawings of the temple'', *Journal of Jewish Art*, I, 1974, pp. 16-27) or Christian ones, such as those of Richard of Saint Victor or Nicolaus of Lyra, all helped answer the obsessive need to know just how the architecture of the absolute, the supreme building really looked.

The most exhaustively detailed study of the appearance and site of the lost temple was that of Benedictus Arias Montanus (1527-1598), whose *Exemplar sive de sacris fabricis liber* appeared in the Polyglot Bible of 1572, in the eighth and succeeding volumes thereof, published again as a single book in the *Antiquitatum Judaicorum* in 1593.[2]

Unsurprisingly, Jesuit collaboration resulted in what may have been the best-known reconstruction, the dual labor of Heronymo Prado (1547-1595) and Juan Bauttista Villalpanda (1552-1608). The first was the Spanish scholar, the second the artist, and they combined their respective talents for the massive three-volume *In Ezechielem Explanationes*. Their book is based in part on the monastic palace of the Escorial, whose design by Juan de Herrera was itself regarded as resulting from the architect's vision of the temple.

A chicken and egg relationship exists between much European palace design and reconstructions of the temple of Solomon, so many royal residences often recall that bleak yet magnificent monastery *cum* palace complex, the Escorial. As their royal residents were often the annointed heirs of David and Solomon, an equivalence between Europe's palaces and Solomon's was not unusual, whether this was the Spanish Habsburgs', the Venetian doges' — with its supposed source in Philo — or Philibert de l'Orme's rambling Tuileries for the Valois. None closely resembled the other, but all these palaces reflected similar powers and related faiths, each striving in its own fashion for identification with divinely Solomonic residence.

A remarkably detailed unpublished topographical view of Jerusalem (New York, private collection), drawn by the artist-priest Liévin Cruyl to illustrate Judas Maccabaeus' victory over Antiochus [Fig. 1], shows the Flemish painter's consultation of Villalpanda's plates which he may well have owned.

Rendered in black and brown ink over black chalk on parchment, the drawing, measuring 200 x 319 mm., was clearly meant to be engraved. A lengthy inscription on the back compares Louis XIV's revocation of the Edict of Nantes (1685) with Judas Maccabaeus' successful revolt and expulsion of the Syrian King Antiochus Epiphanes who had attempted to destroy Israel by Hellenization. Victory resulted in the re-dedication of the second temple by Judas Maccabaeus, built by David's descendant Zerubbabel, ca. 500 B. C.

It is amusing to see how Cruyl has Louis XIV out-Calvinizing Calvin, for it was the reformer who characterized Christian places of worship as temples, referred to in a long inscription on the back as Calvin's satanic temples:

MACHABEUS, ET QUI CUM IPSO ERANT. DOMINO DE PRO-TEGENTE. TEMPLUM/ quidem, & Ciivitatem recepit: aras autem, quas alienigenae per platcas extrúxerant,/ Itemque deliibra demolitus est.(Libro 2)

Machab. cap. 10

Antiochi impÿ Regis Ducibus pulsis, Judae Machabaei fortissi-mi viri heroicum/ ZELUM/ LUDOVICUS MAGNUS piè imitatus

Ex Gallia Calvinum impiissimum expulit, Templa Satanica, in quibus/ Cathedrae Pestilentiae dudum Coulum sacrilege blasphemanerant,/ demolitus est, Orthodoxum Dei Cultum, Catholicam/ avitam Religionem stabilviit, firmavit.

Jude Machabee recouvre le Temple et la Ville de Jerusalem profanés par/ Antioche Roy Paÿeym brisé les Autels et Temples des Idoles, chassé les/ princes des Paÿens par un Zèle & Courage invincible, le quel

1) Liévin Cruyl, **Topographic View of Jerusalem: Judas Maccabeus Victorious Over Antiochus** (New York, Private Coll.).

Louis le Grand imitant a chassé de la France calvin & ses Sectateurs,/ a brisé leur Temples, les Sÿnagoges de Satan les quels aboynt long temps blasphee le Ciel, a retabli la Religion ancienne, & orthodoxe Romaine.

Levinus Cruyl Pbr Gandensis [Ghent]
Delineavit ibid et dedicavit

Now the King has cast himself in a neo-Maccabean role, purifying his nation and his church by expelling the Protestants. The Flemish artist stresses his own priestly calling in the signature ''Levinus Cruyl Pbr'', which was the way all his drawings prepared in France were identified. Joseph Baillio kindly informed this writer that the New York drawing can be dated ca. 1689 on the basis of another drawing in the artist's native Ghent (Museum of Fine Arts), made in that year of the same subject, vertical in format, with an arched top (285 x 165 mm.), inscribed: JUDAS MACHABAEUS HOSTIBUS FUSIS CIVITATEM SANCTAM RECUPERAT TEMPLUMQUE IDOLATRIAE SORDIBVS PVRGATVM ISRAELITIS RESTITVIT [Fig. 2]. A triumphal procession enters Jerusalem, crossing the bridge in the foreground, bearing the temple's treasures, the sacred seven-branched candlestick and the ark.[3]

Subjects drawn from Maccabees were a favorite Counter-Reformation theme, beginning with Raphael's *Expulsion of Heliodorus*, seen later in the century in an engraved series of eight prints by Wierix (LeBl. 84-91), and later works by Rubens and Dorigny. Many seeventeenth-century artists benefited

LIV: CRVYL fecit 1689
IVDAS MACHABÆVS HOSTIBVS FVSIS CIVITATEM SANCTAM RECVPERAT,
TEMPLVMQVE IDOLOLATRIÆ SORDIBVS PVRGATVM ISRAELITIS RESTITVIT.

2) Liévin Cruyl, Judas Maccabaeus (Ghent, Museum of Fine Arts).

3) Liévin Cruyl, View of the Grand Canal and the Ponte Rialto in Venice, (New York, Private Coll.).

from the newly documentary records of the Franciscan Bernardo Amico di Gallipoli, whose *Trattato delle piane et imaggine de sacri edifizi di terra santa*, printed in Florence in 1620, was much consulted for the topography of the Holy Land.

The two studies devoted to Louis XIV show application of the Flemish priest's great topographical skills, developed in Rome, Venice, Genoa and Ghent before coming to France.[4] Cruyl's major activity was in the preparation of highly detailed views of European cities and ports, or battle scenes, but Guy Walton has recently suggested that he may have had very considerable architectural skills and that his high rate of pay in the French royal service could perhaps be connected with Liévin's as yet unknown architectural contribution toward the

designing of Versailles.[5] The artist may have planned to return to Italy but, according to Walton, remained in Paris from the late 1670's or early 1680's, definitely from 1681 onward.

Another unknown drawing by Cruyl (New York, private collection) [Fig. 3], also on vellum, measuring 150 x 215 mm., is similarly in brown and black ink over traces of graphite. A bird's-eye *View of the Grand Canal and the Ponte Rialto*, it is the sort of subject avidly collected in the seventeenth century and ever after. The drawing is inscribed on the back: *Prospectus Celeberrimi Pontis Ripa altae Venetye. Vulgo Ponte Rialto*. Like Cruyl's views of Rome, this topographical rendering may also have been meant to be reproduced in print form, as is suggested by the inscription.

4) Liévin Cruyl, View of Venice (Worcester Art Museum, Worcester, Mass.)

This page probably dates from 1676, the year in which the artist drew a *View of San Marco* [Fig. 4], Worcester Museum of Art, Mass. Langedijk suggested that this page might have been drawn on the artist's way back to Ghent.[6] It is inscribed: *Prospectus aurae S. Marci locorum adjacentium Venetis, a Livino Cruyl Delineatus 1676.*

Seventeenth-century Venice was better known for party than piety, but that city too had an unusually strong identification with the Chosen People. Like so many centers still close to the Byzantine rite, the Serenissima saw herself as a new Jerusalem, many of her churches were named for

prophets following in the Byzantine mode.

The unusual popularity of the theme of the Crossing of the Red Sea — subject of that massive, splendid multi-sectioned woodcut by Titian — could relate to the Venetians' seeing themselves as perpetually preserved by and from the waters, as God's new Jews. A mercantile center, the city-state had provided a leading example of the new commerce in Europe; it was also a center with an unusually large Jewish population, one which intersected in a most complex fashion with Venetian culture.

The Protestant Netherlands, far more genuinely hospitable

36

to the Jews than Venice, were to enjoy a similar combination of commerce and freedom from and of the seas, like Venice a region ever profiting by, yet saved from the waters. The Dutch saw themselves in many a fascinating way as David's descendants. Van de Wall's pioneering iconological study of the *Dutch Portrayal of History* (1952) showed how the Dutch took over Thomas Aquinas' definition of types as "persons, matters or actions taken from the Old Testament, which , by God's purpose and will are so directed that they indicate something of the future (17: 7)."[7] He found (as is in fact often true for earlier art in Venice and the Netherlands) the way in which views of Jerusalem were identical with those of prominent cities in the vicinity, such identification between ancient past and present a constant in the reassurance of faith.[8]

What the great Dutch scholar did not notice is how these comfortably off Protestant patrons and painters in the Lowlands commissioned or volunteered an unprecedentedly large variety of Old Testament subjects, many of these seldom, if ever shown on a large pictorial scale, and if so, only recently in Venice. Before then, these images had to appear in scholastic compilations of 5152 images selected in the thirteenth century, prophetic juxtapositions of Old and New Testament subjects vignetted in the massive *Bible Moralisée*. Three centuries later these subjects reappeared in the exhaustively illustrated mid-sixteenth century French Bible issued by Bernard Salomon, who was known as le Pétit Bernard due to the diminutive format of his hundreds of tiny woodcut vignettes. This, significantly, was the work of a secret Protestant who gave equal weight to almost every episode, without any reference to medieval scholastic thought.

Dutch Protestant artists, and the buyers of their works, seem to have rejoiced in the representation of sordid, all too human scenes from the first Testament, more likely selected for their lubricity than for any "redeeming social features", though doubtless these are to be found, if not in new Protestant

literature, then in that of the Counter-Reformation. Often deliberately ugly and awkward, they often verge upon the burlesque. In this they recall the humorous art of the Middle Ages, when the classical gods were reduced to Classic Comics, lowered to mortal state. So too were the patriarchs brought down to earth, often stripped of the heroic and the awesome, often shown as just folks, and very often the worst ones.

Other than their sexual *frisson* (as in the popularity of such subjects as Judah's seduction by his daughter-in-law Tamar), these images were designed to stress the human solidarity between the People of the Book and their self-proclaimed heirs in the Lowlands. Only they could love their putative ancestors, warts and all, in these veristic images of the lowest Biblical common denominator, where, but for the sake of God, go thee and I, the viewer challenged (if one may mix Testaments) to throw the first stone.

Whatever Dutch Baroque thoroughness failed to represent among a host of little-known or -wanted Old Testament subjects was taken up in the next century. Then the French Académie Royale was forced to select the most arcane Biblical episodes to test the inventive compositional and narrative powers of candidates for the Prix-de-Rome, to select the young painter who would go to Italy as "Pensionnaire du Roi." Boucher's First-Prize-winning submission in 1723 shows how *Evilmerodach frees Jehoiachin from Prison* (Columbia Museum of Art, Columbia, South Carolina) (Kings 2, 25, 27; Jeremiah 53, 31), a subject that is not known to have ever been done before as an independent painting.

In summary, these two unknown drawings by Liévin Cruyl touch upon many subjects close to Rachel Wischnitzer's life-long interests and will, with their accompanying comments, I hope be accepted in homage to her many achievements. I hope too that, before it is too late, the Bible's view of Jerusalem's temple be taken to heart by Israel: "My house shall be called a house of prayer for all peoples." (Isaiha 56: 7).

My very warmest thanks to Mr. Joseph Baillio for his generous provision of the Latin transcriptions and translations and of the drawing's technique and size. He also notified me of the sheets in Worcester and in Ghent.

[1] For the identification of Venetian and other governments with that instituted for the Hebrews when Moses or Joshua occupied the position of a king, and seventy-two were elected by the people and from the people, thus representing the principle of democracy, see S. Sinding-Larsen, "Christ in the Council Hall: Studies in the Religious Iconography of the Venetian Republic", *Acta ad Archeaologiam et Artium historiam Pertinentia*, 5, Rome, 1974, pp. 152 ff.

[2] For a fine survey of the *Vision of the Temple, The Image of the Temple of Jerusalem in Judaism and Christianity*, see the book of that title by H. Rosenau, London, 1979. For a monumental study, see T. A. Busink, *Der Tempel von Jerusalem von Salomo bis Herodes*, Leiden, 1970. See also J. Gutmann, ed., *The Temple of Salomon*, Missoula, 1976. Associations between the design of the Temple of Solomon and that of the royal palace have been studied by R. Taylor. See his *Architecture and Magic. Considerations on the Idea of the Escorial, Essays in the History of Architecture Presented to Rudolf Wittkower*, London, 1967, pp. 81-109, especially pp. 90-95, where the Escorial is seen as a re-creation of the temple of Solomon, and

Philip II as the biblical king (p. 90). See also J. Rykwert, *On Adam's House in Paradise*, New York, 1972, p. 122.

³ It was published in *Gent, duizend jaar kunst en cultur*, 1975, Cat. No. 259, plate 92.

⁴ For Cruyl's activities in the Lowlands between 1660 and 1664 and in Ghent in 1678, see P. Bergmans, ''Liévin Cruyl et sa vue panoramique de Gand en 1678'', *Bulletin de la société d'histoire et d'archéologie de Gand*, 22, No. 1, 1914, pp. 36 ff. See also K. Langedijk, ''Eine unbekannte Zeichnungsfolge von Lieven Cruyl in Florenz'', *Mitteilungen des Kunsthistorischen Instituts in Florenz*, 10, 1961-1963, pp. 67-94. The artist's Roman years (1664-70) are studied by

H. Egger, ''Lieven Cruyls Romische Veduten'', *Medelingen van het Nederlands Historisch Instituut*, Rome, 8, 1927, pp. 183 ff.

⁵ For Cruyl in France, see G. Walton, ''Lievin Cruyl: The Works for Versailles'', *Art the Ape of Nature*, New York, 1981, pp. 425-437. For the artist's drawings in France, see also F. Lugt, *Louvre, Cabinet de Dessins, Inventaire général de dessins des écoles du nord, Ecole Flamande*, I, Paris, 1949, Cat. Nos. 540-552.

⁶ Langedijk, *op. cit.*, p. 86.

⁷ H. van de Wall, *Drie eeuwen vaderlandsche geschied-uitbeelding 1500-1800, een iconologische studie*, The Hague, 1952, I, p. 299.

⁸ van de Waal, *op. cit.*, p. 300.

RALF BUSCH

Constantin Uhde als Synagogenarchitekt

''Angesichts des Ringens, das heute weltumgestaltende Geschehnisse mit einer Wucht aufrollen, wie sie die Geschichte unseres Weltteils kaum tiefer greifend und weiter ausholend aufzuweisen hat, erfaßt uns ein ehrfurchtvolles Staunen vor dem unwandelbaren, unerschütterlichen Bestehen unseres Volkes.''

So beginnt Rachel Bernstein-Wischnitzer ihre Abhandlung über Synagogen im ehemaligen Königreich Polen[1], in der sie die Geschichte und Funktion der Synagogen mit dem sie beseelenden Glauben in einer untrennbaren Einheit sehen läßt. Von nun an (1916) hat sie das Thema der Synagogenarchitektur zu ihrem Lebenswerk heranreifen lassen[2], das 1964 eine fundamentale Zusammenfassung fand[3]. Der norddeutsche Raum mit frühen Synagogen der Emanzipationszeit, z.B. dem Reformtempel in Seesen, hat darin Berücksichtigung gefunden.

Inzwischen ist in dieser Landschaft manches wiederentdeckt worden. Die barocke Synagoge in Celle und die ehemalige, jetzt wieder museal erlebbare aus Hornburg (Landesmuseum Braunschweig) lassen architektonische Entwicklungen erkennbar werden, die längst als verschüttet galten.

Auch über den Synagogenarchitekten Edwin Oppler in Hannover, der die Romanik verstärkt in seine Formensprache aufnahm[4], wissen wir heute gründlich Bescheid.

Sein Zeitgenosse im benachbarten Braunschweig, Constantin Uhde, blieb dagegen eher unbeachtet. Doch muß auch er als Architekt gewürdigt werden, dem synagogaler Bau nicht fremd war; zwei Synagogen hat er errichtet (Braunschweig und Wolfenbüttel), eine weiter entworfen (Dortmund). Gerade letztere Entwürfe sind betrachtenswert, aber bisher unveröffentlicht. Constantin Uhde (Braunschweig 1836-1905)[5] war

derjenige Architekt Braunschweigs, der in der zweiten Hälfte des 19. Jahrhunderts diese Stadt nachhaltig gestaltet hat. 1873/74 errichtete er in Braunschweig eine Synagoge und ein Gemeindehaus (letzteres ist bis heute erhalten, die Synagoge wurde ein Opfer der sog. Reichskristallnacht)[6]. Das Äußere der Synagoge [Fig. 1] war in Sandsteinquadern ausgeführt, beim Gemeindehaus wurde für die Wandflächen gelber Klinker verwendet. Es sind hier ausschließlich romanische Formen verwendet worden, allein die geschwungenen Zinnen über dem Dachgesims lassen an maurische Elemente denken. Auch das Innere hat den Gedanken des ''romanischen Domes'' sehr bewußt aufgegriffen.

Schon K. Steinacker hat bemerkt, daß diese Fassung noch etwas unsicher wirkt, besonders die Anregungen des maurischen Stils, der längst im Synagogenbau wirkte und selbst in Niedersachsen bereits vertreten war[7], sind hier kaum aufgegriffen worden. Eine, wenn auch entfernte Nähe zum Försterschen Bau in Wien zu sehen[8], liegt nicht sehr nahe, wenn man andere Bauten Uhdes aus dieser Zeit betrachtet[9].

Beachtung verdient die städtebauliche Situation. Das zur Verfügung stehende Grundstück lag an einer Straßenkreuzung (Steinstraße/Knochenhauerstraße). Uhde bindet die Synagoge in die Knochenhauerstraße ein, wogegen das Gemeindehaus auf die Kreuzungsecke gesetzt wird; sein Eingang, wenig betont, kommt nur dann ins Blickfeld, wenn man sich dem Gebäude vom Eiermarkt oder von der Petersilienstraße her nähert. Die Synagoge dagegen liegt nicht im Blickfeld. Ihre hohe Fassade ist in die Straßenflucht eingebunden und läßt die Kuppel nicht erkennen [vgl. Fig. 1].

Zu einer völlig anderen Lösung kommt C. Uhde beim Bau der Synagoge in Wolfenbüttel (1892-93)[10]. Sehr zu recht ist betont worden, daß dieser freistehende Bau von bis dahin bekannten

1) C. Uhde, Synagoge, Braunschweig (1873/74).

Gestaltungen abweicht. Die beiden Westtürme wirken fast minarettartig. Während der Bau in Braunschweig in Sandstein ausgeführt wurde, ist hier in Wolfenbüttel verschiedenes Baumaterial (Kalkstein, rote und schwarze Ziegel) verwendet worden [Fig. 2].

Die Turmformen der Fassade sind deutlich orientalisierend. Das Langhaus mit Rundbogenfenstern ist dagegen ganz schlicht gehalten. Eine befremdliche Besonderheit ist der sich im Osten befindende Schornstein, der turmartig ausgeführt ist. Das dreischiffig angelegte Gebäude ist im Inneren [Fig. 3] durch die Bemalung ebenfalls stark orientalisierend gestaltet. Auch

der in die Apsis hineingestellte Toraschrein fühlt sich dieser Tradition mit ihren maurischen Einflüssen verpflichtet, die Uhde auf einer Spanienreise kennengelernt hatte.

Bemerkenswert ist, daß C. Uhde in Wolfenbüttel auf einen Kuppelbau verzichtet, der sich in dieser Zeit allenthalben durchgesetzt hatte. Es ist daher erforderlich, eine allgemeine Standortbestimmung für diesen Bau vorzunehmen, d. h. einen kurzen Blick auf die Synagogenbautheorien des 19. Jahrhunderts zu werfen.

Die ersten Anfänge bürgerlicher Gleichstellung gehen mit der Übernahme des allgemein herrschenden klassizistischen

40

2) C. Uhde, Synagoge, Wolfenbüttel (1892-93), Vorderansicht.

3) C. Uhde, Synagoge, Wolfenbüttel, Inneres mit Blick nach Osten.

Stils einher, was zunächst nur einen Ausdruck jetzt erst möglich gewordener Repräsentation versinnbildlicht.[11]

Die eigentliche Phase der Emanzipation setzt erst in den 40er Jahren des 19. Jahrhunderts ein und findet den Weg zum orientalisierenden Stil, der an den Ursprung und an eine eigene Nationalität der Juden anknüpfen will, sich also deutlich von der sonst verbreiteten Architektur absetzt. Bemerkenswert erscheint, daß derartige theoretische Überlegungen keineswegs nur von jüdischer Seite ausgingen.

Wir beobachten in den ersten Anklängen dieser Zielrichtung architektonische Lösungen, die noch unsicher sind. G. Sempers Synagoge in Dresden, um 1838-1840 gebaut, ist in diesem Zusammenhang der Schlüsselbau. Außen noch überwiegend im Rundbogenstil gehalten, beschränken sich die orientalisieren-

den Elemente auf das Innere. Hans Semper, der Sohn des Architekten, hat später diesen Bau im Einklang mit der von seinem Vater formulierten Gebäudelehre für jüdische Tempel gesehen. Ein solches Programm ist nie bekannt geworden[12], man kann aber feststellen, daß derartige Gedanken nahe lagen und vielfältig wirkten.

Dagegen setzt E. Oppler in Verbindung mit der Planung seines ersten Synagogenbaus 1862-65 in Hannover eine eigene Theorie, die allerdings erst posthum 1882 publiziert wurde[13]. Er sah im romanischen Rundbogenstil die Zugehörigkeit der Juden zur deutschen Nation am besten ausgedrückt. In seinen profanen Bauten schloß er sich dagegen überwiegend dem gotischen Stil an. Was den jüdischen Kultbau betrifft, so beruft er sich auf frühe Synagogenbauten in Worms und Prag.

41

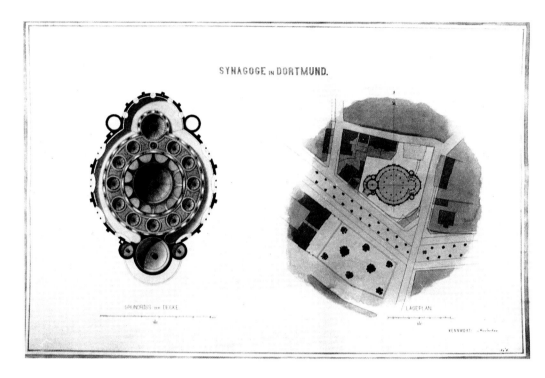

4) C. Uhde, Entwurf für eine Synagoge in Dortmund, Lageplan und Grundriß der Decke.

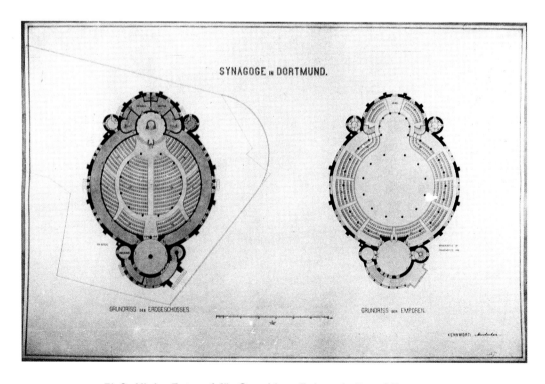

5) C. Uhde, Entwurf für Grundrisse Erdgeschoß und Emporen.

6) C. Uhde, Entwurf für Gesamtansicht.

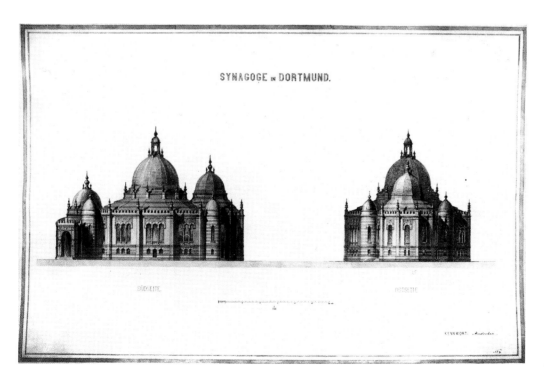

7) C. Uhde, Entwurf für Süd- und Ostseite.

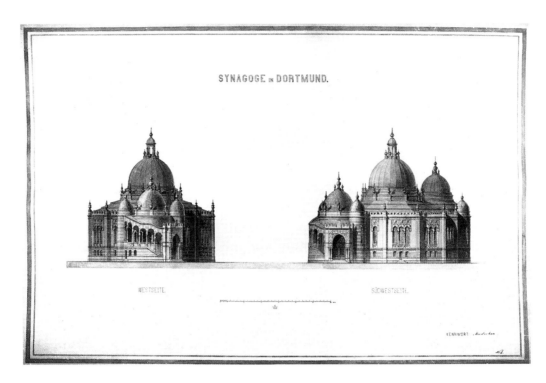

8) C. Uhde, Entwurf für West- und Südwestseite.

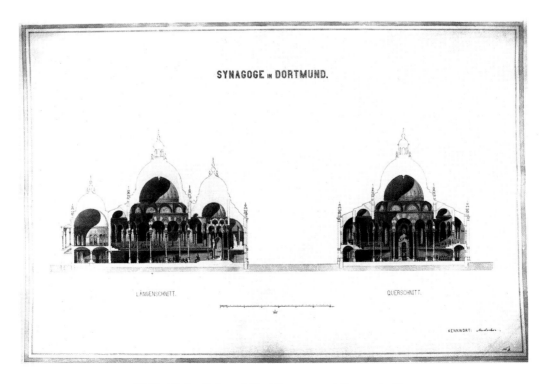

9) C. Uhde, Entwurf für Längen- und Querschnitte.

10) C. Uhde, Entwurf für Portal.

11) C. Uhde, Entwurf für Detail von der Südseite mit Neben-
eingang.

Der jüdische Architekt Oppler wendet sich also einer ''deut-
schen'' Lösung zu und verwirklicht diese in den Synagogen in
Hannover (1862/65), Breslau (1865/66), Schweidnitz (1872),
Hameln (1877) und gleichzeitig in Bleicherode. Hinzu treten
noch Entwürfe nicht gebauter Synagogen für Nürnberg (1868),
München (1871/76) und Karlsbad (1874). Er ist somit als
''Synagogenarchitekt'' zu bezeichnen; leider starb er unerwar-
tet schon 1880.

Fühlte sich C. Uhde im benachbarten Braunschweig als sein
Nachfolger? Uhde hat außerhalb Braunschweigs nur wenig ge-

wirkt. Mit der Synagoge in Wolfenbüttel hat er sich zweifelsoh-
ne gegen die Opplersche Theorie gestellt und eine eigenständi-
ge Lösung gefunden.

Von hier aus hat er sich an einem weiteren Wettbewerb,
diesmal für die Synagoge in Dortmund, beteiligt (1896). Diesen
hat er zwar nicht für sich entscheiden können, doch sind die
Entwürfe erhalten geblieben[14], bisher aber nicht publiziert. Sie
hier vergleichsweise heranzuziehen ist reizvoll, zumal sie kurz
nach dem Wolfenbütteler Bau entstanden sind. Der Wettbewerb für Dortmund wurde 1895 ausgeschrieben, die Ausfüh-

45

rung 1900 vollendet. Es lagen 59 Einsendungen vor.[15] Die dort dann verwirklichte Lösung ist entschieden worden durch die städtebauliche Nachbarschaft zur Oberpostdirektion, die 1895 im gotischen Stil errichtet worden war. Dieser ''Anpassung'' entsprach der Entwurf von C. Uhde nicht [Figs. 4-12].

Er entschied sich für einen Rundbau mit hoher Kuppel. Im Osten ist eine halbrunde Apsis mit weniger hohen Kuppel angefügt. Im Westen bildet ein runder Raum den Eingang. Die hohe Kuppel mit Laterne, die weiteren sechs Nebenkuppeln [Fig. 6] sowie auch Details im Grundriß bis hin zur Sitzaufteilung [Fig. 5] erinnern an barocke Lösungen, wie sie etwa aus der Dresdener Frauenkirche bekannt waren. Dies ist aber nebensächlich angesichts einer sonst total orientalisierenden Gestaltung und Dekoration. Uhde hatte sichtbare Schwierigkeiten, diesen monumentalen Bau auf dem unglücklich geschnittenen Grundstück zu plazieren [Fig. 4]. So kommt es zu dieser eigentümlichen Lage des Portals, das, an den runden Eingangsraum angesetzt, nach Südwesten weist [Figs. 5 und 10] und damit erst nach dem Betreten der Eingangshalle den Zutritt zur ''Männersynagoge'' vom Westen öffnet. Das Äußere, die gebänderten Mauern, Bögen und Säulen sowie die Ornamente sind rein maurisch gehalten. Diese Architektur hatte C. Uhde auf seiner Spanienreise 1888 erlebt und jetzt konsequenter als in Wolfenbüttel umgesetzt, was sich an einem Detail [Fig. 11] genau nachvollziehen läßt. Das Innere [Fig. 12] betont in seinen hellen, leichten Farben diese stilistische Hinwendung, die erkennen läßt, daß C. Uhde einen Bau geplant hat, der ebenbürtig neben den Besten dieser Zeit und Stilrichtung hätte bestehen können.

Die Entwürfe für Dortmund zeigen, daß C. Uhde nicht an E. Oppler anknüpfte, daß er seiner Synagogenbautheorie nicht anhing. Aber es ist auch erkennbar, daß Uhde sich von Braunschweig über Wolfenbüttel bis hin zu den Entwürfen für Dortmund konsequent zu einem Anhänger des maurischen Stils entwickelte. In diesem Sinne fühlte er sich sicher auch als Synagogenarchitekt. Wohl nur unter dieser Voraussetzung scheint er sich an dem Wettbewerb in Dortmund beteiligt zu haben.

Neben C. Uhdes Entwürfen ist auch seine Baubeschreibung erhalten geblieben, die hier im Wortlaut (ohne die Kostenberechnung) folgt.

''Erläuterungen

Die Grundrißanlage

Wesentlich bestimmend für die Anordnung des Grundrisses mußten die sub B II bis V vorgezeichneten Bedingungen des Wettbewerbes sein. Die größte Schwierigkeit lag in der Orientierung der Synagoge von West nach Ost bei Innehaltung der Bauflucht parallel mit dem Hiltrop-Wall, da beide Richtungen in einem spitzen Winkel nach Westen zusammenlaufen. Weil nun das Allerheiligste im Osten liegen muß, so war der Haupteingang im äußersten Westen des Grundstückes geboten und dieser, in der Fluchtlinie des Hiltrop-Walles gelegen, mußte mit der West-Ost-Richtung in Verbindung gebracht werden.

Vorhalle

Die Täuschung über die Richtungsveränderung des Eintretenden wurde am leichtesten durch einen kreisförmigen Grundriß der Vorhalle bewirkt.

Um weitere Richtungsverschiedenheiten zwischen den Bauteilen einerseits und dem Hiltrop-Wall und der Wisstraße andererseits zu vermeiden, ist auch den übrigen Räumen der Synagoge die Kreisform zu Grunde gelegt. Zudem aber ist diese die einfachste und übersichtlichste im Inneren und zugleich die relativ billigste in der Ausführung.

Raum für die Gemeinde

In den Hauptraum für die Gemeinde gelangt man entweder direkt durch die Vorhalle — besonders in der warmen Jahreszeit zu benutzen — oder durch die an der Kreisperipherie unter den Frauenemporen umlaufenden Kleiderablagen, die zugleich als Wandelgänge zu benutzen sind.

Die Kreisform des Hauptraumes ist für die central nach dem Allerheiligsten (der ideellen Ostrichtung) orientierten Sitze die möglichst beste, so daß alle Gemeindemitglieder das Allerheiligste, wie auch den Geistlichen sehen können. Ob eine Almemor — vielleicht in der Mitte der ganzen Anlage aufzustellen — beliebt wird, hängt von dem dortigen Ritus ab. Die für die Männer geforderte Zahl von 750 Sitzen à 58/100 ist selbst bei Aufstellung einer Almemor reichlich vorhanden. Am Ende der Kleiderablagen befinden sich beiderseits die Toiletten.

Das Allerheiligste

Dieser um einige Stufen erhöht liegende, 3/4 kreisförmige Raum kann bis in seine Mitte, wo die Bundeslade steht, von der ganzen Gemeinde gesehen werden. Die Estrade hat auch die geforderte Fläche von 69-70 m².

Die Frauen-Emporen

sind von der äußeren Vorhalle durch zwei Treppen zu erreichen. Man gelangt von diesen in die obere Vorhalle und von hier auf die Emporen. Auch führen noch die beiden Treppen zum Chor hinauf. Über denen der Männer, liegen an den Enden der

Emporengänge die Toiletten für die Frauen, deren Zugänge noch durch 4 Tapziehe verhängt werden können. Die 450 geforderten Plätze sind, in den verlangten Abmessungen 60/100 vollständig vorhanden.

Orgel und Chor

Hinter bzw. über dem Allerheiligsten liegt die Orgel, rechts und links von dieser die ca. 70 Sitze für die Chorsänger.

Nebenräume

Die Zimmer des Predigers und Cantors sind durch Nebenzugänge gesondert zu erreichen, während dieselben in direktem Zusammenhang untereinander und mit dem Allerheiligsten stehen. Die Zu- und Ausgänge der Synagoge — davon 5 vorhanden — sind so gelegt, daß, im Falle von Gefahr, ein jeder Besucher auf kürzestem Wege ins Freie gelangen kann.

Das Äußere

Das Material. Die Wahl des Materials für das Äußere erscheint bedingt durch den Wunsch, die Schauseiten von dem vielen Kohlenstaub, der sich in dortiger Gegend auf allen Gebäuden niederschlägt, längere Zeit rein zu halten bzw. reinigen zu können. Es ist nicht zu verkennen, daß sich für eine öftere Reinigung hart gebrannte Ziegelsteine und Terracotten besser eignen als irgendwelche Quader, die nur durch Überarbeitung zu reinigen sind, während erstere nur abgewaschen zu werden brauchen.

Stil

Über den Stil, in dem eine Synagoge erbaut werden sollte, gehen die Ansichten der Jetzt-Zeit vollständig auseinander. Historisch ist es begründet, daß Synagogen in dem jeweiligen Stil der Zeit und des betreffenden Landes erbaut wurden. Demnach wäre jede Stilart zulässig. Trotzdem sollte durch den Stil der Synagoge auf den orientalischen Ursprung des Volkes und der Symbolik seiner Religion hingewiesen werden. Läßt man diesen Grund gelten und berücksichtigt zugleich die oben angedeutete Materialfrage, so ist der für das gelieferte Projekt gewählte Stil des sog. *Mudechar* wohl berechtigt. Diese Stilart, die Vermischung des orientalischen Stils mit den Formen der Renaissance, also dem Stil des Abendlandes wurde in Spanien vielfach im 15. Jahrhundert nach dem Abzuge der Mauren benutzt. Dieselbe eignet sich besonders auch deshalb gut für den vorliegenden Zweck, weil durch die Satzungen der Religion figürliche Darstellungen verboten sind, die hier durch Pflanzenornamente ersetzt werden.

Das Innere

Der innere Aufbau und die Deckenkuppel- und Gewölbebildung entspricht vollständig dem Grundriß und der äußeren Silhouette. Über jedem Raume — der Vorhalle, dem Hauptraum für die Gemeinde und demjenigen für das Allerheiligste, sowie über den Treppentürmen — erhebt sich je eine Kuppel.

Diese, in Moniergewölben konstruiert, sind feuersicher und billig, geben dem Inneren zugleich den Charakter des Phantasievollen im Verein mit guter Akustik, welche durch die Auflösung der gesammten Decke in viele kleine Teile erreicht wird. Außerdem bedürfen diese Gewölbe geringe Widerlagerstärken der Außenmauern und nur zierliche Unterstützungen im Inneren durch eiserne Säulen, welche das Sehen in der Richtung nach dem Geistlichen und der Bundeslade kaum beeinträchtigen. Somit dürfte durch den Stil und die Construktion der Charakter und Zweck einer Synagoge äußerlich wie auch innerlich zum vollkommen einheitlichen Ausdruck gebracht sein.

Raum für die spätere Erbauung des Gemeindehauses ist gelassen, ebenso wie die Grenzen der Synagoge selbst allseits drei Meter von der Nachbar- und Straßengrenzen abliegen.''

Der Nichtjude C. Uhde plante in traditionalistischen Formen und sucht der jüdischen Geschichte Rechnung zu tragen. Das Preisgericht entschied sich jedoch für eine völlig andere Lösung und zog den Entwurf Uhdes nicht einmal in die engere Wahl. Er empfahl — aus städtebaulichen Gründen — sogar eine Abweichung von der West-Ost-Achse. Diesen Gedanken hat die jüdische Gemeinde bei der Ausführung des Baus verwirklicht — eine fast revolutionäre Tat.

[1] In: *Das Buch von den polnischen Juden*, hsg. von S. J. Agnon und A. Eliasberg, Berlin, 1916, S. 86 ff.

[2] Man vgl. die Hinweise bei: L. A. Mayer, *Bibliography of Jewish Art*, Jerusalem, 1967, Nr. 2803-2877 A.

[3] *The Architecture of the European Synagogue*, Philadelphia, 1964.

[4] P. Eilitz, ''Leben und Werk des königl. hannoverschen Baurats Edwin Oppler'', *Hannoversche Geschichtsblätter*, N. F. 25, 1971, S. 131 ff.

[5] K. Steinacker, ''Constantin Uhde'', *Braunschweigisches Magazin*, 1906, S. 13-22 und 29-34.

[6] R. Busch, ''Der ehemaligen jüdischen Gemeinde Braunschweigs zum Gedanken'', *Veröffentl. des Braunschweiger Landesmuseums*, 11, 1977; H. Hammer-Schenk, ''Synagogen in Deutschland'', *Hamburger Beiträge zur Geschichte der deutschen Juden*, Bd. 8, 1981; R. Hagen, ''Lessings 'Nathan' und die jüdische Emanzipation im Lande

Braunschweig'', *Lessing-Akademie Wolfenbüttel*, 1981, Nr. 162-163.

[7] Zuerst in Hildesheim von 1849. Der Zentralraum gehörte zwar dem Rundbogenstil an, aber die querliegende Eingangshalle zeigt deutlich orientalisierende Element nicht nur mit den beiden Türmen in Minarettform.

[8] H. Künzl, *Islamische Stilelemente im Synagogenbau des 19. und frühen 20. Jahrhunderts*, Frankfurt/M, 1984, S. 256. Zeitgenossen haben allerdings das orientalische Elemente deutlicher gesehen; vgl. Hammer-Schenk, *op. cit.*, S. 327.

[9] Verzeichnis bis Steinacker, *op. cit.*, S. 33 f.

[10] Hammer-Schenk, *op. cit.*, S. 369; Künzl, *op. cit.*, S. 384; Hagen, *op. cit.*, Nr. 165 und 166.

[11] Vgl. Wischnitzer, *op. cit.*, S. 158-161.

[12] Hierzu Künzl, *op. cit.*, S. 175-185.

[13] Hammer-Schenk, *op. cit.*, S. 199 ff.; ergänzend H. Hammer-Schenk, ''Edwin Opplers Theorie des Synagogenbaus. Emanzipationsversuche durch Architektur'', *Hannoversche Geschichtsblätter*, N. F. 32, 1979, S. 101-113.

[14] Im Braunschweigischen Landesmuseum, dem ich für die Genehmigung zur Veröffentlichung danke. Dort sind auch alle weiteren Abbildungen für diesen Aufsatz zu finden (Figs. 1-3).

[15] Vgl. hierzu Hammer-Schenk, *op. cit.*, 1981, S. 415 ff.

GABRIELLE SED-RAJNA

La danse de Miryam

Dans l'*Encyclopaedie Judaica* publiée à Berlin en 1931, l'entrée *Haggada*[1] renferme le paragraphe suivant: ''Die Vorbilder für die figürliche Illustration findet die Haggada in der bestehenden christlichen Bibelillustration deren Kern einen Jüdischen Bilderzyklus enthalten haben mag.''

L'auteur de l'article, Rachel Wischnitzer-Bernstein, fut sans doute étonnée de voir cette théorie hardie — avancée plus sur fond d'intuition que sur base de preuves tangibles —, être confirmée de manière spectaculaire un an à peine après la parution de l'article. L'événement qui a fourni la confirmation de la thèse de Rachel Wischnitzer était, bien entendu, la mise au jour, en 1932, des peintures de la synagogue de Doura Europos.

Avant la découverte de Doura, les recherches sur les origines de l'iconographie biblique étaient arrivées à un *consensus* dont les points principaux se résument comme suit:

— L'Antiquité tardive a produit une illustration narrative fondée sur le récit biblique, visualisant le texte épisode par épisode, de manière fidèle dans tous ses détails;
— nombre d'épisodes sont enrichis d'éléments dont la source n'est pas la Bible, mais une littérature juive spécifique connue sous le nom de *midrash*;
— une partie de cette littérature ayant été connue par les Pères de l'Eglise syriens ou grecs, les écrits de ceux-ci étaient considérés comme les sources les plus probables des dites illustrations. Cette hypothèse était renforcée par le fait qu'avant 1932 on ne connaissait que des monuments et des manuscrits chrétiens pourvus de telles images bibliques.

La découverte de Doura invitait à réviser toutes les hypothèses. Les peintures présentaient, en effet, un ensemble biblique élaboré dont aucun monument chrétien n'offrait l'équivalent. Ces peintures, antidatant d'un siècle les plus anciens témoins chrétiens, correspondaient parfaitement au type d'illustrations défini plus haut: fidélité au texte et présence cumulée d'éléments midrashiques. Qui plus est, du fait que Doura présente une sélection répondant à un programme, il semblait évident que ceux qui avaient conçu ce programme disposaient d'un répertoire plus large de séquences narratives. Autant dire que Doura n'était elle-même qu'une étape dans une évolution déjà en route. Cette constatation invitait à faire reculer la date de création de l'hypothétique archétype jusqu'aux alentours du IIe siècle. Le lieu d'une telle création ne pouvait être Doura, petite ville reléguée aux confins orientaux de l'Empire, située hors des grands circuits culturels, et dont les peintures n'ont été visibles que pendant onze ans, de 245, date de leur achèvement, à 256, année de la prise de Doura par les Parthes. Rapprocher le lieu de cette création de celui où les textes qui ont inspiré cette iconographie furent mis par écrit, à savoir la Judée et la Galilée, semblait dès lors une hypothèse plus acceptable. Elle était par ailleurs renforcée par certains éléments des peintures mêmes de la synagogue. La façade du Temple surmontant la niche, est en effet en tous points identique à celle que portent les monnaies de Bar Kokhba frappées en 134, ou à celle qui apparait sur un linteau de Capharnaum. Ces indices suggéraient qu'il s'agissait là de traditions originaires de la Terre Sainte et transmises vers l'Est. C'est une transmission vers l'Ouest qui a été probablement responsable de la dissémi-

1) «La création d'Eve», Haggadah de Sarajevo, fol. 3v, a.

3) «L'expulsion du Paradis. Les labeurs d'Adam et d'Eve», Haggadah de Sarajevo, fol. 3v, b.

2) «La création d'Eve», Antependium de Salerne, XIe siècle (D'après R. P. Bergman, *The Salerno Ivories*.)

4) «L'ivresse de Noé», Antependium de Salerne, XIe siècle (D'après R. P. Bergman, *The Salerno Ivories*.)

nation de certains de ces éléments iconographiques en Europe et de leur intégration dans la décoration de monuments destinés à des chrétiens. De tels monuments sont attestés en Occident à partir du IVe siècle, et leur diffusion est continue dans l'Empire, à Byzance, dans l'Ouest jusqu'aux îles britan-

niques et dans le Nord jusqu'aux pays germaniques, pendant tout le moyen-âge.

Dans le domaine juif les traces d'une telle transmission sont perdues. Entre Doura, ou son modèle, et le XIVe siècle où l'iconographie biblique réapparait dans les Haggadot, le hiatus semblait être total. C'est cette apparente absence de continuité qui a incité beaucoup de chercheurs, et Rachel Wischnitzer elle-même, à suggérer que la tradition avait été réellement rompue: les artistes juifs du moyen-âge n'auraient eu à leur disposition aucun autre modèle que les manuscrits chrétiens contemporains.

Toutefois des recherches récentes[2], une analyse approfondie des documents, invitent à remettre en question le bienfondé de cette théorie. Une comparaison des images bibliques des Haggadot avec celles des Psautiers, dont on les a le plus souvent rapprochées, montre que, en réalité, les affinités sont plutôt superficielles. Elles concernent les styles — phénomène d'époque nécessairement partagé par les artisans de tous bords vivant dans le même milieu — et aussi l'organisation en cycles préfixés au texte. Mais sur le fond, les divergences l'emportent sur les affinités. La sélection des scènes est différente de part et d'autre, et différentes sont aussi les formules de représentation. Toutefois, de nombreuses formules employées dans les Haggadot sont similaires, non pas à celles de l'art chrétien contemporain, mais à celles des monuments de l'Antiquité tardive évoqués plus haut. De plus, chacune des Haggadot renferme des scènes apparentées non pas à un seul, mais à cinq ou six monuments, d'époques diverses et d'origine différente.

Pour mieux illustrer notre propos, nous examinerons quelques scènes choisies parmi les peintures de la très célèbre Haggada de Sarajevo.

Les deux pages qui évoquent l'oeuvre des six jours de la Création (follios 1v-2r) présentent une composition qui est, sauf erreur de notre part, sans parallèle. En revanche, la création d'Adam, le sixième jour, reprend une formule attestée aussi dans les Octateuques byzantins du XIIe siècle[3]. La création d'Eve [fol. 3r, a; Fig. 1] présente une formule qui s'écarte du texte hébreu: Eve n'est pas formée d'une côte d'Adam, mais émerge de *son côté*. Les deux interprétations possibles du terme hébreu *zela*, sont envisagées dans la Genèse Rabba[4], et dans l'iconographie ancienne les deux sont attestées. Dans la récension de la Genèse de Cotton, la création de la femme a lieu à partir de la côte prise à l'homme. Une autre récension dont les témoins sont les ivoires de Salerne du XIe siècle[5] et les Octateuques[6], visualise l'alternative [Fig. 2]. C'est à cette tradition qu'appartient aussi la Haggadah. L'image inférieure de la même page (folio 3v, b) réunit deux épisodes: à droite Adam et Eve se couvrent et se cachent devant la voix de Dieu; à gauche ils sont déjà hors du Paradis et vacquent à leurs occupations: Adam travaille la terre, Eve tient la quenouille [Fig. 3].

Le premier épisode est formulé comme dans la Genèse de Vienne[7]. Dans le second, Eve avec la quenouille a des parallèles dans la Genèse de Cotton et les monuments qui en dérivent: les mosaïques de Saint-Marc à Venise[8] et un manuscrit du XIVe siècle de l'*Histoire Universelle*, conservé à

5) «L'ivresse de Noé», Haggadah de Sarajevo, fol. 6r, a.

Vienne, qui provient également de Venise[9]. Il est intéréssant de relever que les deux récensions, celle de la Genèse de Cotton et celle de la Genèse de Vienne, si manifestement divergentes en général, se rencontrent dans le cycle de la Haggada. Toutefois, les affinités avec la tradition véhiculée par la Genèse de Vienne sont plus nombreuses. Ainsi dans l'épisode de l'ivresse de Noé, tous les témoins de la récension de la Genèse de Cotton présentent les deux fils de Noé, Sem et Japhet, s'approchant pour couvrir leur père, non pas à reculons comme il est écrit (Gen. 9, 23), mais ayant seulement la tête détournée[10]. Dans la Genèse de Vienne [11], et les ivoires [Fig. 4], au contraire, ils s'approchent à reculons. Il en est de même dans la Haggadah de Sarajevo [fol. 6r, a; Fig. 5].

Dans le songe de Jacob [fol. 10r, b; Fig. 6], le nombre réduit des anges — les deux qui sont indispensables au récit — et le ciel ouvert au sommet de l'échelle, sans aucun symbole de la divinité, était probablement la formule originale. Les deux anges sont encore visibles à Doura[12] et aussi dans la peinture correspondante de la catacombe de la Via Latina[13]. Certes, la partie supérieure de la peinture est perdue dans les deux monuments, mais il est vraissemblable que l'échelle était surmontée par un fragment de ciel, comme le montre encore la scène sur la plaque d'ivoire de Salerne [Fig. 7] et celle de l'Octateuque du XIIe siècle[14]. L'ajout d'un ange — voire de deux anges[15] — dans les Haggadot, ou celui d'un buste du Christ dans l'art chrétien du moyen-âge, résultent de préoccupations doctrinales propres aux tendances théologiques médiévales.

Dans le cycle de Joseph, il y a deux scènes qui méritent une attention particulière. Otto Pächt avait déjà signalé leur intérêt

6) «Le songe de Jacob», Haggadah de Sarajevo, fol. 10r, b.

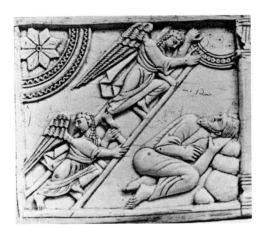

7) «Le songe de Jacob», Antependium de Salerne, XIe siècle (D'après R. P. Bergman, *The Salerno Ivories*.)

8) «La femme de Putiphar cherchant à séduire Joseph», Haggadah de Sarajevo, fol. 13v, a.

et les implications quant à la filiation des traditions iconographiques. Dans l'épisode qui se déroule dans la maison de Putiphar [fol. 13v, a; Fig. 8] les Haggadot juives[16], la Genèse de Vienne (fol. 16r) et trois Bibles exécutées à Saint-Jean-d'Acre[17] sont les seuls manuscrits à représenter la femme de Putiphar s'efforçant de séduire Joseph, assise sur son lit. Tous les documents dépendant de la Genèse de Cotton ainsi que l'art chrétien du moyen-âge représentent la séductrice debout. Cette coïncidence montre que là encore, les Haggadot reflètent une tradition ancienne, qui leur est propre et qui rejoint celle qui était à la source de la Genèse de Vienne. La deuxième scène est celle du banquet offert par Joseph à ses frères (fol. 16r, a). O. Pächt[18] a justement noté que la scène ne peut être identifiée que grâce à la lecture du Targum palestinien et non pas par le texte de la Bible. Cette scène apparait aussi dans la Haggadah Catalane[19], et dans une copie tardive des homélies d'Ephrem le Syrien dont O. Pächt pense qu'elle dérive d'un manuscrit ancien originaire de la région même où Ephrem vivait.

Le modèle antique de la Haggadah comprenait également les illustrations de l'Exode. Plusieurs images présentent des ressemblances manifestes avec les scènes correspondantes des Octateuques, ou celles des ivoires de Salerne. La plus parlante de ces similitudes est l'illustration de la danse de Miryam dans la Haggadah (fol. 28r, b) et la même scène dans l'Octateuque du XIIe siècle conservé au Vatican [Fig. 9, 10].

Il est même probable que le modèle renfermait un cycle d'illustrations du Pentateuque tout entier. C'est au moins la conclusion que suggère la mise en forme de l'épisode de Moïse bénissant le peuple avant sa mort (Deut. 33, 1) dans la Haggadah (fol. 31v, a) et, de manière identique, dans la Bible de Léon[20], datée de 960.

Les quelques sondages que nous venons d'effectuer nous ont amenées à évoquer à titre de comparaison des documents d'origines extrêmement variées: Doura, du IIIe siècle, et les peintures de la Via Latina à Rome, du IVe siècle, pour le songe de Jacob; la Genèse de Vienne, originaire d'Antioche ou de Jérusalem, du VIe siècle, pour la scène d'Adam et Eve se cachant devant Dieu; l'ivresse de Noé et la femme de Putiphar au lit; les Octateuques faits à Constantinople aux XIe et XIIe siècles pour la création d'Adam, la création d'Eve, la danse de Miryam; la récension de la Genèse de Cotton, du Ve siècle, provenant d'Alexandrie, pour Eve tenant la quenouille, enfin la Bible de Léon de 960 pour la scène de Moïse bénissant le peuple.

Les exemples évoqués n'épuisent pas les comparaisons possibles. Ils fournissent simplement un échantillonnage qui montre l'invraisemblance de l'hypothèse considérant l'un ou l'autre, ou encore l'ensemble des documents évoqués comme ayant été la source directe du peintre de la Haggadah. La seule supposition satisfaisante est celle d'un modèle unique, renfer-

9) «La danse de Miryam», Haggadah de Sarajevo, fol. 28r, b.

10) «La danse de Miryam», Vat. gr. cod. 746, fol. 194v. (D'après K. Weitzmann, *Studies in Classical and Byzantine Manuscript Illumination*.)

mant toutes les scènes mentionnées, conservé et transmis directement en milieux juifs. Cette même tradition, reprise partiellement et en dehors de la filière directe, apparait sporadiquement dans les documents chrétiens à travers une série d'intermédiaires qui sont peut-être perdus ou restent encore à découvrir.

Que le modèle originel ait été juif, est prouvé par le caractère même de la Haggadah de Sarajevo. En effet, il y a de nombreuses scènes dont l'identification est incomplète à la lumière du texte hébreu, ou à la lecture de la traduction grecque de la Bible. Il y a des détails qui ne s'expliquent que par la paraphrase araméenne, le Targum, et uniquement selon la version palestinienne de ce texte. Hormis le banquet de Joseph déjà relevé par O. Pächt[21], on peut citer la scène d'Isaac bénissant Jocob [fol. 9v, b; Fig. 11]. Rebecca y assiste en tenant un vêtement dans ses mains: c'est le vêtement reçu par Adam, lorsqu'il a quitté l'Eden et qui fut transmis d'aîné en aîné jusqu'à Esaü; il fut enlevé à ce dernier lorqu'il vendit son droit d'aînesse et remis à Jacob par Rebecca[22]. Seul le Targum dit du Pseudo-Jonathan[23] précise que le sarcophage de Joseph fut immergé dans le Nil (fol. 26r, b), comme il signale aussi le fait que la fille de Pharaon descendit elle-même au Nil pour y découvrir l'enfant Moïse (fol 26r, b)[24]. Pharaon sauvé de la mer (fol. 26r, a) est également un thème du midrash que l'art chrétien ignore[25]. Par ailleurs, il y a des épisodes dont l'importance ne paraît que dans la perspective de la tradition juive. Ainsi la sortie d'Isaac allant à la rencontre de Rébecca, qui serait à l'origine de l'institution de la prière de *minhah* [fol 8r, b; Fig. 12].

Certes, la preuve matérielle qui permettrait d'ériger en certitude ce faisceau de vraisemblances manque, et manquera peut-

11) «Isaac bénissant Jacob», Haggadah de Sarajevo, fol. 9v, b.

12) «Isaac allant à la rencontre de Rebecca», Haggadah de Sarajevo, fol. 8r, b.

être toujours. Mais la force des arguments croît de jour en jour. S'il était possible d'affirmer en 1931, qu'il y avait, dans l'Antiquité tardive, une iconographie biblique créé en milieux juifs, les recherches récentes permettent aujourd'hui d'avancer d'un pas. Elles permettent de formuler la thèse de l'existence d'une tradition d'imagerie biblique conservée et transmise directement, par la médiation des communautés juives de l'Italie du Sud ou de l'Afrique du Nord, jusqu'aux artistes juifs de la Catalogne du XIVe siècle. Ce sont ces traditions qui ont servi à la composition des cycles bibliques des Haggadot.

[1] Volume VII, colonne 807.

[2] Nous avons longuement développé ce problème dans notre récent ouvrage, *La Bible hébraïque*, Fribourg-Paris, Bonn, New York, 1987.

[3] Vatican, Bibl. Apostolique, Vat. gr. 747, fol. 19r; Istanbul, Bibl. du Sérail, fol 42v.

[4] Genèse Rabba, Viii, 3.

[5] Cf. R. P. Bergman, *The Salerno Ivories*, Cambridge, Mass., 1980.

[6] Vat. gr. 747, fol. 37r, reproduit dans Bergman, *op. cit.*, fig. 57.

[7] Vienne, Österreichische Nationalbibliothek, cod. theol. gr. 31, fol. 1v.

[8] O. Demus, *The Mosaics of San Marco in Venice*, Chicago, 1984; K. Weitzmann, H. Kessler, *The Cotton Genesis. British Library Codex. Cotton Otho B. VI*, Princeton, 1987, fig. 60 et 66.

[9] Cf. K. Koshi, *Die Genesisminiaturen in der Wiener ''Histoire Universelle'' (Cod. 2576). Wiener Kunstgeschichtliche Forschungen*, Vienne, 1973.

[10] Cf. Weitzmann, Kessler, *op. cit.*, figures, 134, 135, 138.

[11] Folio 3v.

[12] C. H. Kraeling, *The excavations at Dura Europos. Final Report. VIII, The Synagogue*, New Haven, 1956, pl. XXVI.

[13] A. Ferrua, *Le pitture della catacomba di Via Latina*, Cité du Vatican, 1960, pl. XXV.

[14] Smyrne, fol. 41v.

[15] Notamment dans la Haggadah Catalane, Londres, Brit. Libr. Or. ms 2884, fol. 4v, b. Cf. Sed-Rajna, *La Bible hébraïque*, *op. cit.*, fig. 59

[16] La Haggadah d'Or. Brit. Libr. Add. ms 27210, fol. 6v, d. Cf. B. Narkiss, A. Cohen, A. Tcherikhover, *Hebrew Illuminated Manuscripts in the British Isles*, Londres, 1982, fig. 129; Haggadah Catalane, fol 7r, b. Cf. Sed-Rajna, *op. cit.*, fig 85.

[17] H. Buchthal, *Miniature Painting in the Latin Kingdom of Jerusalem*, Oxford, 1957.

[18] O. Pächt, ''Ephraimillustration, Haggada und Wiener Genesis'', in *Festschrift Karl Swoboda*, Wiesbaden, 1959, pp. 213-21.

[19] Folio 9v, b, cf. Sed-Rajna, *op. cit.*, fig. 96.

[20] Léon, Cathédrale San Isidoro, Ms. 2. Cf. H. Kessler, *The Illustrated Bibles from Tours*, Princeton, 1941, fig. 98, 99.

[21] Cf. l'article cité dans la note 18.

[22] Targum du Pseudo-Jonathan sur Genèse 27, 15-23, cf. la légende à la figure 57 dans Sed-Rajna, *op. cit.*

[23] Sur Gen. 50, 26. Cf. la légende à la figure 101 dans Sed-Rajna, *op. cit.*

[24] Cf. J. Gutmann, ''Josephus' Jewish Antiquities in Twelfth Century Art: Renovatio or Creatio?'', *Zeitschrift für Kunstgeschichte*, 48, 1985, pp. 434-41.

[25] Cf. B. Narkiss, ''Pharaoh is Dead and Living in the Gates of Hell'', *Journal of Jewish Art*, 10, 1984, pp. 6-13.

ZIVA AMISHAI-MAISELS

The Iconographic Use of Abstraction in Jankel Adler's Late Works*

The tendency towards abstraction in Jankel Adler's late works has been analyzed in the past primarily in stylistic terms. Various influences have been discerned to explain his shift in style and much has been made of his own influence on British artists during and after World War II.[1] However, it has not been remarked that Adler's use of abstraction was often very idiosyncratic, and that there are many paintings which juxtapose figurative to abstract elements as though setting up contrasts between two levels of reality [e.g., Figs. 1-2]. This goes beyond the play between abstraction and figuration common to many artists between the two World Wars, and merits a study of what exactly Adler's abstract forms meant to him. For this purpose, it is important to determine what kind of an artist he was and when he first turned to abstraction.

Born near Lodz in Poland, Adler was a prominent figure in German art in the twenties, friendly with both Otto Dix and Paul Klee and moving with ease from his early Expressionism to the more objective approach of the Neue Sachlichkeit.[2] From the start, he had been involved in attempts to create a modern Jewish art, often embellishing the Jewish village scenes he painted with Hebrew or Yiddish inscriptions.[3] In 1933, with the rise of Hitler to power, Adler fled Düsseldorf for Paris and began to experiment — apparently for the first time — with abstraction, producing a series of biomorphic works strongly influenced by Klee, Picasso, Jean Arp, and Auguste Herbin.[4] The transition to abstraction at just this moment is illuminating. Adler had been on close terms with Klee since 1931 without it having influenced his art.[5] He had just undergone a traumatic change in his life, leaving not only the country in which he had become an established artist, but his German wife, Betty Kohlhaas, and their little daughter, Nina. This separation had

been caused because he was Jewish, yet this painter of Jewish themes did not continue with this type of subject matter or express his longing for his child in his art. Instead, he took up the semi-abstract forms that he had developed in the backgrounds of paintings from the early 1930's which had been fraught with anxiety, and turned them into ghost-like, sometimes frightened, abstracted figures, whose biomorphic forms seem completely unconnected to his life.[6] It would seem that at this critical point in his life, Adler retired into an abstract world of art to distance himself from his fears by concentrating on purely formal problems. Yet Adler himself was apparently unconscious of the reasons for this change in his art, and his pronouncements tend to stress the usual ideas on abstract art common to modern artists.[7] Even his pictorial comment on this artistic development, the *Taming of a Bird,* of 1934, seems inherently playful and ironic. In this painting, two abstracted "figures" play with a rather more naturalistic bird, trying, it would seem, to get him to jump through a hoop. The bird, which is the size and general shape of an eagle, may well symbolize Adler himself, whose name means "eagle" in German, and who had occasionally used this bird as an alter-ego.[8] The "Adler-bird" is shown here learning new tricks in Paris, and is concentrating on them rather than on expressing his own feelings.

That this was not a thoroughly natural development can be seen in Adler's switch back to a figurative style when he returned to Warsaw in 1935, travelling in a sealed train through Germany, and meeting his wife and daughter only on the train on his way there and on his return to France in 1937. In the few works that have come down to us from this and the following periods, he seems to have absorbed abstraction into

55

1) Jankel Adler, «Girl with Rocking Toy», 1941, Israel Museum, Jerusalem.

a new figurative style, flatter and less naturalistic than his previous one.[9] When the war broke out, he enlisted in the Western Polish Army and, after Dunkirk, was evacuated to Scotland, moving to London in 1943, where he associated with English artists while retaining Polish and Jewish affiliations.[10]

During this last period, Adler returned to abstraction in a series of works in which he tried to express his feelings as a refugee hiding in a besieged land. One of the earliest of these works is *Girl with Rocking Toy*, of 1941 [Fig. 1], in which the picture space is divided into two rooms separated by a wall, one of Adler's favorite compositional schemes during the war.[11] On the left, the ''toy'' inhabits a confined geometric interior,

divided by a ''wall'' from the flat red and black compartment on the right which is occupied by a more naturalistically rendered girl. The juxtaposition of the two realities, with the forms of the ''toy'' echoing those of the girl, recalls similar juxtapositions in the works of Picasso, the best known of which is *Model with Surrealistic Sculpture*, of 1933. At first glance, the geometric forms from which the toy is constructed are also reminiscent of Picasso's *An Anatomy*, also of that year.[12] But this is not merely a meeting of two realities with playful or sarcastic comments on the artist's personal life, as is the case in Picasso's works, since the forms of the ''toy'' also recall those Klee had been using for years, especially those in the *Fate*

56

2) Jankel Adler, «Woman with a Still Life», 1942, Naftali Bezem collection, Tel Aviv.

3) Jankel Adler, «Jews in Hiding», 1943, present whereabouts unknown.

4) Jankel Adler, «Girl Leaving Room», 1943, present whereabouts unknown.

of a Child, of 1937, with its suggestion of tragedy, and the broken and fearful figures in *Outbreak of Fear*, of 1939.[13] The abstracted ''toy'' is thus really a person, whose destroyed body can be patched together, but which can never return to its original form. The result of the confrontation between the two realities is a feeling of anxiety: each figure is isolated and trapped in its own space, but the formal similarity between them suggests that the fate which befell the ''toy'' may soon befall the woman. This anxiety is heightened by the narrow flat bright red space in which she is confined, a space which impinges on her body the more one looks at the painting.

In the works of 1942, it is the broken abstract form — sometimes recalling a still life on a chair as had the statue in Picasso's etching, sometimes more closely approaching a human form — which occupies a narrow space that is never as dark and confining as is the wider room inhabited by the more naturalistic figure. In the most expressive of these works, *Woman with a Still Life* [Fig. 2], the blue-faced woman closely

resembles one of the *Two Orphans*, of the same year, which Adler painted upon hearing that the parents of his friend Josef Herman had been killed in the Holocaust.[14] She sits behind a table on which a group of abstract objects appear almost as debris, in a dark constricted room, which is all the darker as it is divided from the lit area containing the abstract figure by a ''wall'' — a piece of wood attached to the canvas. The artist suggests that she lives in hiding in the dark, afraid of the fate that awaits her outside, which is suggested by the broken forms of the abstract figure. This feeling is reinforced by the yellow bird atop his cage beside her. Is it comforting her in her isolation, or do the sharp lines pointing towards the bird indicate that she will silence it rather than let it betray her?[15]

The element of anxiety in this work is repeated throughout the war years in other paintings, in which single figures are confined to dark rooms and often set beside the ''broken'' forms of a statue or still life. Sometimes, as in the case of *Woman in a Room*, of 1943, the forms seem completely

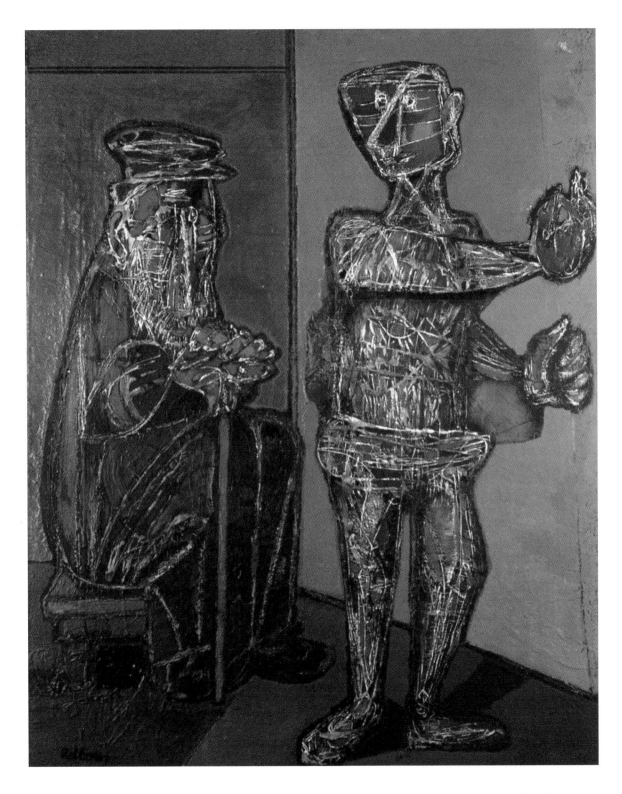

5) Jankel Adler, «Two Figures», 1944, Mr. and Mrs. Jacob Schulman collection, Gloversville, New York.

6) Jankel Adler, «Two Figures«, 1941, present whereabouts unknown.

7) Jankel Adler, «Sketch for Destruction», 1943, present whereabouts unknown.

innocent, and it is the contrast between the blue tones of the entire painting and the bright red patches that invade the woman's head and are scattered like spots of blood over her body, the chair and the table that create a feeling of foreboding.[16] At other times, as in *Old Man looking into a Room* and *Metamorphosis*, both of 1944, the human figure has shrunk to a barely discernible, ghostly head at the top or bottom of the painting, yielding its place to the more aggressive shapes of the abstract ''still life''.[17]

The meaning of this confinement in a dark space and the reasons for the feelings of anxiety these ''neutral'' subjects arouse become clear from a series of drawings Adler did in 1943. One of these sketches [Fig. 3] narrates two episodes of a story in a straightforward manner, and supplies the key to the paintings. Above, Jews hide in a small dark room, the women turning their fearful gaze towards the spectator, as they do in the interiors examined above. Below, a couple

leaves the safety of its home, whose door, with its protecting mezuzah, is clearly delineated at the left, and is caught in a Nazi searchlight.[18] In a slightly later sketch, these figures are naked and their forms have been highly fragmented as they undergo abstraction.[19] Another sketch in this series is also divided into two parts [Fig. 4].[20] The scene on top involves the breakdown of the split composition we examined in the paintings: the woman in the dark room bursts through the partition, which now has a doorknob, in exactly the same pose of outstretched arms and head turned to the spectator as that of the bearded Jew leaving his hiding place. In leaving her room, she passes the abstract ''broken'' figure whose head seems to be raised, its mouth open in a cry. At the same time, the girl herself is being fragmented into geometric planes. This scene is placed above an abstraction of a figure lying on the ground, which has been completely broken up into abstract forms in a manner strongly recalling Klee's *Outbreak of Fear*.[21] This reading of the

60

figure is borne out by Adler's undated sketches of figures lying on the ground who may be dead or badly wounded. Adler tried by means of abstract lines to wipe out or cover over their bodies, at the same time reinforcing the suggestion of wounds.[22] From here, it is but a short step to the fragmented body on the ground in the lower half of the 1943 sketch. The combination of scenes on this page would then again suggest a narrative progression: the fleeing woman, on leaving her hiding place, is turned into a dismembered body.

The similarities in pose and the narrative development in these sketches strengthen the assertion that *Woman with a Still Life* and its related compositions depict refugees in hiding, and that the fragmented abstract forms express — as in *Girl with Rocking Toy* — a dismembered human body. As such, these works reflect life in occupied Europe as well as Adler's own experience in the war and his fears as a refugee ''in hiding'' in Britain. This complex meaning is further elucidated in *Two Figures*, of 1944 [Fig. 5], in which the youngest of the two men stands in a pose very similar to that of the trapped Jew and the fleeing woman in the 1943 sketches.[23] He is set beside the huddled and worried bearded Jew from the 1943 sketch of Jews in hiding, in a closed, dark room. The younger man stands against a lighter background, separated from the old man as the abstract statues had been separated from the hiding women [Figs. 1-2]. He seems about to leave the shelter of the room, pointing towards the light blue area to the far right. Instead of having a broken form, this young man's body is crisscrossed by white lines which look like scars left after a beating. His tortured form suggests the fate of those who dare to leave their place of refuge, yet his need to brave this danger may parallel Adler's joining the Polish army to defend, but ultimately to leave behind, the rest of Polish Jewry, including his family.

This kind of development in Adler's works, and his use of ''stylistic'' elements to convey expressive meaning in an almost symbolic fashion, is further elucidated in *Destruction*, of 1943, and its related sketches and paintings. The earliest dated sketch in this series, from 1941, depicts a woman holding a rod with one hand and her head with the other while standing beside a dead woman lying on the ground. Neither the story nor the mis-en-scène are clear, but the feeling of despair and destruction is evident [Fig. 6].[24] The figure on the ground here is rendered broadly, and it will soon be replaced by the fragmented figure Adler developed at this time in *Girl with Rocking Toy*.

This fragmented ''dead'' figure is combined with the interiors we have examined in a drawing of 1943 which has been identified as an early sketch for *Destruction* [Fig. 7]. Here a much more abstract woman raises her hands to her head in anguish, as she stands beside a shattered mirror and a

8) Jankel Adler, «Sketch for Destruction», 1943, present whereabouts unknown.

crouching ''broken'' body.[25] The composition strongly recalls that of the living woman beside a corpse in the sketch from 1941. The next sketches for *Destruction* are even more abstract, but their meaning is still clear [Fig. 8]. There are now two abstracted but unbroken despairing figures, and they hold between them a broken or destroyed figure on a litter of planks. This figure is composed of the same shapes which form the other figures, and its death and dismantlement causes them to raise their heads and cry out in protest.[26]

This is much less clear in the painting [Fig. 9], where the figures have been set against a dark background with a red moon which rises over a destroyed landscape, rather than over a dead body. The meaning is thus more generalized, and should be connected, at least in part, to Adler's experiences during the blitz in Poland and England. On the other hand, the artist added a detail here which broadens his meaning in another direction. The legs of the two figures are enmeshed in a flaming line which strongly recalls barbed wire: the figures are not only trapped, but the specific trap involved has strong Holocaust connotations.[27]

However, no sooner was the connection to the actual destruction of the war and the Holocaust made, than he shied

61

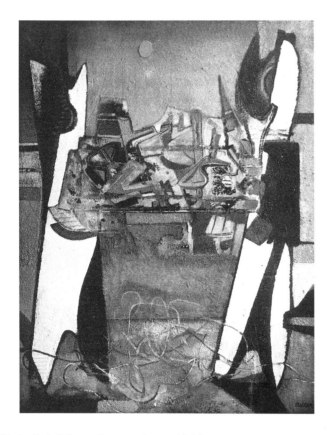

9) Jankel Adler, «Destruction», 1943, private collection.

10) Jankel Adler, «Head», 1938, Benjamin D. Bernstein collection, Philadelphia.

away from it, returning to the idea of objects on a table beside two women in a sketch and in a still more figurative painting of 1944.[28] Although the red background and the sharp objects on the table still lend the painting an ominous atmosphere, and the gesture of one girl repeats that of the figures leaving their hiding places in the 1943-44 works, the subject has been neutralized, and without its association to the other works of this period, one would not normally connect this work either with the war or with the *Destruction* series.

This is equally true of two other paintings of 1943, which combine the image of the bird that we encountered in *Woman with Still Life*, of 1942 [Fig. 2], with the fragmented figure, but without the living woman. Adler had begun to build up a symbolism of birds from his earliest works, in one of which he had defined the bird as a ''Totenvogel'', a bird of ill omen, or, literally, a ''bird of the dead.''[29] This meaning apparently resurfaced in the paintings he did in relation to the Holocaust. In 1938, the year of Kristallnacht, the annexation of Austria

and the Munich agreement, he painted the head of a girl [Fig. 10], which — like Klee's *Stricken from the List*, of 1933 — has been ''crossed out'' to indicate that she has been ''eliminated'' or murdered.[30] On her cheek, as though whispering in her ear, and forming a part of the Cubistic fragmentation of her face, appears a bird who seems to be warning her of impending disaster. This chirping bird reappears, as we saw, in 1942 in an ambiguous context in *Woman with Still Life* [Fig. 2].

This bird also appears beside fragmented figures in two major related works of 1943, *Beginning of the Revolt* and *No Man's Land*, both of which recall the mood of *Destruction*.[31] *Beginning of the Revolt* [Fig. 11] develops the idea of *Head*, 1938. The warning bird now perches on a head which is much more fragmented but still has the same round staring eyes, and hints of a nose, ear and mouth. Sharp axe-like weapons grow out of the head as though its lid had been removed, and this seems to amaze the bird, who had thought the frightened,

11) Jankel Adler, «Beginning of the Revolt», 1943, private collection.

broken head incapable of such a gesture.[32] The name, *Beginning of the Revolt*, connects the work with the Warsaw Ghetto uprising of April 1943, and the imagery — once deciphered — is a clear response to that event, undertaken after most of the ghetto's inhabitants had been deported as a final, desperate gesture of defiance. The outcome — the total destruction of the ghetto — seems to lie behind the related work, *No Man's Land* [Fig. 12], an all blue, twilight painting with a glowing orange moon.[33] Here the bird sits on a fragmented seated "figure" whose head is very close to that of the figures in *Destruction*, split in the center and crying out in despair, echoing the cry of the bird. The latter, a witness to destruction, can only turn towards the moon, calling on it and the heavens to behold the pitiful, broken remains of life in no-man's land. The feeling of desolation is intense, and it is heightened by the contrast between the living bird and its destroyed "abstract" perch.

Whereas Adler had developed the abstract fragmented form in the early years of the war as his major image of destruction, in 1944-45 it was increasingly replaced by the bird, the witness to destruction who warns of it and mourns it simultaneously. As such, the bird appears in a *Still Life*, of ca. 1944-45, flying over Jewish symbols — the tablets of the Ten Commandments on which are inscribed stars, the words "Chai 18" which symbolize life, and one of the names of God — towards a gold relief of a Menorah, which appears under a "broken" figure.[34] In like manner, the bird demands artistic expression of the destruction it has witnessed. In 1944, it flies into the closed and barred red room in which *The Poet* has taken refuge, bringing him news from the outer world in the form of a "song" — an amorphous patch of blue emanating from the bird's mouth. The poet, his head resting on one arm in the pose of melancholia, has not yet taken up the pen and paper before him, but raises his other hand as though to question the bird.[35] Whereas in 1945 *The Night Birds Attracted to the Lamp* enter the room joyously bearing tidings of the war's end, in *Girl with Bird*, of 1946 [Fig. 13], the situation is more ambiguous.[36] Here the bird perches on a fragmented form as it had in *Beginning of the Revolt*, seemingly explaining things to the troubled girl standing beside this "statue," or instructing her on how to reconstruct it. In this painting, Adler blends the main motifs he had used during the war: the closed room, the contrast between the girl and the fragmented figure, and the bird, combining them in such a way that they seem entirely neutral, unless one is aware of the meaning of each motif in his work.

The switch from joy at the war's end suggested in *The Night Birds* to the anxiety and need to come to grips with destruction expressed in *Girl with Bird* was apparently caused by Adler's receiving the news in 1945 that most of his family in Poland had perished in the Holocaust.[37]

That the war remained on his mind during the following years is evident from *Nude*, of ca. 1947, where two birds fly out of a red background to remind a girl of past disasters.[38] She herself seems to be a reconstructed survivor, determined to live life to the full. But her smooth body is scarred, and under her pink flesh one can still perceive the fragmentation to which she had been subjected. Sadly, assuming the customary pose of melancholia, she gazes off into the distance, remembering.

In 1948, Adler painted *Treblinka* [Fig. 14], which may serve to epitomize his attempts to deal with the horror and destruction of the Holocaust.[39] This highly enigmatic painting has an equally enigmatic name, as Adler used the Polish spelling, *Tremblinka*, when he exhibited it in 1948, causing confusion for English speakers by seeming to add the word "tremble" to the name of the camp.[40] The abstracted forms of the figures in this painting seem to have more in common

12) Jankel Adler, «No Man's Land», 1943, Trustees of the Tate Gallery, London.

with Henry Moore's sketches of 1948 for his *Upright Forms* than with the title.[41] On the left, what appears to be an image of Siamese twins joined at the waist gazes down at the green object held out to it by a small "winged" figure. They apparently stand in a room, surrounded by darkness in which suggestions of half-formed, ghost-like heads seem to float. This painting will only make sense when it is realized that here, as in *Destruction*, Adler based himself on a simple genre scene which had special meaning for him: an illustration for Stefan Themerson's book on the artist published in 1948 [Fig. 15].[42] In the illustration, a child with enormous eyes as his only facial feature raises wing-like arms to his head in fright as he contemplates a lizard on the floor. He is protected by two women, who are superimposed on each other: their bodies merge at the waist and, although the lower half of each body

is still visible, they already suggest the "Siamese-twin" effect of the two-headed figure on the left of the painting.

The story here, taken from Adler's childhood memories, is elucidated in Themerson's text, and could stand as a symbol for all that has been said above. At the age of four, Adler saw a small green lizard, and was told that its name was "Mak," the same name as that of a playmate who had apparently died. He told Themerson the tale in 1944, and showed him a drawing of it,[43] but constantly changed the subject when the author asked what had become of the lizard, who — for the artist — was a metamorphosis of his dead friend. This lizard is the source of the green object in the painting presented by the winged child, whose own face is greenish, to the "Siamese twins", the two women from the illustration. Themerson connects this story with Adler's memories of Lodz, the Jewish

64

"world from which destiny has torn him," a world which calls out to him — as had the bird to the poet in the painting of 1944 — "Remember us, the people who were your environment, the people who have remained in the place from which you have escaped!" The author then describes Lodz for the reader. He refers first to the statistics of the *Everyman Encyclopedia* of 1913, and then to the *Lodzer Zeitung* of November 16, 1939, which proclaims that on pain of death, fine or imprisonment, Jews must wear yellow armbands and be indoors from 5 p.m. to 8 a.m. Themerson hints here at the connection between the Lodz of Adler's childhood and that of the Holocaust, but — taking his cue from Adler — he does so in a quotation *in German* which would have been incomprehensible to the average English reader. But he goes on to make his meaning clearer:

> For the second time Jankel Adler finds his way on that same kitchen floor where the first lizard had appeared. But this time the floor, the kitchen, the flat, the house, and the street of the city of Lodz are distant and remote, saturated with blood, covered with ashes; he encounters them only in the newspapers. And this time the prehistoric boy Mak does not change into an ingenuous lizard but into big ichthyosauruses: J.A.'s pictures. These pictures in which the metamorphosis into painting of J.A.'s *philosophy*, perhaps of his *suffering* or his *life*, still continues.

This connection with the past becomes still clearer when the original Polish version of Themerson's text, published in London in *Nowa Polska* in November 1944, is taken into account.[44] First of all, it is important to understand that the story of Mak originated during the war years, and that the process of "Mak" — the metamorphosis of death into another form of life — was recognized by Themerson as the style used by Adler in his wartime paintings, as it was later in *Treblinka*. Secondly, there is a major difference between the original and the later English translation concerning the information on Lodz. To the first line of the above quotation is added the information that Adler saw Mak for the second time forty years after he had seen him the first time, i.e., in 1939, at the outbreak of the war. Furthermore, after the statistics from the encyclopedia and from the *Nouveau Petit-Larousse Illustré* of 1933, Themerson quotes from Julian Tuwim's poem on Poland, citing his nostalgic lines on Lodz, full of poetic imagery.[45] This connects Tuwim with Adler as artists belonging to the same circle, and thus helps to explain *The Poet*, painted the year Themerson's article was published.

Moreover, in the same number of the magazine, several pages further on, there appeared a selection from Yankel Wiernik's pamphlet *A Year in Treblinka*, and the title uses the Polish spelling with an "m" as Adler later did![46] Wiernik's

13) Jankel Adler, «Girl with Bird», 1946, **present whereabouts unknown.**

article opens with a description of his being haunted by nightmares, especially by phantoms of the children he was unable to save from the gas chambers he had been forced to build, whose bodies he often had to bury. His only comfort is the chirping birds, the only beings in the world who still love him. The imagery he uses forms a direct parallel to the bird imagery in Adler's paintings, and may well have fascinated the artist into reading this article — and probably the pamphlet which was issued at this time — which tells of the horrors of the death camp and the revolt in it on August 2, 1943. When, under the continuing influence of Wiernik's text, Adler decided to do a painting on Treblinka, he did not turn to his own dismantled wartime images, but to an abstract version of the story of Mak, which not only involved the use of a neutral object to block out an image of death, but had also appeared together with Wiernik's article and had apparently become

14) Jankel Adler, «Treblinka», 1948, Gimpel Fils, London.

associated in his mind with it. He depicts a phantom or angel-child holding the lizard and asking, as Adler had, "What is it?" of the women, already stripping to enter the black gas chambers infested by the spirits of burnt victims. This child's question echoes those of the children in the death camp as described by Wiernik:

> I suffered most when I looked at the children, accompanied by their mothers or walking alone, entirely ignorant of the fact that within a few minutes their lives would be snuffed out under horrible tortures. Their eyes glowed with fear and still more, perhaps, with amazement. It seemed as if the question: "What is this? What for and why?" were frozen on their lips.[47]

Even the "Siamese-twin" image of the women can be explained with reference to the text of Wiernik's pamphlet, in his description of the German squad leader who rounded up Jews in Warsaw: "With a sadistic smile he contemplated the great accomplishment of his mighty country which, at one stroke, could chop off the head of the loathsome hydra."[48] The hydra, an image of the Jewish people in Wiernik's pamphlet, is a many-headed beast who grows back two heads when one has been chopped off. At Treblinka, Adler seems to imply in 1948 — the year of the establishment of the State of Israel — the Germans succeeded in chopping off the head of the Jewish people, but in its place two immediately grew in, and it is this resurrected being, set on an optimistic pink background, who looks down at Mak, at the metamorphosis of the dead child.[49] *Treblinka* thus becomes a symbolic abstraction of Holocaust death, which yet suggests the hope of metamorphosis and resurrection.

In analyzing the development of abstraction in Adler's works, it becomes apparent that he used this style as a distancing device in two different ways. His early use of it before the war was a means of completely immersing himself in art, and thus disregarding the events taking place around him, including his trauma on leaving Germany and his family. At the end of the thirties and especially after the outbreak of the war, unable any longer to "hide" in art in this way, he began to use abstraction not simply as a style, but as one with a clear iconographic meaning. Since he found it extremely difficult to express the destruction of the war and the Holocaust directly, he turned to abstraction to "portray" this destruction from a safe distance, repeatedly playing back and forth between levels of reality as well as between neutral and war-related themes.

Although this was undoubtedly a fully conscious action, Adler does not seem to have stated what he was doing verbally, any more than he was willing at this time to tell Themerson

15) Jankel Adler, «Two Women and a Child beside a Lizard», 1948 (from Stefan Themerson, *Jankel Adler: an artist seen from one of many possible angles*, London: Gaberbocchus Press, 1948, p. 11).

what had happened to Mak. Instead, he explained the change in his art in more positive terms:

> In times of creative potentiality [...] there has always been a spiritual idea that leads the way. Very often that idea [...] drew its strength from the spiritual world and abstract terms. In times of great cultural achievements, naturalistic forms were never used. [...] In such times there was a striving to find a form, a synthesis which, if accomplished, stands above the every-dayness, the episode, and becomes part of our being [...].

It is perhaps for the first time in the history of plastic art that the viewer of works of art is drawn in on the process of creativeness itself. [...] Looking [at pictures][...] has been raised to the stage of seeing. But how many people can see? For seeing means understanding of connections. [...] The painting of today has no longer the task to reflect what the eye sees, but to create an image which would enrich our mind (soul) and our capacity of imagination.[50]

However, after having examined just what he chose to abstract, it emerges that the problem is not lofty ideals that need to find abstract expression, but painful realities, and that the "understanding of connections" is vital to a decipherment of his art. Here again, he echoes Klee, who said in 1915 à propos World War I: "The more horrible this (today's) world, the more abstract the art, while a happy world produces an art bound to the earth."[51]

[1] See, for instance, Düsseldorf, Städtische Kunsthalle, *Jankel Adler*, Nov. 1-Dec. 8, 1985 (exhibition catalogue), pp. 194-99, 208-13, 247-48. I would like to thank Milly Heyd for reading and making valuable comments on this paper.

[2] For Adler's early life, style and iconography, see *Jankel Adler*, Düsseldorf, 1985, *op. cit.*, pp. 13-27, 39-44, 47, 49, 51, 53-64, nos. 1-69, pp. 182-94, 201-8, 214-21, 232-48, and 253; and A. Klapheck, *Jankel Adler*, Recklinghausen: Aurel Bongers, 1966, pp. 26-7, 34, 38-9, 41, 47-8.

[3] See, for instance, *Jankel Adler*, Düsseldorf, 1985, *op. cit.*, nos. 2-3, 5, 9-12, 14, 31, 35, 41, 43-6, 57, 63, 68-9.

[4] For examples and a discussion of his biomorphic style, see *ibidem*, nos. 70-8, and pp. 194-5, 208-9 and 247; Tel Aviv Museum, *Jankel Adler*, Dec. 23, 1985-Feb. 11, 1986 (exhibition catalogue), p. 13; Jerusalem, Israel Museum, *Jankel Adler*, Oct.-Dec. 1969 (exhibition catalogue), no. 22; Munich, Galerie Wolfgang Ketterer, *Jankel Adler*, [ca. 1972] (exhibition catalogue), no. 4; and *Litterarische Bletter*, vol. 12, Feb. 22, 1935, pp. 120-1. Some of these works have been tentatively dated, I think mistakenly, to ca. 1930 or 1932.

[5] Even his later article on Klee does not stress Klee's use of abstraction (Jankel Adler, "Memories of Paul Klee," *Horizon*, vol. 6, Oct. 1942, pp. 264-7).

[6] For examples of such forms in the backgrounds of his earlier works, see *Family*, of ca. 1930, and *The Purim Players*, of 1931 (*Jankel Adler*, Düsseldorf, 1985, *op. cit.*, nos. 64 and 68), and note that in both paintings the figures have extremely anxious expressions on their faces.

[7] For Adler's comments on abstraction, see *ibidem*, pp. 31-2 and 196; S. L. Schneiderman, "Fun Yidishn Monparnas (A Shmues mit Yankl Adler," *Litterarische Bletter* [in Yiddish], vol. 10, Sept. 20, 1933, p. 614; and the end of this paper.

[8] *Jankel Adler*, Düsseldorf, 1985, *op. cit.*, no. 76 and p. 44. Adler's bird-imagery was strongly influenced both iconographically and stylistically by Max Ernst's use of this theme, but the intricate relationship between their work deserves a fuller investigation than is possible within the context of this article.

[9] Klapheck, *op. cit.*, p. 18; *Jankel Adler*, Düsseldorf, 1985, *op. cit.*, pp. 29-34, and nos. 62 and 80; *Jankel Adler*, Tel Aviv, 1985-6, *op. cit.*, no. 59. See also I. M. Neumann, "Yankel Adler," *Litterarische Bletter* [in Yiddish], vol. 12, Feb. 22, 1935, pp. 116-7; *Jankel Adler*, Munich, 1972, *op. cit.*, nos. 3, 5-7; and New York, Galerie Chalette, *Jankel Adler*, Nov.-Dec. 1959 (exhibition catalogue), nos. 7 and 13.

Unfortunately, most of the works from this period have apparently been lost.

[10] *Jankel Adler*, Düsseldorf, 1985, *op. cit.*, pp. 34-6. Adler was released from the Polish army after a heart attack (*ibidem*, pp. 34 and 249).

[11] *Ibidem*, no. 85. This composition is rare in his earlier works, where, however, a secondary space outside a room is often indicated by a view through a window or a door (e.g., *ibidem*, pp. 63 and 248, and nos. 4, 7-9, 11, 15, 37, and 46). In the few early examples where the division into two inhabited spaces does occur (e.g., *ibidem*, pp. 58 and 242; and *Jankel Adler*, Munich, 1972, *op. cit.*. no. 9), the composition deals almost exclusively with male-female relationships, and the men — in the last case in a state of sexual arousal — are separated from the women.

[12] New York, Museum of Modern Art, *Pablo Picasso, A Retrospective*, 1980 (exhibition catalogue), p. 310. The Picasso model becomes very clear in the *Venus of Kirkcudbright*, of 1943, and the *Homage to Gabo*, of 1946, in both of which the woman and the statue occupy the same space, and in neither of which the artist is primarily interested in expressing the tensions of the war (*Jankel Adler*, Düsseldorf, 1985, *op. cit.*, no. 100; Klapheck, *op. cit.*, p. 63). See also Munich, Michael Hasenclever, *Jankel Adler, Bilder und Zeichnungen*, Sept. 22—Oct. 22, 1977 (exhibition catalogue), no. 18; London, Gimpel Fils, *Jankel Adler*, [ca. 1956] (exhibition catalogue), no. 3; and a later version in Klapheck, *op. cit.*, p. 66.

[13] Düsseldorf, Kunstsammlung Nordrhein-Westfalen, *Paul Klee*, 1964 (exhibition catalogue), p. 49; and C. Giedion-Welcker, *Paul Klee*, London: Faber and Faber, 1952, p. 128. See also *Paul Klee par lui-même et par son fils Félix Klee* [Paris?]: Libraires Associés, 1963, p. 150.

[14] *Jankel Adler*, Düsseldorf, 1985, *op. cit.*, nos. 86-7a and 89; and New York, Jewish Museum, *Jewish Experience in the Art of the Twentieth Century*, Oct. 16, 1975-Jan. 25, 1976 (exhibition catalogue), p. 23. See also S. W. Hayter, *Jankel Adler*, London: Nicholson and Watson, 1948, pl. 17.

[15] The threat to the bird is carried out in *Children with Dead Bird*, of 1942 (Jerusalem, The Jewish National Museum Bezalel, *Jankel Adler*, July 26-Sept. 6, 1947 [exhibition catalogue], no. 23). The feeling that the objects on the table are "broken", rather than simply cubistic renderings of stringed instruments and other objects, is heightened by their being surrounded by naturalistic objects: the bird and cage on the left, the fruit on the right, the woman behind the table

and the chair in front of it.

[16] *Jankel Adler*, Düsseldorf, 1985, *op. cit.*, no. 98. See also *ibidem*, nos. 88, 101, and 108; and a painting of 1944 in which the nude woman raises her arms fearfully as though to protect herself (B. C. Roth, *Die Kunst der Juden*, Frankfurt/M.: Ner Tamid, 1964, vol. 2, p. 131).

[17] *Jankel Adler*, Düsseldorf, 1985, *op. cit.*, no. 112; and Hayter, *op. cit.*, pl. 34. Note that in both French and Polish, languages in which Adler was fluent, the still life is a "dead nature" (nature morte, martwa natura).

[18] *Jankel Adler*, Munich, 1977, *op. cit.*, no. 24. The mezuzah, repeated on the right-hand border, is affixed to the doorpost and is thought to bless and safeguard a Jewish home.

[19] *Ibidem*, no. 23. The sketches are numbered, which may denote the sequence in which they were done.

[20] *Ibidem*, no. 26. The pose of these fleeing figures, particularly in this sketch, recalls that of Picasso's semi-abstract bathers of the late twenties, who were, however, trying to get *into* a cabana, rather than to leave it (e.g., *Pablo Picasso...*, New York, 1980, *op. cit.*, p. 265).

[21] The similarity to Klee is particularly striking when it is realized that Klee began using these broken shapes to depict dismembered bodies as early as World War I (*Paul Klee par lui-même...*, *op. cit.*, p. 16), a fact that Adler, who was very close to Klee in 1931-33, may well have known. This kind of division of broken forms is markedly different from Adler's abstraction of reclining figures, which are usually more organic, divided but less "broken." See, for instance, *Jankel Adler*, Munich, 1972, *op. cit.*, nos. 15, 48v, 51, and 58; and *Jankel Adler*, Düsseldorf, 1985, *op. cit.*, no. 73.

[22] Tel Aviv, Stern Gallery, *Jankl Adler*, May 1973 (exhibition catalogue), opp. no. 27; and New York, A. M. Adler Fine Arts, *Jankel Adler*, Apr. 16-June 6, 1981 (exhibition catalogue), unpaged, entitled posthumously *The Dream*.

[23] *Jewish Experience...*, New York, 1975, *op. cit.*, no. 6. For a sketch of ca. 1943-45 combining these two figures, see *Jankel Adler*, Munich, 1972, *op. cit.*, no. 34.

[24] *Jankel Adler*, Munich, 1977, *op. cit.*, no. 21, mistakenly called *The Astrologer*.

[25] *Jankel Adler*, Munich, 1972, *op. cit.*, no. 39. The anguished head of the standing figure recalls that of the "screaming" statue in the 1943 sketch of the woman leaving her room [Fig. 4].

[26] *Ibidem*, nos. 40-1.

[27] *Jankel Adler*, Düsseldorf, 1985, *op. cit.*, no. 95. There are interesting similarities between this painting and one of Henry Moore's sketches from 1940-1 (K. Clark, *Henry Moore Drawings*, London: Thames and Hudson, 1978, pl. xiv), but it is not clear whether Adler knew this drawing, although his abstract figures, especially those with "crying" heads, suggest that he was well acquainted with Moore's sculpture of the late thirties. See also the Moore-like dismembered reclining figure, mistitled *Still Life* (*Jankel Adler*, New York, 1959, *op. cit.*, no. 12). For Ernst's influence on the background of this painting, see *Jankel Adler*, Düsseldorf, 1985, *op. cit.*, p. 198.

[28] Tel Aviv, Tel Aviv Museum, *Jankel Adler*, November 1947 (exhibition catalogue), no. 53: *Two Women*; and Hayter, *op. cit.*, pl. 37. The gesture of the figure with hands extended was further developed in *Girl at the Table*, of 1945 (*Jankel Adler*, Düsseldorf, 1985, *op. cit.*, no. 88), where the girl's expression is more serene as she extends her arms in longing. She is still, however, confined to a small dark room.

[29] *Jankel Adler*, Düsseldorf, 1985, *op. cit.*, no. 2. See also *ibidem*, nos. 1, 10, 24-5, 56, and 76. See also *Trainer of Birds*, *A Strange Bird*, and *A Flying Bird*, all exhibited in Poland in 1935 ("Bilder-Oisshtelung

fun Jankel Adler," *Litterarische Bletter* [in Yiddish], Feb. 22, 1935, p. 128 [back cover of special Adler issue], nos. 25, 30-1, and 47), and *Two Figures with Birds*, of ca. 1938 (*Jankel Adler*, Munich, 1972, *op. cit.*, no. 5), and *Standing Girl*, of 1940 (*Jankel Adler*, Munich, 1977, *op. cit.*, no. 13). In the last example the bird flies away from the girl.

[30] *Jankel Adler*, Tel Aviv, 1985, *op. cit.*, p. 23; and M. Plant, *Paul Klee, Figures and Faces*, London: Thames and Hudson, 1978, pl. 31.

[31] *Jankel Adler*, Düsseldorf, 1985, *op. cit.*, no. 96 and p. 195. See also a smaller undated variation on this theme, *Night* (*Jankel Adler*, Munich, 1977, *op. cit.*, no. 36). For the influence of Ernst on these works, see *Jankel Adler*, Düsseldorf, 1985, *op. cit.*, pp. 198 and 252.

[32] The broken head appears in a less stylized form in *The Seer*, where the button-like eyes stare into space, while the head has been cleaved in two on top (*Jankel Adler*, Düsseldorf, 1985, *op. cit.*, no. 97). The way this head is broken appears to have been borrowed from Klee's late works, e.g., *Mother and Child*, of 1938 (Hannover, Kestner-Gesellschaft, *Paul Klee*, June 27-Aug. 17, 1980, no. 29) and his *Broken Mask*, of 1934 (G. di San Lazzaro, *Klee*, London: Thames and Hudson, 1957, p. 195).

[33] Both paintings were exhibited with *The Mutilated* and *Destruction* in the summer of 1943 (London, Redfern Gallery, *Adler*, June 3-July 3, 1943 [exhibition catalogue], nos. 2, 13, 15-6), so that Adler apparently painted and named them in direct response to events.

[34] Hayter, *op. cit.*, pl. 25. This may be the *Bird and Cabalistic Sign* exhibited in Brussels, Palais des Beaux-Arts, *Jankel Adler, Peintures (1944-45)*, Oct. 12-23, 1946 (exhibition catalogue), no. 1. The word "Chai" (meaning "alive") is made up of letters whose numerical value is 18.

[35] *Jankel Adler*, Düsseldorf, 1985, *op. cit.*, no. 111. The bars are three-dimensional as they had been in the *Two Rabbis*, of 1942 (*ibidem*, no. 93), one of Adler's most explicit comments on the Holocaust during the war. This third dimension is only fully apparent when the paintings themselves are examined. The "poet" here, an alter-ego of the artist, is a development of the figure in a closed room analyzed above [e.g., Figs. 1-5]. He may also refer to Julian Tuwim, whose poetry and articles on Polish Jewry were being published at the time in *Nowa Polska* (vols. 2-3, 1943-4, *passim*, especially "My, Zydzi Polscy..." [We, Polish Jews], vol. 3, Aug. 1944, pp. 491-4). For his connection to Adler see below.

[36] *Jankel Adler*, New York, 1959, *op. cit.*, nos. 11 and 17; and *Jankel Adler...*, Brussels, 1946, no. 26.

[37] *Jankel Adler*, Düsseldorf, 1985, *op. cit.*, p. 37. Only a single niece and nephew survived.

[38] *Ibidem*, no. 113.

[39] In Adler's two other clear confrontations with this subject, *Two Orphans* and *Two Rabbis*, of 1942 (*ibidem*, nos. 89 and 93), and in related themes, such as his sketches of refugees discussed above, he had described victims in a way that would generate pity and sympathy on the part of the spectator. In the paintings discussed in this article, he dealt with destruction and his treatment was thus markedly different. For a further discussion of his Holocaust- and war-related works, see my forthcoming book on the influence of the Holocaust on the visual arts.

[40] *Jankel Adler*, Düsseldorf, 1985, *op. cit.*, no. 115; London, Gimpel Fils, *Adler*, June 1948 (exhibition catalogue), no. 5; and London, Arts Council, *Adler*, 1951 (exhibition catalogue), nos. 51 and 79. See, however, London, Waddington Galleries, *Adler*, Mar. 1-26, 1960 (exhibition catalogue), no. 13, "Study for *Treblinka*," as opposed to the same gallery's exhibition on Sept. 5-30, 1961, no. 2: *Tremblinka*.

[41] E.g., Clark, *op. cit.*, no. 247.

[42] Stefan Themerson, *Jankel Adler: an artist seen from one of many possible angles*, London: Gaberbocchus Press, 1948, p. 11. See also the illustrations on pp. 13, 17, 21, 23, 25, 27, 29-30, where the figures become progressively more abstract, and the naturalistic artist is often juxtaposed to the kind of abstract figures we discussed above.

[43] For the drawing, see *Jankel Adler*, Munich, 1972, *op. cit.*, no. 2. The word "mak" in Polish means poppy. For the following discussion in the text, refer especially to Themerson, *op. cit.*, pp. 10, 18, 22 and 24.

[44] Stefan Themerson, "Z wielu możliwych spojrzeń na artystę — Jedno," *Nowa Polska*, vol. 3, Nov. 1944, pp. 762-7. My thanks to Avigdor Poseq for translating this text for me. The text was illustrated on p. 764 with Adler's *Metamorphosis*, whose connection to Adler's war imagery was discussed above.

[45] Julian Tuwim, "Z Kwiatów Polskich," *Nowa Polska*, vol. 2, Sept. 1943, p. 622. This poem had appeared opposite an article by Themerson.

[46] Jankiel Wiernik, "Rok w Tremblince," *Nowa Polska*, vol. 3, Nov. 1944, pp. 788-96. The book was issued simultaneously in 1944 in several different languages, including Polish, Yiddish and English.

[47] *Ibidem*, p. 789; and Yankel Wiernik, *A Year in Treblinka*, New York: General Jewish Workers' Union of Poland, n.d., pp. 14-5. The "ghosts" in the black background, reminiscent of the *Old Man Looking into a Room*, of 1944 (*Jankel Adler*, Düsseldorf, 1985, *op. cit.*, no. 112), recall Wiernik's long descriptions of the cremation of the dead and the living.

[48] Wiernik, *A Year in Treblinka*, *op. cit.*, p. 6.

[49] See Middleton's report on how proud and happy Adler was at the rebirth of Israel (M. Middleton, "Jankel Adler," *World Review*, n.s. no. 35, Jan. 1952, p. 32). Adler had just had a show in Jerusalem (July 26-Sept. 6, 1947), and, according to Teo Otto, he planned to move to Israel with his wife and child and build a new life there (Klapheck, *op. cit.*, p. 20). He died in April 1949, before he could carry out his plans.

[50] New York, Meltzer Gallery, *Jankel Adler*, Oct. 18-Nov. 14, 1955 (exhibition catalogue), unpaged, translated by J. Sonntag, and dated there to ca. 1943.

[51] *Jankel Adler*, Düsseldorf, 1985, *op. cit.*, pp. 249-50, from Paul Klee, *Tagebücher*, Cologne: M. DuMont Schauberg, 1957, p. 323. See also Thoene's comment on Klee: "When the immense horror [World War I] was over, he shut himself up in the confined space of his colors and forms" (P. Thoene, *Modern German Art*, Harmondsworth: Penguin, 1938, p. 73). This book, which was well known among avant-garde artists during the war, could well have reinforced Adler's own tendencies in this direction.

KURT SCHUBERT

Die Weisen von Bne Braq in der Haggadaillustration des 18. Jahrhunderts

Rachel Wischnitzer war die erste, die erkannte, daß der Proselyt, der die berühmte Amsterdamer Pesach-Haggada von 1695 anfertigte, als Vorbild für seine Kupferstiche Mathaeus Merians *Icones Biblicae* benützte.[1] Er, der sich selbst auf der Titelseite Abraham bar Jakob aus der Familie unseres Vaters Abraham nannte, war offenbar noch zu wenig mit jüdischen Vorlagen und jüdischer Ikonographie vertraut, als daß er für einige Motive auf nicht passende christliche Vorlagen hätte verzichten können.[2] Die Maler des 18. Jahrhunderts, die sich vorwiegend der Amsterdamer Vorlagen bedienten, hatten daher einige Mühe, ihre Darstellung dem Inhalt der Haggada anzupassen.[3] Besonders problematisch und schwierig war die Darstellung der fünf Weisen von Bne Braq, die eine ganze Nacht über den Auszug aus Ägypten diskutierten, denn Abraham bar Jakob wählte dafür die Meriansche Darstellung des Gastmahls, das Joseph seinen Brüdern in Ägypten gab.[4]

Bei Merian sitzt Joseph mit seinen Brüdern in einem Prunksaal an einem die ganze Breite des Bildes ausfüllenden Tisch, insgesamt elf Personen, was schon von der Anzahl der Teilnehmer her nicht gut zu den fünf Weisen von Bne Braq paßt. Der Speisesaal, in dem vier Diener die Tischgesellschaft bedienen, bietet Ausblick auf ein Schloß linker Hand, auf einen französischen Garten mit Brunnen und ein weiteres Schloß im Hintergrund. Nur Joseph trägt einen Turban, alle anderen Personen sind ohne Kopfbedeckung [Fig. 1]. Wie Wischnitzer mit

Recht hervorhebt, finden sich ''Ansätze zur Judaisierung des Stoffes schon in der Ausgabe von 1695''.[5] Abraham bar Jakob stellte alle Personen bedeckten Hauptes dar, wie es sich für eine jüdische Tischgesellschaft gehört. Ebenso verlegte er alles in einen geschlossenen Raum, der nicht durch hereinflutendes Tageslicht, sondern durch Kerzen künstlich beleuchtet wird, um das nächtliche Ereignis von Bne Braq anzudeuten [Fig. 2]. Die zweite Ausgabe der Amsterdamer Pesach-Haggada von 1712 geht noch in einem weiteren Detail auf den Text der Pesach-Haggada ein.[6] Anstelle eines der drei Fenster befindet sich rechts im Hintergrund ein Mann mit einem Kind in einer Tür, wohl eine sehr unkonventionelle Darstellung der Schüler, die die Weisen von Bne Braq darauf aufmerksam machen, daß es schon Morgen sei und somit Zeit ist, das Morgengebet zu sprechen [Fig. 3].

Bereits Fisher wies im Rahmen des von ihr herausgegebenen Ausstellungskataloges darauf hin, daß die Maler des 18. Jahrhunderts das Motiv der fünf Gelehrten von Bne Braq dem Text der Haggada anzupassen versuchten, daß sie dabei aber stark von ihrer Amsterdamer Vorlage abhängig blieben[7]. Sie erwähnte z. B. eine 1769 in Amsterdam handgeschriebene und illustrierte Pesach-Haggada von Jehoschua ben Mordechai Wolletz, in der dieser — zur zusätzlichen Aktualisierung und zur Betonung der Gelehrsamkeit der bei Tisch Sitzenden — ein Bücherregal mit großen Talmudfolianten hinzufügte,[8] es gelang

1) «Gastmahl Josephs mit seinen Brüdern in Ägypten», Matthäus Merian, Die Bilder zur Bibel, hsg. von Peter Meinhold, Hamburg, 1965, 57.

צודה חכמים מסובין בבני ברקומספרים מצרים מצד כל חללה

3) «Die Weisen von Bne Braq», *Pesach-Haggada*, Druck, Amsterdam 1712, 5v.

2) «Die Weisen von Bne Braq», *Pesach-Haggada*, Druck, Amsterdam 1695, 4r.

ihm jedoch nicht, die Anzahl der bei Tisch Sitzenden wesentlich zu verringern. In Amsterdam 1712 sind es neun Personen, bei Jehoschua ben Mordechai nur acht — immerhin um eine Person weniger [Fig. 4].

Für eine Pesach-Haggada, die Joseph ben David aus Leipnik (Mähren) 1733 in Darmstadt hergestellt hat, diente ebenfalls die 2. Auflage der Amsterdamer Haggada als Vorbild; auch bei ihm befinden sich neun Männer um den Seder-Tisch.[9] Ebenfalls 1733 schrieb und malte er in Darmstadt eine weitere Haggada.[10] Hier sitzen acht Männer um den Tisch und zwei Diener kommen durch die offene Tür rechts im Hintergrund, um Speisen und Getränke zu bringen. Die Fenster aus der Amsterdamer Vorlage fehlen vollends [Fig. 5]. Später allerdings hat sich auch Joseph ben David so weit durchgerungen, daß er die kanonische Fünfzahl erreichte. In einer 1738 in Altona hergestellten Haggada sitzen noch sechs Personen um den Tisch.[11] Den Hintergrund bildet eine Mischung der Amsterdamer Fassungen von 1695 und 1712. Neben drei Fenstern rechts sieht man eine offene Tür, durch die jedoch nicht ein Mann mit einem Kind, sondern etliche Männer eintreten [Fig. 6].[12] In der 1740 ebenfalls in Hamburg/Altona hergestellten Haggada ist die Fünfzahl der Gelehrten von Bne Braq auch in der Illustration endlich erreicht.[13] In gewisser Hinsicht ist sie ähnlich der Haggada von 1733, doch ist die Ausführung wesentlich prächtiger. Der 1733 nur angedeutete Gang, aus dem die Diener mit den Speisen kommen, ist nunmehr ein Wandelgang mit Statuen zwischen den Pfeilern [Fig. 7].[14]

צורת חכמים מסובין בבני ברק ומספרים ביציאת מצרים כל הלילה

4) «Die Weisen von Bne Braq», *Pesach-Haggada*, Jerusalem, Jewish National and University Library, 4°540, 3r, 1769.

Ein anderer aus Mähren stammender Maler und Kalligraph, der es in Wien bis zum Hofbibliotheksschreiber gebracht hat, war Aharon Schreiber Herlingen.[15] Er führte den Titel eines "Officialis in Bibliotheca Caesaraea Viennensi''; auf der Titelseite einer 1749 in Wien geschriebenen Pesach-Haggada nannte er sich ''Schreiber in der Bibliothek des Reiches in der Residenzstadt Wien''[16] und auf den in kalligraphischer Mikrographie geschriebenen fünf Megillot in den Titelbuchstaben des ''Canticum Canticorum'': ''Ahron Wolf, kayserl. und königl. Bibliothecschreiber in Wien, anno 1748''.[17] Er gehörte höchstwahrscheinlich einer vor der Vertreibung der Juden im Jahre 1670 in Wien ansässigen Familie an, die als Folge der Vertreibung zunächst nach Preßburg und dann nach Mähren ausgewandert war. Im Jahre 1663 verstarb in Wien ein Joel Stein ben Jakob

5) «Die Weisen von Bne Braq», *Pesach-Haggada*, New York, Jewish Theological Seminary, Mic 8253, 3r, 1733.

6) «Die Weisen von Bne Braq», *Pesach-Haggada*, Amsterdam, Rosentaliana, Ms. 382, 5r, 1738.

Herlingen, von dem auf seinem Grabstein vermerkt ist, daß er eine Synagoge gegründet hat.[18] Bei den Behörden war er offenbar sehr angesehen, sonst hätte er sich nicht im Jahre 1754 um eine Stelle als Inspektor für die Wiener Judenschaft und die nach Wien kommenden fremden Juden bewerben können.[19] Allerdings erhielt er diese Stelle nicht, weil ''derzeit die angetragene Separierung der Judenschaft aus erheblichen Ursachen nicht wohl zu bewerkstelligen befunden worden seye''. Im Jahre 1762 muß er bereits tot gewesen sein, da in einem Schreiben eines Anonymus an Maria Theresia empfohlen wird, daß der ''verwittlibten Bibliothecsschreiberin Veronica Aaronin'' erlaubt werden soll, einen koscheren Gasthof einzurichten.[20]

In der Darstellung der Szene der fünf Weisen von Bne Braq

war Herlingen stark beeinflußt von der 1. Auflage der Amsterdamer Haggada aus dem Jahre 1695. Die Szene spielt in einem geschlossenen Raum, in dem keinerlei Tür sichtbar ist, die vier servierenden Diener sind aber durchwegs auf zwei reduziert. Ebenso sind die Kerzen auf dem Leuchter heruntergebrannt, um anzudeuten, daß die Nacht schon fortgeschritten ist und der Morgen anbricht. Doch hatte auch Herlingen seine Probleme mit der Anzahl der bei Tische Sitzenden. In der Bolaffio-Haggada aus dem Jahre 1749 sind es noch sechs Personen [Fig. 8].[21]

In zwei Pesach-Haggadot aus den Jahren 1751 und 1752 wurde auch dieser Mangel behoben und um den Tisch herum sitzen nur mehr fünf Personen [Fig. 9].[22] Die Anpassung an den

7) «Die Weisen von Bne Braq», *Pesach-Haggada*, London, British Library, Sloane 3173, 5v, 1740.

8) «Die Weisen von Bne Braq», *Pesach-Haggada*, Triest, Privatbesitz der Familie Bolaffio, S. 5, 1749.

Text der Haggada ist also gelungen, wenn sich auch sonst der Zeichner nach wie vor am Amsterdamer Vorbild von 1695 orientierte. Daß Herlingen in dieser Hinsicht nicht konsequent blieb, beweist eine ebenfalls in Wien 1751 hergestellte Haggada, in der wiederum sechs Männer um den Tisch versammelt sind, die hier aber nur von einem Diener bedient werden.[23]

Ein weiterer Schreiber und Maler, der in Hamburg/Altona wirkte, war Jacob ben Jehuda Lebh, auch Jacob Sopher aus Berlin genannt. Über ihn wissen wir biographisch viel weniger als über Aharon Schreiber Herlingen. Die wichtigsten biographischen Angaben können wir seinen Selbstbezeichnungen auf den Titelblättern und Kolophonen entnehmen. Er stammte aus Berlin, wo sein Vater als *šammaš* tätig war. In Hamburg wirkte er ab 1720 und lebte im Jahre 1748 sicher nicht mehr.[24] Mei-

stens hielt er sich bei der Darstellung des Themas der Weisen von Bne Braq an die Amsterdamer Auflage von 1712; so z.B. in einer Pesach-Haggada aus dem Jahre 1728, wo acht Gelehrte gemeinsam um den Tisch sitzen;[25] neun statt fünf Gelehrte sind es in einer Haggada von 1729;[26] sieben Gelehrte in einer Haggada von 1740;[27] sechs Gelehrte in einer Haggada von 1740,[28] allerdings fehlen hier die Schüler in der Tür, dafür ist der anbrechende Morgen durch in der Luft fliegende Vögel angedeutet. Ein Jahr später allerdings kopierte Jacob ben Jehuda Lebh für die Szene der Weisen von Bne Braq die erste Auflage (Amsterdam 1695): Hier wie dort sitzen neun Gelehrte um den Tisch.[29] Offenbar aus Platzgründen ließ er den Diener weg, der in der Amsterdamer Auflage von 1695 neben dem Anrichttisch steht und anscheinend ein Gefäß reinigt [Fig. 10].

אוֹכְלִין חָמֵץ וּמַצָה הַלַּיְלָה הַזֶּה כֻּלּוֹ מַצָה שֶׁבְּכָל הַלֵּילוֹת אָנוּ אוֹכְלִין שְׁאָר יְרָקוֹת הַלַּיְלָה הַזֶּה מָרוֹר שֶׁבְּכָל הַלֵּילוֹת אֵין אָנוּ מַטְבִּילִין אֲפִילוּ פַּעַם אֶחָת הַלַּיְלָה הַזֶּה שְׁתֵּי פְעָמִים • שֶׁבְּכָל הַלֵּילוֹת אָנוּ אוֹכְלִין בֵּין יוֹשְׁבִין וּבֵין מְסֻבִּין הַלַּיְלָה הַזֶּה כֻּלָּנוּ מְסֻבִּין :

עֲבָדִים הָיִינוּ לְפַרְעֹה בְּמִצְרָיִם וַיּוֹצִיאֵנוּ יְיָ אֱלֹהֵינוּ מִשָּׁם בְּיָד חֲזָקָה וּבִזְרוֹעַ נְטוּיָה וְאִלּוּ לֹא הוֹצִיא הַקָּדוֹשׁ בָּרוּךְ הוּא אֶת אֲבוֹתֵינוּ מִמִּצְרַיִם הֲרֵי אָנוּ וּבָנֵינוּ וּבְנֵי בָנֵינוּ מְשֻׁעְבָּדִים הָיִינוּ לְפַרְעֹה בְּמִצְרָיִם וַאֲפִילוּ כֻּלָּנוּ חֲכָמִים כֻּלָּנוּ נְבוֹנִים כֻּלָּנוּ זְקֵנִים כֻּלָּנוּ יוֹדְעִים אֶת הַתּוֹרָה מִצְוָה עָלֵינוּ לְסַפֵּר בִּיצִיאַת מִצְרָיִם וְכָל הַמַּרְבֶּה לְסַפֵּר בִּיצִיאַת מִצְרַיִם הֲרֵי זֶה מְשֻׁבָּח :

מַעֲשֶׂה בְּרַבִּי אֱלִיעֶזֶר וְרַבִּי יְהוֹשֻׁעַ וְרַבִּי אֶלְעָזָר בֶּן עֲזַרְיָה וְרַבִּי עֲקִיבָא וְרַבִּי טַרְפוֹן שֶׁהָיוּ מְסֻבִּין בִּבְנֵי בְרַק וְהָיוּ מְסַפְּרִים בִּיצִיאַת מִצְרַיִם כָּל אוֹתוֹ הַלַּיְלָה עַד שֶׁבָּאוּ תַלְמִידֵיהֶם וְאָמְרוּ לָהֶם רַבּוֹתֵינוּ הִגִּיעַ זְמַן קְרִיאַת שְׁמַע שֶׁל שַׁחֲרִית :

אָמַר רַבִּי אֶלְעָזָר בֶּן עֲזַרְיָה הֲרֵי אֲנִי כְּבֶן שִׁבְעִים שָׁנָה וְלֹא

9) «Die Weisen von Bne Braq», *Pesach-Haggada*, Jerusalem, Israel Museum, 181/9, 2v, 1751.

ו הגדה

בְּיָד חֲזָקָה וּבִזְרוֹעַ נְטוּיָה וְאִלּוּ לֹא הוֹצִיא הַקָּדוֹשׁ בָּרוּךְ הוּא אֶת אֲבוֹתֵינוּ מִמִּצְרַיִם • הֲרֵי אָנוּ וּבָנֵינוּ וּבְנֵי בָנֵינוּ מְשֻׁעְבָּדִים הָיִינוּ לְפַרְעֹה בְּמִצְרָיִם • וַאֲפִילוּ כֻּלָּנוּ חֲכָמִים כֻּלָּנוּ נְבוֹנִים כֻּלָּנוּ זְקֵנִים כֻּלָּנוּ יוֹדְעִים אֶת הַתּוֹרָה מִצְוָה עָלֵינוּ לְסַפֵּר בִּיצִיאַת מִצְרַיִם וְכָל הַמַּרְבֶּה לְסַפֵּר בִּיצִיאַת מִצְרַיִם הֲרֵי זֶה מְשֻׁבָּח

צוּרַת הַחֲכָמִים מְסֻבִּין בִּבְנֵי בְרָק וּמְסַפְּרִים בִּיצִיאַת מִצְרַיִם כָּל הַלָּיְלָה :

10) «Die Weisen von Bne Braq», *Pesach-Haggada*, Amsterdam, Rosentaliana, Ms. 573, 6r, 1741.

Etlichen Schreibern und Illustratoren des 18. Jahrhunderts gelang trotz Reduzierung der Anzahl der bei Tisch Sitzenden nicht die volle Anpassung an den Text der Haggada, nach dem es sich eben um nur fünf Gelehrte handelte. Eine Haggada, aus Ittingen von 1729, die nicht signiert ist, aber Jakob ben Michael Mai Segal aus Innsbruck zugeschrieben wird,[30] zeigt (fol. 7r) acht Gelehrte um einen rechteckigen Tisch, der fast den gesamten Raum ausfüllt. Auf die Amsterdamer Vorlagen weist die Rückwand, die aber den Vorlagen gegenüber sehr frei gestaltet wurde. Eine Tür führt in einen weiteren Raum mit einem Leuchter. Vor dem einzigen Fenster außen befindet sich ein Mann,

offenbar ein Schüler, der kommt, um auf die Zeit des Morgengebets aufmerksam zu machen.[31] Von Jakob ben Michael Mai Segal signiert ist eine Haggada, die von ihm 1731 in Frankfurt/M. hergestellt wurde und sich heute im Besitz des Jüdischen Museums von Frankfurt/M. befindet. Das Bild der Weisen von Bne Braq (fol. 5r) unterscheidet sich aber in manchen Einzelheiten von der soeben besprochenen Darstellung aus Ittingen von 1729. Um einen Tisch sitzen sechs Gelehrte, im Hintergrund befinden sich zwei Fenster, aber keine Tür.

Auch Meschullam Simmel kam in einer 1719 in Wien hergestellten Haggada nicht über die Amsterdamer Vorlage von

11) «Die Weisen von Bne Braq», *Pesach-Haggada*, Kopenhagen, Jüdische Gemeinde (ohne Signatur), 5r, 1739.

12) «Die Weisen von Bne Braq», *Pesach-Haggada*, Hamburg, Staats- und Universitätsbibliothek, Cod Levy 22, 6r, 1751.

1695 hinaus, die er fast getreu kopierte.[32] Da wie dort befinden sich neun Männer um den Tisch. Ebenso nahezu vollkommen abhängig von der Amsterdamer Vorlage von 1695 war ein gewisser Pinchas, der 1747 eine Pesach-Haggada für den Markgrafen von Ansbach hergestellt und dafür 150 Gulden erhalten hatte.[33] Auch bei ihm sitzen neun Gelehrte um den Tisch. Schmuel ben Zwi Hirsch Dresnitz stellte ebenfalls in einer 1748 in Nikolsburg hergestellten Haggada neun Gelehrte rings um den Tisch dar,[34] sonst variiert er stark seine Vorlage, die Amsterdamer Haggada von 1695. Der Tisch und die rund um ihn sitzenden Gelehrten füllen nahezu den gesamten zur Verfügung

stehenden Raum, so daß knapp Platz für zwei Diener bleibt, von denen einer Wein eingießt und ein anderer Speisen bringt. Im Hintergrund befinden sich in der Wand auch nur zwei Fenster. Chajim ben Ascher Anschel, der sich für die Titelseite seiner 1748 in Wien hergestellten Haggada von der Darstellung der Vermehrung der Israeliten in Ägypten in der Venezianischen Pesach-Haggada von 1609 anregen ließ, hielt sich bei der Darstellung der Weisen von Bne Braq an die Amsterdamer Haggada von 1695.[35] Allerdings stellte er die Fenster im Hintergrund anders dar als seine Vorlage.[36]

Aus den bisher behandelten Beispielen von Pesach-Hagga-

13) «Die Weisen von Bne Braq», *Pesach-Haggada*, Darmstadt, Hessische Landes- und Hochschulbibliothek, Cod Or 7, 5v, 1769.

hergestellt hat.[37] Fol. 5r zeigt im Vordergrund einen großen rechteckigen Tisch, um den die fünf Gelehrten mit vor sich aufgeschlagenen Pesach-Haggadot sitzen. Allerdings ist der Tisch noch viel zu groß und hätte leicht auch mehreren Personen Platz bieten können. Man hat den Eindruck, daß die aufgeschlagenen Pesach-Haggadot und die Becher den leeren Platz auf dem Tisch ausfüllen sollen. Von rechts kommen zwei Schüler, die darauf aufmerksam machen, daß die Zeit für das Morgengebet schon gekommen ist. Nach der Amsterdamer Vorlage von 1695 wären statt der Schüler Diener mit Speisen und Getränken zu erwarten. Die drei Fenster im Hintergrund sind noch eine Reminiszenz an die Vorlage [Fig. 11]. In einer weiteren von Uri Feibusch ben Isaak Eisik Schatz Segal 1751 in Altona geschrie-

14) «Die Weisen von Bne Braq», *Pesach-Haggada*, ~~Cincinatti, Hebrew Union College, Ms. 450, 5v, 1743.~~

Jehuda Löbh, Kopenhagen 1769 Cod. Or. 7,5v

dot aus dem 18. Jahrhundert geht eindeutig hervor, daß die Erreichung der vom Text her geforderten Fünfzahl der miteinander diskutierenden Gelehrten dadurch erschwert bzw. unmöglich gemacht wurde, daß die von Abraham bar Jakob benützte Vorlage aus Merians *Icones Biblicae* eben die große Anzahl der Brüder Josephs beim Gastmahl in Ägypten und nicht die fünf Weisen von Bne Braq berücksichtigte. Nur Künstlern, die den Mut und die Phantasie hatten, sich von der Vorlage weitgehend unabhängig zu machen, gelang es bei ihren Darstellungen, dem Text der Haggada gegenüber der Bildvorlage den Vorzug zu geben. Am stärksten noch von der Vorlage beeinflußt ist die Szene in der Haggada der Jüdischen Gemeinde Kopenhagen, die Uri Feibusch ben Isaak Eisik Segal 1739 in Hamburg/Altona

15) «Die Weisen von Bne Braq», *Pesach-Haggada*, Druck, Venedig, 1599, 4v.

16) «Die Weisen von Bne Braq», *Pesach-Haggada*, Venedig, Druck 1609, S. 8.

benen und illustrierten Pesach-Haggada hat er sich bereits vollends von der Vorlage gelöst und beschritt eigene Wege.[38] In einem barocken von Säulen getragenen Prunksaal, der mit Brokatvorhängen geschmückt ist, sitzen an einem Tisch die fünf diskutierenden Gelehrten. An der Rückwand befindet sich ein Bücherregal mit Folianten zur Veranschaulichung der Gelehrsamkeit der Diskutanten. Links im Hintergrund zeigt ein Blick ins Freie die aufgehende Sonne und zwei Schüler, von denen einer mit erhobener Hand auf die aufgegangene Sonne weist. In der ins Freie führenden Öffnung steht noch ein gebeugter Mann, der über der rechten Schulter einen langen flammenden Lichtanzünder trägt. Offenbar verläßt er die Szenerie, da draußen schon der Morgen angebrochen ist [Fig. 12].

Noch prächtiger als die letztgenannte Pesach-Haggada ist

diejenige, die von Jehuda Lebh den Elijahu hakkohen aus Lissa (Lesnitz/Polen) 1769 in Kopenhagen angefertigt wurde.[39] Die heftig miteinander diskutierenden fünf Gelehrten sitzen um einen Tisch mit aufgeschlagenen oder geschlossenen Büchern. Auf einem ist zu lesen: *Seder haggada šel pesach*. In der Tür stehen zwei Schüler, die mit erhobener Hand auf den morgendlichen Himmel weisen. Hier hat sich der Künstler, der in anderen Darstellungen von der Amsterdamer Vorlage beeinflußt war, von dieser aber vollkommen frei gemacht, um den Text der Haggada lebendig zu veranschaulichen [Fig. 13].

Ganz anders als die aschkenasischen Haggadot ist jene illustriert, die Jakob Chai ben Joseph Israel Conigliano 1743 angefertigt hat.[40] Hier ist der Einfluß der beiden gedruckten Haggadot aus Venedig von 1599 und 1609 eindeutig. Links um einen Tisch sitzen die fünf Gelehrten, während von rechts kommend Diener die Speisen auftragen [Fig. 14]. Anstelle der fünf Weisen stellt die Auflage von 1599, 4v eine Pesach-Tischgesellschaft mit mehreren Personen dar. Dazu passen auch die Diener, die die Speisen auftragen [Fig. 15]. In der Auflage von 1609 sind es nun tatsächlich die fünf Weisen mit aufgeschlagenen Büchern auf dem Tisch, während von rechts die zu erwartenden zwei Schüler den Raum betreten. Ein Blick durch das Fenster läßt ebenfalls die aufgehende Sonne erkennen [Fig. 16]. Jakob Chai ben Joseph übernahm fast die ganze Szene aus der Auflage von 1599, bezüglich der geforderten Fünfzahl aber hielt er sich an jene von 1609.

Es gibt wohl keine Szene in der Illustration der Pesach-Haggadot aus dem 18. Jahrhundert, die wie die fünf Weisen von Bne Braq wegen der Benützung der Amsterdamer Vorlage eine Entsprechung zum Text der Haggada nur schwer ermöglicht; auch für die übrigen Szenen wäre ein Vergleich lohnend, der aber einer anderen Gelegenheit vorbehalten bleiben soll. Hier sollte nur ein Denkanstoß weiterentwickelt werden, den Rachel Wischnitzer schon 1931 richtungsweisend gegeben hat.

[1] Rachel Wischnitzer-Bernstein, "Von der Holbeinbibel zur Amsterdamer Haggadah", *Monatsschrift für Geschichte und Wissenschaft des Judentums*, 75 (NF 39), 1931, S. 269-286, bes. S. 275-277.

[2] Y. Fisher (Hsgb.), *Illustrated Haggadot of the Eighteenth Century*, (Research and Text: Haviva Peled-Carmeli), Jerusalem, 1983, S. 15: "Abraham bar Ya'akov was a German priest from the Rhineland who moved to Amsterdam and converted to Judaism there". Vgl. auch *Encyclopaedia Judaica*, Berlin, 1928, S. 488.

[3] K. Schubert, "Das jüdische Element in der Illustration der Pesach Haggadot des 17. und 18. Jahrhunderts", *Kairos*, 17, 1985, S. 279-287.

[4] M. Merian, *Die Bilder zur Bibel* (Facsimile-Ausgabe, hsgb. von P. Meinhold), Hamburg, 1965, Abb. 57.

[5] Wischnitzer, *op. cit.*, S. 279.

[6] Wischnitzer, *op. cit.*, S. 283.

[7] Fisher, *op. cit.*, S. 22f.

[8] *Pesach-Haggada*, Jerusalem, Jewish National and University Library 4°540, 3r; Fisher, *op. cit.*, S. 48, Abb.55.

[9] *Pesach-Haggada*, Jerusalem, Jewish National and University Library 8°983, 4r; Fisher, *op. cit.*, S. 49, Abb.56. Datierung nach S. Zucker (Einleitung zur Facsimile-Ausgabe), Jerusalem, 1985, S. 1. Die zweimalige Angabe 1712 auf der Titelseite dürfte sich auf das Erscheinungsjahr der 2. Auflage der Amsterdamer Haggada beziehen, die dieser Seite als Vorlage diente.

[10] *Pesach-Haggada*, New York, Jewish Theological Seminary, Mic 8253, 3r.

[11] *Pesach-Haggada*, Amsterdam, Rosentaliana Ms 382, 5r.

[12] Dem Joseph ben David aus Leipnik ist auch eine Pesach-Haggada zuzuschreiben, die 1734 in Darmstadt entstand und die sich heute im Jüdischen Historischen Museum in Amsterdam befindet, Ms 22. Das Kolophon (fol. 19v) nennt Joseph Melammed aus Darmstadt. Eine wesentliche ikonographische Besonderheit hat fol. 3r mit der von Joseph ben David voll signierten Hs Amsterdam, Rosentaliana 382, 5r gemeinsam: in der Tür zum Raum, in dem sich die Weisen von Bne Braq befinden, sind mehrere Schüler sichtbar, dies bedeutet eine wesentliche Veränderung gegenüber Amsterdam, Auflage von 1712.

[13] *Pesach-Haggada*, London, British Library, Sloane 3173, 5v.

[14] Über Joseph ben David aus Leipnik in Mähren sind nur die wenigen biographischen Details bekannt, die aus seinen Kolophonen erschlossen werden können. Aus seiner Selbstbezeichnung als *mellamed* im Jahre 1734 (Anm. 12) dürfte hervorgehen, daß er zumindest zu dieser Zeit auch als Lehrer tätig war. Auf Grund der Kolophone lebte er in Frankfurt/M., Darmstadt und Altona. Sein letztes bekanntes Werk ist die *Pesach-Haggada* aus dem Jahre 1740 (Anm. 13). E. G. L. Schrijver, *The Rosentaliana Leipnik Haggadah*, Jerusalem, 1986 (Einleitung zur Facsimile-Ausgabe).

[15] Abraham Naphtali Zwi Roth, "Ha-tzajjar ha-ammami Aharon Schreiber Herlingen", *Jeda Am*, 5, 1958/59, S. 73-79.

[16] *Bolaffio Haggada* (Privatbesitz Triest), Wien, 1749.

[17] Wien, Österreichische Nationalbibliothek, Cod Ser Nov 1594. Von Aharon Schreiber Herlingen sind auch noch weitere derartige mikrographische Meisterwerke bekannt; vgl. K. Schubert, in: K. Lohrmann, *1000 Jahre österreichisches Judentum*, Eisenstadt, 1982, S. 344.

[18] B. Wachstein, *Die Inschriften des alten Judenfriedhofs in Wien*, I, Wien, 1912, S. 430f., Nr. 569.

[19] A. F. Pribram, *Urkunden und Akten zur Geschichte der Juden in Wien*, I, Wien, 1918, S. 348-350, bes. S. 350 (Anm. 2), Nr. 163.

[20] Pribram, *op. cit.*, S. 365.

[21] *Bolaffio Haggada* (Privatbesitz Triest), Wien, 1749, S. 5.

[22] *Pesach-Haggada*, Jerusalem, Israel Museum 181/9 2v; 181/52, 2v. In der *Pesach-Haggada* des Jewish Theological Seminary in New York, Mic 8963, 2v, die Aharon Schreiber Herlingen in Wien 1751 hergestellt hat, sind es fünf Gelehrte, in Mic 4477, 2v, ebenfalls Wien 1751, sechs Gelehrte.

[23] *Pesach-Haggada*, Amsterdam, Rosentaliana, Ros 463, 2v.

[24] Van de Schrijver, *Jacob ben Jehuda Leib*, Amsterdam, 1985 (Dissertation, Manuskript), S. 13.

[25] *Pesach-Haggada*, Amsterdam, Rosentaliana, Ros 383, 6r.

[26] *Pesach-Haggada*, Jerusalem, Israel Museum, Ms 181/51, 4v.

[27] *Pesach-Haggada*, Cincinatti, Hebrew Union College, Ms 445, 6r.

[28] *Pesach-Haggada*, London, British Library, Add 18724, 6v.

[29] *Pesach-Haggada*, Amsterdam, Rosentaliana, Ros 573, 6r.

[30] Ch. Benjamin, Einleitung zur Facsimile-Ausgabe *The Copenhagen Haggadah*, Altona-Hamburg, 1739 (Privatbesitz, Israel): Jerusalem, 1986.

[31] Benjamin, *op. cit.*

[32] *Pesach-Haggada*, Jerusalem, Jewish National and University Library, 8°5573, 6v. Von Meschullam Simmel stammen u.a. auch zwei Widmungsblätter an Kaiser Karl VI. und seine Frau Elisabeth, Wien, Österreichische Nationalbibliothek, Cod hebr 223. 224 und ein Seder tiqqune sabbat, Wien, 1715: London, British Library, Add 11433.

[33] M. Krieger, ''Die Ansbacher Hofmaler des 17. und 18. Jahrhunderts'', *Jahrbuch des historischen Vereins für Mittelfranken*, 33, 1966, darin: Juda Löw Pinchas (1727-1793), S. 239-257, bes. S. 241f.

[34] *Pesach-Haggada*, Parma, Bibl. Palatina, Ms 147, 4v.

[35] *Pesach-Haggada*, Jerusalem, Israel Museum 181/53, 4r. A. Scheiber, ''The Jewish Artistic School of Kittsee'', *Journal of Jewish Art*, 7, 1980, S. 44-50; M. Ayali, *The Kittsee Haggadah (1770)*, Tel Aviv, 1987.

[36] Ohne Angabe des Schreibers ist die 1733 in Mitteleuropa hergestellte und sonst nicht näher bestimmte *Haggada* der Jewish National and University Library Jerusalem, 8°4017. Fol. 5v zeigt acht Gelehrte, die miteinander diskutieren, rund um einen Tisch, der fast das ganze Bild ausfüllt. Im Hintergrund sind nur eineinhalb Fenster zu sehen. Auch hier ist die allerdings variierte Vorlage die Amsterdamer Haggada von 1695.

[37] Benjamin, *op. cit.*, Uri Feibusch, 1720-1795, lebte bis etwa 1755 in Hamburg/Altona, übersiedelte dann nach Kopenhagen, wo er den Namen Philip Isac Levy führte.

[38] *Pesach-Haggada*, Hamburg, Staats- und Universitätsbibliothek, Cod Levy 22, 6r.

[39] *Pesach-Haggada*, Darmstadt, Hessische Landes- und Hochschulbibliothek, Cod Or 7, 5v.

[40] *Pesach-Haggada*, Cincinatti, Hebrew Union College, Ms 450, 5v.

URSULA SCHUBERT

Die rabbinische Vorstellung vom Schaubrottisch und die Bibel von S. Isidoro de Leon, a.d. 960 (Real Colegiata, cod. 2, fol. 50r)

Die biblischen Angaben vom Aussehen des Schaubrottisches und der sich darauf befindenden Schaubrote im Buch Exodus (25, 23-30 und 37, 10-15) entsprechen nur in höchst ungenauer Weise allen bildlichen Wiedergaben, die in frühmittelalterlichen christlichen und spätmittelalterlichen jüdischen Handschriften enthalten sind. Offensichtlich war die Bibel nicht der einzige Text, der von den Illustratoren für die Darstellung der Kultgegenstände herangezogen wurde. Eines der ältesten Bilder des Schaubrottisches findet sich im Codex Amiatinus[1] aus dem frühen 7. Jahrhundert; das beigefügte Wort "Mensa" schließt jedes Mißverständnis aus [Fig. 1]. Der Tisch ist perspektivisch verkürzt wiedergegeben, oben auf der Tischplatte stehen in zwei Reihen nebeneinander offensichtlich je sechs kelchförmige Gefäße, die die Schaubrote enthalten. Als Textgrundlage könnte hier das Buch Leviticus (24, 5f) herangezogen werden, wo von zwölf Broten die Rede ist, die in zwei Schichten auf den Tisch vor den Herrn gelegt werden. Wenn aber auf jede der beiden Schichten entsprechend dem Bibeltext Weihrauch gegeben werden soll (Lev 24, 7), so läßt sich die Realisierung dieser Vorschrift unter den gegebenen Umständen schwer vorstellen.

Wie mit allen biblischen Texten begannen die rabbinischen Gelehrten sich auch bald mit der Frage nach der Bereitung und dem Aussehen der Schaubrote sowie ihrer Anordnung auf dem Schaubrottisch zu beschäftigen. Die ausführlichste Stellungnahme findet sich in der Mischna, Menachot (XI, 4-5)[2]. Der inhaltlich schwer verständliche Text kann in dem Sinn gedeutet werden, daß die jeweils paarweise gebackenen Schaubrote, deren Ränder oder auch Ecken man vor dem Backen hörnchenartig umbog, in der Weise auf den Tisch gelegt wurden, daß die Länge der Brote der Breite des Tisches entsprach. Weiters legte man, laut diesem Text, die Schaubrote so auf den Tisch, daß in der Mitte zwischen den beiden Schaubrotreihen ein Zwischenraum frei gelassen wurde, "sodaß die Luft dazwischen hindurchstreichen konnte". Außerdem ist in Menachot (XI, 6) von vier Gestellen die Rede, von denen, nach dieser Auffassung, jeweils zwei als Stützen für je eine der beiden Schichten der Schaubrote gedient haben; also lagen diese offensichtlich nicht nebeneinander sondern übereinander, inner- oder außerhalb ihrer Schüsseln auf dem Tisch. All diese theoretischen Überlegungen der Rabbinen blieben aber keineswegs nur auf die Kommentare beschränkt, sondern wurden von den Illustratoren hebräischer Handschriften als Hinweise für ihre Darstellungen herangezogen. Und wie die Texte verschiedene Möglichkeiten für die Art der Anordnung der Brote auf dem Schaubrottisch offen ließen, so scheinen auch die Illustratoren sich für verschiedene Varianten der Darstellung entschieden zu haben. Aber der Anstoß für die voneinander abweichenden

1) «Codex Amiatinus I», Florenz, Biblioteca Laurenziana, I, fols. 2v-3r, Northumbrien, Anfang 7. Jh.

2) «Bibel», Mailand, Biblioteca Ambrosiana, Ms. C 105 sup., fol. 1v, Spanien, 14. Jh.

Wiedergaben des Schaubrottisches dürfte sicher nicht vom Bibeltext, sondern von der rabbinischen Deutung ausgegangen sein.

In spanischen mittelalterlichen hebräischen Handschriften sind die Tempelsymbole in der Regel als Doppelblatt in freier Anordnung auf die ersten Seiten vor den Pentateuch gesetzt. In der Darstellung der Schaubrote in der Handschrift aus Mailand (Bibl. Amb. C 105 sup. fol. I)[3] [Fig. 2] sind die Schaubrote in zwei Reihen — offenbar in Gefäßen — ohne irgendein Gestell frei schwebend über dem Schaubrottisch angeordnet. Rechts davon ist sehr ungenau die Menora, der siebenarmige Leuchter, angedeutet, im Feld darunter statt der Bundeslade mit den sich darüber befindenden Cheruben nur die tragbaren Gesetzes-

tafeln. Als Ausnahmefall wurde — ebenfalls in Spanien, im frühen 14. Jahrhundert — auch einer Pesach-Haggada eine Darstellung des Schaubrottisches vorangestellt (Parma, Bibl. Palatina, Ms. parm. 2411, fol. 3r)[4] [Fig. 3]. Dabei wurde das Brot auf hohen Trägern in vier Reihen auf dem Tisch angeordnet, so daß jede Reihe aus drei Broten besteht. Unter dem Tisch steht zweimal deutlich ''Tisch'', in jedem einzelnen Brotbehälter ''Brot'' geschrieben. Eine ganz andere Darstellungsweise des Schaubrottisches und der Schaubrote findet sich im Regensburger Pentateuch[5] [Fig. 4]. An die Stelle, wo sich in spanischen hebräischen Handschriften die Darstellung der Bundeslade mit den Cheruben befindet, ist hier eine zweigeteilte Tafel gesetzt; in die sechs kleinen Felder jeder Hälfte ist deutlich

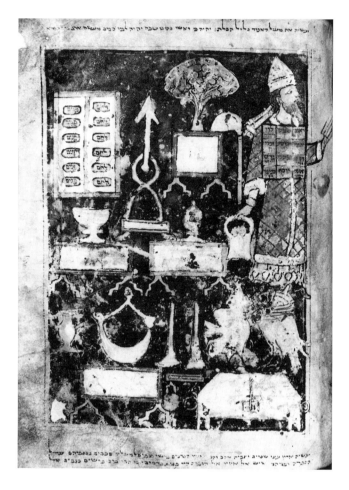

3) «Pesach-Haggada», Parma, Biblioteca Palatina, Ms. parm. 2411, fol. 3r, Spanien, 14. Jh.

4) «Regensburger Pentateuch», Jerusalem, Israel Museum, Ms. 180/52, fol. 156r, Bayern, um 1300.

abwechselnd ''Schau'' und ''Brot'' geschrieben. Aber die Bundeslade ist auf demselben Blatt in der rechten unteren Ecke wiedergegeben. Man erkennt deutlich die Stangen, an denen sie getragen wurde. An der Vorderseite befindet sich, wie bei einem Opferaltar, ein Schloß, was beispielsweise in der Wiedergabe der Bundeslade im Pentateuch von Tours[6] eine Parallele hat und auf das Alter dieses Typus schließen läßt. Ebenso wie im Pentateuch von Tours (fol. 127v) sieht man über dem Deckel der Bundeslade im Regensburger Pentateuch die Cheruben. Zum Unterschied von spanischen hebräischen Handschriften ist hier die Abbildung der Tempelsymbole mit der Darstellung des Hohepriesters Aaron verbunden, der — in seine hohepriesterlichen Gewänder gekleidet — im Begriffe ist, den

siebenarmigen Leuchter anzuzünden, der sich auf der gegenüberliegenden Seite (fol. 155v) befindet.

Die Verbindung der Darstellung Aarons bei der Ausübung einer hohepriesterlichen Funktion mit einer Darstellung der Tempelsymbole hat eine unerwartete Parallele im Frontispiz zum Buch Leviticus der spanischen Bibel in der Colegiata von S. Isidoro in Leon [Fig. 5] aus dem Jahre 960[7], hinter der eine westgotische Bibel aus dem 5. Jahrhundert als Archetyp vermutet wird[8]. Die Bibel wurde von Florentius und Sanctius im Kloster SS. Peter und Paul in Valeranica in Altkastilien geschrieben und illuminiert; die Illustrationen sind in der Regel direkt beim Text in die Schriftkolumne eingefügt, was den Konservativismus dieses Bildtyps verrät[9]. J. W. Williams erwägt die Mög-

85

5) «Bibel», Leon, Real Colegiata de S. Isidoro, cod. 2, fol. 50r.

6) «Bibel», Leon, Real Colegiata de S. Isidoro, cod. 3, I, fol. 50r, Kastilien, 1162.

lichkeit, daß die ursprüngliche Bildvorlage, die hinter einer Reihe von heute verlorenen aber aus Berichten bekannten und von Williams angeführten illustrierten Bibelhandschriften steht, jüdischen Ursprungs war. Williams sah in dem sich an der Westwand der Synagoge von Dura Europos[10] befindenden Bild des Tempels, in dessen ummauertem Vorhof ebenfalls der hohepriesterlich gekleidete Aaron steht, eine Parallele zum Leviticusbild der Bibel von S. Isidoro de Leon von 960. Seine Meinung wurde durch die Tatsache bestärkt, daß es in der spanischen Bibel Mißverständnisse, zumindest aber eine Verwechslung der Legenden gibt, was beweist, daß die Vorlage nicht mehr verstanden wurde. In der Bibel von 960 auf fol. 50r, ebenso wie in Dura Europos, ist die gemauerte Stiftshütte mit einem durch Vorhänge verhängten Eingang dargestellt. Zum Unterschied vom Codex Amiatinus ist die Trennung zwischen Heiligtum und Allerheiligstem nicht klar vollzogen, denn die Bundeslade mit

ihren Tragstangen steht innerhalb des Heiligtums vor dem Vorhang, der das Allerheiligste vom Heiligtum trennt. Die Menora ist offenbar um ihren Ständer gebracht und hängt unter dem Vorhang; auch sind die drei Querarme auf einen einzigen reduziert. Außer dem siebenarmigen Leuchter befanden sich, wie die Beischriften im Codex Amiatinus beweisen, im Heiligtum der Rauchopferaltar und der Schaubrottisch. In der spanischen Handschrift steht der Rauchopferaltar in der Mitte des Heiligtums und Aaron vor ihm. Aber die zweigeteilte Platte hinter Aaron versinnbildlicht ohne Zweifel einen Schaubrottisch, über dem nicht zwei, sondern nur eine Reihe von Schaubroten in ihren Schüsseln in der Luft gleichsam schwebt. Die Platte des Schaubrottisches ist durch eine Beischrift als ''Labrum'' bezeichnet. Daraus geht hervor, daß der Kopist die Vorlage nicht mehr verstand, denn wie auch die Darstellung im Codex Amiatinus beweist, befand sich das Labrum im Vorhof des Tempels.

7) «Bibel», San Millan de la Cogolla, Madrid, Real Academia Historica, cod. 2, fol. 58v, Altkastilien, 1200-20.

nung zwischen dem Schaubrottisch und den Gefäßen für die Schaubrote durchgeführt. Den Schaubrottisch beließ er im Heiligtum und setzte ihn links neben die Bundeslade über die Köpfe der Figurengruppe; den Turm von sieben Gefäßen für die Schaubrote setzte er hingegen auf eine Art Säule vor die Mauer, die das Heiligtum umschließt. Aaron selbst steht hier nicht beim Rauchopferaltar, sondern beim Labrum, das seinen Platz vor der Mauer verloren hat und in das Innere des Heiligtums versetzt ist. Die Kopien der spanischen Bibel von 960 zeigen somit, daß das Verständnis der einzelnen Kopisten für die Darstellung des Schaubrottisches gemäß der Vorlage deutlich im Schwinden begriffen war. Aber — wie Williams von seiner Seite aus ebenfalls annahm — entsprach selbst die Darstellung des Schaubrottisches in der Bibel von 960 nicht mehr der vermutlich illustrierten Vorlage aus dem 5. Jahrhundert.

Es konnten somit die verschiedenen Elemente des Schaubrottisches, wie sie der hier dargelegten Ikonographie entsprechen, nur auf Grund des Mischna-Textes formuliert worden sein. Auf der anderen Seite ist dieser Typus von Schaubrottisch sonst nur in mittelalterlichen hebräischen Handschriften belegt. Aus diesen Gegebenheiten muß der Schluß gezogen werden, daß zumindest für die Incipit-Seite zu Leviticus in der Bibel von S. Isidoro de Leon, a.d. 960 — das heißt für die angenommene westgotische Vorlage aus dem 5. Jahrhundert — eine jüdische Bildvorlage zur Verfügung stand[14].

Daß es aber ein beckenartiges Aussehen hatte, ist auch aus einer entsprechenden Darstellung der Sacra im Regensburger Pentateuch zu schließen.

Nach der Meinung von Williams[11] sind die beiden illustrierten Bibelhandschriften — einerseits die in Leon, San Isidoro, vom Jahre 1162[12] [Fig. 6] und andererseits jene von San Millan de la Cogolla[13] [Fig. 7] aus dem ersten oder zweiten Jahrzehnt des 13. Jahrhunderts — entweder direkt oder durch gemeinsame Vorlagen indirekt mit der Bibel von 960 verwandt. In beiden Fällen gibt die Incipit-Seite zum Buch Leviticus die Bibel von 960, fol. 50r, wieder. Die Darstellung des Schaubrottisches und der sich darüber befindenden Schaubrote stimmt mit der Vorlage besser in der Bibel von 1162 (I fol. 50r) [Fig. 6] überein. In der Bibel von San Millan de la Cogolla (I fol. 58v) [Fig. 7] hingegen hat der Kopist offenbar selbständig eine räumliche Tren-

[1] Florenz, Bibl. Laur. cod. Amiatinus I, fol. 2v-3r. Eine gute Literaturübersicht bei E. Revel Neher, ''Du Codex Amiatinus et ses rapports avec les plans du tabernacle dans l'art juif et dans l'art byzantin'', *Journal of Jewish Art*, 9 , 1982, S. 6-17.

[2] Siehe Übersetzungen von J. Cohn, *Mischnajot*, V, Basel, 1968, S. 154-158; H. Danby, *The Mischna*, Oxford, 1974, S. 507f.

[3] A. Luzzatto, L. Mortara Ottolenghi, ''Description of Decorated and Illuminated Manuscripts in the Ambrosian Library'', *Hebraica Ambrosiana*, Mailand, 1972, II, S. 129-132.

[4] G. Tamani, ''Elenco dei manoscritti ebraici miniati e decorati della 'Palatina' di Parma'', *La Bibliofilia*, Florenz, 1968, S. 112f.

[5] Jerusalem, Israel Museum, Ms. 180/52, fol. 156r, um 1300; B. Narkiss, *Hebrew Illuminated Manuscripts*, Jerusalem, 1969, S. 96.

[6] *Pentateuch von Tours*, Paris, Bibliothèque Nationale, Ms. nouv. acq. lat. 2334, fol. 76v u. 127v, Anf. 7. Jh.

[7] *Bibel*, Leon, Real Colegiata S. Isidoro, cod. 2, fol. 50r.

[8] J. W. Williams, *Frühe spanische Buchmalerei*, München, 1977, S. 24.

[9] J. W. Williams, ''A Castilian Tradition of Bible Illustration'', *Journal of the Warburg and Courtauld Institutes*, 28, 1965, S. 66-85, bes. S. 71

[10] C. H. Kraeling, ''Excavations at Dura Europos, Final Report, VIII, part I'', *The Synagogue*, New Haven, 1956, S. 125-131, pl. LX.

[11] Williams, *op. cit.*, 1965, S. 66-68.

[12] *Bibel*, Leon, Real Colegiata de San Isidoro, cod. 3, I-III.

[13] *Bibel*, Madrid, Real Academia Historica, cod. 2, Altkastilien, 1200-20. Ich danke der Real Academia Historica für die bereitwillige Übersendung der Photographien von allen erbetenen alttestamentlichen Illustrationen dieser Handschrift.

[14] Rachel Wischnitzer hat schon vor der Aufdeckung der Synagoge von Dura Europos (November 1932) die Möglichkeit erwogen, daß es in hellenistischer und frühbyzantinischer Zeit einen jüdischen Bibelbilderkreis gegeben hat; vgl. R. Wischnitzer, ''Von der Holbeinbibel zur Amsterdamer Haggadah'', *Monatsschrift für Geschichte und Wissenschaft des Judentums*, 75 (NF 39), 1931, S. 269-286, bes. S. 270 (Anm. 1).

PHILIPP P. FEHL

The *Stadttempel* of the Jews of Vienna: Childhood Recollections and History*

I

Rather late in life Professor Moshe Barasch and I met and soon discovered to our mutual delight and melancholy comfort that we were born in the same year (1920) and that we share memories not just of the horrors which our generation, to the extent that it survived, is destined to live with and — such as one can — to meditate upon, but also of a Jewish childhood which is reflected in the fragments of the broken mirror that hold the images of our early past with a singular glow of blessedness.

Moshe Barasch was born and lived as a child and a youth in Czernowitz, or Černovcy, or Cernăuţi (the very number of these names, all at one time or another official designations of one and the same town, points to the complexity of its life) and I in Vienna, which does not need the recommendation of many names to bespeak the confusions, tribulations, and triumphs of its history. In the homes our parents provided, our lives were, if not exactly defined by the synagogue, still lived within the reach of its shelter and affected by the shadowy proximity of densely crowded Jewish cemeteries.

They were touched by a sense of ancientness and belonging and by certainties regarding the dignity, the proper joys, and the duties of men that transcended religious and national boundaries. These certainties spoke to us — depending on where we were — in the voice of the theater, the concert hall, and the museum, as well as in that of the synagogue. The voices were differently accented, of course, and their ranges and intensities varied, but the hopes that mattered, the thrust, as it were, of our prayers, and of our awe and pleasure in the presence of poetry, was the same.

Jewish Czernowitz and Jewish Vienna, in the generalizations of hindsight in which history often is perceived, readily appear in the twilight of irreconcilable differences. Here the town of the true Jews, vintage Jews, as it were, resistant to compromise with the gentile world, and there the Jews of the modern world, interesting, perhaps, but also unreliable, and even eager to escape definition in their identity as Jews.

Barasch and I, in our happy conversations, which were really an intermingling exchange of recollections, saw the past and Vienna and Czernowitz and much else in quite a different light; it was much more beautiful at either end of the spectrum. Our view of a childhood that was so abruptly and cruelly terminated by events that will never seem to us, no matter how old we get to be, to have occurred long ago, necessarily looks across the abyss that separates us from the people we loved and with whom we lived in our innocence, through a veil of tears. These are, of course, not tears to be ashamed of, not even in an historian. But if our view is frankly and gratefully supported and colored by sentiment and longing, are we for that reason also flawed observers and, howsoever understandably, poor judges of our own memories?

Tears, we might respond, do not always obscure vision; there are times when they act like lenses and we see a truth more clearly because we are capable of weeping. This is certainly so in the theater that Aristotle thought worthy of his analysis. Is it all that different on the stage that is explored by historians and, in particular, by the historian of art who is concerned in the innermost sense of his calling with the sense and the truth of works of fiction which were produced to inspire pity and disinterested fear, and love, and hope?

The works of art which here concern us, synagogues, or "temples" as we called them, by and large were not triumphs of architecture — synagogues rarely are and perhaps should not even be that — but they were lovable and were loved by many, for a complexity of reasons. These are compounded of art and faith, ritual practice, habit, sentiment, and even sentimentality, that predilection for the exercise of tender emotion that is despised by those who pride themselves on their lack of it, but that cannot be bad as long as we distinguish sentimentality, as I think we should, from what, with a nice precision of taste, one used to call "false sentimentality."

Barasch and I, each in his own way, offer eyewitness accounts of synagogues that mattered in our lives. We do so in the form of memories that were instructed and enlarged upon by our concerns as historians. Our memories come in the form of a lump, in more ways than one. But then, so also did we encounter the sense, the life, and the faded beauty of the synagogues we wish to talk about in a conglomeration of emotions and architectural forms. We are loath to separate out and to package and label the different elements which make up this whole as, perhaps, the conventions of the profession might find desirable.[1] Our concern for our subject, even if unuttered, goes back further even than the time of our apprenticeship in the history of art. It may have helped to confirm us in our doubts about the ultimate efficacy or usefulness of an art history that prides itself on being an exact science and to this end objectivizes the relationship between the student of a work of art and the life of the work of art itself. Purged of the force of sentiment that alone will jump the hurdle of the grave, history itself becomes dead, a mechanical exercise that may be reliable within limits but cannot celebrate a memory or find access to works of art that come to life in the world of fiction through our compassion. As a result, it would seem, an anxiously unsentimental science of art defeats its own purpose. Its exacting exactitude keeps it from encountering the passionate reality of the object it professes to study. It perceives not the work of art itself but only its measurable shell.

But be that as it may. In the task at hand, at least, it is obvious that we have a particular obligation to the dead whom we can only serve if we refrain from crowding them. We must not, in the process of looking at buildings and their history, lose just what we set out to reconstruct. Our purpose is as much to see the works of architecture in question in the transfiguring light of the people and the functions they served, as it is to salute the shades of those whose prayers, spoken and sung and lived within these premises, gave substance to the nameless and immeasurable presence of this light.

"There cannot be many art historians left, if ever there were many," Barasch and I said to each other with a sigh, "who still can speak to the subject as witnesses as, however haltingly, would we." "Let us therefore do it," we continued with a kind of relief that we had reached this point of resolve, "while there still is time."

II

We turn to the Vienna of my childhood, the Vienna as I knew it then. Physically it is still, by and large, the same. But I lived my life in an environment in which Jews mattered, not so much in their capacity as Jews, as that the majority of the people whom we knew with any kind of intimacy were Jews, with whom we shopped, and ate, and, in the "Gymnasium", went to school where even many of our professors were Jews — and they are there no more. There was for the Jews, at least, a certain naturalness about the Jewish presence in Vienna. There were about 170,000 Jews in the city which counted two million inhabitants; these were Jews who were counted as members of the Jewish faith, no matter whether they practiced it or not, as long as they did not register a conversion to another religion or took upon themselves the trouble and burden of declaring themselves to the authorities as being without defined religion, "konfessionslos," as they were called by a terminus technicus which, I suppose, still obtains.[2] In addition there were then in Vienna many people of Jewish extraction who were not Jews but among whom there were again many who continued to live among Jews and carry on a normal course of civic life with them. They were, if not co-religionists, still, in a peculiar way, fellow Jews, in the same way as they were fellow Austrians. Certain professions, certain activities had a preponderance of Jews in them, doctors, above all, and lawyers, but since the sense of fellowship among colleagues outweighed religious differences in a society where, by and large, one did not debate religion, this was by many not at all deemed unreasonable or remarkable. The preponderance of Jews in the professions named was explained, by the Jews at least, by the fact that these were traditional fields of excellence and interest for Jews. We were good at them and the chosen callings had a certain dignity; Jewish students often worked harder than their gentile colleagues and they therefore deservedly reached the places they competed for. But even that was rare in my hearing; it was one of the facts of life in Vienna that Jews would frequently be found in certain fields of endeavor, academic or otherwise, and not so in others where, perhaps, they would have been held back (if they insisted on entering them in the first place), just as they had an opportunity to prosper in others. But I must add that in the time I lived in Vienna hardly anybody ever prospered at anything — if we measure prosperity in terms of earthly goods.

Similarly the density of the pattern of Jewish residences in Vienna was established by tradition. Most Jews in Vienna congregated in the Leopoldstadt, the second district of Vienna, which is named after the Emperor Leopold I who in 1670 expelled the Jews from Vienna. It was there where the former ghetto had been located and it was to this area that the Jews eventually returned when they were grudgingly and with demeaning restrictions re-admitted to the city.[3] Later immigrants who were free to move where they wished, settled, or at first settled, among their already established co-religionists. There was hardly a Jew in Vienna who, if he did not live in the Leopoldstadt, did not have a relative there. We hardly knew anything about the grim origins of the Leopold-stadt and its name. It had happened so long ago, in a barbaric age, we thought, in a different Vienna.

And, indeed, the city I knew and loved was the Vienna that had been established in the second half of the nineteenth century, when the city walls were replaced by the majestic boulevards of the Ringstraße and an endless stream of immigrants, workers, craftsmen, and traders from all over the empire, with many Jews among them (who now enjoyed the same rights as anybody else) poured into the capital which grew immensely in size. New streets with closely packed buildings sprung up everywhere, the results of a building boom which still was sufficiently well regulated so as not to offend the dignity of the capital city. This new town gently enclosed the old city which shone within it like a gem. When I was a boy the new town was itself turning old, and even shabby. Among the streets of Vienna the Ringstraße was to me especially attractive and will always remain so. Built nobly, in an eclectic Renaissance style, it was sinking into the ancientness it had affected, and honored, in its beginning. Historicism, as it were, was maturing into history and the two Viennas, the old and the *quondam* new, blended and were fading in unison into a kind of perfection that was tinged with regret.

It was not difficult for a Jew to feel at home in such a city and to look back upon its past as being a part of his own as well. Two or three generations of quiet, constructive residence go a long way among immigrants to create in them the conviction of permanence and belonging. In a way, among new immigrants, the Jews could consider themselves pioneers. When their first wave arrived, in the fifties and sixties of the nineteenth century, they already found in Vienna a relatively small but thriving community of Jews, the descendants and the many dependents of the so-called

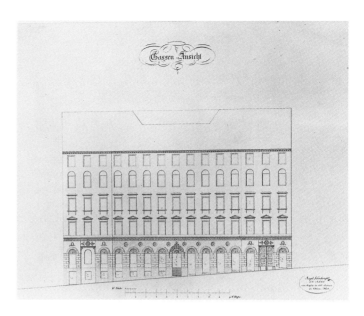

1) Joseph Kornhäusel, «Stadttempel», Vienna. Apartment house and access to synagogue. Elevation. First project. Collection Albertina, Vienna. Photo Albertina.

tolerated Jews, Jews who were granted residential privileges in Vienna for the good of the empire, members of banking firms and entrepreneurs distinguished by their wealth and influence. The leaders of this community enjoyed the confidence and to a certain extent also the respect of the government; some of them even were created noblemen, without their having to convert to receive the honor.

In 1823 these Jews, after skillfully conducted negotiations, were granted the opportunity of building a whole block of flats and administrative offices that would also contain a *mikvah* (the ritual bath), a school, a kosher butcher shop, and above all, in its very center, a synagogue. This is the famous *Stadt-tempel* of Vienna.[4] It is a gem of a building in a delicate neo-classical style, an oval hall circled by twelve tall Ionic columns that help support two galleries for women. To the east, adjacent to each other, are the *bema* and the *Aaron Ha Kaudesch* (Thora Shrine). The room is covered by a dome crowned by a lantern. The entire complex [Figs. 1, 5-11] is the work of the architect Joseph Kornhäusel who had been chosen with care and who clearly took a consummate interest in the perfection of his unusual commission.[5] The building was completed in 1826 and consecrated in a ceremony of splendor and dignity that seems to have moved non-Jews who attended as well as Jews.[6]

The order of the service in this temple was developed according to convictions regarding the dignity and the beauty

2) Statue of Josef von Sonnenfels, Vienna. Photo: Michael Kreiter.

3) Seitenstettengasse with «Stadttempel». Photo: coll. Pierre Genée.

of the service of God which corresponded to the quiet and elegant simplicity of the temple's interior. It was the work of two men, the temple's first spiritual leader, Isaac Noah Mannheimer (1793-1865), and Salomon Sulzer (1804-1890) its first cantor who from its inception served the temple not only as a singer but also as a creator of sacred music[7]. The work of these two men, as well as of Mannheimer's immediate successor, Adolph Jellinek (1821-1893), established a form of divine worship that became exemplary for almost all the temples which were subsequently established in Vienna (at the end of the century there were well over forty of them) and influenced religious practice all over the Habsburg Empire and even far beyond.[8] Unlike the worship of the reform movement of the Jews of Germany, though it was instructed by its precedent, it did not seek to change but rather to elevate and clarify, to let speak out, with the help of art, the ritual one had inherited. The purpose was high-minded and, like so much else that was lovable in Austria, conciliatory, and capable of serving and nourishing the religious needs of many comers from different lands of the Habsburg Empire. Except for the absolutely orthodox who congregated not in a temple but a temple-like building they defiantly called a ''Schul,'' the Jews of Vienna acquiesced in the *Stadttempel* ritual and found a home in it. My father once took me along to the ''Schul'' I just mentioned (it was called the ''Schiffschul,'' after the Schiffgasse in the Leopoldstadt where it was located[9]) for the celebration of the Bar Mitzvah of a young relative. I was so astonished by the intensity of the service, the multitude that packed the large hall, the shouting of the prayers, the prodigious Hebrew learning and power of song of the Bar Mitzvah boy, the self-evident certainty that defined everyone's conduct, the shaking of the bodies in the rhythm of the prayers they knew by heart, and the seeming irregularity of it all that I could hardly believe my eyes and ears. ''They are very strange,'' I said to my father but he said, ''No, they are just pious.'' He respected them but he too would not have joined them. They were, I think, too pious, too demandingly pious for the kind of life he tried to lead as a good Jew who was not exclusively a Jew.

My parents were born in Moravia and came to Vienna as children. My father came from an old and once great Jewish town, Nikolsburg, no more than seventy kilometers away from Vienna, but now in a different world. My mother came from a small, Czech-speaking village called Žižkov. Her parents had moved there, from a nearby Jewish town, Kostel, where there was no living to be made, to open a store and trade with the farmers.[10] In Kostel — as in Nikolsburg — the Jews spoke German, with a Jewish local color, almost a family accent, but not Yiddish.

My father was a skilled artisan, a maker of uppers for shoes, who would work for shoemakers who commissioned the work. The two professions were carefully separated and it so happened that in Vienna a fair number of the leather workers who made uppers were Jews but shoemakers hardly ever. My father, I think, thought of his work primarily as an art but not so of the making of shoes. That was mere labor. As long as women would wear shoes whose uppers went up high to cover a part of the calf the prosperity of his art, as well as his shop, was assured, for the uppers would be decorated with a variety of suitable fancy patterns. That was the fashion. But when silk stockings were introduced into women's wear and the female leg became its own ornament, the uppers, of course, dropped below the ankles and my father's skills were no longer needed. He was like a saddler master in a country without horses. All this happened before I even can remember. He still eked out a living by working with the new kind of uppers, as commissions came his way, but more and more these were produced in factories. He could not bear to be idle and when he had nothing else to do he would design and cut model uppers from paper, just in case they might again be needed. But it was a true joy to see him when he actually had a skin in his hand

4) Kornhäusel, «Stadttempel». Portal, present state.

to cut an upper, for then economy and art were joined; he examined the skin like a sculptor who looks at a block to see what kind of figure there is in it, and then the knife would cut with precise elegance and the upper would emerge from the skin of which all usable parts had been put to use.

That was the life of my father who was a man of few words but a good-natured and fine observer. He spoke with the work of his hands.

We lived near his shop, in the twentieth district of Vienna, a proletarian neighborhood where my father had moved from the Leopoldstadt when he established his shop to be nearer the

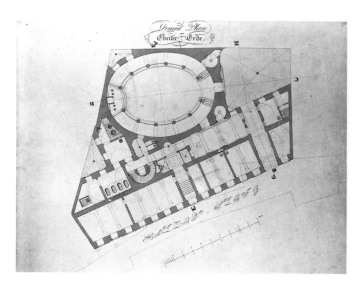

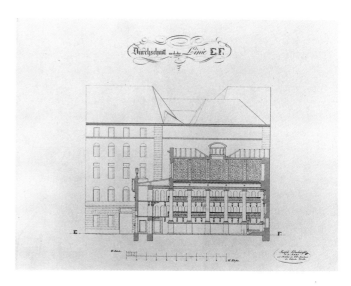

5) Kornhäusel, «Stadttempel» with apartment house. Ground plan. First project. Collection Albertina. Photo: Albertina.

6) Kornhäusel, «Stadttempel» with apartment house. Section: Alternate project. Collection Albertina. Photo: Albertina.

shoemakers whom he hoped to gain as clients; there were already too many cutters of uppers in the Leopoldstadt.

My grandmother, my mother's mother, also lived with us. In late middle age she had become blind but this did not affect her bearing which was erect and very alert. She needed no help about the house and only gentle guidance when we went out together on walks. She never complained about her blindness; it would have been an offense to God, and bad manners as well. So assured was she in the exercise of her piety that it, perhaps, never even occurred to her to complain.

The religious life of my family was a matter of simple practice and my grandmother's presence in it was its cornerstone. Quite in the tradition of the Viennese synagogue, we were anything but zealously religious but my parents kept a kosher house. The way we lived was governed not so much by what we chose to do as by what we refrained from doing. We did not touch pork if it was served when we ate out of the house; my father, for a long time, did not open his shop on Saturdays; we children did go to school on Saturdays, but we did not touch a pen or pencil to write, we did not turn on the lights in the house as it was getting dark on Saturday afternoons until we could see three stars, and so on. And we shared the persuasion of many Jews that there were certain things that Jews, no matter how low they sank, still could not get themselves to do; especially, they would not commit

murder.[11] If, as happened in two instances in my recollection, Jews were accused of murder, it was clear to the Jews of Vienna that these must be charges trumped up by anti-Semites, and signatures were collected to challenge the indictment. Considering the circumstances — and the nature of anti-Semites — the Jews were surely right in their presumptions. Normally, however, anti-Semitism, though it was in places virulent, did not cross our path. We knew it existed and deplored it, but it was, to many of us, so incomprehensible that we took it to be a form of brutish ignorance, a survival from the Dark Ages, or a throwback to them that eventually would be touched by education, and good sense would dissolve it. This kind of thinking was the fruit of the Enlightenment that had transfigured and shaped the lives of the Jews of Austria, and our synagogue services, but also, in a different constellation, the lives of the Austrians themselves. There were many of them who welcomed the emancipation of the Jews and looked upon all men as brothers. We need but recall the chorus of Beethoven's Ninth Symphony to see that this persuasion was not just a mouthing of platitudes.

Enlightenment, however, is a frail flowering and cannot be dependend upon. In a diary entry of 1852 one of my favorite authors, the Austrian poet Franz Grillparzer, who is taking the waters in a Hungarian spa, marvels in dismay about how long it takes for enlightenment to have an effect on people:

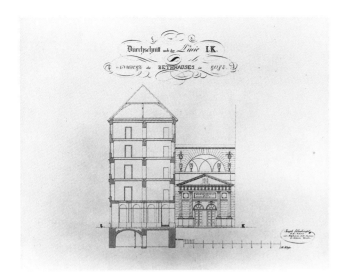

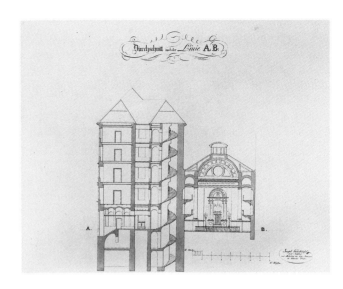

7) Kornhäusel, «Stadttempel». Section, with courtyard entrance. Elaborate alternate project. Collection Albertina. Photo: Albertina.

8) Kornhäusel, «Stadttempel». Section showing «Aaron Ha Kaudesh». Elaborate alternate project. Collection Albertina. Photo: Albertina.

How far away the Hungarians still are from the blessings of civilization, becomes evident, not when we converse with the uneducated (for their ignorance is natural) but when we come to talk to people who have received a not inconsiderable amount of schooling. Such a person complained to me today that the authorities had hanged his swineherd, who was as perfect a swineherd as he had ever had. … A Public official from Ödenburg, who joined us, opined that the Austrians must learn to understand that the robbers of Hungary are quite different from those of the Habsburg crownland: they never do anyone any harm and only kill Jews and Rumanians. Beyond that they are content to abscond with a few animals from the abundance of herds of sheep and swine, to break into winecellars, and on occasion, to rob a traveller. The police who persecute them are unjust and for that reason they are quite properly hated by the populace.[12]

I can match Grillparzer's astonished account with a story of the time my wife and I, after the war, were graduate students at the University of Chicago. We lived in a housing project for married students with children and my mother came to visit us. A number of children were playing in the yard. They had tied a tin can to the tail of a cat and now, with obvious enjoyment, observed the tortures suffered by the desperately frightened animal. Their mothers were sitting on the steps of their houses and were watching the scene and making entries in notebooks. They were engaged in an experiment for which they got paid. They were to see what their children would be up to when left uncontrolled for a certain length of time. ''And these are educated people?'' said my mother in dismay when I explained the situation to her; ''Und das sind gebildete Menschen?'' I can still hear her voice as I write these lines. Her astonishment had the same resonance as that of Grillparzer. Whether she spoke from her conviction as a Jewess or simply as the kind of ''civilized person'' Grillparzer had thought he could take for granted among the educated, was here, happily, one and the same. Her response was formed by the language and the hopes that prospered, at least in certain circles in Austria, in the early half of the nineteenth century, the period that saw the building of Kornhäusel's *Stadttempel* in Vienna.

The tradition, and the commonplaces in which its commitment was articulated, was the delayed fruit of the reforms initiated by the Emperor Joseph II who had given his ''Toleranzpatent'' to the Jews in the name of enlightened humanity, the *Menschlichkeit* he wished to serve. We know that some of this was a myth and that Joseph's reforms also were the result of authoritarian simplifications and, perhaps, a tyrannical temper. But a myth is not a lie. It can speak more clearly than the mere facts of history and, if it uses the vocabulary of love and justice, transcend them. I never could

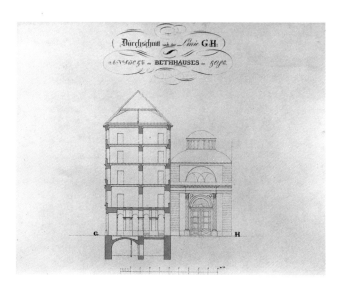

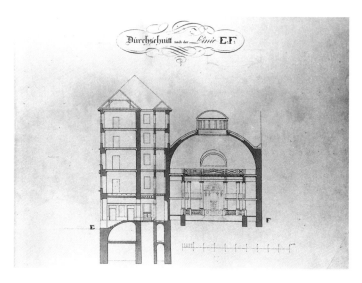

9) Kornhäusel, «Stadttempel». Section, with courtyard entrance. Collection Albertina. Photo: Albertina.

10) Kornhäusel, «Stadttempel». Section, with «Aaron Ha Kaudesh», as built. Collection Albertina. Photo: Albertina.

pass the equestrian monument of Joseph II in front of Austria's National Library without emotion. I did not know then that it was quoting in its form and sense the equestrian statue of Marcus Aurelius on the Capitol, but now that I know it, the statue of Joseph which gladly subordinates itself to that of the philosopher-emperor only speaks to me the more clearly of love and justice. The right hand of each emperor is extended in a gesture of greeting and of bidding peace and order. "It is," says Nathaniel Hawthorne in *The Marble Faun* of the gesture of Marcus Aurelius, "a command that [is] in itself a benediction."[13] This sense was perceived by Zauner, the sculptor of Joseph's monument and saluted in the statue he fashioned.[14] Kornhäusel, in the building of the *Stadttempel* did the same in responding to the language of classical architecture. By subordinating his work to great example it also partakes of its truth. What is before us also points beyond itself. On feast days the interior of the *Stadttempel* looked like an ideal stage set for *The Magic Flute* turned into the reality of architecture.

III

Before we visit this temple of the universal God worshipped by Jews, let me quickly take you to the temple where my family and I regularly worshipped, the temple in the Kluckygasse of the twentieth district where we lived. On Saturdays and the High Holidays it was unheard of to take any kind of

transportation to the synagogue or to walk a great distance to it. This is, of course, the pious reason for the existence of so many temples in Vienna of which now there is only one left, the *Stadttempel*. None of the other temples followed the *Stadttempel* in the form of its classical architecture. We had Gothic, Romanesque, Moorish and all sorts of composite temples. The one in the Kluckygasse, of which not even a good picture survives, was built at the beginning of this century in a quasi-Romanesque style with a tower at each side; it looked squeezed, for it was flanked by apartment houses with which it formed a virtually flush front.[15] The classic style of the *Stadttempel* evidently represented to later architects a facile internationalism, the Romanesque demonstrated belonging (and, indeed, a Jewish presence in Austria can be documented to the tenth century, if not beyond);[16] the Gothic, in turn, showed intensity and purity of faith, while the Moorish recalled the age of glory and learning of the Jews in Spain. Moreover it had the advantage of not also recalling a Christian church. But once one was inside one of those temples, no matter how the architecture was structured, it was the *Stadttempel* that took over, as if by proxy. The distinguished clerical dress of the rabbi and cantor, the top hats (on holidays) of the members of the temple board, the choir, the measures of the music, the ordering of the service, the worthiness of the sermon, its restrained delivery, the rabbi's demeanor of the scholar that he was — none of that had anything to do with medieval art and life but, in a local adaptation, reflected the traditions of the

96

11) Kornhäusel, «Stadttempel». Interior view. Photo: coll. Pierre Genée.

12) Kornhäusel, «Stadttempel». Lantern, exterior view, present state. Photo: Nikolaus Vielmetti.

Enlightenment and the culture of the Ringstraße. It was not appropriate, for example, unless one was very pious, to unfold one's talith (the prayer shawl) and wrap oneself in it. It was, as a rule, not even ample enough to permit this. One wore it about the neck and shoulders as a narrow band, folded and neatly ironed, with a gold or silver border on top. Often it was not made of wool but of silk. It was handsome, but it looked more like a sash, a piece of full-dress equipment, rather than a Jew's prayer garb. It made its own sense; at prayer we appeared before the Lord dressed at our best, dressed up and not disguised as the kind of Jews we were not. I saw my father only once at prayer with his talith wide open. It was on the Day of Atonement, directly after the prayer for the dead had been recited. Children, if their parents were still alive, inevitably were sent out of the temple while this prayer was recited but this time I came back to my father just a little before he had cause to expect me. His eyes were filled with tears and his talith which he had placed on his head was all about him, almost like a tent. I was still quite little and he saw that I saw his tears and pulled me close to him, under the shelter of his tent. It was a moment of unspoken, unexpected and essential intimacy and I am grateful for it and its enlightenment to this day.

The relation between cantor, choir and the public was well ordered, and yet those parts of the public prayers which broke forth at the appointed places like a great storm of reciting voices, each moving at its own speed, were altogether unrehearsed and undirected. Only when the storm died down did cantor and choir (there never was an organ) take over in a kind of musical dialogue between *recitativo* and song. It was

a musical experience, a kind of dramatization, in harmonic form, of the content of the ancient prayers, a recalling of Hebrew antiquity itself; we heard its celebration, its echo and elaboration in terms of what, in a musical city like Vienna, one had good reason to consider the laws of music proper. All this was the result of the pioneering work of Sulzer in the *Stadttempel*. If one was of good will it had something wonderfully evocative of the joy of God about itself, of repentance, of yearning for salvation. The sublimity of prayer in musical accents embraced us like a noble assurance that we were indeed, in so remembering them, the children of Abraham, Isaac and Jacob. Many of the melodies were not difficult to retain and my mother, who had a good voice, would sometimes sing them at home, to our joy and wonder.

The services, though high-minded and committed in their conduct, as a rule, were anything but solemn in their effect. The audience was too lively, too much there with bursts of occasional shouts of *amen*, with a steady coming and going of people who were exercising the Jewish birthright of their individuality before God; but none of this disturbed. It was expected and it was rather a challenge to the cantor and choir to drown out unwanted noises by a sudden improvisation of choral joy and so recall the audience, without coercion, to its cooperative role in the conduct of the services in which all were called upon to take their part in a reasonably measured pattern. We were, indeed, at such moments a team performing in praise of God.

The memory of the music of Sulzer which in the days of my childhood was still loved and treasured by many, particularly

13) Kornhäusel, «Circus Gymnasticus» in the Prater, Vienna. Design for the exterior. Collection Albertina. Photo: Albertina.

among the older people, has now fallen unto hard times. Musicologists, especially ethno-musicologists, look upon it with disdain, for the melodies, like the art of the Ringstraße or even the *Stadttempel* itself, are not ''authentic''; In their harmonization they see not a new originality but a falsification, the product of a hypocritical elitism that insisted on preserving ancientness by casting it into a socially acceptable new form. Rather than preserving the music of the Jews, some claim, Sulzer trivialized it.[17]

These are hard words and charges to which, far too long,

the ethos of the Victorians has been subjected. It is easy to see the flaws and inherent contradictions in a spiritual and educational enterprise that endeavored to give so much to so many, for it was built on compromise; but one does not then see it very well. I still was privileged in my impressionable youth to see and hear and to sympathize with the dying glory of the Victorian Jews, if we may call them so, of Vienna. I also heard the arguments of their detractors, gentiles and Jews alike, who detested compromise and insisted that the whole concern of the temples of Vienna was some sort of capitalist

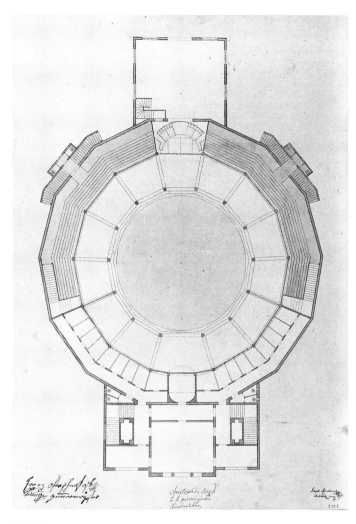

14) Kornhäusel, «Circus Gymnasticus» in the Prater, Vienna. Ground plan. Collection Albertina. Photo: Albertina.

or ethnic lie. In such a view the attempt of the *Stadttempel* and its dependent sygagogues in the outer districts to serve the divine with the help of eclectic art and classically styled oratory was a pastiche and persiflage, a stupid attempt at once to flatter one's rich and upward-mobile parishioners and to deceive the gentiles with lying protestations of adherence to their alien decorum. Jews who were not themselves believers curiously still would insist that those who were should act out their faith in fervent spontaneity, in pictures, as it were, painted in stark colors and not in pastels. The former demonstrated the strength of ancestral convictions, the latter, in aiming to please the eye and ear, showed only weakness and vacuity.

I also lived through most of the first year of the Nazi occupation of Vienna. The Nazis did not argue, they just murdered the remnant of the Jewish Victorians as well as so many other Jews, the critics of the Victorians included. But the arguments of the critics have survived more readily intact, and even at times more blatantly formulated, than has the memory of these largely forgotten last descendants of the Enlightenment. All I can do is try to paint what I remember of the pictures they painted on the canvas of the love of God.

IV

And so I take you to the *Stadttempel* on the walks I took there when I was a youth. Approaching the temple, usually from my walks on the Ringstraße in the approaching dusk, I went past the Burgtheater (which was also a foundation of Joseph II) and sometimes paused to look at a statue nearby, in the "Rathauspark", of Josef von Sonnenfels who had been one of the emperor's favorite counsellors and was responsible for the creation of the high-minded, classical program of the Burgtheater which turned it, for a time, into one of the most inspiring theaters of the German stage.[18] Sonnenfels, who was a jurist, also revised the Austrian penal code. It is to his credit in particular that torture was abolished in Austrian procedures of judicial inquiry.[19] At Sonnenfels' feet, in a perhaps otherwise unremarkable monument, were placed the instruments of torture which he had reduced to uselessness [Fig. 2].[20] I knew that Sonnenfels was born a Jew in Nikolsburg, my father's hometown. His father converted to Catholicism and Sonnenfels was baptized when still a child but it seemed to me, as it did to other Jews, that in his career, that was only possible because he had turned Catholic, he remembered the tradition of Israel.

My way then would take me past the Opera and on a meandering road, getting lost in the narrow, dark streets of the oldest parts of Old Vienna, past the imposing structure of St. Stephen's which I never fully entered, but only peeked inside, because Jews should refrain from visiting churches, and then, into the incipient dusk, down towards the river round about and past the little Romanesque church of St. Rupert, the oldest church in Vienna, into the Seitenstettengasse where the temple is located.

The temple was carefully hidden within the premises of a block of apartments [Fig. 1, 3]. It is fully enclosed by them and an outsider, if he were not told, would never know that there is a temple within. But the apartment block, which is also the work of Kornhäusel, has a certain aura of dignity and reticence of its own; it is faintly reminiscent in its regularity and very sparse classical ornament of blocks of flats on the Rue de Rivoli in Paris. Entering through a gateway that can hardly be called a portal, one found oneself among Jews directly; and a sense of family surrounded, as it still surrounds the Jewish worshipper approaching the temple [Fig. 4]. One washes one's hands at a fountain, crosses the courtyard and suddenly enters, from darkness and a kind of confinement, through a great gate with a Hebrew inscription above, into the splendor of the fully lit oval interior that is crowned by a dome but dominated in accents of jubilation by the imposing view of the *Aaron Ha Kaudesch* (the Thora Shrine) which is topped by the radiance of the tablets of the Ten Commandments [Figs. 9-11].

My visits usually were on Friday evenings or on the eve of holidays, when the Temple was filled. I often did not come to services on time; there was so much to see on the way, and to salute. The service then was in full swing, the voice of the cantor lucid and strong in the familiar melodies, the choir young and lively in its song, and a good many elderly gentlemen in the audience wore top hats. Women and girls, many of them beautiful and festively dressed, looked down from the ladies' galleries, or read in their prayer books, or, discretely and charmingly, talked to each other. Everything was as in the temple in the Kluckygasse, only more choice, older, and more self-evident; the classical interior helped convey the impression that all this was here for ever, and that it had been here since the beginning of time, that is, of modern time, or the time of the *Menschlichkeit* that was initiated by the emancipation of which the temple was such a lovely witness. Presiding over the assembly was the pale and dignified countenance of Vienna's chief rabbi, Dr. David Feuchtwang. I knew him, that is, I saw him, and heard him preach, when he was in his seventies. His presence inspired a loving respect. I marked each one of his gestures (which ever were sparing) and each of his words, though I could not always follow his exposition.[21] It was as lucid as it was learned but I sometimes paid attention more to his manner than his argument. It showed his power of self-control and directed us to the sense of his words which followed his thought with a beautiful precision. He was a savant, an Assyriologist, as well as a learned rabbi and the two vocations merged in him into one, in keeping with a tradition of learning in which scholarship commits us to the humanities and the humanities commit us to God. I was ever so proud that Dr. Feuchtwang, who also came from Nikolsburg, had celebrated the marriage of my parents, as had his father that of my paternal grandparents. I have found in Wininger's *Große Jüdische National-Biographie* which was published in 1927 in Czernowitz (the town, we recall, to which Professor Barasch's article is dedicated) the entry which Dr. David Feuchtwang devoted to the memory of his father, Dr. Meyer Feuchtwang. It is a beautiful tribute of filial piety and it also reflects what both of these men, father and son, thought of the duties and character of learning. I translate the last lines:

His philosophical equanimity and restrained scholarly temperament kept him from drawing attention to himself. He was truly an eminent man, a splendid chancel orator and a universal savant. Nonetheless, short of his dissertation (on Plato), he never published a single line.[22]

Such were some of the men in Israel who guided the spiritual welfare of the Jews of Austria.

V

History at once corrects and falsifies recollections. The architectural history of the *Stadttempel* has been explored repeatedly, with firm results, and equally so the social history of its origin. But when I lived in Vienna and grew up there, a Viennese child of Austrian Jews, who looked upon Austria still in the givenness or, better, the past givenness of the Habsburg monarchy of their forebears' and their own lives, I saw the "Tempel" and the lives and memories that clustered about it not historically but as a given fact, one might almost say, of nature. It seemed to me ancient and timeless all at once, as was the language of its classical architecture and — in another dimension of memory — as was the promise of Revelation that defined us as God's chosen people.

This does not mean, however, that I was not aware of the basic circumstances of the "Tempel's" relatively recent origins. I well knew the date of its dedication (1826 — not even a hundred years before I was born) and the names of its first preacher and first cantor, Isaac Noah Mannheimer and Salomon Sulzer, respectively. All this was engraved on two memorial tablets which still can be seen in their old places in the entrance hallway. The inscriptions moved me, as they still do, by their reticent, somewhat archaïc and yet flowery language.[23] Even the rhythmic sound of the protagonists' ancestral names in which Hebrew and German are naturally joined into one flowing utterance conveyed a sense of faded memory and elevation. These were Jewish names of old Austria, such as they also appeared on weathered shields over the entrances to old stores and businesses and, of course, on old tomb stones [Figs. 15-23].[24]

My brother and I were taken by our parents on visits to the cemeteries on certain occasions when it was customary to pray at the graves of relatives. I remember practicing my reading both of German and Hebrew letters in early attempts to decipher the inscriptions on head stones. When we paused at the rows of tombs which had been singled out for special honors awarded to the dead (be that for contributions to the

15) Tombs in the «Währinger Friedhof», Vienna. Photo: Nikolaus Vielmetti.

16) Tombs in the «Währinger Friedhof», Vienna. Photo: Nikolaus Vielmetti.

life of the Jewish Community or to the City of Vienna), we were moved with a grateful pride — with a sense of wonder and of belonging — so close were their memories to our lives and so overgrown with stories and legends of Old Vienna. These were passed on to us by my grandmother and by relatives so old as to have been there, or who seemed to have been there, when these ancient worthies lived. All the narrators quite justly drew a line in their accounts between the ''time before the war'' (which was the land of memory) and the largely incomprehensible, shabby, and uninteresting present.

This way of speaking surely contributed to my seeing the hundred and some years that had accumulated from the foundation of the ''Tempel'' to the time of my youth in Vienna as an eternity. To the young, of course, even decades seem like centuries, but this was not the decisive factor. Everything, no matter how recent, that had its roots in the Habsburg monarchy seemed ancient to me and my contemporaries. It belonged to the other side of the great divide which was marked by the foundation of the Austrian Republic of 1918. As a child of the republic I felt that I could not, without making elaborate historicizing qualifications, understand the loyalties and customs of my elders. They had lived and become what they were in what seemed to me the feudal age [Fig. 24].[25] But if I could not understand them I could still love them and respect their ways, as relics of a by-gone age, and delight in their speech which seemed to me, in the way they placed their accents, different from my, as it were, republican German.

In short, the little I did know about the history of the

''Tempel'' only helped to remove it for me into a time beyond history. Kornhäusel's drawings [Figs. 1, 5-10, 12], which I here reproduce from the large store of his designs for the Tempel in the Albertina (developed in four stages of evolvement), may help to make comprehensible what I saw as, as it were, timebound timelessness in architecture when I visited the ''Tempel'' and found there a kind of nourishment — always a little astonished and yet as if coming home.

It is, of course, easy to spot the hallmarks of the building's period style and to place it ''in its time.'' Kornhäusel's classicism sports a kind of past modernity, an elegance of fashion that he bestowed on all his buildings. The trait is evident, for example, in the decidedly ''snob'' character of the Riding Circus he designed for the Vienna ''Prater'' [Figs. 13-14].[26] Its refined severity is deliberately stylish, not inappropriate for an acrobat concerned with showing off his riding skills, and attuned, perhaps, to the atmosphere of the classicizing cafés of the period. Transfigured to greater glory, this elegance also hovers, like the exhalation of a fine perfume, over the recherché perfection of Kornhäusel's interior of the town palace of Duke Albert of Saxe-Teschen which we know as the Albertina.[27]

The Stadttempel, however, was Kornhäusel's one and only significant ecclesiastical commission. It seems to me, in retrospect, that in response to a task that of necessity transcends stylishness, he used everything art offered him to create just that impression of timelessness that my memory has preserved. An impressionable worshipper (who, in

17) Tomb Hermann Wertheim. «Währinger Friedhof», Vienna. Photo: Nikolaus Vielmetti.

All of these effects (which are hallmarks of classicizing as well as of classical art) are encountered optimally in the generous response to the kind of worship the building was designed to serve and even to elicit. Only then will a classicizing style have the chance to overcome itself through art and the work become what it strives to be, namely classical. Exactly because it is well styled, the *Stadttempel* is capable of rising to a world of truth that is above style and time; or better, it opens up that world to us because it so intelligently and lovingly points to it.

There was a rich treasure of temple utensils, candelabra, the menorah, silver vessels, precious curtains, canopies, etc. that would be displayed and used at appropriate times: Sabbaths, holidays, weddings, and other festive and memorial occasions. They partook, by virtue of the preciousness of their materials and their exquisite workmanship, and by their very age, of the marvel of timelessness and enhanced the dignity of the "Tempel" with a special festive splendor. Some of these still exist and some have been replaced. An album of sixteen steel engravings which was published soon after the dedication of the *Stadttempel* showed, next to views of the architecture, Kornhäusel's detailed designs for the *Aaron Ha Kaudesh*, the Tablets of the Law above it, the candelabra and other ornaments and ritual requisites. Short of a few architectural views (which continue to be re-published from older sources where they happened to have been used for illustrations), nothing, as far as I know, is known any more of the pictures in this album. All copies of the edition seem to have disappeared, though it is possible that some survive in places that are not known to the *Stadttempel*'s keepers or its historians.[28] Perhaps this notice will help to bring a copy to light again.

The building underwent a number of renovations which somewhat altered its interior appearance.[29] The most radical of these (undertaken largely for practical reasons) was effected in 1895. It determined the appearance of the "Tempel" until the sacrileges and devastation of 1938. In a complete restoration of 1963 the building was carefully gone over and where it was readily feasible, forms that had in the course of time been changed or destroyed were replaced or reconstructed in keeping with Kornhäusel's original work; the most decisive changes of 1895, however, were retained. The result is a possibly amiable compromise between the building I knew as a child, in the vitality of its givenness, and Kornhäusel's precise drawings. There also now floats a touch of modernism through the restored building, as if the architect had attempted to interpret Kornhäusel's classicism from the position of Adolf Loos. Ornamental bands, where they are restored, lack the liveliness of the original craftsmanship, not so much, perhaps, because the restorers did not work well but

ecclesiastical architecture, would seem to be the architect's ideal patron) here perhaps has better eyes than the analyzing historian of art.

The work, rich, ornate, and yet simple and dignified, is designed as a festive shell for ritual song, prayer, and the word of the preacher; and the accoustics, for that matter, are superb. Exterior and interior are related to each other with a keen sense of decorum, joined to drama in the progress from reserve to jubilation, from darkness to light. The elliptical prayer room, the dome, the lantern and the rectangular articulation of the containing walls all unite effortlessly, yet with a clear individualization of the parts in their relation to the whole.

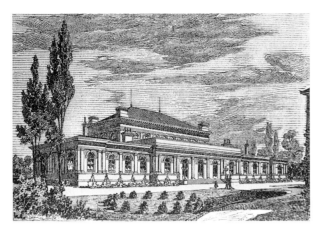

18) Ceremonial Hall, «Zentralfriedhof», Section I («Erstes Tor»), Vienna. Wood engraving. Collection Nikolaus Vielmetti. Photo: Nikolaus Vielmetti.

19) Ceremonial Hall, «Zentralfriedhof», Vienna, Section I. Condition after 1945 (Razed ca. 1981). Photo: Nikolaus Vielmetti.

rather because they defined ornament as a mere patterned addition to flat surfaces.

Mutatis mutandis, the result reminds me of the restoration of the burnt out interior of the Vienna opera. One must be glad that it was done, but in spite of the loving attention lavished on the project, it points away, in an all-purpose sort of way, from the imaginatively abundant decorative wealth of the opera house we knew to a cautiously still-undefined but functionally oriented future.[30]

VI

Three years after the opening of the *Stadttempel* on March 18th, 1829, a document defining and regulating the religious services to which the temple was dedicated was ratified by a committee of dignitaries who were responsible for its management. By virtue of their wealth, social position and concern these men — Josef Biedermann, Moritz Königswarter, Jakob Lövy and Siegmund Wertheimstein — were also the chief representatives of the Jews before the authorities.[31] To make the document as binding as possible it was also to be signed by the heads of the households that were permitted to reside in Vienna. A majority of these (including six women) affixed their names to this instrument of administration which was then presented to the government for its approval. As there was reason to expect, approbation was obtained and the document, which is entitled "The Statutes of the House of Prayer of the Israelites in Vienna", became legally valid.[32]

The "Statutes," though they are ostensibly concerned solely with the government of the temple, are, in fact, rudimentary articles of the self-government of the Jewish community. Next to prayer they extend to all events of Jewish life which involve ritual and communal affairs, from circumcision and Bar Mitzvah for male children and the new ceremonies for the naming and confirmation of girls, to weddings and the grave. Also regulated are the various fees that help to support the temple and most importantly the registry of births, weddings, and deaths. The latter was an official function which bestowed upon the community, without its being admitted in so many words, the character of a public entity.

De jure, the Jews of Vienna were not allowed a corporate existence but only a "tolerated" status as individuals in the city. The document is therefore cautiously phrased so as, on the one hand, not to rock the boat of "toleration" but, on the other, also to promote the official recognition of their dignity and rights as human beings and loyal subjects of the emperor. If one accepted the spirit of the Enlightenment which, under Joseph II, had made a lasting impression on Jews and gentiles, such a recognition was long overdue. There was, in particular, a sorry discrepancy between police regulations regarding the Jews of Vienna and the appreciative acceptance which at least certain segments of polite society accorded to Jews and Jewesses who joined and even advanced the cultural life of the city and its caritative cares.[33]

It is for reasons of this political compromise between the realities of the laws obtaining and the hopes of the Jews of Vienna for a life of freedom in dignity that the nineteenth

20) Tomb Adolph Fischhof. «Zentralfriedhof», Vienna, Section I. Photo: Nikolaus Vielmetti.

21) Tomb of the poet Ludwig August Frankl. «Zentralfriedhof», Vienna, Section I. Photo: Nikolaus Vielmetti.

century surely would usher into the world, not only for them but for all the unjustly oppressed, that the very title of the "Statutes" speaks of a House of Prayer (*Bethhaus*) rather than a of a temple.

Similarly the rabbi of the congregation is referred to not by this or any comparable title which presupposed, in the eyes of the authorities, the existence of a community with residential rights (instead of privileges) but rather he is styled, by a subterfuge in which the government concurred, a teacher (*Religionslehrer*).[34]

But this is not the only direction of compromise or appeasement in which the document abounds. Not all the influential Jews of Vienna were in favor of the reforms in the practice and style of Jewish worship which, in keeping with the reforms then flourishing in Germany and France, were advocated by the partisans of change.[35]

The redaction of the "Statutes," which was the work of Mannheimer,[36] must in itself have been a school in the art of reconciling opposites for the sake of the common good. There are numerous provisions which show that they were worked out in heated debates in committee meetings. The sentences still bear the scars of them. Others, in turn, are almost self-contradictory in what, on the one hand, they advocate and, on the other, make fairly impossible to achieve without constant friction. Over virtually all of them is poured the oil of Mannheimer's circumspect piety, reasonableness, and good will. In

104

22) Tomb of the actor Adolf von Sonnenthal. «Döblinger Friedhof», Vienna, Section I. Photo: Nikolaus Vielmetti.

23) Family vault, Baron Guttmann. «Zentralfriedhof», Vienna, Section I. Photo: Nikolaus Vielmetti.

the introduction to the document, however, we meet Mannheimer virtually as a chancel orator, expounding his view of Judaism and its proper practice, honoring tradition with winged words but also rejecting its abuses, as he saw them and as a majority of his congregation, led by his example, eventually would come to see them.

The ''Statutes'' are the foundation upon which Mannheimer and Sulzer and others in many years of dedicated work developed the service of the ''Tempel'' and, with it, a form of Jewish life which, as the century progressed, became exemplary not only for the Jews of the Habsburg Empire (who naturally looked to Vienna for a model) but even far beyond the confines of Europe.[37]

The ''Statutes'' were read from the chancel on an interim day of Passover, April 20th, 1829, and after that were considered binding on the Congregation and its officers. They were not, however, published in print until 1926 when the Jewish Community of Vienna offered a facsimile edition of the manuscript on the occasion of the 100th anniversary of the dedication of the *Seitenstettentempel*. This festive publication was accompanied by a searching historical essay and biographical sketches of the signatories of the document by Bernhard Wachstein.[38]

Since the publication is now difficult to find and the text (in German script) offers occasional obstacles to smooth reading, I present, at the end of these recollections, a transcription of

24) Isaac Noah Mannheimer, «*Festgebete der Israeliten*», 4th ed., vol. III, 1868. Title page and p. 186. Family prayer book, the author. Photo: Photographic Services, University of Illinois at Urbana-Champaign.

the complete ''Statutes.''[39]

It remains to point out once more that when Wachstein wrote his study confidence in the validity of the tradition of the ''Tempel'' was already in full retreat. Wachstein makes it clear that, with all of his appreciation of the labors of Mannheimer and Sulzer and their successors and the challenges they met and overcame, he considers the experiment of the *Stadttempel*, by and large, a failure. Instead of confirming Jews in their love of God, the origins of the ''Tempel'' only heralded the waves of religious indifference and even apostasy which beset the history of the Jews in the modern world. The Enlightenment, as he saw it, had no sense for the historical individualization of nations and thus deprived the Jews of a proper defense of their uniqueness. Only insofar as the ''Tempel'', through compromise, also made allowances for traditions of Judaism which the Enlightenment was not equipped to comprehend did it serve the survival of Jews who now were able to live, and chose to live, in an desegregated environment.[40]

When such a position is taken (and there is ample reason for it) the "Statutes" fall apart. Passages which abound in admonitions to behave worthily in the "Tempel", to pray silently, to avoid conversations, to obey the sexton's call to order, smack of condescension to the lower classes and bespeak a blindness to the vitality and the needs of their "unspoiled" Judaism. Or, to add just one more example of these seemingly perverse values: the regulations specify that the *Religionslehrer* must have studied philosophy before they address themselves to the more obvious requirement that he must be well grounded in (Judaic) theology.[41]
Does this not show that the "Statutes" put the cart before the horse, in a frivolous lust for assimilation?

But I would encourage readers to look at the document — and the history of the "Tempel" — in a less critical way.

Mannheimer was a deeply religious man who followed in the footsteps of the sages of Judaism, Christianity, and Islam who had responded positively to the challenge of philosophy to received religion. He took it for granted that the best of philosophy and the truth of Revelation were reconcilable and that the two branches of human knowledge worked towards the same end.[42] Philosophy, without the love of God, thus is seen to decay into sophistry, just as religion, without the assistance of philosophy, will sink into mere enthusiasm and superstition.

Add to this the perhaps not altogether unwarranted propensity of the historians of the Renaissance (up to and including the time of the Enlightenment) to look upon the Middle Ages as the period in which darkness descended upon the civilized world and the memory of true things became distorted and was eclipsed.[43]

In such a view, even if one made interesting exceptions, the Jews, who until fairly recently had been confined to ghettos, must have appeared, with all due respect for their suffering and perseverance, as period pieces from a past one could only congratulate oneself to have left behind. It was then the humble duty of a true *Religionslehrer* — and not arrogance on his part — to return his flock, in the setting of the altered circumstances that obtained, to the life of ancient dignity which was led by our forefathers in Biblical freedom, before the great Dispersion, the *galuth*. Mannheimer made this point movingly clear in his sermons (cf. our Appendix).[44]

He painted, perhaps, a romantic picture of the history of the Jews but the lessons he draw from it were true and magnanimous. His work suited the spiritual needs of the majority of the Jews of Austria in the nineteenth century and beyond. It also articulated them with a new clarity and in happy moments, bestowed upon them a singular beauty.

Moreover, it helped shape the trust and the hopes which were needed to support the mutual civility and on occasion even love with which Jews freely came to move in a select world of Christians whom they had cause to respect and cherish, not the least for the fact that this world had come, largely on its own, to recognize them as equals.

Needless to say: that this was possible meant that formidable hurdles of habits, commitment to tradition, prejudice and even common sense had to be overcome; different ones for Jews and Christians but still a task of consequence for each party in this new co-existence. Only too often the civilized ease in which one lived together was maintained or defended with generalizations about what it meant to be "Austrian" or "Viennese" that offended reason and wit. But, by and large, it worked and became in itself a school of truth and tact and wit.

Who would then have thought that anti-Semitic prejudice ever could prove victorious over reason and the Jews' longstanding record of civic loyalty? To most of us it was not comprehensible even in 1938, when all one held dear — including one's language and the right to live — was at the mercy of those who prided themselves on being merciless.

And yet the *Seitenstettentempel* again performs its old function and its old ritual, faded still more than when I knew it as a child, continues faithfully to be observed in the restored building. The small Jewish community it serves is chiefly composed of new settlers who, as in former times, still come largely from what used to be the territories of the Habsburg monarchy, and from Eastern Europe in general.

My wandering ways on occasion take me to Vienna. If the opportunity offers I attend services at the "Tempel" on Friday evening. The approach to the building is now forbidding. As at so many synagogues all over Europe policemen with rifles at the ready guard the access to the street in order to protect the worshippers from terrorist attacks. When I see them I cannot help recalling the police who once brutalized and arrested Jews in the same place. I would remember them even without the macabre spectacle of a seeming threat.

But in the hallway and in the interior of the Tempel the same warmth surrounds me that I remember from so long ago. If I can, I take the same seat I used to choose when I was young. I sometimes see the "Tempel" filled with ghosts so that there hardly is any room for the living, even though the dead take care not to be in the way.

When the cantor, in the old familiar melody, pronounces the Sabbath blessing over the wine, two or three children are called upon to ascend the podium for the ceremony and to drink from the great silver chalice, as we used to when we were little, at the service in the Kluckygasse.

The last time I saw this ceremony the children were so very

lively, so trustingly responsive to the song of the old cantor, so at home in the aura of the ''Tempel'', and yet so concerned about showing their respect by standing still, even as they squirmed and surreptitiously greeted their mothers in the women's gallery, that it seemed to me that all was as before and time had come full circle. The ''Tempel'', in spite of everything, is still alive and still offers the gift of Mannheimer's and Sulzer's inheritance to children who are (at least within the confines of the ''Tempel'') without conflict, both Jews and, quite simply, Viennese children. May God protect them, and keep them, and give them Peace.

VII

The document transcribed below consists of forty manuscript pages. I have followed the spelling of the text throughout but have expanded difficult abbreviations. In the instances in which the scribe switched from German script to Latin characters (either for emphasis or because he responded to the Latin origin of a word) the word is spaced wide. Words underlined in the original are underlined in our transcription. Words in Hebrew are reproduced from the text.

The transcription was made from the facsimile edition published in 1926.[45] The original is now on permanent loan at the Central Archives for the History of the Jewish People in Jerusalem. It consists of twenty unnumbered sheets in folio, stitched into a cover of marble paper. The text itself — the last five lines of it — ends on the pre-penultimate page. The rest of that page and the penultimate page are taken up by signatures and the last signature appears all by itself on the ultimate page (which is otherwise empty). I am grateful to the Institut für Judaistik of the University of Vienna for the use of its copy of the facsimile edition in the preparation of this transcription.

Statuten für das Bethhaus der Israeliten in Wien

Einleitung.

Schon seit vielen Jahren ist in den angesehensten israelitischen Gemeinden, die Herstellung der Gotteshäuser in ihre Würde und Feyerlichkeit, ein Gegenstand der allgemeinen Aufmerksamkeit geworden.

Indem der Gottesdienst immer mehr sank und vernachlässiget wurde, je nachdem die Bildung unter den Glaubensgenossen sich verbreitete, ward es Jedem fühlbar, daß die bisherige Einrichtung der Bethhäuser, den Ansichten und dem Bedürfnisse eines geläuterten gottesfürchtigen Sinnes nicht entspreche.

Das Band der Eintracht und der Anhänglichkeit ward immer lockerer, die Klage über das Unbefriedigende der Andachtsanstalten immer lauter, die Forderungen der Wohlgesinnten, die vorzüglich um der Jugend willen, eine schleunige Abhülfe wünschten, wurde immer dringender und ließen sich nicht mehr abweisen. —

So entstanden in dieser Angelegenheit manigfaltige Versuche in Deutschland, über deren Werth oder Unwerth größtentheils bereits die Zeit und der Erfolg entschieden haben. — Manches ward begonnen, und Weniges ward vollendet, — Manches ins Leben gerufen, das sich nicht konnte erhalten, — weil man einerseits jede Läuterung als Neuerung abwies, andererseits wirklich die Gränzen der Mäßigkeit überschritt, und das Ansehen und die Würde der bestehenden alten Form nicht zu würdigen geneigt war. —

Als nun das neuerbaute israelitische Bethhaus in Wien, im Monathe N i s s a n des Jahres 5586 — April 1826 — eröffnet werden sollte, kamen alle jene Wünsche und Erwartungen auch hier zur Sprache, und die Vertreter der hiesigen israelitischen Einwohner, als Leiter der gemeinschaftlichen Angelegenheiten, setzten als Regel und Grundsatz fest, daß in dem neuerbauten Gotteshause:

1tens der Gottesdienst nach allen bestehenden Formeln, Regeln und Vorschriften, in so fern sie eine gesetzliche Autorität für sich haben, ohne alle Abänderung abgehalten werden solle, daß aber

2tens die äußere Ausstattung des Gotteshauses, das Verhalten der Bethenden im Gotteshause, der Vortrag der überkommenen Formeln, von allem Störenden und Unwürdigen gereinigt, und

3. jedes Mittel zur Wiederbelebung der Andacht und des religiösen Sinnes, zur Aneiferung im Guten, zur Befestigung der Bande der Eintracht, und der Anhänglichkeit, aufs sorgfältigste solle in Anwendung gebracht werden, zu welchem letzten Zwecke, die Einführung der religiösen Vorträge und Gebethe in der Landessprache, die dem bestehenden hebräischen Gottesdienste sollten hinzugefügt werden, als besonders wirksam und wohlthuend anerkannt wurde. —

Von solchen Ansichten ausgehend, unternahmen die Leiter der gottesdienstlichen Angelegenheiten in hiesiger Gemeinde, dieß schwere Werk, im Vertrauen auf Gottes Schutz und Beystand.

Mehrere Jahre sind bereits seitdem verflossen, und die Zeit und der Erfolg haben auch hier entschieden.

Das Wort Gottes, das da ausging von dem Gotteshause, fand eine willige Aufnahme; die Sehnsucht nach dem Heiligthume wurde mehr als früher aufgeregt, und fand ihre Befriedigung, die Feste des Herrn wurden wieder mit Feyerlichkeit begangen, und es sind die heilsamen Wirkungen der neubelebten Andacht, aufs manigfaltigste sichtbar geworden. —

Da nun aber das Wandelbare der menschlichen Ansichten seinen Einfluß selbst in den heiligsten Angelegenheiten geltend macht; hingegen eben in gottesdienstlichen Dingen, dieser Wandelbarkeit am wenigsten irgend ein solcher Einfluß darf gestattet werden, so haben die Vertreter der israelitischen Einwohner Wiens, als Leiter deren gemeinschaftlicher Angelegenheiten, in Berathung mit mehreren wohlgesinnten und sachverständigen Männern beschlossen:

Die Regeln, die bisher mit so gutem Erfolge sind angewendet worden, und deren Zweckmäßigkeit die zeitherigen Erfahrungen haben bewiesen, so wie die in gleicher Ansicht noch hinzuzufügenden Vorschriften, in aller Ordnung und Bestimmtheit zu sammeln und nieder zu schreiben, und sie für die Zukunft, als gültige N o r m anzuerkennen und zu befolgen; damit die Würde und Feyerlichkeit des Gottesdienstes gegen jeden Angriff der Zeit gesichert sey, und das Gedeihen und Bestehen derselben nicht anheim gegeben werde, den zufälligen Ansichten und Neigungen der daran Theilnehmenden, oder der eben so zufälligen Geschicklichkeit und Willensrichtung der dabey mitwirkenden Individuen.

So möge denn die Gnade Gottes auch diesem Unternehmen sein Gedeihen geben, daß es bestehen möge, wie es in guter Absicht unternommen ward, und ein Zeugniß gebe dem kommenden Geschlechte, von dem Streben seiner Vorfahren, die da bedacht waren, zu gründen ein Gotteshaus in Israel zum Heil und Segen. —

E i n t h e i l u n g.

Die S t a t u t e n für die gottesdienstlichen Angelegenheiten zerfallen in d r e y Haupteintheilungen:

C a p i t e l I.
Die Verwaltung betreffend, und zwar:

a. ihre Ernenung, Zusammensetzung und Dauer;
b. ihre F u n c t i o n e n in Leitung des Gottesdienstes,
c. in der Aufsicht über L o c a l i t ä t e n und Ausstattung des Aeußeren,
d. über innere Ruhe und Ordnung,
e. über die zum Gottesdienste angestellten Individuen,
f. über O e c o n o m i e;
g. Ihr Verhältniß zu den Vertretern.

C a p i t e l II.
Die zur Besorgung des öffentlichen Gottesdienstes angestellten Personen betreffend, und zwar:

a. den Religionslehrer, in seinen F u n c t i o n e n als Lehrer und als Seelsorger,
b. den Vorbether,
c die Gehülfen des Vorbethers und den C h o r,

d die Aufseher im Bethhause, oder Gehülfen der Vorsteher desselben,
e die Bethhausdiener.

C a p i t e l III.

Regeln für die **Religions = Gemeinde**. —

*

C a p i t e l I.

V o n d e r V e r w a l t u n g.
§ 1. So wie nach den gesetzlichen Normen, alle gemeinschaftlichen Institute der hiesigen israelitischen Einwohner, unter die Obsorge, Verwaltung und Leitung der **Vertreter** gestellt, welche letztere dafür, sowohl den vorgesetzten hohen Behörden, als der hiesigen israelitischen Gemeinschaft, verantwortlich sind, so stehet auch das Bethhaus in allen seinen Beziehungen, nähmlich hinsichtlich der liturgischen Einrichtungen, der äußeren Ordnung, der Erträgnisse und Kosten derselben, u.s.w., unter der Aufsicht und Verwaltung der jeweiligen **Vertreter**, denen nach bestehender hoher Vorschrift, für diese, sowie für sämmtliche im Hause No. 494, gestifteten Anstalten, die **Repräsentanten** zur Mitaufsicht beygegeben sind.

2. Da jede Anstalt jedoch, einer unmittelbaren Leitung und eines Vorstandes über die Einzelheiten derselben bedarf, so wird diese spezielle Leitung des Bethhauses an vier, von den Vertretern, immer auf drey Jahre zu ernennende **Bethhaus = Vorsteher** übertragen, welche jedoch nach Ablauf dieser Zeit, wieder neu bestätiget werden mögen, daher ihr Amt solange bekleiden können als ihre Privat = Verhältnisse es gestatten, und sie zur Beförderung der mit Ersterem verbundenen frommen und gemeinnützigen Zwecke, sich bereit finden lassen, ihren Beruf mit Eifer und Thätigkeit zu vollziehen.

§3. Den Bethhausvorstehern ist nun die Führung aller vorkommenden gewöhnlichen Angelegenheiten des Bethhauses überlassen, wie solche in den folgenden §§ näher bezeichnet sind.
Wichtigere Gegenstände jedoch, als z.B. Aufnahme der im Bethhause anzustellenden Individuen, Vermehrung der Aus-

lagen, Abänderung der für die Bethplätze festgesetzten Miethpreise, u.s.w., so wie solche Gegenstände, die zur Kenntniß der vorgesetzten hohen Behörden zu bringen sind —, haben sie den Vertretern vorzulegen.

4. Die Functionen der Vorsteher, sind abwechselnd, immer von Einem derselben, unter dessen Verantwortlichkeit, durch einen Monath, und nach einer fest zu setzenden Reihefolge zu besorgen.

5.Jeden Monath, und zwar am letzten Donnerstage desselben, ist eine Sitzung zu halten, worin der d i r i g i r e n d e Vorsteher:

a. über die laufenden Geschäfte referirt,
b Vernachlässigungen und Mißbräuche welche etwa statt gefunden, anzeigt,
c Vorschläge zu deren Abhülfe macht,
d das etwa sich ergebende Außergewöhnliche zur Berathung vorlegt, und
e. sodann die Verwaltung seinem Nachfolger übergiebt.
f. Auch außer dieser bestimmten Sitzung, kann der Vorsteher im Dienste, wenn er es für nöthig findet, die anderen Vorsteher zur Berathung berufen.
g. Einer der Vertreter wird zur besonderen Mitleitung des Bethhauses bestimmt, der in solchen Angelegenheiten, die zur Kenntniß der Vertreter zu gelangen haben, ohne daß es eben Zeit und Umstände gestatten, sie ihnen insgesammt vorzulegen, Einsicht zu nehmen, und sie bey Rechtfinden zu bestätigen hat.
h Bey besonderen Veranlassungen zu Feyerlichkeiten, oder anderen momentanen Einrichtungen, haben die Vorsteher /: wenn der Gegenstand nicht in Gemeinschaft mit sämmtlichen Vertretern berathen und festgesetzt werden kann :/ ihre Beschlüsse wenigstens zweyen Vertretern, und wenn die Einrichtungen mit Geldauslagen verbunden sind, dem Haus = Administrator und Kasseführer der religiösen Anstalt, zur Beystimmung mit zu theilen.
i Wenn die erwähnten Vorfälle eine denselben angemessene Einrichtung der Liturgie erfordern, haben die Vorsteher den Religionslehrer ihren Berathungen bey zu ziehen.
k Bey verschiedenartigen Ansichten über Einen oder den andern Gegenstand, haben sämmtliche Beysitzende ihre Meinungen abzugeben, worauf der Beschluß nach der Stimmenmehrheit zu fassen ist.
l. Die Vorsteher sind verpflichtet, über jede Verhandlung ein geordnetes Protokoll zu führen, das zugleich als C h r o n i k der Anstalt, als Regulativ für die Folge in ähnlichen Fällen, dienen kann.

6 Die Functionen der Vorsteher bestehen in der Aufsicht im Bethhause, in der speziellen Verwaltung der Empfänge und Auslagen, und in der Anordnung und Leitung der gottesdienstlichen Angelegenheiten überhaupt, nach der deßhalb festgesetzten Ordnung. —

Demnach hat der im Dienste befindliche Vorsteher zu wachen:

a. daß die Vertheilung der gottesdienstlichen Functionen gehörig geordnet, und
b. daß das Bethhaus, wie es der Würde desselben, und seiner heiligen Bestimmung zukommt, bis auf die kleinsten einzelnen Theile, stäts in dem reinlichsten und anständigsten Zustande erhalten werde.
c. daß zu jeder Zeit, der bestimmte Beleuchtungs = Bedarf vorräthig, und bey jeder vorkommenden Feyerlichkeit die nöthigen Requisiten in Bereithschaft seyen.
d. daß sämmtliche zum Bethhause gehörigen Geräthe und Requisiten, in gutem Zustande erhalten, sicher aufbewahrt, und die Evidenzhaltung derselben mit der hierüber zu verfassenden I n v e n t u r, unter Verantwortlichkeit des, mit der Aufbewahrung beauftragten Individuums, wenigstens alle drey Monathe statt finde.
e. daß zur Sicherheit des Bethhauses überhaupt, sowohl gegen Feuersgefahr, als gegen Diebstahl, die geeignetesten Mittel vorgekehrt, und zu diesem Ende, die genaueste Aufsicht, nach dem Verlöschen der Beleuchtung, und sorgfältiges Abschließen aller Thüren und Zugänge, dem hiemit Beauftragten zur Pflicht gemacht werde.

7 Die Vorsteher haben die Aufsicht über die angestellten Individuen, und denselben jede Vernachläßigung ihrer Pflichten, auf gebührende Weise zu rügen, oder nöthigen Falls die Anzeige an die Vertreter zu machen.

8. Die Anfangsstunden und die Dauer des Gottesdienstes für den laufenden Monat, sowohl für die Sabbathe und Feste, als für die Wochentage zu bestimmen, und über die pünktliche Befolgung dieser Bestimmung zu wachen, welche jedesmal nach der üblichen Ankündigung des Neumondes, der Versammlung, durch den Vorbether, in der Art mitzutheilen, daß sich diese Zeitbestimmung, für die tägliche Morgen = und Abend = Andacht, von jenen der Sabbathe und Festtage, deutlich unterscheiden lasse.

9. Im Innern des Bethhauses haben die Vorsteher die vorgeschriebene Ordnung, die ehrerbiethigste Stille und Ruhe, so wie die Gerechtsame jedes Inhabers eines Bethplatzes aufrecht zu erhalten. — Die Aufseher sind ihnen als Gehülfen in diesem Geschäfte, unter genauer Beachtung der ihnen dessfalls zu ertheilenden Instruktion, zugegeben.

10 Beyde, sowohl Vorsteher als Aufseher haben sorgfältig dahin zu wirken, daß während des Gottesdienstes, so wie vor- und nach demselben, im Bethhause keine Streitigkeit oder Störung vorkomme; sie haben also nöthigenfalls zur Ruhe und Ordnung zu ermahnen, doch aber Jedermann mit Höflichkeit und Schonung zu behandeln und sich im Bethhause selbst keineswegs in Wortstreit oder Erörterungen einzulassen, sondern die Urheber der Störung sind außerhalb des Bethhauses, etwa durch Einladung bey einer Sitzung, von ihrem Unrechte zu überzeugen, zu einem besseren Benehmen zu ermahnen, und die Sache auf eine gütliche und versöhnende Art auszugleichen; — im entgegengesetzten Falle jedoch, wenn ihre Bemühung zur Schlichtung der Streitigkeit vergeblich wäre, sich an die Vetreter zu wenden, die durch die ihnen zu Gebothe stehenden Mittel, dem Beleidigten Genugthuung verschaffen, und die Einigkeit herzustellen sich bestreben werden.

11. So wenig als dem monathlichen Vorsteher gestattet werden kann, ohne anderweitige gemeinschaftliche Verfügung eine Abänderung der bestehenden Ordnung zu unternehmen, oder irgend eine Weisung zu ertheilen, die mit der angenommenen Art und Weise nicht übereinstimmt, eben so wenig kann es einem von den anderen Vorstehern zustehen, willkührlich in die Funktionen des monathlichen Vorstehers einzugreifen, und Anordnungen zu treffen, wofür nur der Vorsteher im Dienste verantwortlich ist. —

12 Wenn ein Vorsteher, der den monathlichen Dienst zu übernehmen hat, durch Abwesenheit oder Krankheit hieran verhindert wird, so ist er durch freundschaftliche Uibereinkunft, oder durch das Loos, für den laufenden Monath, durch einen andern Vorsteher zu vertreten.

13. Die Vorsteher fungiren bey allen gottesdienstlichen Handlungen, beym Ausheben, Vorlesen und Einheben der T h o r a h , und es wird ihrer Uibereinkunft überlassen diese Funktionen unter sich nach einer bestimmten Ordnung fest zu setzen. —
Bey feyerlichen Gelegenheiten haben sie den Ehrenplatz nach den Vertretern und Repräsentanten.

14. Der monathliche Vorsteher hat, außer der Besorgung und Verrechnung aller Empfänge und Ausgaben, auch die C o n t r o l l e über den Verkauf der מצות ; und hat deren Ertrag, so wie den der freywilligen Spenden, erheben zu lassen, und über beydes Rechnung zu führen.

Zur Erzielung der Genauigkeit und Richtigkeit der dießfälligen Vormerkungen im Bethhause, hat der dienstthuende Aufseher zu ebener Erde, dieselben zu verzeichnen. — Die Spenden an andere wohltätigen Anstalten müssen alle an die Bethhaus = Vorsteher entrichtet werden, die dann monatlich, dem betreffenden Vereine, sein Q u a n t u m gegen Bescheinigung abgeben.

15 Es ist dahin zu trachten, daß mit Abschluß des Monaths, das laufende Geschäft berichtigt, sämmtliche Beträge eingehoben, und diese, so wie die gesammte Verrechnung, an den Nachfolger im Dienste übergeben werden.

16 Die Rechnung an die Vertreter legen die Vorsteher gemeinschaftlich alle Monathe, und übergeben die überflüssigen Gelder, an den, mit der C a s s e führung beauftragten Vertreter, gegen Empfangsbestätigung ab. —

17 Dagegen ist den Vorstehern von den eingegangenen Geldern, nach Maßgabe des genehmigten jährlichen Uiberschlages, der ungefähre monathliche Bedarf, zur Verrechnung, gegen Interimsschein auszufolgen.
Unvorhergesehene oder außerordentliche Ausgaben, wenn sie zusammen monathlich die S u m m e von D r e y s s i g Gulden C o n v e n t i o n s = M ü n z e übersteigen, bedürfen einer besonderen Zustimmung von Seiten der Vertreter.

18. Mit jedem Jahreswechsel, und zwar dermahlen beym Beginnen der religiösen Jahresabtheilung רח ניסן , haben die Vorsteher, beym Vermiethen der Plätze, den Vertretern den E t a t vorzulegen, die Uiberschläge für das kommende Jahr umständlich anzufertigen, die Ausgaben für die angestellten Individuen, für die R e q u i s i t e n und Beleuchtung zu berechnen, und sich die Anweisung für den genehmigten Jahresbedarf, in monathlichen Q u o t e n , in ihr Protokoll vormerken zu lassen.

19. Sämmtliche Berechnungen und Auseinandersetzungen, sowohl zwischen den Vorstehern beym Monathschlusse, als zwischen Vorstand und Vertretern, müssen mit gehörigen, klassenmässig gestempelten Belegen, Quittungen, und saldirten Rechnungen, versehen seyn.

20. Bey dem Umstande, daß der kostspielige Bau des Wohn = und Bethhauses, und die inneren Einrichtungsstücke des letzteren, durchaus nur mit aufgenommenen Geldern bestritten werden mußten, deren C a p i t a l s = und Zinsenzahlung, dem Bethhause gleichmäßig obliegt, wird es schließlich den Bethhausvorstehern zur Pflicht gemacht, wie dieß auch von den hohen Behörden den Vertretern ausdrücklich vorgeschrieben ist, sich die möglichste Vermehrung des Ertrages, und Verminderung des Kostenaufwandes angelegen seyn zu lassen, bey den Einnahmen und Einkassierungen für das Bethhaus, und

andere gemeinnützige Anstalten, die erforderliche Thätigkeit anzuwenden, damit denselben nichts von den einzubringenden Erträgnissen entzogen werde; und so gegenseitig bey den Ausgaben, ohne jedoch die dießfalls eingeführte, anständige Einrichtung zu beschränken, auf die möglichste O e c o n o m i e, und Vermeidung alles überflüssigen Aufwandes zu sehen; damit einerseits alle dem Bethhause gebührenden Zuflüsse, zur Bestreitung seiner Verbindlichkeiten und Lasten gehörig eingehen, und andererseits die einfließenden Beträge nur ihrem Zwecke, und ihrer Bestimmung gemäß, angewendet werden mögen.

———————— ✳ ————————

Capitel II.
Von den zu dem Gottesdienste angestellten Individuen.

Von dem Religionslehrer.

21 Der Religionslehrer muß als Lehrer und Seelsorger in der Lehre wie im Leben, die Würde seines Standes aufrecht halten, die Lehren der Religion gewissenhaft befolgen, seiner Gemeinde als Beyspiel und Muster im Sittlichen, wie im Gottesdienstlichen vorgehen, und in allen öffentlichen Dingen, alles Anstößige, und jedes Aergerniß gewissenhaft vermeiden.

22 Der Religionslehrer ist von den Vertretern zu wählen, und über seine Wahl und Anstellung können diese Statuten weiter nichts festsetzen, als in so fern es sich um die erforderlichen Eigenschaften zum gottesdienstlichen Amte handelt. — Ohne daher hier weiter in diesen Gegenstand einzugehen, bestimmen diese Regeln als Erforderniß:

> **Wissenschaftliche Bildung**, und zwar:
> **Philosophisches Studium,**
> **Umfassende theologische Kenntnisse,** sowohl der **Bibel**, als **deren Erklärer,**
> **Eine ausgebildete, gewandte Sprache**, und
> **Einen bewährten sittlichen Character.** —

23 Die Bethhaus Vorsteher können seine Amtsführung nur in Bezug auf die gottesdienstliche Anstalt c o n t r o l l i r e n, ohne ihn seinem Verhältnisse zu den Vertretern, zu den obrigkeitlichen und Schul = Behörden, zu entziehen.

24 Als Lehrer hat derselbe in seinen öffentlichen Vorträgen, das reine ursprüngliche Judenthum zu lehren, in faßlicher verständlicher Sprache und Darstellung, wie sie der Zeit, der wissenschaftlichen Bildung und dem Bedürfnisse der Jugend, und des größeren Theiles der Religionsgemeinde, angemessen ist.

25 So wenig es auf gelehrte Abhandlungen über religiöse Dinge, oder auf Auseinandersetzung der Ceremonial = und Rechtslehren abgesehen ist, so sehr hat er sich dagegen angelegentlich zur Pflicht zu machen, in seinen Vorträgen:

> **Frömmigkeit,**
> **Sittlichkeit,**
> **Menschenliebe,**
> **Vaterlandsliebe** und
> **häusliche Tugenden**

zu empfehlen und einzuschärfen. Hierbey hat er alles Fremdartige in der Lehre, das dem Geiste der israelitischen Religion zuwider ist, strenge zu vermeiden. —

26. Er hat deßhalb auch um jeder Entfremdung vorzubeugen, sich in den Sabbath = Vorträgen an dem Wochenabschnitt סדרה , oder הפטירה , und in den Fest = Reden, an das Fest und seine Bedeutung: מענין החג , wo möglich genau zu halten.

27 Er hat in seinen Vorträgen, die israelitischen Schriftgelehrten und Schrifterklärer: מפרשים zu benützen, damit wenigstens aus seiner Behandlungsweise hervorgehe, daß er das Studium und die Anwendung derselben, nicht verabsäume. —

28 Er hat alle Persönlichkeiten, alles Verletzende oder Beleidigende sorgfältig zu vermeiden, und sich von dem Tone des Sittenrichters besonders in c a u s e l l e n Fällen möglichst entfernt zu halten.

29 Uiberhaupt, wenn auch die Vorträge seiner Einsicht Amtsklugheit und Treue ganz übergeben sind, so hat er sie doch ganz so einzurichten, daß er jeder C e n s u r nicht nur für das Ganze, sondern auch für jeden einzelnen Ausdruck verantwortlich ist.

30 Vorläufig ist die Ordnung: daß an jedem zweyten Sabbathe, und immer am ersten Festtage, Vorträge gehalten werden, noch bey zu behalten; bey einer bevorstehenden Erweiterung und Ausdehnung der Anstalt, soll indessen darauf Bedacht genommen werden, daß die religiösen Vorträge ein integrirender Theil des Gottesdienstes seyen, der nicht nur in Rücksicht seiner Wirksamkeit und seines Einflusses, sondern auch in Rücksicht des Zusammenhanges mit den übrigen Bestandtheilen des Gottesdienstes, unerläßlich ist. —

31. Die Dauer der Vorträge, ist höchstens auf eine Stunde, und wo möglich kürzer, etwa auf 3/4 Stunden bestimmt.

32. Da es Zweck und Bestimmung der Anstalt ist, so wie es

auch im Geiste des Judenthums liegt, das häusliche und Familienleben, so viel möglich mit dem gottesdienstlichen Leben zu vereinigen, und die feyerlichen Epochen des Lebens, durch die Weihe der Religion zu heiligen, so wird dem Religionslehrer die Pflicht auferlegt — und der Gemeinde ihrerseits diese Verfügung als N o r m mitgetheilt — auch alle im häuslichen Leben vorkommenden Fälle, die zu religiösen Feyerlichkeiten geeignet sind, mit geziemender Feyer zu begehen. —

33. Dahin gehören:

a. **Trauungen**,
b. **Beschneidungen** /: die jedoch nur in den Wohnungen und nicht im Bethhause vorzunehmen sind :/.
c. **das Nahmengeben der Mädchen** als Einsegnung.
d. **Glaubensbekenntnisse der Jünglinge und Mädchen** bey hiezu erreichtem Alter. —
e. **Fürbitten** für Kranke und Wöchnerinnen.
f **Dank = oder Bittgebethe** in besonderen Fällen.
g die herkömmliche **Todtenfeyer:** הזכרת נשמות
h **Leichenreden.**

34. Bey allen diesen feyerlichen Veranlassungen, hat der Religionslehrer, ohne auf den Stand und die Verhältnisse des Hausvaters Rücksicht zu nehmen, und ohne Anspruch auf ein Honorar zu machen, von Amtswegen zu fungiren.

35. Die Formulare für diese verschiedenen Amtsverrichtungen, werden diesen Statuten als Beylagen angeheftet, und es ist keineswegs der Willkür überlassen, von denselben abzuweichen, es sey denn, daß der Religionslehrer einverständlich mit dem Vorstande und den sämmtlichen Vertretern, eine Abänderung für zweckmäßig oder nothwendig halte.

36. Jedoch ist demselben ganz freygestellt, außer den Formularen, und nebst denselben, wo es die speziellen Umstände, der Zweck der Erbauung, und der größeren Wirkung nothwendig machen

[In another hand the following alternatives are here added to complete the sentence]: das freye Wort zu gebrauchen, freye Vorträge zu halten. [Then two further alternatives (for ''Wort'') are offered: ''Vortrag'' and ''Rede''].

37. In Rücksicht der Leichenreden aber, — in so fern sie nicht bey **allen** Verstorbenen gehalten werden sollen, — hat derselbe in jedem besonderen Falle, die Weisung von den Vertretern einzuholen, die den sittlichen Ruf des Verstorbenen, und seine wohltätige gemeinnützige Wirksamkeit zu berücksichtigen haben.

38 Uiber alle, unter den Israeliten allhier vorkommende Geburten, Trauungen und Sterbefälle hat der Religionslehrer genau und gewissenhaft, nach den landesobrichkeitlichen Vorschriften, die P r o t o c o l l e zu führen.
Wo sein Beystand erfordert wird, ist nach beendigter Handlung, selbe in das Protokoll einzutragen; in anderen Fällen, solches durch Einholung der nöthigen D a t a auszufüllen.

39 Die Geburtszeugnisse, Trau = und Todtenscheine sind auf Verlangen, von dem Religionslehrer in Form eines Auszuges aus dem Protokolle auszustellen, und von zweyen Vertretern, unter Beydrückung ihres Amtssiegels, mit zu fertigen.

Von dem Vorbether:

40 Der Vorbether hat den herkömmlichen hebräischen Theil des Gottesdienstes, auf eine, dem Sinne entsprechende würdevolle, zur Erbauung geeignete Weise, vorzutragen.

41 Es ist derselbe jedoch nur zum Vortrage der Gebethe:

an S a b b a t h - T a g e n,
an **Festtagen** und **deren Vorabenden**
und **bey feyerlichen Handlungen** verpflichtet.

Bey den Morgengebethen hat er mit: ברכו , bey den Abendgebethen mit: לכה·דודי , am ט״ו etc. mit: תפלת ערבית zu beginnen.

42 Es muß derselbe, abgesehen von den, zu einem erbauenden Vortrage gewöhnlich erforderlichen Eigenschaften, der hebräischen Sprache und deren c o r r e c t e r Aussprache, vollkommen mächtig seyn, so wie er auch der deutschen Sprache und Schrift kündig seyn soll.
Er muß in seinem Leben die Würde seines Amtes aufrecht zu erhalten wissen, und kein Vergehen sich zu Schulden kommen lassen, das auf irgend eine Weise seinen Stand entwürdigt. Er darf auch kein anderweitiges Geschäft betreiben. Ein Gleiches gilt von denen, die an Wochentagen im Bethhause vorbethen.

43 Jeder Gottesdienst hat in der Regel dieselbe Würde und dieselbe Feyerlichkeit. — Äußere Umstände, stärkerer Besuch, oder die Willkühr des Vorbethers oder Vorstehers, dürfen in dieser Rücksicht, nie eine Abänderung m o t i v i r e n, daß etwa ein Theil ungewöhnlicher Weise hervorgehoben, ein anderer vernachläßiget, daß etwa an Einem Tage alle Feyerlichkeit beseitigt, und eine gewisse Eilfertigkeit sichtbar werde, und an einem anderen, ohne weitere besondere festliche Veranlas-

sung, ein größerer Aufwand von Kunst, Kraft und Zeit eintrete; sondern es muß die Gleichmäßigkeit des Gottesdienstes, sowohl in Rücksicht auf denselben, an verschiedenen Sabbathtagen als auch in Rücksicht auf dessen einzelne Theile, strenge aufrecht erhalten werden.

44 Zur Erreichung dieses Zweckes ist:

a. eine bestimmte Ordnung festzusetzen, welche Stücke der Liturgie zu einer besonderen Gesangsweise sich eignen, als z. B.: קדושה, לכה דודי , alle Psalmen, u.s.w., und welche nach herkömmlicher oder angenommener M o d u l a t i o n vorgetragen werden.
b. Ist für die Sabbathtage eine besondere Weise, und für die Festtage eine feyerlichere, die dem Gesange mehr Raum läßt, als N o r m zu bestimmen.
c. Hat der Vorbether einverständlich mit dem Vorstande und Religionslehrer, eine bestimmte Art und Weise hierüber fest zu stellen, und sich sodann genau hieran zu halten, ohne daß es demselben benommen ist, nach Ablaufe eines Zeitraumes, das Eine Tonstück mit einem anderen zu vertauschen. —
d. Haben die Vorsteher zwey Musikverständige zu ernennen, und zu ersuchen, die C o n t r o l l e über das Musikalische des Gottesdienstes zu übernehmen, welche dann bey neu einzuführenden größeren Tonstücken, der Probe beyzuwohnen, und besonders darauf zu sehen haben, daß die Gesangsweise sich nicht von den angemessenen würdevollen Styl entfernen, am wenigsten aber Veranlassung gebe die Gebethe nur zur Unterlage einer glänzenden künstlichen Musik zu machen.
e. Ist /: wie schon im C a p i t. I, § 8 enthalten :/ die Stunde, in welcher der Gottesdienst beginnen, und wie lange er beyläufig dauern soll, zu bestimmen, und der Vorbether hat sich genau darnach zu halten, um zur bestimmten Stunde anzufangen, und seinen Vortrag so einzurichten, daß er die dazu festgesetzte Zeit nicht überschreite.

45 Der Vorbether ist ämtlich verpflichtet, sowohl seine Gehülfen, als auch den C h o r zu üben, denselben die neuen M e l o d i e n einzustudiren, und für das genaue Zusammenstimmen möglichst zu sorgen, da jede Störung oder Profanirung des Gottesdienstes, demselben als Vernachläßigung angerechnet würde.

46 Der Vorbether hat mit darüber zu wachen, daß sowohl seine erwachsenen Gesangsgehülfen, als auch die Chorknaben eine religiöse und sittliche Lebensweise führen, und sich besonders während des Gottesdienstes, mit dem gehörigen äußeren Anstande betragen, in welcher Aufrechthaltung der Sittlichkeit,

ihn die Vorsteher des Bethhauses jederzeit zu unterstützen haben.

47 Der Vorbether ist verbunden, alle bisher im Bethhause eingeführten, und künftig noch einzuführenden Gesänge und Musikalien, wo möglich in den, von deren Verfassern abgegebenen Original = Exemplarien, oder doch in reinen correcten Abschriften, in das Archiv der hiesigen Tolerirten abzuliefern, die daselbst sorgfältig aufzubewahren sind, und deren Verzeichnung und Aufbewahrung von den Bethhausvorstehern c o n t r o l l i r t werden soll.

48 Eine umständliche Uibersicht der angenommenen L i t u r g i e, mit spezieller Beziehung auf die einzelnen Festtage, nach welcher sich der Vorbether zu richten hat, wird diesen Statuten als Beylage angeheftet.

49 In Rücksicht der abzuhaltenden Gebethe oder Formulare, in so fern sie nicht auf alle Festtage und Ereignisse im Voraus bestimmt werden können, hat der Vorbether die nöthigen Weisungen von dem Religionslehrer zu erhalten.

50 Bey ämtlichen Handlungen, Beschneidungen, Trauungen etc. ist der Vorbether eben so wie der Religionslehrer sich einzufinden verpflichtet.

51 Die bisherigen hebräischen Segenssprüche: מי שברך, für die bey der T h o r a h Aufgerufenen, so wie besonders noch für die Brautleute, Confirmanden: בר מצוה Wöchnerinnen, Kranke etc. werden durch die im § 32 à 36, angegebenen Funktionen des Religionslehrers, nicht aufgehoben, sondern vielmehr, bey solchen Gelegenheiten dem Vorbether übertragen, und zwar nach Formeln, welche für die verschiedenen Gelegenheiten ausgewählt, oder neu verfaßt, und den übrigen Formularien beygefügt sind. —

52 Es ist daher der Vorbether verpflichtet, sich genau an diese Formulare zu halten, und weder beym Gottesdienste selbst, noch bey den Fürbitten, Segenssprüchen u. s. w. eigenmächtig etwas hinzuzufügen, wegzulassen, abzuändern, oder Formulare ohne Verständigung mit Religionslehrer und Vorstand einzuführen. —

Von den Gehülfen des Vorbethers und dem C h o r.

53 Die Gehülfen des Vorbethers und die Chorknaben, so wie alle Personen, die zum Gesange gehören, sind dem Vorbether untergeordnet, und müssen demselben, — was den Dienst betrifft — in jeglicher Rücksicht sich fügen, da derselbe für ihre

geziemende Aufführung verantwortlich ist; sie müssen zu seiner Disposition stehen, sowohl zu den Uibungen, als zur Ausführung, so oft er sie fordert.

54 Die Bethhaus = Vorsteher werden zu jeder Zeit darauf bedacht seyn, daß die abgehenden Chorknaben immer durch andere taugliche ersetzt werden.

55 Die Spenden die für die Gehülfen und Chorknaben eingehen, werden von den Vorstehern eingezogen, und durch den monathlichen Vorsteher nach folgendem Maaß = stabe vertheilt: — Wenn die Gehülfen nicht besonders bedacht worden sind — theilen dieselben mit dem Chore dergestalt, daß die beyden Gehülfen Ein Drittel des Betrages, die Chorknaben zusammen; zwey Drittel erhalten. — Sind der Vorbether und das Gesangspersonal insgesammt bedacht worden, so erhält der Vorbether die Hälfte des Betrags, die Gehülfen erhalten Ein Drittel des Restes, und der Chor die restirenden zwey Drittheile. — die beyden Gehülfen haben ihren Antheil wieder unter sich, in der Art zu theilen, daß davon dem ersten Gehülfen zwey Drittel, und dem zweyten: Ein Drittel des Betrags zufällt. —

56 Der erste Gehülfe hat die Aufsicht über die Chorknaben, über die Musikalien, Gebethbücher, und gottesdienstlichen Gewänder des Chors; und hat für die Erhaltung, Ordnung und Aufbewahrung letzterer Gegenstände, Sorge zu tragen.

Von den Aufsehern beym Gottesdienste.

57 Den Aufsehern ist, laut vorstehenden §9 die Inspektion zur Aufrechthaltung der Ordnung, und zugleich die Assistenz bey den verschiedenen gottesdienstlichen Functionen übertragen, und nach einer, unter ihnen selbst festzusetzenden Ordnung, haben wenigstens v i e r derselben, an den Sabbath = und Festtagen, und an deren Vorabenden gegenwärtig zu seyn.

58 Da die Aufseher aus freywilligem Antriebe bloß aus Liebe und Eifer für die Beförderung der guten Sache, und mit Aufopferung, diesen Dienst verwalten, so verspricht man sich von ihnen, daß sie nach Maßgabe der ihnen ertheilten detaillirten Instruction:

a. Jede Störung wo möglich verhüthen, oder doch sogleich aufmerksam wahrnehmen, abstellen, oder anzeigen werden.
b. daß sie sich an den, der Gemeinde vorgeschriebenen Regeln halten,
c. durch zeitweises Herumgehen die nöthige Aufmerksamkeit auf alle Anwesenden richten;

d. bey vorkommenden Störungen, wie bereits im § 10, erwähnt, in höflichen Worten zur Ruhe auffordern, und wenn die Warnung überhört wird, sie wiederholen, sodann aber dem Vorsteher die Anzeige machen werden, ohne sich je in Erörterungen oder Streitigkeiten einzulassen.

59 In Rücksicht ihres Dienstes bey den gottesdienstlichen Functionen, beym Aus = und Einheben der T h o r a h, bey קידוש‎, פתיחת‎ האָרין‎, הגבה‎ וגלילה‎ und bey Trauungen, haben dieselben zur gehörigen Zeit in Bereitschaft zu seyn, und hiebey nach der, bis jetzt eingeführten Weise zu assistiren; der Aufseher zu ebener Erde hat auch die Beträge der מצות‎, und der den verschiedenenen wohltätigen Anstalten zugesicherten Spenden, vorzumerken.

60. In Verhinderungsfällen des Einen oder andern, haben sie für Stellvertreter aus ihrer Mitte zu sorgen. —

Von den Bethausdienern.

61 Es sind zwey ordentliche Bethhausdiener anzustellen und zu besolden.

62 Es müssen dieselben bewährte, rechtliche Männer seyn denen man die Einkassirungen der Gelder, mit Sicherheit anvertrauen kann, und die der deutschen Sprache und Schrift kundig sind.

63 Dieselben sind außer den ihnen angewiesenen, in der Beylage bezeichneten Dienstverrichtungen im Bethhause, noch in allen damit verbundenen Anliegenheiten zur Verwendung sowohl der Vorsteher als des Religionslehrers, bestimmt.

64 Sie haben bey jedem Gottesdienst an Fest = und Wochentagen gegenwärtig zu seyn, die ihnen allda aufgetragenen Verrichtungen genau zu vollziehen, die Einkassirungen persönlich zu bewerkstelligen, und zu den Versammlungen zu berufen.

65 Sie müssen nicht nur jedes anvertraute Geschäft pünktlich, und ohne Verzögerung ausrichten, sondern auch verschwiegen seyn, — und nichts zur öffentlichen Kunde bringen, — was sie im Dienste erfahren, oder was ihnen zur Besorgung anvertraut wird. —

66 Derjenige von ihnen, welcher mit der Einkassirung beauftragt ist, muß ein besonderes Vormerkebuch haben und die einkassirten Gelder täglich an den Vorsteher im Dienste — gegen dessen im erwähnten Einkassirungsbuche bey zu setzende Empfangsbestätigung abzuliefern. —

Capitel III.
Von der Gemeinde.

67 Alle Anwesenden im Bethhause, haben die bestehende Ordnung, und die unterm 18ten July 1826, bekanntgemachte Vorschrift genau zu befolgen:

a. die ihnen angewiesenen Plätze, ohne Geräusch oder Störung einzunehmen,

b. sich auf denselben, in der größtmöglichen Stille und Ruhe zu verhalten,

c. jedes, den Anstand und die Würde des Amtes, auf irgend eine Weise verletzende Benehmen zu meiden;

d. jedes laute Mitbethen, jedes Intoniren, und Einhalten zu unterlassen, und sich, wo die Gemeinde laut bethet, an die Weise des Chors zu halten, und

e. der bestehenden äußeren Ordnung, in jeder Rücksicht: als beym Aufstehen, Beugen, Knien u.s.w. sich zu unterziehen. —

68 So wie es sich von selbst versteht, daß hier kein Unterschied der Person gelten kann, so werden die mit der Aufsicht Beauftragten, aufs bestimmteste angewiesen, keinen solchen Unterschied zu beachten, und im Uibertretungsfalle, jeden, ohne anderweitige Berücksichtigung, auf seine Pflicht aufmerksam zu machen, und zur Ordnung anzuhalten.

69 Da den Aufsehern hiebey alle anwendbare Schonung und Höflichkeit empfohlen ist, erwartet man um so mehr von den Besuchern des Bethhauses, daß sie jeder Erinnerung, die von Jenen ausgeht, nachkommen, und in keinem Falle, irgend eine Widersetzlichkeit oder einen Wortstreit im Gotteshause sich erlauben werden.

70 Wenn jemand von einem der Aufseher sich beleidigt glaubt, so steht es demselben frey, nach beendigtem Gottesdienste dem Vorsteher die Anzeige zu machen, der ihm in sofern die Klage gegründet ist, gewiß die geforderte Genugthuung verschaffen wird.

71 Bey Vermiethung der Bethplätze, jedoch nur zur eigenen Benützung, haben hier Tolerirte und deren Familienglieder, so lange sie das Miethgeld gehörig entrichten, den Vorzug vor hier ansässigen Dienst = Individuen, und diese wieder vor fremden, sich nur mit Pässen hier aufhaltenden Personen. —
Der von Einem oder dem Andern gewählte Bethplatz, wird ihm, ohne Unterschied seines Standes —, unter obiger Voraussetzung der pünktlichen Berichtigung des Miethgeldes, nicht aufgekündet, und unbestreitbar gelassen.
Jeder Inhaber eines Bethplatzes, hat auf die Benützung der gottesdienstlichen Einrichtungen, und auf den Beystand der beym Gottesdienste fungirenden Personen, bey vorkommenden Ereignissen in seinem Familienleben, Anspruch zu machen.

72. In dieser letzteren Beziehung, hat jedes Mitglied der Religionsgemeinde bey sich ereignenden Ehebündnissen, Geburten, und Sterbefällen, die Anzeige an den Religionslehrer zu machen, und zwar:

a in der gehörigen Zeit
Bey Trauungen, wenn der obrigkeitliche C o n s e n s erfolgt ist, bey Geburten längstens zwey Mahl 24 Stunden nach derselben, bey Sterbefällen sobald als möglich.
b in der gesetzlichen Form, nach der in den Geburts = Trauungs = und Sterbe = büchern eingeführten Vorschriften und Anweisungen, die hierbey geheftet sind. — Bey Trauungen ist das Heuratsbewilligungsdekret, bey Todesfällen der Schein des Todtenbeschauers vorzuzeigen; oder die Eintragung der Sterbefälle in die Bücher nach dem, im Israelitenspitale geführten Register vorzunehmen. Der Religionslehrer hat bey solchen Functionen, daran der Vorbether Theil zu nehmen hat, sobald ihm selbe bekannt werden, auch den letzteren davon in Kenntniß zu setzen.

73. In diesen Fällen sowohl, als in Betreff der sonstigen Fürbitten, für Wöchnerinnen, Kranke und Verstorbene, hat jeder Bemittelte eine Gebühr /: ohne das den fungirenden I n d i v i d u e n zugebundene freywillige Honorar :/ zum Besten des Gotteshauses zu entrichten, und zwar:

für Trauungen f ü n f z e h n b i s f ü n f z i g G u l d e n C o n v. M z e.
'' Beschneidungen V i e r, b i s Z e h n G u l d e n — detto
'' sonstige Einsegnungen und Fürbitten:
Z w e y b i s F ü n f G u l d e n i n C o n v. M ü n z e.

In jedem Falle ist die Handlung, erst nach erfolgter Anweisung des Bethhaus = Vorstehers, vom Religionslehrer und Vorbether vorzunehmen.

74. Sollten besondere Umstände zu dem Wunsche Veranlassung geben, daß Eine oder die andere Trauung nicht im Bethhause vollzogen werde, so ist dem Religionslehrer einverständlich mit den Bethhaus = Vorstehern, die Vollziehung derselben nur dann gestattet, wenn der ihm angewiesene Ort, zu einer solchen feyerlichen Handlung geeignet ist. Die Abgabe an das Gotteshaus ist sodann dennoch zu entrichten.
Beschneidungen werden nur in den Wohnungen, erforderlichen Falls in den Schulzimmern des Hauses, niemahls aber im Bethhause vorgenommen.

75. Bey allen solchen feyerlichen Veranlassungen, können laut

§ 35, 51, und 52, nur die angeführten Formeln, und die bestehende, oder neu einzurichtende Art und Weise in Anwendung kommen, und der Unterschied des Standes oder der Person, kann in dieser Rücksicht keine Abänderung in der Weise oder Form motiviren oder entschuldigen.

So ist jede Trauung auf dieselbe Weise zu vollziehen, mit derselben Feyerlichkeit und Ausstattung des Bethhauses /: wozu indessen die Beleuchtung nicht gehört, die jeder Festgeber auf seine Kosten einrichten mag :/ und jede Fürbitte, in derselben Form abzuhalten.

76. Auch kann kein Mitglied der Gemeinde irgend ein Vorrecht geltend machen, wo es die bestehende Ordnung nicht erlaubt; — so ist z.B. jedem das am Sterbetage der Aeltern, oder bey sonstigen Gelegenheiten gewöhnliche Vorbethen untersagt, so wie auch das Kadisch = Gebeth nur von dem Vorbether laut gebethet wird, die Leidtragenden aber ohne Unterschied es leise mitzusprechen haben.

77. Bey Trauungen stehen eine bestimmte Anzahl Plätze zur Disposition des Festgebers, über welche derselbe frey verfügen kann.

78. Bey anderen Familienfesten, kann der Festgeber auf die üblichen Vorrechte Anspruch machen; so ist jedem Bräutigam am Sabbathe vor, und nach der Trauung, jedem Knaben der בר מצוה wird, jedem Hausvater, am Sabbathe wenn die Frau aus dem Wochenbette ihren ersten Gang ins Bethhaus macht, so wie Jedem an den Sterbetagen seiner Aeltern, eine עליה ohne weiters um den für חיובים bestimmten Minimum = Preis zu überlassen. —

Die gesammten vorstehenden Statuten für das israelitische Bethhaus in Wien, sind in lebhafter Anerkennung ihrer Nothwendigkeit, und ihrer durch mehrere Jahre erprobten Zweckmäßigkeit, auch für die Folgezeit bestimmt und festgesetzt worden.

Es haben daher die Vorsteher des Bethhauses, so wie sämmtliche Mitglieder der Religionsgemeinde und die bey dem Gottesdienste mitwirkenden Individuen sich genau darnach zu halten, und die jeweligen Vertreter und Repräsentaten, über deren Befolgung sorgfältig zu wachen.

Im Falle jedoch, daß wider Verhoffen unter den Bethaus = Vorstehern, und selbst unter den Vertretern und Repräsentanten, einst eine Lauheit und Vernachläßigung in dieser Angelegenheit, eintreten sollte, so hat der aus den hiesigen Tolerirten gewählte Ausschuß welchem die Revision der C a s s a = Rechnungen von den hiesigen israelitischen gemeinschaftlichen Anstalten obliegt, an die Aufrechterhaltung des Gotteshauses zu erinnern, und wenn es die Noth erheischt, alle dienlichen Maßregeln zu veranlassen, um dasjenige, was in den vorliegenden Statuten für das Gedeihen dieser wichtigen Anstalt festgesetzt ist, in ungehemmter Anwendung und Ausübung zu erhalten.

Gegenwärtige zur künftigen Norm zusammengestellte Regeln und Bestimmungen, sollen zur mehreren Bekräftigung, sowohl von den Vertretern, den Repräsentanten, und den dermahligen Bethhaus = Vorstehern, als auch von sämmtlichen hier tolerirten Familienhäuptern unterzeichnet, der vorgesetzten hohen Behörde zur Genehmigung vorgelegt, und sodann zur allgemeinen Befolgung und Darnachrichtung, kundgemacht, dieses unterfertigte Original = Exemplar aber in dem Archive der hiesigen israelitischen Einwohner aufbewahrt werden.

Wien am 18. M ä r z 1829. —

D i e   V e r t r e t e r   u n d   R e p r a e s e n t a n t e n   d e r   i s r a e l i t i s c h e n   E i n w o h n e r   W i e n ' s.

[Here follow three pages of signatures in two columns. The transcriptions used below are based on the identifications established by Bernhard Wachstein.]

Max Edler v Hönigsberg
Marcus Ritter v: Neuwall
I. Edler v Liebenberg

I L Hofmann
M L Biedermann

H. E. v Wertheimstein
Samuel Lewinger
Joachim Leidesdorff
Moyses Koblenzer
Carl Hirschmann
B. Landesmann

Sigmund E Wertheimstein

Jacob Wartfeld

Jacob Lövy

Joseph Biedermann

Moritz Königswarter

Carl Leidesdorf

L G Goldstein

Salomon Mayer

118

Bernhard Spitzer
M. Bunzel
Moritz Hürsch
Ludwig Eppinger
    gelesen M Reittlinger

M H Weikersheim

Dr. Oesterreicher
gelesen Ernst Wertheim
Herm. Todesco
gelesen M. M. Baumgarten
W. I. Nassau
Dr. Wertheim
I. Pontzen

gelesen, J. Hayne Med. Dr.

Arnold Engel
Samuel Gottlieb
Elisabeth Sichrovsky

Bernhard Grünebaum
Moyses Sidwers

gelesen M Stern
gelesen M L Schlesinger
gelesen Joachim Heim

Anton Schnapper
Bernhard Wertheim
gelesen Angelus Sinzheimer

gelesen Joseph Simon

Jos. Haikes

gelesen Salomon Joseph
    Wertheimer

=   I. Figdor

=   Marcus A. Leidesdorf
=   Marcus Luzzatto
gelesen Joseph Reiter
Benedict D. Arnstein
      S. P. Wertheimer
M. D. Schiel
Herrman Schlesinger

Magdalena Leidesdorff

Amalia Kohn

Ascher Matzel

gelesen Ignatz Beer

Jacob Reichenstein
Julie Landauer
gelesen Herrman
Herzenskron
Adam Markbreiter
Joseph Arnstein
gelesen Salo Camondo

      August Leon
Herz Ph: Schinow
gelesen Rosalie Levi
gelesen Jacob Wertheimer

Rosalie Trebisch

David Semler

Isaac Noah Mannheimer's Preface to His Collected Chancel Orations [delivered at the *Stadttempel*], 1835.[45]

Vorwort.

Indem ich hiermit den vorliegenden ersten Band meiner gottesdienstlichen Vorträge, deren Erscheinen bereits vor einem Jahre angekündiget ward, einem größeren Publikum, als für das sie ursprünglich bestimmt waren, übergebe, ist es mein innigster Wunsch, daß sie fortan der menschlichen Anerkennung und des göttlichen Segens im gleichen Maße sich mögen zu erfreuen haben, als sie deren bereits sind gewürdiget worden.

Ich gebe das Beste, was ich habe, und glaube daher, mit aller Zuversicht, die jedes redliche Streben gewährt, mich eines günstigen Erfolges versichert halten zu dürfen; nur möchte ich diesen Erfolg nicht nach dem Lobe und Beifalle bemessen, der mir werden könnte, sondern das für meinen Gotteslohn und Segen halten, wenn das Wort in den Herzen einen Anklang und in den Gemeinden Israels eine freundliche Theilnahme, Anerkennung und Nachahmung fände, und wie auch immer, auf die eine oder andere Weise, werkthätig ins Leben träte.

Daß es einer solcher Anregung bedürfe in Israel, wird wohl Niemand in Abrede stellen.

Noch hat der Gottesdienst nur in den wenigsten Gemeinden sich der Erneuung im Geiste zu erfreuen, die nun schon seit mehr als zwanzig Jahren von den Edelsten und Besten in Israel beabsichtiget ward. Es hat sich dieses Streben als wohlthätig, segenreich, über die Maßen segenreich bewiesen, trotz aller Hemmungen, denen es hin und wieder unterlag; es hat sich als das einzige Mittel zur Einigung, Bindung und Kräftigung im Geiste bewiesen, trotz allen Voraussetzungen, daß es als ein Mittel zur Trennung und Entzweiung sich beweisen werde; — und doch hat es nicht die Anerkennung und weniger noch die Nachahmung gefunden, deren es sich vor allem hätte erfreuen sollen, um sich in seiner ganzen segenreichen Kraft zu bewähren. Noch wird in den wenigsten Gemeinden Israels das Wort Gottes faßlich, verständlich und eindringlich gelehret und geprediget. Noch ist der unselige Zwist, in den das heutige Israel gerathen ist, nicht geschlichtet. Noch halten die Einen fest an Satzungen, in denen kein Geist ist, die kein Leben haben und kein Leben geben, und bannen den Geist aus den Schulen und die Andacht aus den Tempeln; noch halten die Andern fest an dem unseligen Wahne, daß nicht der Glaube, sondern das Wissen, nicht was wir im Geiste ahnen, schauen und erkennen, sondern im Geiste verneinen und verläugnen, uns erhöhen und verherrlichen müsse, und in der Zerstörung und Verwüstung

des Überkommenen und Überlieferten, nicht in seiner Auferbauung und Verklärung, das Heil zu hoffen sey! Die Einen löschen das Licht aus, die Andern zünden es nicht wieder an.

Beiden zu begegnen, war von jeher mein Bestreben. Ich bin seit zwanzig Jahren Lehrer des göttlichen Wortes in Israel. Für seine heiligsten Angelegenheiten, nicht für das, was Menschen in ihrer Menschlichkeit berührt, wollte ich reden und wirken und die Herzen gewinnen. Daß ich das Menschliche im Menschen nicht übersehen, und auch wohl beherziget habe, daß wir Menschen sind, bevor wir Isrealiten werden, — das Zeugniß glaube ich mir selber geben zu dürfen, und die vorliegenden Blätter werden seine Beglaubigung und Bestätigung seyn. Aber darum war ich nicht minder darauf bedacht, das Judenthum als solches zu lehren, es in seinem Geiste, in seiner Weise zu verbreiten, und mit seinen Tröstungen und seinen Segnungen die Herzen zu füllen, und die Seelen zu gewinnen, um sie ihm in Wahrhaftigkeit wieder zuzuführen. Darum habe ich Gottes Wort zu meinem Quell und Born gemacht, aus dem ich habe geschöpft. Darum habe ich die Propheten zu meinen Meistern erkoren, und daran meine Kraft gesetzt, was sie mit Engelzungen geredet haben, mit einer schwachen Menschenzunge ihnen nachzureden; — und dazu hatte mir Gott eine »gelehrige Zunge« gegeben. Darum habe ich in den Büchern der Weisen meines Volkes emsig nachgesucht, und Jedes mir sorgfältig aufgehoben, das den Keim und Kern des Lebens in sich trug. Darum habe ich in der Geschichte meines Volkes mir stets Rath und Trost geholet, wenn mir irgend Eines nicht recht gefallen wollte. Darum habe ich das Leben meines Volkes, das ich auf seinen Höhen und in seinen Niederungen habe kennen gelernt, — denn es führte mich mein Beruf in die Hütten und in die Palläste, und überall, ich daf es sagen, schlossen sich mir die Herzen auf, — zu meinem Grund und Boden mir erkoren, den ich urbar machen wollte, und dahin mein Wort gerichtet, wo es das Leben verschönern, verklären, veredeln und heiligen könne.

Daß nicht Alles Wurzel fasset, was wir den menschlichen Herzen anvertrauen, und nicht Alles reifet, was die Herzen fassen — ist eine Erfahrung, die ich mit so vielen meines Gleichen habe machen müssen, und die wohl die Selbstgefälligkeit, wo sie aufkommen wollte, aber nicht das bessere Selbstgefühl in mir hat niederschlagen können.

Es ist das Alles, was ich denen, die danach verlangen, über meinen Beruf und meine Befähigung zum Lehrer und Prediger in Israel zu sagen weiß, und ich fühle mich verpflichtet, Allen, die mit mir und nach mir sich diesem heiligen, segenreichen Berufe widmen, und an die dieses Vorwort eigentlich gerichtet ist, dieselbe Weise, als die erprobte und bewährte, zu empfehlen.

Ich gehöre nicht zu denen, die das Alte, weil es alt ist, und das Todte, weil es todt ist, ehren, und mit den Mumien der Vergangenheit einen Götzendienst treiben, und sie wie ein Heiligthum hegen; gehöre aber auch nicht zu denen, die mit den Blumen und Blüthen, die sie auf ihren Spaziergängen durch die Litteratur gepflückt, dem an Leib und Seele schwer erkrankten Volke zu helfen, und den alten Schaden zu heilen gedenken. Ich fordere Selbständigkeit des Geistes und lebendige Kraft des Wortes von den Lehrern meines Volkes, wie ich die freie Kraft und Regsamkeit des Lebens für mein Volk in Anspruch nehme, wo ich sie immer verkürzt und beschränkt sehe.

Zwar sollen und dürfen wir nie vergessen, daß wir als Schüler und Jünger, als Neulinge in der Kunst, die wir erst seit Kurzem betreiben, von den Meistern der Kunst gar Vieles lernen können, und dankbar jede Anleitung und Unterweisung zu empfangen haben, die uns in ihren Schulen geboten wird; dürfen aber auch das nie vergessen, daß wir im Heiligthume Gottes auf eigenem Grund und Boden stehen, und fürs heimische Leben die Saat des Lebens streuen, und von unsern Vätern einen Schatz empfangen haben, den wir zu wahren von Gott berufen sind. Es wäre Verrath an uns und unserem Volke, an Gott und der ewigen Wahrheit, so wir, wie es so Manche in der Art haben, mit einem Federzuge die ganze Vergangenheit unsers Volkes oder ein Paar Jahrtausende, die in der Mitte liegen, wegstreichen wollten, um von heute ein neues Leben anzufangen, das mit dem Gestern und Ehedem in keinem weiteren Zusammenhange, in keiner weiteren Verbindung steht.

Darum kann ich der Entfremdung im Geiste, der flachen schöngeistigen Richtung eben so wenig das Wort reden, als den bodenlosen Theorien, den luftigen Schwindeleien, der angestrichenen Alterthümlichkeit, mit der wieder Andre ihre Blößen decken, und die Kluft in den Herzen zu füllen, sich bemühen. Mit leeren Formen und Satzungen füllen wir die Herzen nimmer, und mit leeren Phrasen auch nicht. Ärger als Pharisäer und Saducäer sind mir die, die je weniger sie selbst die Ceremonien halten, um so mehr auf das Ceremonienwesen dringen, und je weniger sie selbst von dem Talmud und den Rabbinen wissen, um so mehr ihre Weisheit rühmen und preisen.

An der lautern Wahrheit des göttlichen Wortes und der ewigen Weisheit sollen und müssen die Herzen sich kräftigen und die Seelen im Glauben sich zu Gott erheben. Vom eigenen Gute zehren, ist immer besser als vom Almosen leben, und den eigenen Boden anbauen immer besser, als auf fremdem Grund und Boden eine dürftige Ährenlese halten. Wer dem eigenen schaffenden Geiste was zumuthet, dem wird er seine Kraft nicht versagen, und der braucht keine Behelfe und keine Täuschungen der Kunst. Schlafend und träumend gibt uns Gott das Wort des Heiles ohnehin nimmer ein. Wer auf solche Erleuchtung hoffet, und die im Geiste scheuet, dem eignen Geiste Nichts zumuthet, und, wo er ihm was zumuthet, sich von ihm verlassen fühlt, — den hat Gott nicht berufen und nicht befähiget, der gebe das heilige Amt lieber ganz und gar dahin, und treibe sonst eine menschliche Kunst, an der er sich minder versündiget. Zum Spaten und zur Hacke, um das tägliche Brot damit zu ge-

winnen, wollen wir Gottes Wort nicht herabwürdigen, und zur Ehrenkrone, die uns die Stirne schmücket — auch nicht.

Das gilt vom Geiste der Lehre und der Richtung des Lehrers, und gilt auch von der Form.

An jedem menschlichen Werke ist die Form ein Unerläßliches. Wir fassen Gedanken in Formen. In so fern wir von höheren Wahrheiten reden, die nicht Jedem faßlich sind, und der Wahrheit ihren Eingang, dem Worte seine Geltung sichern wollen, ist es nötig, daß wir die Wahrheit in eine faßliche Form, in eine geregelte Form, in eine gefällige Form kleiden. Die Willkür schaffet nirgends Heil, und wir reden nicht, um uns am Klange und Schalle unserer Worte zu erfreuen, sondern um Wahrheit zu schaffen in den Herzen.

Nur wollte ich damit keineswegs behaupten, daß alles Heil in der einen abgeschlossenen Form zu suchen, und die schulgerechte Homiletik die alleinseligmachende sey; vielmehr wollte es mich bedünken, als wenn eben jenes Aneignen einer uns nicht ganz eigenthümlichen Form der Armuth des Geistes gar zu oft zum Deckmantel diene, ohne sie je zu verhüllen, geschweige denn zu verhüthen; — denn die Form kann keine Gedanken schaffen, und bindet vielmehr den Geist, als daß sie ihn frei mache.

Die Hauptsache in dieser Beziehung bleibt immer die innere Verbindung der Gedanken, nicht der Faden, der sich von außen um das Ganze schlingt, und ihm eine gewisse Einheit gibt. Die Gedanken müssen in sich zusammenhängen, folgerecht aus einander sich entwickeln; sie müssen wie Lichtstrahlen in einem Brennpunkte sich einigen. Daher wir auch nie einen Gegenstand wählen, und der Gemeinde zur Beachtung und Beherzigung vorlegen sollen, von dessen innerer Lebenskraft wir nicht selber durchdrungen sind. Wo das ist, da ordnen sich auch die Gedanken und fügen sich, für jeden Gedanken findet sich das rechte Wort, und es wird dem Ganzen die Rundung, dem Einzelnen die Haltung, dem Gedanken die Klarheit, dem Worte die Kraft auch nicht fehlen und nicht ausgehen. Alle übrigen Kunstgriffe und Regeln sind — Behelfe, und jeder Behelf ist störend, und wirkt hemmend auf die schaffende Kraft des Geistes ein. Wo das Gedächtniß sich anstrengt, da ruht die schaffende Vernunft, und es tritt derselbe Fall ein, wenn der ordnende Verstand sich obenan stellt. Jede schöpferische Kraft ist, — wo sie was anders als eine rohe Kraft ist, und die gehört nicht in den Tempel Gottes und nicht vor den Altar des Herrn, — zugleich eine ordnende, nach organischen Gesetzen schaffende, und die innere Fülle schließt die äußere Rundung und Vollendung keinesweges aus.

Es kommt viel darauf an, wo und wann und wem wir Gottes Wort zu predigen haben; ob die, die es hören und fassen sollen, an eine gewisse Form gewöhnt sind, oder an das freie Schalten des Geistes; ob sie ferner die Achtung und Würdigung des göttlichen Wortes mitbringen in den Tempel Gottes, oder ob es ihnen solche Achtung und Würdigung erst abgewinnen muß, und wir mithin nur eine bloße Empfänglichkeit voraussetzen dürfen. Letzteres dürfte vorläufig noch der Fall seyn. Da muß der lebendige Geist das Seine thun; die starre Form wird es nimmer über sie vermögen.

Mit diesem Bekenntnisse vertraue ich nun mein Wort dem Schutze Gottes und der Freundlichkeit der Menschen an, und hoffe, so Gott die Zeit und Kraft dazu verleihet, die Vorträge über die übrigen Wochenabschnitte und die restlichen Vorträge in zwei gleichen Bänden nachfolgen zu lassen.

Schließlich bemerke ich nur, daß manche Rüge und Erinnerung, die sich auf öffentliche Einrichtungen in unserem Gemeinwesen oder auf unsere gottesdienstlichen Angelegenheiten beziehet, bereits ihre Erledigung gefunden hat. — Dank sey es dem wohlwollenden und wohlmeinenden Sinne meiner Gemeinde im Allgemeinen und ihrer Führer und Leiter ins Besondere, die sich der Wahrheit stets zugänglich und geneigt bewiesen haben. Wenn ich dennoch das Wort wieder aufgenommen habe, wie es zu seiner Zeit gesprochen ward, so geschah es einerseits, um die Gemeinde und die, die ihr Wohl in Händen haben, von der siegenden Kraft der Wahrheit zu überzeugen, und ihnen einen Maßstab zu geben, um das Ehedem mit dem Heute zu vergleichen; andrerseits aber auch, um andern Gemeinden, für die das Wort nunmehr bestimmt ist, die gleiche Überzeugung zu verschaffen, und dem Worte, das einmal als recht und wohlthuend sich bewährt hat, auch in weitern Kreisen seine Anerkennung zu sichern.

Wien, im Juli 1835.

Mannheimer.

* Rudiments of this essay were first presented in a paper read in the session ''Sentiment and the Historian of Art'', which was organized by the International Survey of Jewish Monuments in conjunction with the XXVIth International Congress for the History of Art of the Comité International d'Histoire de l'Art, convened at Washington, D. C., 11th to 18th August, 1986. I wish to acknowledge my gratitude for the help I received in reviewing and collecting materials pertaining to the history of the *Stadttempel* to Professor Kurt Schubert and Dr. Nikolaus Vielmetti of the Institut für Judaistik of the University of Vienna, to Professor Artur Rosenauer and Dozent Dr. Walter Krause of the Kunsthistorisches Institut of the same university, and to Professor Konrad Oberhuber and Dr. Richard Bösel of the Graphische Sammlung Albertina who introduced me to the collection of Kornhäusel's drawings and took me on unforgettable walks through the private apartments of the Albertina where Kornhäusel's architecture can be appreciated at its best. Without the help of my wife, Maria Raina Fehl, who accompanied me on my journeys to Vienna and shared, from a wealth of her own memories of a Jewish childhood in Vienna, in the adventures and melancholy cares of such a return, writing this essay would have been even more difficult than it was. Her own studies, furthermore, provided valuable information on the history of the Jews of Austria. Raina Fehl joins me in saluting Rachel Wischnitzer, whose life's work has been an inspiration to us in tending the Survey of Jewish Monuments and studying synagogue architecture.

[1] The argument in favor of such a separation was fully developed by A. Riegl, *Der moderne Denkmalskultus: sein Wesen und seine Entstehung*, and has rarely been challenged. For recent discussions and, by and large, endorsements, see E. Bacher, ''Denkmalsbegriff, Denkmälermasse und Inventare,'' *Deutsche Kunst und Denkmalpflege*, XXXVIII, 1980, pp. 121-25; A. Emiliani, ed., *La terra promessa: Chiesa, città, campagna. Il patrimonio artistico e storico della chiesa e l'organizzazione del territorio*, exhibition catalogue, Bologna, 1981 (with an Italian translation of Riegl's *Denkmalskultus* and a critical introduction); R. Middleton, ''The architect and tradition — three Boston Lectures: 1: the use and abuse of tradition in architecture,'' *Royal Society of Arts Journal*, CXXXI/5328, 1983, pp. 729-39. For the particular task of representing the social and cultural history of the Jews of Vienna, note especially H. Tietze, *Die Juden Wiens: Geschichte - Wirtschaft - Kultur*, Vienna, 1933. The author rigorously observes the standards for which we here cite Riegl. We would not readily know from reading this book (except, perhaps, from his choice of the topic and the concluding words of his preface) that Tietze himself was a Jew of Vienna who was writing of what in some ways must have been nearest and dearest to him. For Tietze's endorsement and development of Riegl's standards, see his *Die Methode der Kunstgeschichte: ein Versuch*, Leipzig, 1913, pp. 224-40, and his further reflections, with thoughtful qualifications, pp. 450-66. Interestingly, Tietze did not practice this kind of objectivity when he wrote of modern art. The last words of his *Die Juden Wiens* impressively demonstrate the pathos and moral integrity of his personal detachment from the history he tells and should here be allowed to speak for themselves: ''... die Weltgeschichte ist weder ein Weltgericht, noch ein moralischer Traktat; sie ist der Schauplatz von Kräften, die über die einzelnen wie über ganze Nationen hinweggehen.

Völker leben gegeneinander, füreinander, ineinander. Das Wiener Judentum ist vom Überfluß der schönsten und kulturell reichsten deutschen Stadt gewachsen; es hat hier die größte Fruchtbarkeit entwickelt, die irgend einem westlichen Judentum beschieden war. Es hat genommen und gegeben, zersetzt und geformt; es hat gelebt und leben geholfen, so daß es ein Teil von Wiens Vergangenheit und damit von Wiens Gegenwart geworden ist. Ohne Juden wäre Wien nicht, was es ist, wie ohne Wien ihr Dasein in den neueren Jahrhunderten seiner stolzesten Seite verlustig ginge. Kein Eingriff der Welt vermag diesen Lebensprozeß rückgängig zu machen. Sofern wir historisch denken, fragen wir nicht, ob er für den einen oder den anderen Teil vorteilhaft oder nachteilig war; nur daß er war und wie er war, leidenschaftslos und wahrheitstreu zu schildern, war die bescheidene Aufgabe dieses Buches.''

[2] According to Erika Weinzierl's moving epilogue to the facsimile edition of G. Wolf, *Geschichte der Juden in Wien (1156-1876)*, reprint, Vienna, 1974, the number of Jews who could be counted as members of the Jewish Community of Vienna was 169,978 in 1938 and that of Jews in all of Austria 185,246. Wolf's book is not only fundamentally instructive on its subject but also a precious document of Jewish life and hopes in the Vienna of his own times. See also his *Die Juden* (*Die Völker Österreich-Ungarns: Ethnographische und Culturhistorische Schilderungen, VII*), Vienna-Teschen, 1883. On the tradition to which I address myself here it is best to consult Wolf's writings in conjunction with S. Mayer, *Die Wiener Juden: Kommerz, Kultur, Politik, 1700-1900*, Vienna, 1916; 2nd, enlarged edition, Vienna, 1918. See also *Das österreichische Judentum: Voraussetzungen und Geschichte*, ed. Anna Drabek *et al.*, Vienna, 1974. For its language as much as for its learned argument note M. Güdemann, *Jüdische Apologetik*, (Schriften herausgegeben von der Gesellschaft zur Förderung der Wissenschaft des Judentums: *Grundriß der Gesammtwissenschaft des Judentums*), Glogau, 1906. Güdemann, who served the community from 1866 on, was chief rabbi of Vienna from 1894-1918.

[3] At first, returning Jews were forbidden to live in the Leopoldstadt. See Wolf, *Geschichte...*, *op. cit.*, pp. 52-53. Sporadic temporary residence is, however, already on record for 1699. See M. Grunwald, *Samuel Oppenheimer und sein Kreis* (*Quellen und Forschungen zur Geschichte der Juden in Deutsch-Österreich, V*), Vienna-Leipzig, 1912, p. 172. It was only in the early nineteenth century that Jewish residence there recommenced in earnest. On the flood of demeaning regulations and restrictions that governed the life of Jews in Vienna before 1848, see A. F. Pribram, *Urkunden und Akten zur Geschichte der Juden in Wien* (*Quellen und Forschungen zur Geschichte der Juden in Deutsch-Österreich, VIII*), *Erste Abteilung, Allgemeiner Teil, 1526-1847 [1849]*, I, Vienna-Leipzig, 1918, pp. xlxii-clxiv.

[4] On the origins and history of the *Stadttempel* see especially *Studia Judaica Austriaca* (Schriften herausgegeben im Auftrag des Vereins ''Österreichisches Jüdisches Museum,'' ed. K. Schubert), *VI: Der Wiener Stadttempel, 1826-1976*, Eisenstadt, 1978. See also P. Genée, *Wiener Synagogen, 1825-1938*, Vienna, 1987, pp. 46-52. The book contains a representative bibliography. Material on the destroyed synagogues of Vienna is difficult to find and photographs of them, especially views of the interior of the buildings, are often unobtainable. Genée's book is the result of many years of searching for its pictorial documentation and truly a labor of love and learning. I am glad to be able here to give grateful notice of this recently published work. Equally interesting to the student of the history of Vienna's Jews will be the catalogue of the exhibition of works from the remarkable collection Max Berger (Vienna), *''Heilige Gemeinde Wien,'' Judentum in Wien: Sammlung Max Berger* [Historisches Museum der Stadt Wien], ed. Karl Albrecht Weinberger and Felicitas Heimann-Jelinek, Vienna, 1987. Note especially N. Vielmetti, ''Reform und Tradition im neuen Stadttempel in der Seitenstettengasse zu Wien,'' *ibidem*, pp. 30-40, and R. Kassal Mikula, ''Der Wiener Stadttempel'', p. 29.

[5] This included the installation of the *mikvah* in the apartment tract of the building in which the ''Tempel'' is contained. On several of Kornhäusel's architectural drawings in the Albertina the bath and its water ducts are carefully indicated in blue color. Since Kornhäusel had already made a reputation with the building of a bath in Baden (an important spa near Vienna) the Jews of Vienna could be certain that their ritual bath would be elegant and commodious.

[6] On the ceremonies and the inauguration service see Vielmetti, ''Bilder und Dokumente,'' *Studia Judaica Austriaca VI: Bethhaus der Israeliten in Wien*, *op. cit.*, pp. 98-99. See also H. Avenary, W. Pass and N. Vielmetti, *Kantor Salomon Sulzer und seine Zeit: Eine Dokumentation*, Sigmaringen, 1985, pp. 45-53.

[7] Wolf, *Geschichte...*, *op. cit.*, pp. 134-40, pp. 172-75. Avenary, Pass, and Vielmetti, *op. cit.*, *passim*.

[8] On the succession of the chief rabbis of Vienna see J. Allerhand, ''Die Rabbiner des Stadttempels von J. N. Mannheimer bis Z. P. Chajes,'' *Studia Judaica Austrica VI*, *op. cit.*, pp. 5-28. Chajes' successors were David Feuchtwang (1933-36) and Israel Taglicht (1936-1938). Taglicht died, a refugee in England, in 1944. See also A. Willman, ''Famous Rabbis of Vienna,'' in J. Fraenkel, ed., *The Jews of Austria: Essays on their Life, History and Destruction*, London, 1967, pp. 319-26.

[9] Genée, *op. cit.*, pp. 60-62.

[10] My parents' coming to Vienna was in keeping with a pattern of population shifts among Jews in Bohemia and Moravia that had commenced in the fifties of the nineteenth century. For the cares, hopes and needs that caused or accompanied these migrations, see especially the autobiography of A. L. Frankl (1810-94), *Erinnerungen*, ed. Stefan Hock, Vienna, 1910. Frankl, a once well-known poet and essayist, combined his literary concerns with the life of a physician and the office of permanent secretary to the Jewish Community of Vienna. He was a descendant of Koppel Fränkel, the last Jew to be buried in Vienna before the expulsion of 1670. On Koppel Fränkel see our note 24 below. On Frankl see *Studia Judaica Austriaca I: Das Judentum im Revolutionsjahr 1848*, Vienna, 1974, p. 34, and, for his tomb, our Fig. 17. Note also the plethora of picturesque and poetically embroidered ''Ghettogeschichten'' by L. Kompert (1822-1886) in his *Sämmtliche Werke*, ed. Stefan Hock, Leipzig, 1906. The stories, as a rule, lovingly depict the lives of Jews in their ancient, provincial settlements in Bohemia and Moravia, the impact on them of the reforms of Joseph II, and their brave first moves to the countryside (whence, in turn, their children often moved to Vienna). Kompert's sentimental stories are not as far from the truth of history as may be supposed. I still encountered figures straight out of Kompert among the Jews I met when I spent some time as a refugee in Czechoslovakia before the outbreak of the war. On the milieu and its reflection in literature see especially W. Abeles Iggers, ed., *Die Juden in Böhmen und Mähren: ein historisches Lesebuch*, Munich, 1986. On Kompert see also *Studia Judaica Austriaca I*, *op. cit.*, p. 35 and Wilma Iggers, ''Leopold Kompert, Romancier of the Bohemian Ghetto', *Modern Austrian Literature*, VI, ns. 3/4, pp. 30 f.

[11] Allied to this was a repugnance to blood sports. Characteristic for the perseverance of this Jewish trait is an aphorism of Walter Rathenau's (who did not otherwise lead a particularly Jewish life). At the end of a hunt he said to his host that if a Jew were ever to tell him that he enjoyed hunting he could be sure he was lying. If I am not mistaken the story was told (or invented) by Rathenau himself. I should also mention in this context that drunkenness was remarkably scandalous to Jews. It is not so much that it was not done as it was, after a fashion, inconceivable.

[12] F. Grillparzer, *Briefe und Tagebücher*, ed. C. Glossy, A. Sauer, Stuttgart-Berlin, n.d., II, pp. 135-6.

[13] N. Hawthorne, *The Marble Faun*, ed. Boston, 1900, I, p. 230. The same response, in front of the monument of Joseph II, is conveyed in a once much beloved poem, ''Sein Bildnis,'' by Anastasius Grün [Anton Graf Auersperg]: ''Ruhig auf granitnem Sockel schwebt das

Kaiserbild voll Glanz, / Um die Schläfen keine Krone, nur der selbst-errungne Kranz! / Hoch zu Ross, das Antlitz lächelnd, und empor die rechte Hand / Sanft erhoben, wie zum Segen über sein geliebtes Land.'' See A. Grün, *Gesammelte Werke*, ed. L. A. Frankl, Berlin, 1877, II, pp. 369-70.

[14] On Zauner see H. Burg, *Der Bildhauer Franz Anton Zauner und seine Zeit*, Vienna, 1915. The effect of the statue is enhanced by its dedicatory inscription: JOSEPHO II. AUG./ QUI/ SALUTI PUBLICAE VIXIT/ NON. DIV. SED. TOTUS. There is one among the several emblematic bronze reliefs on the posts surrounding the monument which might make a particular impression on a Jew viewing the monument. It records the foundation of the Alms House in 1784 and shows, rising in a glory of rays above the clouds, the two tablets of the Ten Commandments. The inscription reads: ''Dilige Deum super omn. prox. ut te ipsum.'' What I knew best about the emperor when I was young was, next to the many fabulous stories that showed him as a prince charming, the sight of the great gate through which one enters the *Augarten*, an imperial park opened by the emperor to all comers. I passed it or through it every day on my way to school. The inscription over the gate which was and, I trust, still is beloved by many Viennese, reads in accents of magnanimous simplicity: ''Allen Menschen / gewidmeter / Erlustigungs-Ort / von / Ihrem Schaetzer.'' The text supports, as it were, the gesture of Joseph's hand on his monument. See G. Egger, R. Wagner-Rieger, *Geschichte der Architektur in Wien* (*Geschichte der Stadt Wien*, Neue Reihe VIII. 3), Vienna, 1973, fig. 74.

[15] Genée, *op. cit.*, pp. 82-83. No photograph of the interior seems to have survived. An architectural cross section is reproduced by Genée on p. 83.

[16] Wolf, *Geschichte...*, *op. cit.*, p. 1-2. See also K. Lohrmann, ed., *1000 Jahre Österreichisches Judentum* (i.e., *Studia Judaica Austriaca, IX*), exhibition catalogue, Eisenstadt, 1982, pp. 21-24, 69-92, and B. Wachstein, *Hebräische Grabsteine aus dem XIII-XV Jahrhundert in Wien und Umgebung* (Akademie der Wissenschaften in Wien: Philosophisch-Historische Klasse. *Sitzungsberichte*, 181. Band, 1. Abt.), Vienna, 1916; *idem*, *Die Inschriften des alten Judenfriedhofes in Wien, herausgegeben im Auftrag der Israelitischen Kultusgemeinde in Wien*, (*Quellen und Forschungen zur Geschichte der Juden in Deutsch-Österreich*, IV), Vienna, 1912-17.

[17] Even the painstakingly objective study *Kantor Salomon Sulzer und seine Zeit* (Avenary, Pass, & Vielmetti, *op. cit.*) finds that the time for a just critical evaluation of Sulzer's *oeuvre* has not yet come. See p. 10. For characteristically negative modern views (which are in sharp contrast to the appreciations of the nineteenth and early twentieth century), see *ibidem*, pp. 238-42. A first harbinger of a return to a loving understanding of Sulzer's music appears in A. Bankier, ''Synagogaler Gesang in der jüdischen Liturgie und die Bedeutung der Reformen des Salomon Sulzer'', in *Heilige Gemeinde Wien ... Sammlung Berger, op. cit.,* pp. 35-36.

[18] Cf. J. von Sonnenfels (1733-1817), *Briefe über die wienerische Schaubühne...*, [Vienna, 1768], ed. C. Konegen, Vienna, 1884. See also his *Gesammelte Schriften*, Vienna, 1783-87. He also was influential in the management of the ''Akademie der bildenden Künste'' of Vienna and served for many years as its secretary and eventually as its president. On his life and work see F. Kopetzky, *Josef und Franz von Sonnenfels. Das Leben und Wirken eines edlen Brüderpaares*, Vienna, 1882; W. Müller, *Josef von Sonnenfels*, Vienna, 1885; K. H. Osterloh, *Josef von Sonnenfels und die österreichische Reformbewegung im Zeitalter des aufgeklärten Absolutismus* (Historische Schriften, Berlin, Heft 409).

[19] He also advocated, but in vain, the abolition — with certain limitations — of the death penalty. See his essay ''Über die Abschaffung der Folter'' and the accompanying stirring address to the Empress Maria Theresia on the cruelty and uselessness of the death penalty in his *Gesammelte Schriften*, VII, part II, especially pp. 12-36. The other work contained in this volume, a fitting counterpoint, is entitled ''Über die Liebe des Vaterlandes.'' See also his *Grundsätze der Polizey-, Handlungs- und Finanzwissenschaft*, Vienna, 1765-67.

[20] The statue is the work of Hans Gasser. Together with the statues of seven other worthies (by other sculptors) it was commissioned to decorate the ''Elisabethbrücke'' over the river Wien and put in place in 1867. The statues were moved to the Rathausplatz when the river was covered over and the bridge demolished. Soon after the establishment of the Nazi regime the statue was removed from its pedestal and Sonnenfels' name erased. In its place was put a statue of Christoph Willibald Gluck. Sonnenfels' statue was recovered after the war in a mutilated state, was restored and then returned to its former position. Gluck's statue, in turn, languished in a magazine until 1987 (the bicentenary of Gluck's death) when it was placed on the Argentinierstrasse near the Karlskirche. The statue is a perhaps deliberately ''hard-edged'' copy after an original by Vincenz Pilz which graces a corridor of Vienna's *Musikvereinsgebäude*. The copy is signed ''Max Kremser 1940 nach V. Pilz 1865'' and, obviously, for the purpose of replacing Gasser's ''Sonnenfels''. On the early history of Sonnenfels' statue see G. Kapner, *Ringstraßendenkmäler* (R. Wagner-Rieger, ed., *Die Wiener Ringstraße: Bild einer Epoche, IX, 1*), Wiesbaden, 1973, pp. 90-1, and W. Krause, *Die Plastik der Wiener Ringstraße* (*ibidem*, IX.3), Wiesbaden, 1980, pp. 13-5. Subsequent to his death Sonnenfels' fame was eclipsed. It cost some effort to get him included among the worthies on the ''Elisabethbrücke''. On the *fortuna* of his memory see the entry ''Sonnenfels'', in C. von Wurzbach, *Biographisches Lexikon des Kaiserthums Oesterreich* XXXV, Vienna, 1877, pp. 333-5. Prominent among the restorers of Sonnenfels' fame was Ludwig August Frankl, who opened his *Sonntagsblätter* to appreciations of Sonnenfels' accomplishments. On Frankl see note 10 *supra*. A portrait of Sonnenfels is also included among the many figures in high relief surrounding Vienna's monument to Maria Theresia (on the green between the ''Kunsthistorisches'' and the ''Naturhistorisches Museum'') by Caspar von Zumbusch.

[21] David Feuchtwang (1864-1936) was called to Vienna from the rabbinate in Nikolsburg in 1902. He was rabbi in Währing (Vienna's eighteenth district) and after the death of Chief Rabbi Zvi Peretz ben Salomon Chajes in 1927 assumed Chajes' duties. He was named chief rabbi in 1933. Among his publications are his dissertation, *Nachum im Lichte der Assyriologie* [1888], a selection of sermons (*Kanzelreden*, Frankfurt, 1899-1906), and a number of studies, some of them in book form, on Jewish homiletics, the language of the Bible, Old Testament ritual, *topoi* in Biblical and Babylonian narrative and law, and with S. Krauss, *Moses ben Maimon. Aus Anlaß der 800. Wiederkehr seines Geburtstages*, Vienna, 1935. It would be presumptuous to interpret the sparing gestures of Feuchtwang's oratory, which I remember so well, as a reaction to anti-Semites who often mocked the Jewish way of ''talking with their hands.'' Instead, I like to think that his manner was simply professorial, in the best sense of the word. In Austria the heirs of the Enlightenment preferred the Attic style of rhetoric over the Asian as a matter of course. Josef von Sonnenfels (as in his work on the theater) here too had been instrumental in forging a tradition. See his *Von der Bescheidenheit im Vortrage seiner Meinung; eine Rede beim Eingange der Vorlesungen*, Vienna, 1772. See also G. Wolf, *Das Unterrichtswesen in Österreich unter Kaiser Josef II. Nach einer Darstellung von Josef von Sonnenfels*, Vienna, 1880.

[22] ''Seine philosophische Beschaulichkeit und verschlossene

Gelehrtennatur liessen ihn nicht hervortreten. Ein wahrhaft großer Mensch, glänzender Kanzelredner und universeller Gelehrter. Gleichwohl hat er außer seiner Dissertation (über Plato) nie eine Zeile publiziert.'' F. Salomon Wininger, *Große Jüdische National-Biographie...*, Cernăuți, 1925-34, II, pp. 242-3. For the dissertation see M. Feuchtwang, *Summa Platonicae Philosophiae imprimis Ethicae*, Göttingen, 1838. On Israel Taglicht, Feuchtwang's worthy and venerable successor as chief rabbi, see *Studia Judaica Austriaca*, vol. VI, p. 80 and note 8, *supra*.

[23] A drawing proposing the shape and text of the dedication tablet, submitted for approval, is reproduced in Avenary, Pass, and Vielmetti, *op. cit.*, p. 33. Except for the seemingly insignificant but evidently well — pondered replacement of the word *gestattete* with *bewilligte* (the emperor *granted* instead of *permitted* the dedication of the ''Tempel''), the tablet was executed as proposed.

[24] In my childhood there were (as there still are) three Jewish cemeteries in Vienna. The oldest, in the Rossau (Vienna IX, Seegasse 9), was established in the sixteenth century. When the Jews were expelled from Vienna in 1670 the cemetery was bought by the sons of Koppel Fränkel (the last Jew to be buried in Vienna before the expulsion) who made a contract with the city of Vienna to protect the cemetery and its stones as their and their heirs' personal property. The price they paid for the privilege was 4,000 florins, almost a third of the price which was fetched for all the houses combined which the Jews owned in Vienna and at that time had to sell. From 1690 on (some Jewish families having returned to Vienna) the cemetery was again in use. In 1784 it was closed on the order of Joseph II, who relocated all cemeteries outside the city. The cemetery was completely leveled by the Nazis and the bulk of the grave stones dumped on the grounds of the Jewish section of the ''Zentralfriedhof'' (see below). Jews then secretely covered these stones with earth to preserve them from further desecration and, perhaps, to bury them as one buries desecrated Thora scrolls. It was not until a few years ago that this *cache* of stones was rediscovered. Thanks to the magisterial study of the history of the cemetery and the inventory of the graves prepared by Bernhard Wachstein (*Inschriften, op. cit.*), it was possible to return the recovered tombstones to the places to which they belong. This was done with the assistance of the City of Vienna, which respected its commitment to the contract with the sons of Koppel Fränkel (dated 1671 and negotiated by the sons from Fuerth, where they had found refuge). The inauguration of the restored cemetery took place in a moving ceremony in August, 1983.

From 1784 to ca. 1878 the cemetery of the Jews was the ''Währinger Friedhof'' which is now a wilderness and unsafe to walk in because tombs open up beneath the unwary step, but a rehabilitation project is under consideration. The site is now normally closed to visitors.

In 1878 the ''Zentralfriedhof'' of the City of Vienna was opened. A part reached by the gate closest to the city, the first gate (''Erstes Tor''), was reserved for Jews. When this proved insufficient in the twentieth century a supplementary section was opened (''Viertes Tor'') which is still in use. Under the Nazis Christians of Jewish origins could not be buried with other Christians and their graves were placed in a kind of no-man's land between the Christian and the Jewish sections at the ''Viertes Tor.'' The cemetery also contains a new section of Jewish tombs transferred from ancient cemeteries in the provinces where there are no Jews left to tend and preserve the graves. I should here also mention Vienna's ''Döblinger Friedhof,'' where Jews and Christians were buried in common, though by and large in easily identifiable rows of plots. (This is the cemetery where Theodor Herzl was buried.) In the ''Pötzleinsdorfer Friedhof'' a number of Jewish graves also can be found. The Jews of Floridsdorf near Vienna opened a cemetery in 1877. The community joined with that of Vienna in 1907 when Floridsdorf became a part of the city proper.

All the Jewish cemeteries were vandalized under the Nazis (and some later as well), though in varying degrees. The ''Zentralfriedhof'' furthermore became a battlefield when the Russians were fighting for Vienna. Large parts of the Jewish sections are now virtually inaccessible. Other parts, particularly in the proximity of the relatively wide passage ways which traverse the cemetery, are beautifully maintained.

On the older cemeteries see Frankl, *op. cit.*, pp. 30-32; Wolf, *Geschichte, op. cit.*, pp. 39, 50, 197-98, 266; Wachstein, *Inschriften, op. cit.* (with exhaustive documentation of the tomb of Koppel Fränkel — no. 634, Jakob Koppel ben Jeremia Isak ha-Levi [Fränkel] and the protective actions of his sons); and *idem, Hebräische Grabsteine..., op. cit.*, especially pp. 2-3, on the placement of the oldest tombstones in the west wall of the cemetery in the Seegasse. See also P. P. Fehl, ''Life Beyond the Reach of Hope,'' *The College* (St. John's College at Annapolis, Maryland), XXXI (1980), pp. 32-3.

[25] The prayer for the emperor and his family is in keeping with an old tradition in Jewish worship. It is joined to the prayers for the welfare of the community and all of Israel and the prayers for its sages and students of the Law. For the Hebrew model on which Mannheimer based his Austro-Hungarian version in German, see S. R. Hirsch, *The Hirsch Siddur*, ed. Y. Feldheim, Jerusalem-New York, 1978, p. 349, and for notes on its origins, pp. 347-8. Note also *Ethics of the Fathers* (*Pirkey Avoth*), chap. III.v.2: ''Rabbi Chaninah, the Assistant of the High Priests, said: Pray for the welfare of the government, for were it not for the fear of it, men would swallow each other alive.'' Mannheimer's prayer, with obvious adaptations, survived into the period of the republic and is, I believe, still in use. Even as a child with democratic convictions fully ablaze I found the revised version less compelling (perhaps because it is, of necessity, a prayer for the well-being of an abstraction) than the ''Habsburg'' original. The last paragraph of Mannheimer's prayer (where he asks God that we may find a place of honor in our country and the good will of men) was dropped in the course of the later nineteenth century. Evidently the redactors thought there was no longer any need for it or that it would be impolitic, if not unworthy, to acknowledge such a need when we had long been granted equal rights. The original version of Mannheimer's ''Gebet für den Landesvater'' was, of course, offered for Francis I of Austria. See also Wolf, *Geschichte, op. cit.*, p. 135.

[26] The so-called ''Circus Gymnasticus'' established by the circus rider Christoph de Bach in 1808. It was demolished in 1852. On Kornhäusel's work see P. Taussig, *Josef Kornhäusel*, Vienna, 1916, and H. Herzmansky, *Josef Kornhäusel, eine Künstlermonographie* (Ph. D. dissertation, University of Vienna), 1964. On the *Stadttempel* in particular see pp. 258-77. See also Herzmansky's entry on Kornhäusel in *Österreichisches Biographisches Lexikon: 1815-1950*, 16. Lieferung (1966), pp. 132-3; R. Wagner-Rieger in Egger, Wagner-Rieger, *op. cit.*, pp. 124-6; Georg Rizzi, ''Josef Kornhäusel'', in *Bürgersinn und Aufbegehren: Biedermeier und Vormärz in Wien, 1815-1848,* Exhibition Catalogue, Historisches Museum der Stadt Wien, Vienna, 1987, pp. 505-513. On the ''Tempel'' see esp. pp. 508-509, 519. On the interior of the ''Tempel'' see esp. R. Blaha, ''Der Innenraum der Synagoge Wien I, Seitenstettengasse 4: Aufnahmearbeit,'' (a seminar paper, summer, 1977, on file in the Institut für Kunstgeschichte of the University of Vienna). I am particularly grateful to Doz. Dr. Walter Krause who drew my attention to this valuable work. See also Ruth Blaha's contribution to *Studia Judaica Austriaca VI, op. cit.*, pp. 94-5; R. Wischnitzer, *The Architecture of the European Synagogue*, Philadelphia, 1964, pp. 177-9; H. Hammer-Schenk, *Synagogen in*

Deutschland, Hamburg, 1981, I, pp. 160-2; C. Krinsky, *Synagogues of Europe*, Cambridge, Mass.-London, 1985, pp. 186-90.

[27] Cf. Wagner-Rieger, in Egger, Wagner-Rieger, *op. cit.*, p. 125. The work was done for the duke's heir, the Archduke Charles, in 1822.

[28] A copy of the album was in the possession of the Archives of the Jewish Community of Vienna (reported by Taussig, *op. cit.*). A search for the work in the Archives (which are now on permanent loan to the Central Archives for the History of the Jewish People in Jerusalem) was undertaken at the request of Ruth Blaha in 1977 but remained without success. Cf. Blaha, "Innenraum," pp. 1, 23 n.1.

[29] My account here follows Blaha, "Innenraum," p. 2. See also Krinsky, *op. cit.*, p. 189.

[30] A new restoration of the entire complex of the building is in progress at the time of this publication (1988).

[31] A. Pick, "Zur Geschichte der Wiener Israelitischen Kultusgemeinde," in *1000 Jahre Österreichisches Judentum, op. cit.*, pp. 112-5.

[32] On the attitudes, conflicts, and reconciliations which influenced or determined the construction of the "Tempel" and eventually the drawing up of the "Statutes", see especially Vielmetti, "Reform und Tradition im neuen Stadttempel," (*op. cit.*), pp. 30-4. See also Wolf, *Geschichte, op. cit.*, pp. 121-37, and Bernhard Wachstein's review of the "Statutes" and its signatories, reported in note 37, *infra*. I have not been able to consult the here obviously interesting book by S. Husserl, *Gründungsgeschichte des Stadt-Tempels*, Vienna-Leipzig, 1906.

[33] On the "salons" of Jewish ladies and on their function in Viennese society, see Tietze, *Geschichte, op. cit.*, pp. 146-9. See also H. Spiel, *Fanny von Arnstein, oder die Emanzipation. Ein Frauenleben in der Zeitenwende 1758-1818*, Frankfurt, 1962; Susanne Walther, "Der 'zweite Adel'. Kultur und Gesellschaft vor 1848", in *Bürgersinn und Aufbegehren, op. cit.* pp. 314-24. On the increasing openness in the relation of Jews and Christians in Vienna and the Jewish participation in various professions and the life of the arts, see Wolf, *Geschichte, op. cit.*, p. 149-53. On Jewish charities, *ibidem*, pp. 146-8. See also Tietze, *Geschichte, op. cit.*, pp. 129-77. Extraordinary among many remarkable Jews who offered their charities and labor without distinction of religious differences was the pioneering social worker and educator Marie Löwy Kompert (1821-92). She was the wife of Leopold Kompert. See note 10 *supra* and *Österreichisches Biographisches Lexikon, op. cit.*, 16. Lieferung, p. 104.

[34] Curiously, the government, which insisted on continuing the humiliating conditions of the "Judenamt" and other restrictive regulations imposed on the Jews, also wished to advance an enlightened teaching of religion among Jews. The title "Religions-lehrer," which they favored (as they held back that of rabbi), still suggested a position of honor and high responsibility. On the complexity (and, to some extent, irony) of the government's position, see Vielmetti, "Reform und Tradition," pp. 31-2, and Wachstein, "Statuten," cited below in note 37.

[35] The "Statutes," as Wachstein points out ("Statuten," p. 8, cf. note 37 below) were by no means signed by all the heads of "tolerated" households. Some among the signatories who prefixed the word "gesehen," i.e., *vidi*, to their names, may have wished to indicate that they took notice of what they were given to read and sign but did not necessarily approve of it.

[36] Wachstein, "Statuten," p. 8. See note 37 below.

[37] Avenary, Pass, and Vielmetti, *op. cit.*, p. 196-209

[38] *Die ersten Statuten des Bethauses in der inneren Stadt* (herausgegeben vom Vorstand der Israelitischen Kultusgemeinde Wien), with B. Wachstein, "Das Statut für das Bethaus der Israeliten in Wien: Seine Urheber und Gutheißer," Vienna, 1926.

[39] Excerpts have been published before, the largest, with special emphasis on the role of the cantor, by Avenary, Pass and Vielmetti, *op. cit.*, pp. 55-60.

[40] Cf. Wachstein, "Statuten" (*op. cit.*), pp. 7-8. Wachstein here sums up thoughts he developed with delicate understanding and fairness in the introduction to his *Inschriften, op. cit.*, II (1917), pp. xvii-xviii and xxii-xxviii. The relative sharpness of his summary in 1926 perhaps reflects the changed conditions of the times.

[41] The order of the requirements was in Koeping with the decision of the authorities (January 1820) to insist on the philosophical studies of rabbis. See Pribram, *op. cit.*, pp. cxliii-cxliv, n. 354.

[42] The reconciliation of Athens and Jerusalem is, of course, an ancient endeavor of believers touched by the charm of philosophy and Philo Judaeus is, perhaps, their patron hero. For an all-embracing development of the quest note Giovanni Pico della Mirandola's "Oration on the Dignity of Man," transl. E. Livermoore Forbes, introd. by P. O. Kristeller, in *The Renaissance Philosophy of Man*, ed. E. Cassirer, P. O. Kristeller, J. H. Randall, jr., Chicago, 1948, pp. 215-6.

[43] For a refreshingly open-minded re-examination of this tradition, see A. Demandt, *Der Fall Roms: Die Auflösung des römischen Reiches im Urteil der Nachwelt*, Munich, 1984.

[44] Note also the posthumous edition of his chancel orations, I. N. Mannheimer, *Gottesdienstliche Vorträge, gehalten im israelitischen Bethause in Wien*, ed. S. Hammerschlag, Vienna, 1876.

[45] See note 37, *supra*.

[46] *Gottesdienstliche Vorträge über die Wochenabschnitte des Jahres. Gehalten im israelitischen Bethause zu Wien von I. N. Mannheimer*, Vienna, 1835, vol. I, pp. iii-xii.

MOSHE BARASCH

Reflection on Tombstones: Childhood Memories

I should like to introduce these somewhat personal reflections with a word of thanks to Professor Philipp Fehl. It was he who urged me to go back in my mind to my childhood days, and to revive the sense of wonder, a little fear and a strange attraction to the forms I saw in the Jewish cemetery. I hope I may thus be able to pay homage to a culture, past and lost, which, though "primitive" in certain respects, held many hidden treasures and was to me a rich source of inspiration. Often it seems to me that this irrevocably lost culture has not yet received the full attention it deserves. Professor Fehl, it should be gratefully said, also set the particular tone of these reflections, combining what little professional observation I can offer with memories and the sense of a personal involvement. What I should like to present are mainly questions. The answers I unfortunately do not know, and some of them will perhaps never be known. The questions, however, may suggest an abundant creativity concealed behind primitive forms.

The following observations are devoted to a single and rather limited subject: the images found on some of the tombstones in the Jewish cemetery of Czernowitz, the town where I was born and reared. I shall have to rely largely on personal memories, and on stories I heard as a child and adolescent.[1]

Before I start with my reflections I should like, first, to indicate the historical span of time "covered" by the few monuments I have in mind. Czernowitz, located on the eastern slope of the Carpathian mountains, is not one of the very old Jewish communities; in the wealth of its history it cannot compare with the famous Jewish communities of central Europe, like Prague or Worms. This is of course reflected in the

tombstones in the Jewish cemetery. So far as I know, no Jewish funerary monument, either in Czernowitz or in the neighboring communities, precedes the mid-eighteenth century. Most of the "old" tombstones in that region were produced in the early or mid-nineteenth century. My second preliminary remark concerns what we are used to calling the "level of artistic achievement." Not too much should be expected. I shall have to describe the artistic character of the monuments as "primitive," without going into a discussion of what the term means, fully aware that the meaning is far from obvious. We can now turn to our subject proper.

I shall begin with whatever little I know about the social conditions in which the tombstones were produced, and the people producing them lived and worked. I shall then turn to some observations concerning the major artistic components of the monuments themselves.

The first thing that should be noted is that all the tombstones I shall mention are of local production. In Czernowitz there was, of course, no import of tombstones. For the local Jewish community that would have been far too expensive in financial terms and far too difficult in terms of transport. In general, I am not aware of any import or export of Jewish tombstones to or from Eastern Europe in the nineteenth century (though in the twentieth this may have partly changed). Czernowitz was surely not wealthy enough to form an exception. What is more important is that there seems to have been no immigration of highly trained tombstone carvers. It may be dangerous to make any positive, final statement about that fact, but there are no documents hinting in any way at such an immigration, nor have I ever heard any oral reference to such a movement of artisans. The assumption that there was no influx of tombstone carvers agrees well with the rather low esteem in which these craftsmen were held in the Jewish community.

As a type of professional (sometimes, only semi-professional) artisan, these carvers constituted an interesting phenomenon. Both the social conditions of their work and the patterns of what, for want of a better term, we should call their training (that is, how they acquired and transmitted their skills) are worthy of careful study. The tombstone itself was known by its traditional Hebrew name, "Mazewe," and, in my native Yiddish, the carvers were commonly called "Mazewe-Schläger." *Schläger* is a term describing what the carver's activity looks like to an outside observer: it means "hitter" or "striker." In literal translation, the generic name of these carvers would, then, mean "tombstone hitters" or "tombstone strikers." Who were they, and how were they trained?

So far as I could see, the "Mazewe-Schläger," particularly those belonging to the orthodox segment of the community, were not organized in any body, whether of modern or semi-medieval form. The general public, especially in the more orthodox sector, did not regard their occupation as a full-fledged profession. In the nineteenth century — if we are to trust the memories of some of the older survivors of the community — at least some of the carvers were earning their living partly by doing some other jobs. According to oral traditions, the reliability of which I cannot check, these jobs often had something to do with the business of death: I heard stories in my youth about tombstone carvers who worked in the *Hevra kadisha*, the community organization taking care of funerary services; some, I was told, were grave diggers. Later on, owing to a rapidly growing community, tombstone carving became a full-time occupation, even a business.

It goes without saying that there was no formal institution for training tombstone carvers. Originally, the profession seems to have been mainly a matter of family tradition. To be sure, this was partly true also for many other occupations. But, if my childhood impressions do not mislead me, with tombstone carvers this seems to have been the case to a much greater degree than with most other professions. Even after the First World War, two families in downtown Czernowitz, that is, in the part of the city populated mainly by orthodox Jews, still kept alive the tradition of tombstone carving as a genuine family business and occupation. These families, Picker and Steinmetz, had exercised the same profession for several generations. The name of the latter (literally: stone carver) seems hardly accidental (though this was, of course, a common name). Dr. Diamant, the Czernowitz lawyer dedicated to the study of Jewish folklore, knew the last of the Picker family who was still a traditional tombstone carver, and told me about him in my youth. The then already elderly Picker

had acquired his skills by helping his father in the carving of tombstones. It should be noted that, as a rule, tombstone carvers did not carve any other objects, nor did they indulge in any other medium of the visual arts. But the descendant of the Picker family I have just mentioned seems to have been an exception. According to local tradition, some of the wall paintings in the "Groisse Shuhl" (great synagogue) in downtown Czernowitz were done by him.

The profound economic changes that took place during the nineteenth century, needless to say, also affected the tombstone carvers. During most of the century, so the story is told, these carvers did not have a regular "business" of their own; the carving of tombstones was an intermittent activity. Ancient (oral) lore has it that early in the century the family of the deceased would even have to acquire the stone slab themselves and bring it to the carver.[2] The latter would only provide his work, originally done in the own backyard.

In the later nineteenth century, with the growth of the Jewish population in Czernowitz, the conditions of the Mazewe-Schläger changed in all respects. Yet only around the turn of the century did tomb stone carvers physically separate their private homes from the place where they worked, so that the tombstone carver's "workshop" came into being. It was only in the twentieth century that the production of tombstones became a fully commercial enterprise.

II

The artistic treatment of these tombstones is rather modest. The basic shapes of the objects as a whole and of the essential features of their decoration were of course narrowly prescribed by tradition. Yet an attentive observer will enjoy a considerable amount of variation in the shapes and motifs that distinguish between one piece and the other. The process of shaping the traditional Jewish tombstone is essentially focused on two fields: the script, and some decorative motifs (which, in turn, may be divided into purely ornamental patterns, on the one hand, and certain figural motifs, on the other). The varying proportions in which the two basic components are combined circumscribe the formal variations of the tombstones here reviewed.

The script, of course, is always present. Invariably, it plays a primary part in the overall shape of the tombstone, as a rule occupying the major part of the slab's surface. It is the script to which the observer's attention is to be directed. Some of the old tombstones are devoid of any decorative forms except

1) Tombstone of Barukh, son of Shlomo, Czernowitz, 1794.

the tombstone, the greater the significance of the text in its visual configuration.[3] Nevertheless, one has the feeling that in the Jewish tombstones the significance of the text is particularly striking, perhaps more than required by the need to tell who lies there, and more than seems explicable by the primitive conditions of artistic creation. The script is the essential part of what we see when we look at these slabs.

This is not the proper occasion for reflection on the central position of text and lettering in Jewish visual traditions and lore,[4] and on the cult objects used in Jewish rituals throughout the centuries. Obviously, many artistic energies were oriented towards the treating of script. The rather extensive use of microscript in Jewish culture is a good example[5]. The shaping of letters on rather primitive tombstones is another. Humble as the craftsmen who produced these tombstones may have been, their use of lettering deserves our attention.

At first glance it would seem that the tombstone carvers had no room for variation or invention in the lettering they used. Not only is the square shape of the Hebrew letter prescribed, but the difficulty of producing this shape in stone — for obvious reasons, much greater than in writing on parchment — must preclude any deviations from the minimum of forms to be carved. The careful spectator of the lettering on these tombstones is therefore particularly surprised by the variations he finds. To begin with, two types of "writing" in stone are used in these simple artefacts. In most cases the letters are carved into the flat surface of the slab, they are sunk into the stone. In quite a few tombstones, however, the spaces between the letters are sunken. Among the objects here discussed, we already find the second manner (obviously harder to employ) in the early stages. On a tombstone of 1740 [Fig. 2],[6] one of the earliest in the Jewish cemetery of Czernowitz, we have a fine example of projecting script. So far as I know, tombstone carvers in Czernowitz continued throughout the centuries to employ both methods of carving letters.

The shape of the letters also varies. On many of the tombstones the letter is not plainly quadratic and uniform, but frequently shows a fine distinction between verticals, usually more slender, and horizontals, as a rule heavier and bulkier. Sometimes the verticals are slightly indented, giving the letter a certain organic elegance, as can be seen on a rather elaborate tombstone of 1843 [Fig. 3].[7] It is not difficult to detect the origins of the variations in the individual letter shapes, of which I have mentioned only two examples. What we see on the tombstones are not characters constructed in the geometric manner so well known in the history of European art; the carved letters of the tombstones are clearly derived from scripts written with a quilt pen on parchment. They recall, however faintly, a scribe's hand.

for the script itself. Look, for instance, at the tombstone of one Barukh, the son of Shlomo, done in 1794 [Fig. 1]. In most cases, to be sure, the script is topped by a more or less richly decorated field, and framed by ornamental borders. The text, however, remains the essential part of what we see when we look at the tombstone. Now, the tombstone as an art form gives, of course, primary significance to the text. Moreover, one is probably also safe in assuming that the more primitive

2) Tombstone of Meier, son of Jechiel, Czernowitz, 1740.

assumed. How, then, did the refinements of the Hebrew ritual script (as differing from the normal cursive writing) reach the humble stone carvers? Were there alphabetic model books? So far as I am aware, nothing of such model books is known in Czernowitz of the eighteenth and nineteenth centuries. Were the different shapes of letters transmitted from father to son, as part of the craft of carving? We do not know. One would also be curious to know who decided on the type of letters to be used on a given tombstone: was it the customer (whom we would thus assume to have a high degree of awareness in matters of aesthetics and calligraphy) or was it the stonecarver himself? A study of this seemingly rather limited and marginal problem, should it prove at all feasible, would constitute a valuable contribution both to our knowledge of the tradition of crafts and to our understanding of broader aspects of social and cultural life in Jewish communities of that time.

3) **Tombstone of a Young Woman (name not legible), Czernowitz, 1843.**

III

The decorative parts of the tombstones, consisting partly of certain figural motifs, of course attract most of the art historian's attention. Keeping in mind the rather modest quality of these monuments, one's expectations as to what the free exercise of an artist's skill may provide in them should not be too high. The repertory of motifs is indeed limited; for religious reasons no human figure could be portrayed. And yet one is often surprised by the variations invented by popular fantasy and executed by anonymous stone carvers. Since the present observations are of a somewhat personal character, I take the liberty to mention some of those motifs that struck me most, and which may have helped me to focus my iconographic interests.

On Jewish tombstones, as one knows, the depiction of certain animals is rather common. The heraldic lions facing each other are the motif best known in many fields of Jewish folk art, and we find them also in the cemetery in Czernowitz [Fig. 4].[8] Symmetrically arranged birds (probably peacocks) are also found, though less frequently than the lions. I was, and still am, puzzled by the portrayal of a stag, or hart, unmistakably identified by his antlers, on Jewish funerary monuments. Look at the Czernowitz tombstone of 1810 [Fig. 5], where a hart is juxtaposed to a lion, or the tombstone in a nearby small location, produced in 1830 [Fig. 6], where the stag alone dominates the field of decoration.[9] How did the stag get onto the crest of a Jewish tombstone? We of course knew our Psalms, and we remembered the famous verses that played

A modern art historian cannot help wondering how these variations of lettering reached the tombstones. Writing the quadratic script was, as is well known, a highly regarded occupation. The *sofrim*, the scribes, in the way they saw themselves as well as in their intellectual status and social conditions in the community, were far removed from the tombstone carvers, who performed a kind of manual labor. No direct and specific interaction between these two types can be

4) Tombstone of Rivka, daughter of Yehuda, Czernowitz, 1809.

5) Tombstone of Libzie, daughter of Arieh, Czernowitz, 1810.

such and important part in Christian art and imagery of the Middle Ages.

> As the hart panteth after the water brooks
> so panteth my soul after thee, O God.
> My soul thirsteth for God, for the living God:
> when shall I come and appear before God?
>
> (42: 1-2)

But can we really assume that such an iconographic feat — the personification of the soul in the image of a hart — was accepted both among the tombstone carvers and their customers? We are of course familiar with what historians so often claim: that images such as that of the stag form part of a tradition, and that they were employed as such without necessarily evoking a great deal of conscious reflection. The survival of past objects and the tenacity of past images are, no

132

6) Tombstone of Naphtali, son of Joseph, Siret (Bukowina, not far from Czernowitz), 1830.

out how much conscious reflection was taking place in these rather primitive conditions. Whether or not such a study will prove possible, it would seem that the stag's image could not have reached the tombstone without a rather significant amount of iconographic awareness, both among tombstone carvers and the public at large.

In addition, the stag once again raises the question whether model books were available to our craftsmen. How did the stone carver get the model for his beast? It is precisely because the stag is not so common that the question of how the carvers got a model of his image becomes so pointed. The symmetrical lions are found on many ritual objects; they were executed in a great variety of media. We may assume, therefore, that the stone carvers were somehow more familiar with the image, and knew how to execute it on tombstones. If this is indeed so, the same assumption cannot be made for the considerably less well-known image of the hart.

The bird is another motif that holds the student's attention. One cannot but be surprised by the variety of birds found on tombstones in many Jewish cemeteries, including Czernowitz. Differing from the lions, which were cast in the famous pattern of a symmetrical juxtaposition, on Jewish tombstones birds did not attain a typical compositional form that would deeply and inescapably impress itself upon the cultural memory. Birds, therefore, are more complex images. The very significance of the bird on Jewish tombstones raises interesting questions. Why, and in what function, was it represented? Attempts have occasionally been made to describe such a bird on a tombstone as a "Totenvogel."[11] Not many words need be wasted to show that this is an unacceptable reading. Surely, the bird is not rendered here as an image of death, or as a fearful omen. The bird, it is true, is a common feature in funerary art, appearing on sepulchral monuments of many periods and cultures. But, as one knows, in every period it carried different connotations: as a peacock it could have been understood as embodying the beauty and bliss of paradise, as an eagle it could have been read as the "psychopompos," the bird that carries the souls to heaven.[12] The role of the bird as an image of soul is also well known.[13]

In the Jewish cemetery of Czernowitz one finds different birds, and one cannot help attributing to them different meanings. Take, for instance, a tombstone of 1814 on which two big birds, with extended wings and long tails, are symmetrically affronted [Fig. 7], clearly following the pattern of the heraldic lions. Are they peacocks? And what were they originally meant to convey? Other bird images are less heraldic, but they call for interpretation. An art historian will certainly be attracted by the tombstone of a certain Hannah, the daughter of Hayim, who died in 1852. On her tombstone a seven-branched menorah, of rather unusual shape, is carried by

doubt, powerful forces in every present.[10] Artistic traditions, needless to say, have a tangible influence on the creation of every period. Art historians surely do not need to be told that tradition can be a formative force. And, yet, one cannot help asking whether, in our particular case, we are not taking tradition too much for granted. It would be fascinating to revive the intellectual and emotional world of an eighteenth- or nineteenth-century "Mazewe-Schläger" in Czernowitz, to find

7) **Tombstone of Sarah, daughter of Arieh, Czernowitz, 1814.**

8) **Tombstone of Hannah, daughter of Chajim, Czernowitz, 1852.**

a big bird of an equally unconventional character [Fig. 8]. The bird, spreading its wings, does not fly; broadly squatting, it lowers its head (on a rather long neck) and seems to direct its beak towards its own breast. One of course immediately recalls the story of the pelican who herself tears her breast open with her beak, using the blood pouring from the wound to feed her children, or (in another tradition) to revive them. The Christian interpretation of that story is too well known to require any documentation.

Now, it is perhaps not too difficult to imagine how, in the middle of the nineteenth century, an image of the Christian pelican reached an anonymous Jewish stone carver in a community on the eastern slope of the Carpathian mountains. After all, one recalls, in the middle of the nineteenth century reproductions of famous images, in engravings or woodcuts, were available, and common enough to penetrate even the eastern provinces of the Habsburg monarchy. One can also understand how a humble stone carver, endowed by nature with an intuitive understanding of artistic forms, by sheer empathy instantly perceived the expressive character of the famous image. But how are we to understand that he was able to introduce such an image on a tombstone? Tombstones, it need hardly be stressed, are products of an essentially social art. The customers, and the community at large, must have interpreted the image of the bird in a way that could fit into their own cultural consciousness.

An interpretation of the humble monuments I have tried to conjure up holds, it seems to me, the key to an understanding of a complex and rich community life, a life in which images, however modest, had a significant role to play.

[1] Not surprisingly, there seems to be virtually no scholarly literature on this subject. The only attempt to study these monuments, though not in a professional way, was made by a Czernowitz lawyer interested in Jewish folklore, Max Diamant. The little book in which he summed up the studies to which he had devoted much love, *Jüdische Volkskunst*, was ill fated. Printed in Vienna early in 1938, it was confiscated before it could be bound. A few copies, bound in Czernowitz, were distributed by the author (probably late in 1938 or early in 1939). I wonder how many copies (if any) reached libraries in Western Europe or the United States.

[2] I find it very difficult to either verify or contradict this tradition.

[3] Interesting material can be found in Allan I. Ludwig, *Graven Images: New-England Stonecarving and its Symbols, 1650-1815*, Middletown, Connecticut, 1966, which deals primarily with the carving of New-England tombstones. Though the tombstones of New England are richer in carvings than those in Czernowitz, some striking parallels can be discovered.

[4] So far as I know, there is no comprehensive study of this subject. For some fascinating aspects of the problem in medieval history, see Gershom Scholem, ''Der Name Gottes und die Sprachphilosophie der Kabbala,'' reprinted in the author's *Judaica III: Studien zur jüdischen Mystik*, Frankfurt/M, 1973, pp. 7-70, esp. pp. 31 ff.

[5] Microscript, it should be noted, was a form of decoration that could be found in some of the homes of orthodox Jews. I remember in my grandfather's house an image of the Temple in Jerusalem ''drawn'' in microscript.

[6] See Diamant, *op. cit.*, pl. 21.

[7] Diamant, *op. cit.*, pl. 35.

[8] See the tombstone of 1809 in Diamant, *op. cit.*, pl. 28.

[9] Diamant, *op. cit.*, pls. 25, 22.

[10] E. Shils, *Tradition*, Chicago, 1981.

[11] Diamant, *op. cit.*, p. 60.

[12] Though these connotations are well known, I should like to mention, particularly for the eagle, the still interesting investigations by Franz Cummont, ''L'aigle funeraire d'Hierapolis et l'apothéose des empereurs'', in his *Etudes Syriennes*, Paris, 1917, pp. 35-118.

[13] Georg Weicker, *Der Seelenvogel in der alten Literatur und Kunst*, Leipzig, 1902.

JOSEPH MANCA

Renaissance Theater and Hebraic Ritual in Ercole de' Roberti's *Gathering of Manna*

In the early 1490s Ercole de' Roberti painted an altarpiece that consisted of at least four panels: a large *Pietà* and a three-part predella, including a *Last Supper*, *Gathering of Manna*, and *Abraham and Melchizedek* [Figs. 1-4].[1] The altarpiece, which was probably first installed in the Ferrarese church of San Domenico, is redolent of the world of the Este court and events in late fifteenth-century Ferrara. The *Pietà* [Fig. 1], the main panel, includes portraits of Duke Ercole I, on the left, as Nicodemus [cf. Fig. 5], and the Duchess, Eleonora d'Aragona, at the lower right, as an anonymous mourner. Above the portrait of the Duchess is her brother, Alfonso II of Naples, represented as Joseph of Arimathea [cf. Fig. 6].[2] If the altarpiece dates to 1493 or slightly later, it can be hypothesized that the whole altarpiece, in which every scene refers either directly or typologically to the theme of the Body of Christ, was made as a monument to the Duchess, who died in the autumn of 1493 and was buried in an inconspicuous tomb in the monastery of the Corpus Christi. Eleonora had maintained close relations with the church and monastery of the Corpus Christi; she had also been a consistent patron of the public festival of the Corpus Christi and had commissioned and purchased many smaller works of art on the same theme.[3] Roberti's altarpiece would have served as a public and permanent recognition of the Duchess's support for the worship of the Body of Christ.[4]

While the *Last Supper* [Fig. 2] and the *Abraham and Melchizedek* [Fig. 3] also make references to ducal patronage,[5] it is the *Gathering of Manna* [Fig. 4] that is particularly rich in references to Ferrarese culture and the attitudes and achievements of the patron, Ercole I d'Este. The Gathering of Manna was a rare subject at this time; in the fifteenth century it usually appeared only north of the Alps in editions of the *Biblia Pauperum* or *Speculum Humanae Salvationis* as one of the prefigurations of the Last Supper, along with the Meeting of Abraham and Melchizedek.[6] The architecture and perspective in Roberti's *Gathering of Manna* are unusual in medieval and Renaissance representations of the scene, where cruder, haphazardly arranged tents usually appear. The composition of the *Gathering of Manna*, which in its deep and open space is unusual for Roberti, forcibly recalls theater sets as they appeared in Ferrara at the time. During the 1480s and 1490s the first regular, fully-staged performances of secular drama since antiquity appeared in Ferrara, beginning with the *Menaechmi* of Plautus in January, 1486, and continuing with plays by Plautus, Terence, and Ferrarese contemporaries of Roberti, such as the humanist Niccolò da Correggio.[7] The staging of drama continued throughout the reign of Ercole I d'Este, except when financial difficulties and war intervened. The revival of Roman comedy (the Ferrarese had little interest in tragedy) and classically inspired drama by his contemporaries was one of the outstanding cultural achievements of Ercole I. Notices of his staging of classical drama appear in such diverse places as contemporary diaries, court correspondence, the inscription on the Duke's equestrian monument, and Ariosto's *Orlando furioso*.[8] Every performance made the city buzz with excitement, and there was broad involvement from many quarters, from the artists who designed the sets, to the dancers

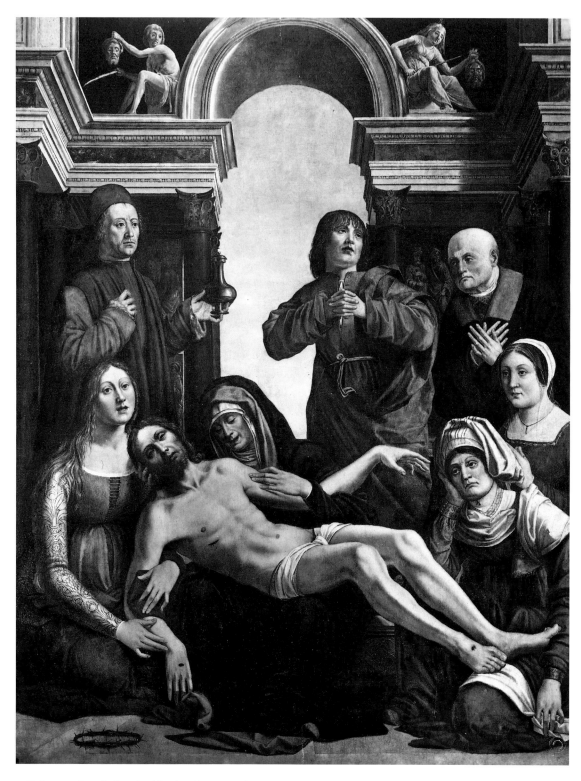

1) Copy after Roberti, «Pietà», Rome, private collection (on deposit at the Galleria Spada, Rome).

2) Ercole de' Roberti, «Last Supper», London, National Gallery.

3) Copy after Roberti, «Abraham and Melchizedek», (formerly) Florence, private collection.

and musicians who played at the *intermezzi*, to the local and foreign courtiers who sat silently in attendance. Thousands of viewers were able to witness each of the performances, which were usually held either outside in a courtyard of the Ducal Palace or in a *salone* of one of the Ferrarese palaces.

The appearance of the stages is known from many sources, including diaries, chronicles, court payment records, and descriptions in contemporary correspondence. Whether the plays were performed inside or out, the stages remained more or less the same. There were usually five or six small painted houses placed in a row across the back, forming the *scena*, and the actors moved in the front on a narrow proscenium.[9] Each of these free-standing huts had one window and one door, from which the actors entered the proscenium. Over the years the stages were designed with such uniformity that in 1502 Isabella d'Este referred to this as the "usual arrangement."[10]

Several factors demonstrate that Roberti's *Gathering of Manna* is a consciously theatrical work. First, the approximate number of the huts and their position behind the planar strip of actors recall the Ferrarese theater sets. There is a disjunction between the figures and the setting, giving the background the passive, decorative appearance that is characteristic for scenic architecture. Moreover, Roberti arranged the huts so that they face the picture plane, rather than the central *piazza*, as would be expected. This arrangement is apparently the same as that

of the Ferrarese theatrical huts, in which a single door in each hut faced the audience.[11] This ''scenic'' orientation of the houses is the same as that used by later designers of stage sets, such as Serlio (*Comic Scene*, 1543; Fig.7), Antonio da Sangallo the Elder (?) (design of ca. 1530, Fig. 8), an anonymous designer of a play in Venice in 1525, and others.[12] The use of huts on Ferrarese stages meant having actors enter and exit a stage from buildings that face an audience; it would have been poor theatrics to have an actor enter the set from the side or back door of a house. In borrowing this scenic solution Roberti gives his *Gathering of Manna* a decidedly theatrical appearance. The use of curtains to cover the doors of the huts also recalls an actual stage practice; this is again an exigency of the theater, where a wooden door would have been inadequate, for it would have allowed the spectators a view into the backstage area. We do not know for certain that in Ferrara curtains were used in plays, but it is likely that they were, for the visual demands of staging required it; moreover, in a contemporary woodcut (Lyons, 1493; Fig. 9) of an imaginative setting of a play by Terence — a rare visual record of a dramatic representation from the period — the actors are shown entering and leaving the *mansiones* through curtains.[13] These factors — the position and number of the huts, their orientation, the strip of actors in the narrow proscenium, and the presence of the curtains — all make Roberti's picture

4) Ercole de' Roberti, «Gathering of Manna», London, National Gallery.

literally scenic; we can presume that Roberti's theater-going contemporaries recognized the conscious theatricality of his painting.

Yet, in its perspectival scheme Roberti's picture recalls not the actual stages of Ferrarese drama, but theoretical reconstructions of Roman *scenae*. Whereas the huts on the Ferrarese stages were probably placed in a flat row, in the *Gathering of Manna* they are pushed back forming a deep *piazza* that foretells the perspectival theater designs of the Cinquecento, such as those of Peruzzi and Serlio [Fig. 7]. This is no coincidence, for the strong theatrical perspective in the Renaissance, whether it appeared in real theaters or in ideal designs, originated in the knowledge that the ancient Romans had made the *frons scenae* in perspective.[14] Roberti would have known of such matters through the Ferrarese court humanist Pellegrino Prisciano, who at about this time wrote a treatise on theater, *Spectacula*, which deals with problems of staging and the archaeological reconstruction of Roman theaters and amphitheaters. Prisciano himself had access to the remarks on theater in the architectural treatises of Vitruvius and Alberti.[15] Vitruvius indicates that the *scenae* of his day were in perspective. In referring to the three types of drama — tragic, comic, and satyric — Vitruvius notes that in comic theater the backdrop should be painted with a *prospectus* ("view") of houses and windows, and in the section on satyric drama he states that the *frons scenae* must represent mountains, trees, rocks, and caves, which could not be accomplished without a perspectival arrangement.[16] The Renaissance interpretations of these brief remarks by Vitruvius form the basis for the nearly universal practice of making theater sets in deep and obvious perspective. As Krautheimer noted, after the mid-fifteenth century "for almost three centuries perspective and stage design became nearly synonymous."[17] Indeed, the first actual (not ideal) theater design painted in perspective was created in Ferrara in 1508 for the performance of a play by Ariosto. But, as regards the fifteenth-century theater sets, practical limitations of space prevented the Ferrarese from placing huts in depth on the stages, while the force of tradition (the previous *sacre rappresentazioni* lacked painted backdrops) kept the Ferrarese from illusionistically painting houses and *piazzas* on their stages. In the *Gathering of Manna,* Roberti was creating,

141

5) Dosso Dossi (?), «Portrait of Ercole I d'Este», detail, Modena, Galleria Estense (perhaps based on a lost original by Ercole de' Roberti).

7) Sebastiano Serlio, design for a «Comic Scene» (woodcut from his *Trattato di architectura* of 1545).

6) Guido Mazzoni, «Pietà, with a Portrait of Alfonso II of Naples», detail, Naples, S. Anna dei Lombardi.

perhaps with the advice of Prisciano, an idealized theater space that, unlike the stage designs of his contemporaries, was in deep perspective and was meant to imitate classical theater settings.

But why did Roberti choose to create a theatrical setting for this particular scene? The answers are found in the ideas that appear in Alberti's and Prisciano's discussions of theater, where several historical and even etymological reasons appear that may have induced Roberti to provide the *Gathering of Manna* with a theatrical setting. Prisciano, who is often thought to be the "ideator" of the iconographic scheme in the *Sala dei mesi* in the Palazzo Schifanoia, was a leading humanist in Ferrara and is known for his active role in the intellectual life at the Este court.[18] It is possible that Prisciano was personally responsible for the spatial invention in Roberti's picture, or at least that he was advising Roberti directly.

In his *Spectacula*, Prisciano remarked that the origins of drama and stage sets are to be found in primitive religious festivals: "Sono adunche alcuni spectaculi ne li quali poeti comici, tragedi, satyrici et simili altri se travalgiano et li loci de questo se chiamano Theatri: perchè si como quelli primi agricoli in li giorni feriali celebravano soi sacrificii a diversi soi dei per boschi, compagne et ville." This echoes a comment that Alberti had already made.[19] The time of the Gathering of Manna occurred during the passage of the Jews across the desert from Egypt into Israel; this time is marked by the Feast of Succoth, the Feast of Tabernacles, for which Jews are

8) Attributed to Antonio da Sangallo the Elder, «Scenic Design», New York, Pierpont Morgan Library (gift of Mrs. Donald Oenslager).

required to build huts as a remembrance of their trial in the desert. Moreover, the Feast of Passover has its origins even more directly in this time of Gathering of Manna. Both of these celebrations would have been known to the Ferrarese from the large Jewish population living in the city.[20] Thus, if Renaissance theorists imagined that rustic religious celebrations were originally acted out as theater, the setting of the *Gathering of Manna* as a theatrical event would have made good historical sense.

The specific event of Succoth can also be connected, through Prisciano's thinking, to the origins of theater. Prisciano knew that the word *scena* in Latin is related to the Greek word for hut, *skene*, and that theaters were so called because of the presence of huts on the stages; he saw the origins of later architectural theaters in crude, rustic stages, and specifically in huts that adorned primitive stages: ''Ma tuto

9) Scene from Terence's *Adelphoe*, French, 1493, woodcut.

143

semper se ornava meravelgiosamente et cohoerivasse sumptuosamente, maxime la scena, se bene da prima si cohoerivasse de fronde de arbori et percio propriamente scena cusi fu nominata *apo tes skenes* che presso greci significa tabernaculo cusi chiamato per farsi umbra: quello li greci chiamano *skene*."[21] Thus the Feast of Tabernacles, *Skenophegia*, or Succoth, would be a particularly apt scene to be rendered as theater since huts, which formed a regular part of the Ferrarese stage decorations, are appropriate to Succoth; and, as already noted, both Succoth and Passover were *giorni feriale* of *primi agricoli*. Note that Roberti's huts are more elaborate than either branchy Succoth huts or Prisciano's imagined rustic structures with *fronde de arbori* of early religious celebrations; the artist has given his huts an architectural and theatrical appearance in order make the scenic nature of the setting clear.

All court artists of the fifteenth century were likely to take every opportunity to pay homage to their employers; this is especially true of Roberti, whose work is documented as having been closely supervised by his Este patrons.[22] There is another reason, perhaps the more important, for believing that the representation of the *Gathering of Manna* is theatrical and is an attempt to flatter Duke Ercole I. Prisciano, in a remark that appears in essential form also in Alberti's discussion of theater (but Prisciano adds the essential and pointed reference to his Duke), notes that just as Moses had brought the people of Israel together into a Brotherhood by having them meet in the temples and at meals in public places, so too did Ercole I unite the citizens of Ferrara by bringing them together in cultured and civilizing gatherings, namely theatrical performances:

> Non tacendo che se Moyse fu lodato, fra le altre excellente cose facte per lui, per haver instituto che in uno templo tuta la gente de soi dovesse convenirse a certi solemni tempi et lie insieme confabulare et mangiare. Et questo a cio che per il convenire insieme, stare, ragionare et cibarsi li animi loro se facessero più miti, più dolci et più prompti e parechiati al fructo de la amicitia. Non mancho nui dovemo laudare vostra Celsitudine [namely, the Duke],

la quale, cum tanti et tanto ordinati spectaculi, congregi questo suo fidissimo et dolce populo; lo delecti, lo amaestri in questo suo mondano vivere, lo inviti al studio et al farsi docti homini ad honore et benefico non mediocre de tuta la Republica.[23]

This remarkable connection of the Duke to Moses makes the connection between the Gathering of Manna and the theater in Ferrara even closer. Indeed, there is a background action in the *Gathering of Manna* that is best explained by this connection between Moses/Duke and theater: hardly necessary for the scene are the background figures of Moses, Aaron, and some Israelites gathering before a temple-shaped hut, which is probably intended to be a kind of forerunner to the "tent of meeting" referred to throughout the book of *Exodus*.[24] Here, then, we have a representation of Moses uniting his people as Prisciano notes that he did, while in the foreground is the staged event of the *Gathering of Manna*. This convivial gathering in the background thus points to the social advantages that result when a leader brings his people together, and this representation would remind Duke Ercole I of his own efforts to bring the Ferrarese together through his sponsorship of theatrical events.

In conclusion, Roberti united several notions in the *Gathering of Manna*: first, that theater originated with early religious festivals such as the Feast of Succoth and Passover; second, that early theaters were originally staged in huts, a practice that is analogous both physically and visually to the celebration of the Feast of Succoth. Finally, Roberti was able to flatter the Duke by reproducing one of the typical Ferrarese stage sets in a painting, which serves as a reference to a major cultural achievement of the Duke. At the same time, Roberti suggests an analogy between the social value of the Duke's patronage of theater and the perspicacity that Moses also revealed. Roberti's depiction of architecture and space as theater thus turns out to be not just a cold and formal borrowing, but a meaningful idea that would have been significant to the artist's contemporaries and, especially, his patron.

---

[1] Of the four pieces, only the *Last Supper* and *Gathering of Manna* are originals; the others are copies. The pictures were all originally on panel; the *Gathering of Manna* was transferred to canvas in the early nineteenth century. I discuss the reconstruction, dating and provenance of the altarpieces in "An altarpiece by Ercole de' Roberti Reconstructed," *The Burlington Magazine*, CXXVII, 1985, pp. 521-524. The predella itself had already been reconstructed by

F. Zeri in "Appunti per Ercole de' Roberti," *Bollettino d'arte*, L, 1965, pp. 72-79. In my reconstruction I was able, given the fact that the *Pietà*'s location was at the time unknown, to make only an estimate of its width, which I deduced from other evidence as being about 20 cm. wider than it actually is. The new information that the panel is 140 cm. wide does not affect my reconstruction of the altarpiece. Yet it now seems possible that the complex consisted of more pieces than the four illustrated here; there were perhaps some small panels of saints along the sides, as in Roberti's earlier Griffoni Altarpiece (see illustrations and reconstructions by R. Longhi, *Officina ferrarese*, Florence, 1956, pp. 43-48 and 155-159, and figs. 59 and 159). It could also have been the case that, if the predella was wider than the *Pietà* overhead, the area on either side of the *Pietà* was occupied by a wide frame instead of painted figures, so that the altarpiece is indeed complete with the four pieces illustrated here. Several other possibilities would explain why the Blumenstihl *Pietà* is slightly wider than the three panels below when laid end-to-end; these are that the *Pietà* was copied in a different scale from the now-lost original, that the copy has been cut down, or that the original *Pietà* was cut down before it was copied. (The predella panels are each about 30 cm. high and 153 cm. long when laid end-to-end, not including the narrow frames that must have separated the *Last Supper* from the two longer predella panels.)

[2] The identification of these figures as portraits has never before been made. For portraits of Eleonora see medals illustrated in G. Hill, *Corpus of Medals of the Renaissance*, London, 1930, nos. 117 and 366. See also a miniature in the Pierpont Morgan Library, illustrated in W. Gundersheimer, *Ferrara: The Style of a Renaissance Despotism*, Princeton, 1973, pl. 14, and Eleonora's portrait in the sculpture group in the Gesù in Ferrara (formerly S. Maria della Rosa) by Guido Mazzoni (see T. Verdon, *The Art of Guido Mazzoni*, New York, 1978, pl. 17). Another portrait of her from ca. 1474 is illustrated in J. Manca, ''Ercole de' Roberti and Baldassare d'Este: Two Portraits in Miniature,'' *Antichità viva*, XXIII, 1984, p. 16.

For portraits of the Duke see Hill, *op. cit.*, 1930, figs. 100, 117, and 364, the portrait in Mazzoni's *Pietà* (Verdon, *op. cit.*, 1978, pl. 16), and the portrait by Dosso Dossi in the Galleria Estense (fig. 5 in this article), perhaps a copy after a lost original by Roberti (see F. Gibbons, *Dosso and Battista Dossi: Court Painters for the Este*, Princeton, 1965, pp. 190-191, and fig. 206); see also the portrait illustrated in Manca, *op. cit.*, 1984, p. 16.

For a discussion of a portrait of Alfonso II, fig. 6 here, see G. Hersey, *Alfonso II and the Artistic Renewal of Naples, 1489-1495*, New Haven, 1969, p. 123 and figs. 169-173 (see his fig. 175, a later portrait of Alfonso by Giorgio Vasari). The group by Mazzoni is in the church of S. Anna dei Lombardi in Naples (formerly S. Maria di Monteoliveto). For illustrations see also Verdon, *op. cit.*, 1978, Figs. 78-81.

[3] Contemporary notices of the Duchess's burial in the monastery of the Corpus Christi appear in B. Zambotti, *Diario ferrarese dall' anno 1476 sino al 1504*, ed. G. Pardi, Bologna, 1934, p. 174, and the anonymous *Diario ferrarese dall'anno 1409 sino al 1502 di autori incerti*, Bologna, 1928, p. 132. Eleonora's interest in the theme of the Corpus Domini is evinced by the large numbers of works on that subject found in her personal collection at the time of her death; the inventory of her pictures is published in G. Campori, *Raccolta di cataloghi ed inventarii inediti*, Modena, 1870, pp. 1-34 *passim*. Other evidence for her support of the public procession of the Corpus Christi and the monastery of the same name appears in the anonymous *Diario ferrarese, op. cit.*, p. 131.

[4] If the idea of an altarpiece serving as a substitute tomb seems strange, it is worth remembering that the *Pietà* commissioned by Alfonso from Mazzoni several years earlier was interpreted by G. Hersey as having a funereal reference, for it contains a portrait of Alfonso as a permanent witness of Christ's Passion, and an inscription on it refers to Alfonso's own death. Hersey notes that the sculpture group ''is the tomb of Alfonso's hopes, and is at the same time his own tomb, at which he himself weeps.'' (See Hersey. *op. cit.*, 1969, p. 124, and illustrations referred to here in fn. 3). Hersey's

interpretation is based largely on inscriptions that accompany the group. The *Pietà* of course immediately suggests itself as a subject made to honor the dead. It was sometimes used as a funeral piece, as in the tomb by Michelangelo in St. Peter's for a French cardinal. Bronzino painted a *Pietà* that was commissioned by Giovanni Battista della Fonte for the tomb of his mother and brother in S. Croce, Florence (see E. Pilliod, ''Bronzino's S. Croce *Pietà*,'' *The Burlington Magazine*, CXXVIII, August, 1986, pp. 577-581).

[5] The *Last Supper* is set in a room that recalls the descriptions of the now-lost interiors of the Ducal Palace; for example, Giovanni Sabadino degli Arienti in 1497 noted ''le cui sale e camere con li cieli ingeniosamente e con egregia arte elaborati de tue arme, insignie e divisie e fronde de ligname relevati, posti richissimamente ad auro fino,'' and the courtyard with the ''pavimento a quadri de candidi e russi marmi,'' which recalls almost exactly the paving in the picture, the gold-decorated walls, and the reliefs (see the full text in W. Gundersheimer, *Art and Life at the Court of Ercole I d'Este: The ''De triumphis religionis'' of Giovanni Sabadino degli Arienti*, Geneva, 1972, pp. 90-91). If this setting of the *Last Supper* in the Estense Ducal Palace seems strange, it ought to be recalled that one day a year, on Maundy Thursday, there was a re-enactment of the Last Supper in the Ducal Palace; thirteen poor men of Ferrara were chosen to act out the main roles and they were served, along with other poor men seated on benches put to the side, by members of the Este family in a great display of pomp, apparent humility, and splendor. This annual ceremony is described at length more than once by the diarist Zambotti (see his p. 272, for example). By thus placing the *Last Supper* in a setting recalling the Ducal Palace, Roberti was certain to flatter the Duke by reminding the viewer of his occasional role as humble servant of the people.

A connection of the *Abraham and Melchizedek* with Ducal interests is also possible. The picture includes a setting that is derived in part from an engraving by Martin Schongauer of the *Intervention of St. James at the Battle of Clavijo* (see C. Minott, *Martin Schongauer*, New York, 1971, pp. 50-52 and illustrations); we know that the Duke was particularly devoted to the Saint and he perhaps sponsored the *sacra rappresentazione* devoted to him in 1476 (see Zambotti, *op. cit.*, p. 11). More importantly the Duke planned a splendid pilgrimage to Santiago de Compostela in 1487, but the Pope cancelled it. The Duke was proud enough of the projected pilgrimage to have the train of followers painted in a large mural in Belfiore, described in detail by Sabadino (see Gundersheimer, *op. cit.*, 1972, p. 69). The event was also described in the anonymous *Diario ferrarese, op. cit.*, p. 123, and in Zambotti, *op. cit.*, p. 184.

[6] The three subjects in Roberti's predella are those of the *Biblia Pauperum*; the *Speculum Humanae Salvationis* added a fourth prefiguration of the Eucharist, the *Sacrifice of the Paschal Lamb*. It is not impossible that the subject of the predella was borrowed from an edition of the *Biblia Pauperum* in the ducal collection, but the inventory of the Duke at this time is not specific enough in its description to allow us to separate editions of the *Biblia Pauperum* from actual Bibles; see G. Bertoni, *La biblioteca estense al tempo di Ercole I d'Este, 1471-1501*, Turin, 1903, *passim*.

M. Davies, National Gallery Catalogues: *The Earlier Italian Schools*, London, 1961, p. 461, and Zeri, *op. cit.*, 1965, p. 78, first noted that the predella subjects are derived from the *Biblia Pauperum*. It is worth adding that the compositions of Roberti's scenes are vaguely related to the arrangements found in the standard edition of the *Biblia Pauperum* of the 15th century; see Manca, *op. cit.*, 1985, p. 522, and comparative illustrations in H. Cornell, *Biblia Pauperum*, Stockholm, 1925, *passim*, and in G. Schmidt, *Die Armenbibel des XIV. Jahr-*

hunderts, Cologne, 1959, *passim*. See also E. Soltesz, *Biblia Pauperum: Facsimile Edition of the Forty-Leaf Blockbook in the Library of the Esztergom Cathedral*, Budapest, 1967.

[7] For the history of theater in Ferrara the best source for documented evidence is still P. d'Ancona, *Origini del teatro italiano*, Turin, 1891, II, pp. 124-136, with a summary of the evidence. Of the many studies of the history of drama in Italy the most helpful are the ones that contain specific studies of Ferrarese theater: L. Zorzi, *Il teatro e la città: Saggi sulla scena italiana*, Turin, 1977, especially pp. 10-50, in Ch. 1, and N. Pirrotti, *Li due Orfei: Da Poliziano a Monteverdi*, Turin, 1969, pp. 357-371. The essential, immediate references from contemporary diarists appear in Zambotti, *op. cit.*, *passim*, and the anonymous *Diario ferrarese*, *op. cit.*, (see the index). Also of use is the study by E. Povoledo, "Las Sala teatrale a Ferrara: Da Pellegrino da Prisciano a Ludovico Ariosto," *Bollettino del Centro Internazionale di Studi di Architettura, Andrea Palladio*, XVI, 1974, pp. 105-138. See also A. Beijer, "An Early Sixteenth-Century Scenic Design in the National Museum, Stockholm, and its Historical Background," *Theatre Research*, IV, 1960, n. 1, pp. 85-155. Povoledo notes the theatricality of Roberti's *Gathering of Manna*, but ascribes it not to the influence of perspectival theater design, but to an attitude toward spatial representation that would itself later bring about the perspectival stages of the early Cinquecento. This suggestion does not give enough recognition to the knowledge that, even if illusionistic and deep scenic design had not yet been carried out on actual stages in the 1490s, it was known by Alberti, Prisciano, and others that the ancients did make their stages in deep perspective; Roberti's picture precedes the *all'antica* stages of the Cinquecento because the knowledge that inspired the design of sixteenth-century stages was already available to Roberti.

[8] For the line of Ariosto see *Orlando furioso*, III, XLVIII; for the inscription on the Duke's equestrian monument see D. Zaccarini, "Il disegno di Ercole Grandi per il monumento ad Ercole I d'Este," *L'arte*, XX, 1917, p. 160: "Antiquorum comedias, ad veteris scene modos, astusque regulit, plurimoque ad spectatorum illaritatem inusitato sumptuosque paratu actibus interposuit." The importance of the theater is attested by the frequent and thorough discussions of the Ferrarese diarists Zambotti and the anonymous *Diario ferrarese* (see their indices).

[9] The *Diario ferrarese*, *op. cit.*, p. 121 describes the stage thus: "[...] fu facta suxo uno tribunale de legname, con caxe V merlade con una fenestra et uso per ciascuna." Zambotti, *op. cit.*, similarly notes (pp. 171-172) for the January, 1486 play: "Fu recitata la comedia di Menichini suxo uno tribunale novo in forma de una citade de asse con daxe dipinte," and the next year (p. 178) as "suxo uno tribunale de legno e d'asse depinto cum caxe in fogia de castello e citade." (To fit the story, Roberti had to paint rustic huts, and his do not imitate in their decoration the painted, crenellated little houses that were on the Ferrarese stages). The stages, depending on whether they were set up in the courtyard of the Palazzo Ducale or in a *salone* inside the palace, seem to have been between 25 or 30 m. wide and only about 5 m. deep at most; the huts were perhaps 3 by 3 m.; for the calculation of the size of the stages and of the huts see Povoledo, *op. cit.*, 1974, p. 113, and Pirrotti, *op. cit.*, 1963, p. 364. For numerous other contemporary descriptions of the stages in Ferrara of the 1480s and 1490s see the literature cited in note 7 above.

[10] Isabella's letter of 1502 is cited from d'Ancona, *op. cit.*, 1891, p. 134. Isabella noted that the huts were "non avantagiate del consueto," that is, that the usual arrangement was not being used.

[11] The descriptions in the diaries again note that the "finestre e usci" were on each hut, obviously facing the spectators. This similar arrangement appears in a later visual record of a *sacra rappresentazione* in Valenciennes in 1547; see E. Königson, *La représentation d'un mystère de la Passion à Valenciennes en 1547*, Paris, 1969. This strip arrangement is equally characteristic of sacred plays, where the stage exigencies are the same.

A scene of the city of Rome in the month of September in the Hall of the Months in the Palazzo Schifanoia contains a row of Roman buildings in a strip and a crenellated wall in the foreground; Zorzi, *op. cit.*, 1977, p. 24, regards this arrangement as having been made *in imitatione antiquitatis* and ideated by Prisciano himself. Whatever the merits of the arguments of Zorzi, who states that Prisciano had by this time full knowledge of antique stage design, the planar arrangement in this view of Rome probably reflects the appearance of contemporary sacred plays. This view of Rome, which like the rest of the fresco has been continuously and erroneously attributed to Roberti, does not necessarily represent classical staging; the arrangement could equally reflect sacred plays, which were customarily staged with a strip of small structures in a plane across a shallow stage. Roberti's *Miracles of St. Vincent Ferrer*, the predella panel of the Griffoni Altarpiece (Vatican, Pinacoteca), has been connected convincingly with this sacred play arrangement by B. Rutledge, "The Theatrical Art of the Italian Renaissance," Ph.D. Diss., University of Michigan, 1973, pp. 45-46; for illustrations see E. Ruhmer, *Francesco del Cossa*, Munich, 1959, fig. 62, and M. Salmi, *Ercole de' Roberti*, Milan, 1961, fig. 9. This predella, like the view of Rome in Schifanoia, also contains houses in a row facing the viewer. Indeed, that arrangement displays the differences between the later *Gathering of Manna*, which in its perspective is of classical inspiration, and the Griffoni predella, which is apparently based on contemporary religious drama.

[12] See Zorzi, *op. cit.*, 1977, for illustrations (fig. 56) and discussion of the Venetian design for the *Betia* of Ruzante (fig. 120). Zorzi, who attributed Fig. 8 of this article to Bastiano da Sangallo, incorrectly stated that it forms part of the collection of the University of Madison, Wisconsin (Elvehjem Art Center). The drawing was once on loan there for an exhibition; it was given by Mrs. Donald M. Oenslager to the Pierpont Morgan Library (n. 1982.75:600). It has also been attributed to Aristotile da Sangallo.

[13] Published in Lyons in 1493 by Joannes Trechel; see T. E. Lawrenson and H. Purkis, "Les éditions illustrées de Terence dans l'histoire du théâtre," in *Le lieu théâtral à la Renaissance*, Paris, 1964 (ed. J. Jacquot), pp. 1-23. They conclude that the woodcuts of 1493 were not reflections of real theaters, but were imaginary settings; the sets must have combined some actual practices used in staging *sacre rappresentazioni* with imaginative theatrics of the designer's own invention.

[14] See Vitruvius, *De architectura* (ed. F. Krohn), Leipzig, 1912.

For the effect of Vitruvius's writings on 16th-century stage design see R. Klein and H. Zerner, "Vitruve et le théâtre del la Renaissance italienne," in *Le lieu théâtral à la Renaissance*, *op. cit.*, pp. 49-60. For the identification of perspective and stage design see also D. Rosand, "Theater and Structure in the Art of Veronese," *Art Bulletin*, LV, 1973, pp. 220-228. Rosand emphasizes the misreading of Vitruvius by Cinquecento stage designers (see especially his p. 221: "Concentrating on the scenic decor, which played a minor role in Vitruvius, dissociating it from the rest of the theater, and magnifying it out of all proportion to its original context, Renaissance artists initiated the development of the modern stage.")

The essential piece of knowledge that led to the representation of theater in perspective is the Romans' practice of using a painted *frons scenae*; both Prisciano and Alberti, in their discussions of ancient *scenae*, reveal that they knew that Roman stages were painted illusionistically.

[15] For information on Prisciano's manuscript see note 18.

[16] See Vitruvius, *op. cit.*, V, 6, 9, as in note 14: "genera autem sunt scaenarum tria: unum quod dicitur tragicum, alterum comicum, tertium satyricum. Horum autem ornatus sunt inter se dissimili disparique ratione, quod tragicae deformantur columnis et fastigiis et signis reliquisque regalibus rebus: comicae autem aedificiorum privatorum et maenianorum habent speciem prospectusque fenestris dispositos imitatione, communium aedificiorum retionibus; satyricae vero ornatur arboribus, speluncis, montibuus reliquisque agrestibus rebus in topeodis speciem deformati."

[17] From R. Krautheimer, "The Tragic and Comic Scene of the Renaissance," in *Studies in Early Christian, Medieval, and Renaissance Art*, New York, 1960, pp. 345-360.

[18] For a biography of Prisciano see A. Rotondo, "Pellegrino Prisciano," *Rinascimento*, IX, 1960, pp. 69-110. That Prisciano was an adviser at the Hall of the Months project in 1469 is deduced from the notice of Francesco del Cossa that he was to consult Prisciano about the payment. Cossa's letter, dated 25 March 1470, is transcribed in Ruhmer, *op. cit.*, 1959, p. 48. That Prisciano had a role as iconographic adviser for the Hall of the Months project was first argued by A. Warburg, "Italienische Kunst und internationale Astrologie im Palazzo Schifanoia zu Ferrara," in *L'Italia e l'arte straniera. Atti del X congresso internazionale di storia dell'arte, 1912*, Rome, 1922, pp. 179-193.

The manuscript of the *Spectacula* is in the Biblioteca Estense, Modena, Lat. 466 (a.x.1.6), and comprises *carte* 17 to 40. A full transcription, except for the Latin prologue, is found in F. Marotti, *Storia documentaria del teatro italiano: Lo spettacolo dall'Umanismo al manierismo*, Milan, 1977, pp. 53-77. See also the study by G. Ferrari, "Il manoscritto *Spectacula* di Pellegrino Prisciano," *La corte e lo spazio: Ferrara estense* (eds. G. Papagno and A. Quondam), II, 1982, pp. 431-449.

It is not absolutely certain that Prisciano had finished his treatise at the time of the making of the San Domenico Altarpiece. The *Spectacula* is datable to between 1486 and 1501. Even if it was not yet finished by the early 1490s, Prisciano had probably already formulated the ideas expressed in it, and he could have shared his thoughts with Roberti. In any case, most of the salient features of the history of Roman theater were already well known through Alberti's and Vitruvius's treatises on architecture, both of which were available even before the 1490s. As regards the date of the *Spectacula*, it is worth nothing that when Prisciano went to Rome in 1501 as an ambassador he had the chance to re-study Roman monuments at close hand; this trip of 1501 apparently led him to include several marginal notes in the manuscript. This suggests that the first, unannotated manuscript was written before 1501. His remark in the prologue that he had to put other Ferrarese things aside, namely his history of Ferrara (*Historiae Ferrariae*, Modena, Biblioteca Estense, a.L.5.16), suggests that the *Spectacula* dates from the 1490s, the presumed time of the *Historiae Ferrariae*. For a full discussion of the date of the *Spectacula*

see Ferrari, *op. cit.*, 1982, pp. 441-442.

[19] Prisciano's *Spectacula* (ed. Marotti), p. 55. Here Prisciano was specifically referring to Greek theater, but the principle can be extended to other primitive peoples, especially the Jews, for reasons noted in the following paragraphs in the text.

[20] Succoth was the first place where the Jews stopped after their departure from Egypt (see *Genesis* 33:17, *Exodus* 12:37 and 13:20, and *Numbers* 33:5). For references to the Feast of Succoth see *Exodus* 16:13. For the story of the Gathering of Manna see *Leviticus* XXIII:43, on the injunction to celebrate the passage by building huts: "You shall dwell in booths for 7 days [...] that your generations may know that I made the people of Israel dwell in booths when I brought them out of the land of Egypt." Creighton Gilbert first suggested to me that the huts in Roberti's *Gathering of Manna* are reminiscent of Succoth booths. Good background on the meaning and context of the Feast of Succoth in the Renaissance appears in J. Fleming, *From Bonaventura to Bellini: An Essay in Franciscan Exegesis*, Princeton, 1982, in his chapter on references to Succoth in Giovanni Bellini's Frick *Saint Francis*. For the meaning of the Feast in later thought see J. Danielou, *The Bible and the Liturgy*, Notre Dame, 1956, pp. 333-347.

[21] Prisciano, *op. cit.*, p. 63. According to H. Liddel and R. Scott's *Greek-English Lexikon*, skene means: 1. A covered, sheltered place; 2. a tent or booth; 3. a wooden stage for actors. The Greek for Succoth is skenophegia. The word skenikos means scenic, of the stage. The Latin scena (or scaena) means, according to the *Oxford Latin Dictionary* (Oxford, 1982), the background against which a play is performed, or the platform on which actors perform, namely the stage.

[22] In 1493 a ducal secretary reported in a letter that the Duke was spending every day from early morning until evening for weeks on end seated across from Ercole de' Roberti, who was busy making cartoons for a fresco cycle to be painted in the Este villa of Belriguardo; for a discussion of the letter see W. Gundersheimer, "The Patronage of Ercole I d'Este," *Journal of Medieval and Renaissance Studies*, 6, 1976, pp. 1-18. In 1494 it is documented that Roberti, while decorating a small room in an Este palace, had prince Alfonso d'Este constantly by his side; see G. Campori, "I pittori degli Estensi nel secolo XV," in *Atti e memorie delle RR. deputazioni di storia patria per le provincie modenesi e parmesi*, 3, III, part II, 1886, p. 573.

[23] Prisciano, *op. cit.*, p. 54. For the similar line of Alberti, which apparently was the source for Prisciano, see Alberti's *De re aedificatoria*, Milan, 1966 (ed. P. Portoghesi), p. 724, where Alberti also refers to the gathering together of the people by Moses in order to make them friendlier and more sociable. Alberti does not compare Moses to any fifteenth-century ruler in this connection, unlike Prisciano, who draws parallels between the Duke of Ferrara and Moses.

[24] As far as I know, this scene does not appear in the early edition of the *Biblia Pauperum* from which this is drawn, nor does it appear in later Renaissance version of the subject. It seems to be an original representation, one intended for a specific occasion and patron.

JACK WASSERMAN

Observations on Two Statues in the Museo dell'Opera del Duomo and the Porta della Mandorla in Florence[1]

In 1904 Giovanni Poggi for the first time connected the two beautiful and enigmatic statues in the Museo dell'Opera in Florence [Figs. 1 and 2] with the lunette of the Duomo's Porta della Mandorla [Fig. 3].[2] His hypothesis took hold immediately and is today unchallenged,[3] despite the absence of a provenance for the statues prior to 1884.[4] The reasons for its endurance are several: the existence of documents dating 1409 and 1414 that refer to an *Annunciation* group in relation to the lunette,[5] the apparent iconography of the museum statues as an *Annunciation*, the presence of the statues in the collection of the Opera del Duomo, and their general dating in the first years of the Quattrocento, when the Porta della Mandorla was under construction.[6] This is not to say that Poggi's hypothesis has been immune to controversy,[7] but its critics have been very few, largely ignored, and silent in the past quarter century. Since I am convinced that the critics are right, it is the purpose of this paper to reopen the controversy by examining very closely the physical structures of the statues as a technique for demonstrating that they were not created for the lunette. Two standard and familiar components of fourteenth- and fifteenth-century sculpture are the points of departure for my discussion. First, as architectural decoration, statues are aligned in profile or else face the beholder directly; second, their principal and subsidiary views are systematically framed by drapery folds, limbs, and, in the case of angels, also

wings. The paper concludes with speculations on the actual sites of the statues and on the missing *Annunciation* group that did occupy the lunette of the Porta della Mandorla.

I

The physical structures of the museum statues show that they were planned to be seen panoramically.[8] The Virgin, for example, although its frontal plane is defined in the orthodox manner, has a second, oblique view on the left. This one is established by the turn of the head and advanced leg [Fig. 4]. It is worth noting that from this direction a distortion in the raised right arm, evident when the statue is seen from the front, is eliminated. Still another oblique view is visible on the opposite side of the figure, where embroidered volumes of folds complement each other synchronously [Fig. 5]. Thus far, there is nothing exceptional in the structure of the statue. The decisive factor is the neat sectioning of the back into two vertical areas [Fig. 6]. One area is rough and appears to echo the shape of the architectural member to which the statue was anchored, evidently a broad pier set on a wider base. The contact between the Virgin and the architectural support is further reflected in the abruptness with which the figure is terminated on the left side [Fig. 7]. The other area of the back,

149

1) «Angel Gabriel». Florence, Museo dell'Opera (Photo: Soprintendenza per i Beni Artistici e Storici).

2) «Virgin Annunciate» (?). Florence, Museo dell'Opera (Photo: Soprintendenza per i Beni Artistici e Storici).

3) Duomo, Porta della Mandorla, Florence (Photo: Author).

whose detailed folds are continuous around the statue [Fig. 5], was, instead, expected to be observed by the beholder. It should be noted that the distinct division of the back into finished and unfinished, seen and unseen sections is carried over into the embroidery of the garment beneath the head [Fig. 8], as well as into the hair at the nape of the neck and the headband [Figs. 9 and 10]. The calculated treatment of the statue in this manner belies a relationship with the lunette of the Porta della Mandorla.

Like the Virgin, the Angel Gabriel has a frontal posture [Fig. 1]: with one foot moved boldly to the side, the statue initiates an opposing motion that is fulfilled in the arm across the breast and in the turn of the head towards right. But when

4) «Virgin Annunciate» (?) (left side). Florence, Museo dell' Opera. (Photo: Soprintendenza per i Beni Artistici e Storici).

151

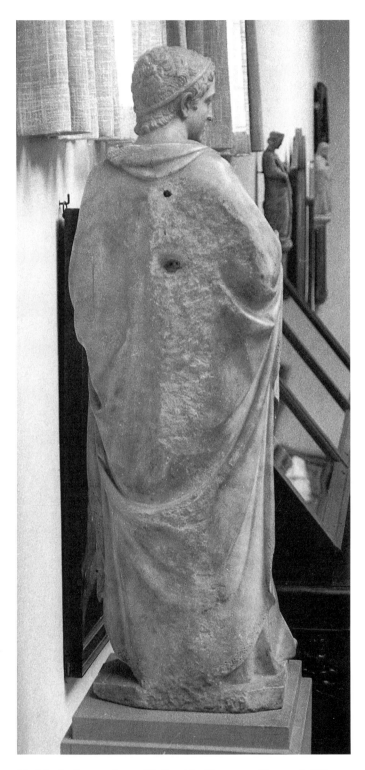

5) «Virgin Annunciate» (?) (right side). Florence, Museo dell'
Opera (Photo: Soprintendenza per i Beni Artistici e Storici).

6) «Virgin Annunciate» (?) (back). Florence, Museo dell'Opera
(Photo: Author).

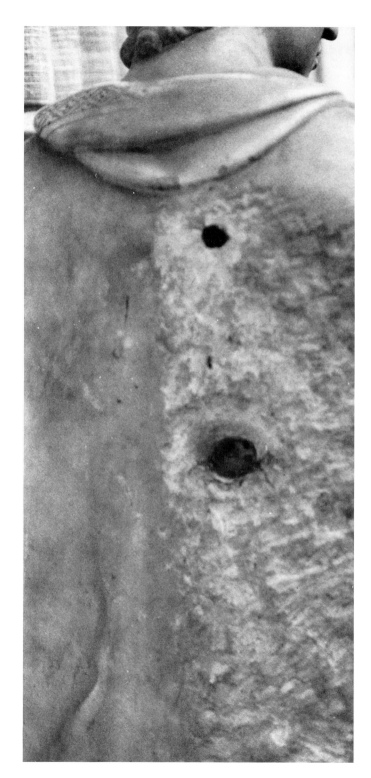

7) «Virgin Annunciate» (?) (left side). Florence, Museo dell' Opera (Photo: Author).

8) «Virgin Annunciate» (?) (back; detail). Florence, Museo dell'Opera (Photo: Author).

9) «Virgin Annunciate» (?) (head; from front). Florence, Museo dell'Opera (Photo: Kunsthistorisches Institut Florenz).

10) «Virgin Annunciate» (?) (head; from rear). Florence, Museo dell'Opera (Photo: Kunsthistorisches Institut Florenz).

viewed from this position the arm seems awkward and its forward action slackened by the heavy sleeve of the garment that sags to form a descending pattern with the arched folds along the left side of the body. The pattern reinforces a contradiction that is evident between the movement of the leg in one direction (leftward) and the reaching arm and turn of the head in the opposite direction (rightward). Furthermore, the folds at the body that bend without interruption around to the rear of the figure contrast radically with those on the other side: these instead hang vertically from the arm, spread widely akimbo. The two sets of folds would seem to have antithetical functions: on the one hand, to assert the body's volume; on the other hand, to enclose and make evident the surface plane.

Therefore, the assumption that the angel had primarily a frontal pose is compromised and can be reclaimed only were it provided with wings that flank the torso symmetrically.

Unfortunately, the wings are lost, but we can judge that they were not arranged that way from the markedly off-center placement of the wing cavities in back [Fig. 11], one of them located just below the head. This curious treatment of the cavities, with the consequent lateral displacement of the wings, creates an essential problem of intention, since the sculptor could easily have spaced them equidistant on either side of the spinal axis.[9] The clue to resolving the problem is contained in the cavity situated below the head. It is inserted into the marble exactly at the upper end of a long and clearly cut ridge [Fig. 12] that methodically divides the back into a rough area and a narrower one containing the well-defined drapery folds that have entered from the front. This concurrence of cavity and ridge cannot be a coincidence, and I would surmise that the wing in the cavity had overlapped the ridge and had followed its descent to the leg. Consequently,

154

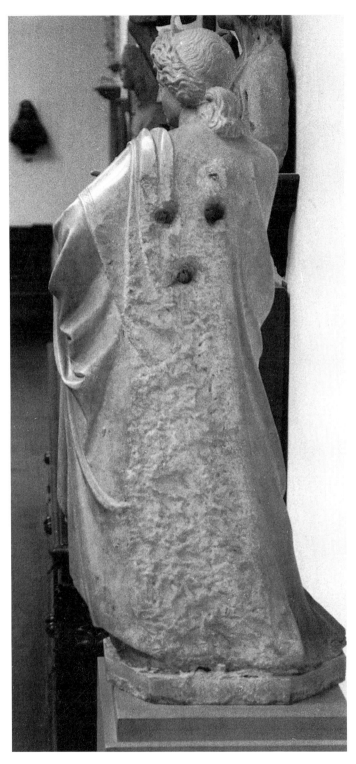

11) «Angel Gabriel» (back). Florence, Museo dell'Opera (Photo: Author).

12) «Angel Gabriel» (back; detail). Florence, Museo dell'Opera (Photo: Author).

the wing must have been perpendicular to the back,[10] in which position it could be paired with the drapery hanging over the arm on the right to frame the visible extent of the statue, continuing from behind, around the side, and along its entire frontal plane.

The construction of the angel is unique and requires an uncommon way of presenting it to the beholder. The fact that the statue was carved to have multiple views might imply a disposition comparable to that of the Virgin [Fig. 2]. Actually, however, the two figures have to be experienced differently because the Virgin has four visible sides and the angel only three. To be sure, a fourth area on the right side of the angel was also worked by the sculptor [Fig. 13], but less precisely,

14) «Angel Gabriel» (detail of drapery on right). Florence, Museo dell'Opera (Photo: Author).

13) «Angel Gabriel» (right side). Florence, Museo dell'Opera (Photo: Kunsthistorisches Institut Florenz).

15) «Angel Gabriel» (detail of drapery on left). Florence, Museo dell'Opera (Photo: Author).

16) Jacopo di Piero Guidi, «Angel Gabriel». Florence, Duomo, Porta del Campanile.

17) Verrocchio, «Doubting of Thomas». Florence, Or San Michele (Photo: Soprintendenza per i Beni Artistici e Storici).

18) Verrocchio, «Doubting of Thomas» (from left). Florence, Or San Michele (Photo: Soprintendenza per i Beni Artistici e Storici).

and so, in accordance with workshop practice, it was not intended to be visible. Note, for example, the detail of the embroidery of the angel's hem, which suddenly turns schematic and disappears altogether [Fig. 14], whereas on the opposite side the embroidery is consistently in focus [Fig. 15]. Now, the position one might conjecture for the angel should satisfy the condition that the full extent of the body, from the wing in back to the drapery hanging over the left arm, is seen simultaneously. One possibility is the profile position with the extended foot in the foreground, as in a late fourteenth-century Angel Gabriel from the Duomo's Porta del Campanile [Fig. 16]. But in the case of the Campanile angel, the body is typically contracted into a relief-like configuration that makes it conform to the frontal plane of the containing tabernacle. The museum angel, on the other hand, is conceived three-dimensionally. Therefore, in full profile its body in front would b e nearly invisible to the beholder. One can conclude that a modified version of the profile position, angled to be slightly oblique, is more suitable for the statue.

In view of the fact that the angel cannot be properly photographed in the Museo dell'Opera, I shall illustrate the position I am proposing with another work that is also part of an exceptional group composition: Andrea del Verrocchio's St. Thomas from the *Doubting of Thomas* at Or San Michele in Florence [Fig. 17].[11] Standing at the edge of a niche, the saint turns inward at a slightly oblique angle to face Christ, leaving a part of the back exposed [Fig. 18]. At this point, I might raise the question of how we would imagine St. Thomas deployed in a site, were it encountered in a museum undocumented. The answer, I believe, would consist largely of the same design characteristics that define the structure of the angel [Figs. 19 and 1]: the pronounced contrapposto, the restrained movement of the arm at the breast, the turn of the head towards right, and the dichotomous treatment of drapery folds. Like the angel, St. Thomas is a three-dimensional statue whose vertical folds on the right confirm its frontal plane, while those on the left arch around the back to establish its volume. Moreover, St. Thomas's visible surface, which in the niche ends in back at a colonnette instead of a wing, is apprehended simultaneously with the body in front [Fig. 17]. Therefore, if the treatment of surface, gesture, and drapery are the products of St. Thomas's deployment in his site, then, by inference, the same treatment of these elements should confirm a comparable disposition for the angel, even allowing for the different themes, the individual personalities of the sculptors, and the seventy critical years that separate the statues. Implied in this conclusion is the direct influence of the earlier work on the St. Thomas, since Verrocchio must have investigated *Annunciation* statuary in the difficult task he faced of adapting his group to a niche that was originally designed for a single statue.[12]

To summarize, the position I am proposing for the angel is determined by the asymmetrical grouping of the wings, which diminishes the primacy of the frontal plane, and by drapery folds that coordinate the front, the left side, a portion of the back, and the nearest wing into an integrated visual experience. To these elements should be added the very noticeable push of the right leg to the side, whose intention, as in Verrocchio's St. Thomas, is to attract and guide the eye of the beholder along the arched folds, the arm at the breast, and the turned head towards the statue's compositional companion. The inevitable conclusion is that the angel, like the Virgin, was intended for a site other than the lunette of the Porta della Mandorla. For that matter, the physical space of the lunette is inadequate to contain the figure, even in frontal position. The depth of the socle strip, whose dimensions I record here for the first time, is 29 cm, to which about 4 cm should be added for the space taken up by the late fifteenth-century mosaic, for a total of approximately 33 cm. The angel, on the other hand, measures 33.6 cm,[13] to which a considerable number of centimeters should be added for the lost wings.[14]

II

My analysis of the two museum statues paves the way to still another conclusion, that they were not conceived as a single group. For instance, comparison with Verrocchio's *Doubting of Thomas* indicates that the angel requires a narrative companion who turns to face it, as Christ does the saint. But the Virgin's attention is directed sideways: therefore, were it displayed as Christ is, it would look away from, and thus be psychologically uncoordinated with, the angel. Moreover, as Claudia Freytag suggested,[15] there is reason to doubt the identity of the Virgin, in which case the two figures are without iconographical coordination as well. Freytag noted the masculinity of the statue's face [Figs. 9 and 10] and the "uncommon garment, which is furnished with a hood in back ... reminiscent rather of representations of Deacons" [Fig. 8]. To be sure, other scholars before her had commented on the anomaly of the head, stressing in particular the masculinity of the hairdo,[16] but no one took the decisive step she did. Nor, for that matter, has anyone since, perhaps because her discussion lacks systematic analysis. Still, the hairdo is unquestionably masculine: closely cropped and arranged in overlapping ringlets, it appears in statues and portrait busts of men (never of women) since at least fifth century B.C. Greece,[17] and it was adopted by such fifteenth-century sculptors as Donatello for the marble *David* and Nanni

19) Verrocchio, «Doubting of Thomas» (from right). Florence, Or San Michele (Photo: Author).

159

20) «Virgin Annunciate» (?) (detail). Florence, Museo dell' Opera (Photo: Author).

21) «Angel Gabriel» (detail). Florence, Museo dell'Opera (Photo: Author).

22) »Angel Gabriel» (detail). Florence, Museo dell'Opera (Photo: Author).

di Banco for the *Isaiah*. In addition to the masculinity of the hairdo, the statue displays the qualities of self-possession, which we traditionally associate with men. These are the effects of the firm set of the head, the erect body, and the oratorically advanced leg.[18] Therefore, Freytag's attempt to change the sex of the statue is well-grounded, but the identity she gives it as a deacon is not, because the garment, although common to male saints,[19] is not the dalmatic. Tentatively, I would identify the statue as St. John the Evangelist. Its raised right hand, the turn of the head, and the book in the other hand (all frequently the attributes of the Virgin Annunciate and, incidentally, also of male saints), as well as the figure's slender, youthful, and beardless aspect are sometimes his.[20]

The angel's base is a final reason for divorcing the two statues because it was consciously and drastically altered to resemble that of the "Virgin." Both bases as we see them today are octagonal and articulated horizontally by flat and curved zones, but this similarity hides important differences. For instance, the base of the "Virgin" is refined and delicate and it shares a rectangular outline with the figure; the angel's base is rough and heavy in proportions and its contours are separate from those that enclose the body's sway and hanging drapery on the right. A more significant difference is found in the folds at the feet. The "Virgin's" [Fig. 20] are attached directly to the base, whereas the angel's adhere entirely to an intermediary surface [Fig. 21], indicating that the octagonal base was an addition. In fact, its *post factum* character was surreptitiously disguised by adapting it in front to an upward curve in the intermediary surface, a deception time has revealed in the form of a crude seam that has developed all around the statue exactly where the new base and the intermediary surface meet [Fig. 22]. It is obvious that this surface was the original base and that it had once an undulating shape, perhaps even representing a cloud.[21]

III

Since the museum statues are compositionally and iconographically independent of each other, it is easy to come to the conclusion that they were conceived for separate sites, which, however, were probably part of a single architectural framework. On the other hand, the identities of the sites are not easy to establish, owing to the absence of documentation.[22] Under the circumstances, I shall merely describe certain minimum requirements they should have.

Reference has been made above to the several viewpoints that characterize the so-called Virgin and to its having been anchored to a broad pier that permitted part of the back to be visible. As the figure apparently is conceived in active rapport

comparable structure, the ''Virgin'' should be located well above head level, from which position [Fig. 23] its long torso would be adjusted proportionately to the observer's eye and the distortions of its elongated upper left arm and aborted forearm visually corrected.[25]

As regards the angel, we noted earlier that it should be deployed in a site nearly in profile with a Virgin Mary facing it.[26] An example of an *Annunciation* arranged in this manner is a thirteenth-century group occupying two adjacent tabernacles on the west portal of the Cathedral of Santa Maria, in Burgos, Spain [Fig. 24].[27] The angel there is somewhat similar to ours in the general form of the drapery and in posture, but it was meant to be seen from two sides only, front and side. Moreover, its wings are symmetrical, which reinforces the frontal plane, and they are small elevated elements that require no significant additional space. Still, using this group and Verrocchio's *Doubting of Thomas* as guides, we might propose as a suitable site for our angel, and for the Virgin with which he was originally paired, a deep niche or, more likely, two ample tabernacles placed at right angles to each other, the angel's unencumbered by a wall in order to make room for its wings. As for the framework that encompassed the angel's site, and also that of the ''Virgin'' in the Museo dell'Opera, two possibilities may be mentioned. One is the facade of the Duomo;[28] the other, and more likely one, a structure inside the Duomo: an altar, tomb, or chapel.[29]

I am aware that my discussion of sites is inconclusive, but the angel and the ''Virgin'' are not the only statues in the Museo dell'Opera one does not know what to do with. For example, two statuettes by Andrea Pisano, believed to represent the Redeemer and Saint Reparata, are also without known locations.[30] In fact, when they were brought to public attention in 1870, the facade or some unidentified altar in the interior of the Duomo were proposed as possible alternative sites.[31]

IV

Be that as it may, my hope is that the primary goal of this study has had a positive issue, namely the liberation of the statues from Poggi's hypothesis, which has tied them for generations to the Porta della Mandorla. If so, then the *Annunciation* group that originally did occupy the lunette has to be reconsidered. But since the group is missing and the documents do not describe it,[32] I can do no more than speculate on its composition. Before proceeding, I should point out that the subject of the Annunciation never appears independently in lunettes; thus there is no model on which to base a reconstruction of the composition. Furthermore, only two figures are required to tell the story, whereas the number of

23) «Virgin Annunciate» (?) (from below). Florence, Museo dell'Opera (Photo: Author).

with a neighbor, it should be included in an architectural ambience that contains two or more statues. As an example, I am reminded of the lower section of the fourteenth-century Arca of St. Peter Martyr in S. Eustorgio, Milan, by the tuscan sculptor Giovanni di Balduccio.[23] The ''Virgin'' matches the four end figures because they also are carved to have several viewpoints, including the one from behind.[24] However, in a

24) Cathedral of Santa Maria (west portal). Burgos, Spain (from O. von Simson, *Das Mittelalter II. Das Hohe Mittelalter*, Berlin, 1972, VI, pl. 423).

statues usually found in lunettes alternate between one and three, which, for esthetic reasons, are adapted to the arched space of the architecture. Specifically, a principal figure dominates the central area, but when more than one statue is involved, smaller flanking figures are included, at times in kneeling position. Therefore, two options are possible for reconstructing the composition of the *Annunciation* in the lunette of the Porta della Mandorla. This first is esthetically unacceptable: it entails a Virgin and angel of equal dimensions placed side by side on the same forward plane of the socle strip (which is how the statues in the Museo dell'Opera would have been arranged, had they been located in a lunette). The second

option requires that a Virgin stand in the center flanked by a kneeling angel on the left and, on the right, possibly by a vase with a lily. Although a vase with a lily is rarely found in this location in *Annunciation* scenes, and the Duomo documents do not mention it, in this particular instance, given the requirement of the architecture, liberties may been taken with the motive. The second reconstruction is the more attractive one, in part because it corresponds better with the ogival shape of the lunette and also because, were it still intact today, it would be integrated compositionally and by a central axis with Nanni di Banco's slightly later *Assumption* relief (1414) in the gable above the lunette [Fig. 3].

V

How long the lost *Annunciation* group had remained intact is a problem that is occasionally debated. The prevalent belief is that it was dismantled shortly before 10 July 1489 because a document that bears this date describes the lunette as empty.[33] But a much earlier date is possible, the clue to which is found in a document of 10 February 1422. It records a payment to a stone cutter ''to brighten up the lily that is held by Our Lady of the portal of the Annunciation,''[34] as the Porta della Mandorla was referred to in the fifteenth century. The document is interpreted as alluding to the *Annunciation* group itself, irrespective of the fact that it places the flower in the Virgin's hand, whereas normally it is held by Gabriel. Is this an error in the document,[35] or should the anomaly be explained figuratively, in the sense that even when the angel holds the lily, it is still recognized as the Virgin's attribute?[36] In my opinion, the document is clear and direct in what it intends to record, that a *Madonna with the Flower*, perhaps holding the Child in her arms, was present in the lunette at the time.[37] If so, then the *Annunciation* group had been removed prior to February 1422.[38]

It could be argued, against this conclusion, that a portal ''of the Annunciation'' must have as its centerpiece an *Annunciation*. But the Opera del Duomo did not seem to think so in 1489, when a new decoration for the empty lunette was being considered and an almost infinite variety of possible subjects was mentioned, apparently without prejudice: an *Annunciation*, a *Madonna and Child*, or ''any other figure'' in mosaic or sculpture.[39] Although the theme of the *Annunciation* was ultimately, and perhaps predictably, selected for the mosaic Domenico and Davide Ghirlandaio placed in the site,[40] initial flexibility was possible because the portal's designation was simply a colloquialism used to distinguish it from the others on the Cathedral, as being located in the direction of the church of the SS. Annunziata.[41] Now, in the period around 1422 the same flexibility may have obtained, if, as I am attempting to demonstrate, the Opera had then considered a replacement for the recently removed *Annunciation* group. The choice of a *Madonna with the Flower* would have been motivated by the Duomo's dedication to Saint Mary of the Flower. This dedication appears in an earlier document of 29 March 1412,[42] in which the flower is described, significantly, as a lily and associated with the "Incarnation of the said son of God, which was announced by the angel on the 25th of the month of March." The document further records the establishment "in perpetuity" of an annual celebration of the Annunciation in the Duomo. Subsequently, on 8 January 1413, a "marble statue of a Virgin Mary with a lily held in her hand" was ordered for the "front and summit of the cathedral."[43] I shall not propose this as the replacement statue, since no further mention of it occurs in the documents,[44] but one with the same symbolical attribute of the lily in its hand would certainly have made a suitable substitute for an *Annunciation* group.

[1] This paper is a revised version of a talk I gave at the annual meeting of the College Art Association of America in New York in 1986. I appreciate the comments and suggestions made on that occasion by Anita Moskowitz and Julian Gardner as, respectively, session chairwoman and commentator.

[2] G. Poggi, *Catalogo del Museo dell'Opera del Duomo*, Florence, 1904, pp. 42ff. In formulating his hypothesis, Poggi was probably influenced by A. Schmarzow's stylistic association, for the purpose of attribution, of the museum statues with several reliefs on the jamb of the Porta della Mandorla ("Vier Statuetten in der Domopera zu Florenz," *Jahrbuch der Königlich Preussischen Kunstsammlungen*, VIII, 1887, p. 146).

[3] For the early literature dealing with the two statues, see L. Becherucci and G. Brunetti, *Il Museo dell'Opera del Duomo a Firenze*, I, Florence, 1969, pp. 255ff. To this literature may be added *Jacopo della Quercia nell'arte del suo tempo* (catalogue notes by G. Chelazzi Dini and G. Previtali), Florence, 1975, pp. 63ff; and *Lorenzo Ghiberti, "materia e ragionamenti"*, Florence, 1978, p. 45ff.

[4] W. Bode in J. Burckhardt, *Der Cicerone*, Leipzig, 1884, II, p. 344, records having seen them in the building of the Opera del Duomo. The statues were subsequently cited in *Atti della Reale Accademia di Firenze*, Florence, 1887, p. 69, nos. 31-32. This publication contains a list that was composed in 1885 and headed (p. 67) "Elenco degli oggetti d'arte appartenenti all'Opera di Santa Maria del Fiore, i quali dovranno essere conservati nel nuovo Museo dell'Opera." The new museum was inaugurated in 1891. According to Becherucci and Brunetti (*op. cit.*, p. 7), the statues probably were in the building of the Opera since the beginning of the fifteenth century.

As for this, it may be possible at least to push the provenance of the statues back from 1885 to 1870. H. Semper ("Donatello, seine Zeit und Schule. Erster Abschnitt: Die Vorläufer Donatellos," *Jahrbücher für Kunstwissenschaft*, Leipzig, 1870, III, pp. 11ff) mentions seeing four statuettes, according to him belonging to the school of Andrea Pisano, in the vestibule of the Opera building. Two of the statuettes he identified as Christ and St. Catherine. They are obviously those that are today known as the Redentore and St. Reparata and attributed directly to Andea Pisano. The other two statuettes he identified as female figures with allegorical meaning. It is possible that he had misinterpreted their iconography and that they were actually the two figures we are discussing in this paper. The reasons are the following: first, Semper noted that they are larger than the Redentore and St. Reparata, as are our two figures, which, incidentally, have the dimensions of statuettes (the angel 1.39 m, the Virgin 1.40 m); second, no such allegorical statues are today preserved in the Museo dell'Opera. Nor were they mentioned in 1884 by Bode (*op. cit.*), nor included in the list of works of art that were to be installed in the new museum of the Opera and published in 1887 in the *Atti* of the Academy of Florence (*op. cit.*), nor, finally, are they found in the 1969 catalogue of the Museo dell'Opera by Becherucci and Brunetti (*op. cit.*). Third, Semper's description of the "allegorical" statues as "rich in grace of movement and in the study of the antique" (*op. cit.*) seems to fit our statues.

[5] The documents were published by C. Guasti, *Santa Maria del Fiore*, Florence, 1887, and again, but more systematically, by G. Poggi, *Il Duomo di Firenze*, Florence, 1909, nos. 371, 372, 374. The documents show that the statues were provisionally set up on the altar of the Trinity inside the Duomo and transferred into the lunette in 1414.

[6] For the most recent discussion of the construction of the Porta della Mandorla, see G. Kreytenberg, *Der Dom zu Florenz*, Berlin, 1974, p. 16.

[7] Only four scholars disputed Poggi's hypothesis, during a circumscribed period between 1951 and 1973. In chronological order: W. Valentiner ("Notes on the Early Works of Donatello," *Art Quarterly*, XIV, 1951, pp. 307ff), H. W. Janson (*The Sculpture of Donatello*, New Jersey, 1957, II, pp. 221f), M. Wundram ("Der Meister der Verkündigung in der Domopera zu Florenz," *Beiträge zur Kunstgeschichte. Eine Festgabe für Heinz Rudolf Rosemann*, Munich, 1960, p. 123, n. 10), and C. Freytag ("Italienische Skulptur um 1400. Untersuchung zu den Einflussbereichen," *Metropolitan Museum Journal*, VII, 1973, pp. 27f). However, these scholars did not create a collective hypothesis that might serve as an alternative to Poggi's. The reason is that, except for Janson's dependence on Valentiner, they all had different objections to placing the statues in the lunette and were unaware of each others contributions.

[8] C. Freytag, *ibidem*, noted, without comment, that the Virgin and the angel "are conceived fully in the round," while from Becherucci-Brunetti, *op. cit.*, we learn that the statues are "not finished in the rear."

[9] I have found no other examples of cavities treated as they are in the museum angel. In the Trecento and Quattrocento cavities are invariably arranged symmetrically (for illustrations, see G. Kreytenberg, *Andrea Pisano*, Munich, 1984, pls. 128-129). When statuary angels

have their original wings, they, too, are arranged symmetrically.

[10] Charles Seymour (*Sculpture in Italy, 1400 to 1500*, London, 1966, diagram on p. 33) proposed a different solution to the problem of the wings. He arranged them along the statue's left side in a symmetrical relationship with the drapery on the right. But his reconstruction presupposes wing cavities intentionally placed furthest from where the wings, themselves, would appear. Moreover, since the cavities are aligned horizontally, his reconstruction presupposes also an improbable wing-support system consisting of two units of different lengths extending protracted and unequal distances behind each other.

[11] The relevant side of the angel in the Museo dell'Opera is located very close to a wall. Another example of the pose in question is found in a fifteenth-century illuminated *Annunciation*, illustrated in *Zenale e Leonardo Milano* (exh. cat.), Museo Poldi Pezzoli, Milan, 1982, p. 61.

[12] The statue is Donatello's *St. Louis of Toulouse*. G. Passavant, *Verrocchio*, London, 1969, p. 20, stated that Verrocchio translated into three-dimensional sculpture ''the usual two-figure composition-scheme of paintings of the Annunciation, the Visitation or the Baptism and arranged the figures round an imaginary center on the central axis of the niche.'' It is more likely that Verrocchio was drawn to three-dimensional representations of the *Annunciation*, because they parallel the composition of the *Doubting of Thomas* (the figures of the angel and St. Thomas have a striking rapport). He may have come upon the angel in the Museo dell'Opera in 1476, when, according to Passavant, ''the idea of a scenic group'' for the *Doubting of Thomas* first arose in his mind. For a discussion of Verrocchio's problem of dealing with the niche, see, in addition to Passavant, C. Seymour, *The Sculpture of Verrocchio*, London, 1971, p. 59.

[13] It should be pointed out that the Virgin's dimensions, at 29.7 cm, are, on the other hand, adequate for the space of the lunette. I would like to thank Dr. Giorgio Bonsanti and Dr. Gastone Petrini for making it possible to ascend the scaffold at the portal. M. Wundram (*op. cit.*) in 1960 had already noted that the lunette is too shallow for the two statues, but he failed to include its dimensions. This left him vulnerable to the erroneous objection of Becherucci-Brunetti (*op. cit.*, p. 256) to the effect that the lunette had been sufficiently ample for the statues before it was reduced by the inclusion of the mosaic in 1490. Moreover, it led him astray as regards the figure of the Virgin, which he also excluded from the lunette for reasons of dimensions. The heights of the statues, on the other hand, present no problem (see *ibidem*).

[14] It is possible that the wings measured about 30 cm in width, or approximately equal to the depth of the angel. This dimension is based on the appearance of the wings of angels that were executed for the facade of the Duomo in 1390-96. They are illustrated in a drawing made at the time the facade was demolished in 1587 (see *ibidem*, pl. 1-b).

[15] C. Freytag, *op. cit.*, p. 28.

[16] Leo Planischig (*Nanni di Banco*, Florence, 1946, p. 18) noted the short curls of the statue, which, according to him, make it ''seem almost ephebe.'' Giulia Brunetti, on the other hand, maintained that the hair treatment makes the figure ''appear as a Hermes or an Olympic winner,'' which she ascribed to the ''incorrect interpretation of the subject of some antique fragment'' by the sculptor (whom she took to be Jacopo della Quercia) and to his ''youthful ardour'' in copying his model. Brunetti's comments appear in ''Jacopo della Quercia and the Porta della Mandorla,'' *Art Quarterly*, XV, 1952, p. 120 and n. 6, and ''Jacopo della Quercia a Firenze,'' *Belle arti*, 1952, p. 4. Her views were repeated by G. Marchini, *Baptisterium, Dom und Dom-Museum in Florenz*, Florence, 1972, p. 56.

[17] The hairdo, adorned with the fillet, is especially reminiscent of Hellenistic Ptolemaic imperial portraits found in the coinage of the period. I would like to thank Profs. Russell F. Scott and Alfred Frazer for making this suggestion. For illustrations of Ptolemaic coins, see J. N. Svoronos, *Die Münzen der Ptolemaeer*, Athens, 1908, IV, *passim*. A Hellenistic figure of a winged Agon has this style of hairdo, as well as a fillet with slanted grooves reminiscent of the angel's fillet (illustrated in M. Bieber, *The Sculpture of the Hellenistic Age*, N.Y., 1955, fig. 289). Another interesting comparison is the Hellenistic head of a boy illustrated in R. Lullies, *Griechische Plastik*, Munich, 1956, pl. 212. The female coiffure in antiquity and in the Renaissance is typically parted in the center and combed back in waves, even in short hair.

[18] A difficulty in giving the statue a masculine identity is the existence of an elevation on the right side of the torso that could be identified as a breast. However, there is no evidence of a matching breast, and, moreover, the elevation does not have the round shape of a breast. I believe that the elevation is simply an effect of the pleat in that area. For a similar treatment of the garment in male statues, see K. Rathe, *Der Figurale Schmuck der alten Domfassade in Florenz*, Vienna and Leipzig, 1910, figs. 13, 19, 50. I would call attention also to the statue of *David* in the National Gallery in Washington, attributed to Donatello, which has full breasts like a female's (illustrated in Janson, *op. cit.*, pl. 21). For a typical example of rounded female breasts in statuary, see J. S. Raspi, *I Pisano e il Gotico*, Milan, 1968, pl. X.

[19] For examples of this type of garment as worn by men, see Becherucci-Brunetti, *op. cit.*, pls. 128-129. A good general survey of drapery in the Quattrocento is A. Meyer-Weinschel, *Renaissance und Antike*, Reutlingen, 1933.

[20] However, there are no preserved Duomo documents citing a statue of St. John to which ours can be related. For an illustration of St. John with these physical attributes, see Donati, *Orvieto*, Orvieto, 1984, p. 55, and P. Thoby, *Le crucifix des origines au Concile de Trente*, Nantes, 1958, pl. L, no. 116. For an illustration of male saints in general with these attributes, see A. Tambini, *Pittura dell'alto medioevo al tardo Gotico nel territorio di Faenza e Forlì*, Faenza, 1982, fig. 35. Incidentally, I found the ''Annunciation'' attributes in another *female* saint, St. Modesta from the west portal of Chartres Cathedral, which might easily be mistaken for a Virgin Annunciate were it seen out of context (ill. in E. Tea, *Medioevo*, Turin, 1957, II, fig. 876).

[21] Examples of angels on clouds, though not common, are found on the Duomo's Porta dei Canonici (see Poggi, *op. cit.*, fig. 58) and in an *Annunciation* group at Bamberg Cathedral (illustrated in O. von Simson, *Das Mittelalter II. Das Hohe Mittelalter*, Berlin, 1972, VI, fig. 213). It is interesting to note that Verrocchio's St. Thomas does not stand on a base at all. A cloud under the angel and the absence of a base under St. Thomas may account for their similar lack of controlling outlines.

[22] Several sections of the Duomo documents are missing, as we learn from Poggi, *op. cit.*, p. L.

[23] Illustrated in *La Basilica di Sant'Eustorgio in Milano* (G. A. Dell'Acqua, ed.), Milan, 1984, figs. 84 and 271.

[24] Illustrated in *ibidem*, fig. 271 (includes the back of an end figure). Incidentally, like the museum statues, all those on the Arca have round cavities in back and tubular supports that link them to piers.

[25] Donatello's *St. John the Evangelist*, commissioned for the facade of the Duomo in 1410, is treated in a similar manner.

[26] The angel's original companion figure is lost or may never have been executed. Or else the sculptor may have worked with other sculptors on a group commission and been assigned only the two statues in the Museo dell'Opera. Therefore, the angel's original mate

may have been executed by another sculptor. A known instance of an *Annunciation* statuary group that consists of statues by different sculptors is found on the Porta del Campanile, although there it was a question of reusing an earlier statue of the Virgin (see Kreytenberg, *op. cit.*, pp. 52ff).

[27] For a close-up illustration of the group, see von Simson, *op. cit.*, pl. 424.

[28] The facade as a site for the two statues in the Museo dell'Opera was suggested more than a decade before Poggi announced his hypothesis, at the time of the inauguration of the new museum in 1891 (*Catalogo del Museo di Santa Maria del Fiore*, Florence, 1891, p. 21). However, there are no traces of our statues in a drawing of the unfinished facade that was made shortly before its demolition in the later sixteenth century (for an illustration of the drawing, see Becherucci-Brunetti, *op. cit.*, pl. I-b). Perhaps the sites were intended to be included in the section of the facade awaiting completion. This is not an unlikely possibility, since there is record of a statue that was commissioned in 1413 for the peak of the unfinished facade (see note 43 below). Note, incidentally, that another angel in the Museo dell'Opera (Becherucci-Brunetti, *op. cit.*, no. 77), executed in 1389-90 for the facade of the Duomo, has three cavities in back that are distributed in the same manner as our angel: two for the wings and one centrally located for the tubular support element.

[29] However, neither G. Richa's survey of the interior of the Duomo (*Notizie istoriche delle chiese fiorentine*, VI, Florence, 1757, pp. 75ff) nor the list of the Duomo's lost works published by W. and E. Paatz (*Die Kirchen von Florenz*, III, Frankfurt am Main, 1952, pp. 392ff) permit the identification of a suitable location for the statues in the interior of the Cathedral.

[30] The statuettes are undocumented. See Becherucci-Brunetti, *op. cit.*, pp. 232f, no. 27, pls. 37-39.

[31] H. Semper, *op. cit.*, p. 12. In Becherucci-Brunetti catalogue (*op. cit.*, p. 232), the statuettes are listed in the Campanile section, but without discussion or citation of documents. The reason appears to be the Andrea Pisano authorship of the figures and the reliefs on the Campanile.

[32] Janson (*op. cit.*, p. 221), following an idea of Valentiner ("Donatello and Ghiberti," *Studies of Italian Renaissance Sculpture*, London, 1950, pp. 44ff), identified the angel in a statue that until recently was located on the left pier above the lunette. However, examination of the statue reveals that it never had wings and so is not an angel.

As regards the assumption that the group is missing, I would point out that many other sculptures executed for the Duomo are lost. For example, an *Annunciation* group of 1388-9, evidently for the Duomo facade (Poggi, *op. cit.*, nos. 57, 58, 63, 76), and three statues that formerly occupied the lunette of the Porta dei Cornacchini, representing the Madonna, St. Barnaba, and St. John the Evangelist (see G. Kreytenberg, "Una Madonna e Due Angeli di Simone Talenti," *Antichità viva*, XIX, 1980, pp. 28ff). Then there are the lost prophets Donatello executed for the Porta della Mandorla and for which he received payments in 1406 and 1408 (see Janson, *op. cit.*, pp. 219f).

[33] Poggi, *op. cit.*, no. 399. For a transcription of the text, see note 39 below. The reason for the removal of the group from the lunette is not known.

[34] Poggi, *op. cit.*, no. 389: "A dì detto soldi 2 portò Antonio da Servi, scharpelatore, per ischiarare il giglio tiene Nostra Donna dela porta della Nunziata." The translation in the text is Janson's (*op. cit.*, p. 222)

[35] Brunetti, *Belle arti*, assumed that the document substitutes the angel for the Virgin because he "has a more feminine aspect". Of course, she was equating the group with the statues in the Museo dell'Opera.

[36] According to Janson, *op. cit.*

[37] This interpretation is consistent with the straightforward way the Cathedral documents prior to 1422 refer to the *Annunciation* statuary group in the lunette: "Nostra Donna quando fu Anu[n]tiata"; "figure nostre domine Anuntiate" adding "et angeli"; and "nostre domine senper Virginis Marie" adding "et figure marmorea angeli Gabriellis" (Poggi, *op. cit.*, nos. 371, 372, and 374).

[38] Based on this same document, Janson, *ibidem*, concluded instead that the statue was removed shortly *after* February 1422. He seems to be implying that the document mentions the group for the last time. Incidentally, Brunetti (*Belle arti*, p. II, n. 1) proposed 1430 as the removal date, based on a document in which Bicci di Lorenzo is reported to be painting the lunette (Poggi, *op.cit.*, no. 396).

[39] Poggi, *op. cit.*, no. 399: "Spectabiles domini consules...et operarii deliberaverunt quod in vacuo existente super porta a parte exteriori, qua itur ad edem dive Marie adnuntiate videcet Servorum, possit confici seu fieri confici per ipsos operarios figura admintiationis beate Marie virginis vel ipsa virgo Maria cum eius figlio ut vulgo dicitur in collo vel alia quecumque figura, prout visum erit dictis operariis in concordia et tam de musayco quam de scultura vel aliter quomodocumque..."

[49] Poggi, *op. cit.*, no. 400.

[41] For documents containing this designation of the portal, see Poggi, *op. cit.*, nos. 372, 374, 376, 381, 384, and 389.

[42] C. Guasti, *op. cit.*, no. 464: "Quarto provisionem infrascriptam...cum maior eclesia Florentia fuerit, ut asseritur, in suo initio fundata et reverentiam et sut nomine beate et gloriose Maria Virginis matris domini nostri Jesu Christi et vulgariter debeat appellari Sancta Maria del Fiore; et flos ac initium nostre redemptionis fuit benigna humilis ac gratiosa Incarnatio dicti Filii Dei, que fuit per angelum Nuntiata die vigesimo quinto mensis martii."

[43] Guasti, *ibidem*, no. 465: "Item quod dicti operarii quam citius fieri poterit et ipsis videbitur, debiant facere poni in parte anteriori dicte ecclesie et in summitate ecclesie figuram beate Marie Virginis de marmore sculptam cum flore lilii in manibus honorabiliter."

[44] See Paatz, *op. cit.*, p. 396, who doubts that the statue was ever executed. However, if the statue of the *Madonna with the Flower* had been executed, it might have been placed in the lunette temporarily, awaiting completion of the facade, in the way the *Annunciation* group that was commissioned for the lunette of the Porta della Mandorla was temporarily set up on the altar of the Trinity.

CARLO DEL BRAVO

L'armonia del Ribera

Credo che poco dopo il 1610 il giovane spagnolo abbia frequentato a Genova Bernardo Strozzi, il Cappuccino. Da lui deve aver imparato l'impasto spesso e solcato che tratterà più volte, per tutta la vita; con lui ha in comune anche i temi prossimi ai Cappuccini, delle sue prime opere. Un tema di beneficenza — l'Elemosina di San Martino per Parma[1], come lo Strozzi ha quelle di San Lorenzo o di Santa Zita —; ed altri poi a Roma di sprezzo dei sensi e contemplazione di Gesù morto[2], forse secondo la recente *Regula perfectionis* di un autore dell'ordine, Benoît de Canfeld[3]. A Roma, fra il '15 e il '16[4], ha già consultato le *Tusculanae*[5] per un rimando di San Gerolamo[6], traendo con intelligenza spunti dalla loro descrizione della cecità di Democrito, per il *Tatto* fra i suoi *Sensi* che con le dita non può vedere i colori di una tavoletta, né i chiari e gli scuri della luce e dell'ombra su una testa di gesso.

Allora egli fu deciso e radicale nella beneficenza e nella noncuranza dei valori del mondo, sull'esempio di eroi cristiani in cui credeva. San Martino[7] aveva regalato al povero metà del suo mantello perché aveva già consumato in beneficenza tutti gli altri suoi averi: e lui a Roma manteneva dei poveri, che gli altri consideravano suoi sfruttatori e mangiapane, e poi per loro fece dei debiti. Il Santo, rimasto con mezzo mantello fece ridere diversi: e lui a Roma fece ridere un uomo di successo, che descrisse per i posteri la miseria dell'arredamento che gli fu anche sequestrato, con dieci mattoni al posto delle seggiole[8].

Autonomo, lui, dalle vedute degli altri, intelligente, scevera nell'opera del giovane Valentin[9] alcuni elementi formali che lo interessano, toni bronzei o lucidi neri, ma non quel suo amore

platonico. E non resta mai costretto nei termini di una vena: il tono di disgusto che usa nei *Sensi* sarà dipeso dall'invito mistico a denudar lo spirito dalle percezioni, ma non era nel potente *San Martino*; e la perduta *Pietà* dipinta a Roma, secondo la tradizione bonaventuriana dei Cappuccini sarà stata pietosissima.

Fuggì a Napoli lasciando lo squallore senza paura e i debiti contratti per far beneficenza, e là aderì subito al molinismo, se fin dai primi tempi rappresentò le sue autorità: i Santi *Pietro*, *Paolo*, e *Giacomo*, per il concorso di Grazia e merito, di fede e opere, a render giusto l'uomo: Giacomo aggiungendo nella sua epistola che la fede a parole o comunque da sola è inutile e morta[10]. Con quel passato drastico, ecco dunque il Ribera per la schiettezza delle opere, senza l'equivoco delle parole — come fra poco sarà per il vangelo, per la fede di cuore e non di ragione, per l'ingenuità dei semplici, per gli inermi, per l'inverso di quel che piace nel mondo.

La dottrina molinista sul libero arbitrio di Cristo come uomo ci permette poi di decifrare i pensieri che aggravano le teste ombrose dei suoi primi Cristi dolenti [Fig. 1]: pensieri di onnipotenza trattenuti dalla costanza pur umana di voler morire[11] per degli immeritevoli, aumentando duramente in noi la comprensione e lo sgomento; e nel *Sebastiano* di Osuna il Ribera implicitamente scarta della vita del Santo[12] la dissimulazione della fede e l'eloquenza con cui convinceva al martirio gli altri, per presentare invece la prova nella sua carne, petto nudo, braccia aperte; e *San Bartolomeo* poteva portar nell'etimo del nome la fede esclusiva nella Grazia[13], ma il macello sanguinoso che

167

1) Ribera, «Ecce Homo». Madrid, Academia de San Fernando.

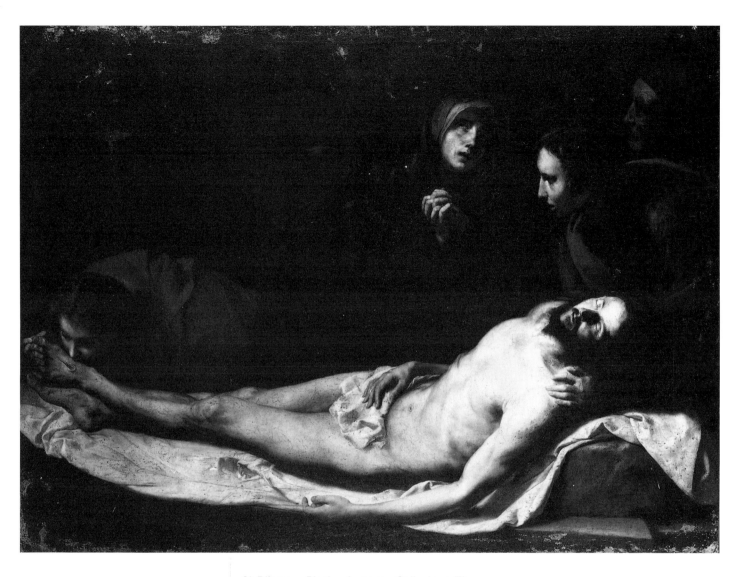

2) Ribera, «Pietà». Lugano, Collezione Thyssen.

affrontò e che il Ribera espone fino in fondo, conclama pure il suo merito.

Ma la dottrina molinista non spiega da sola il significato dei Santi *Pietro* e *Gerolamo* di Osuna: giacché Pietro in luogo deserto[14] e Gerolamo che risente l'alto monito — la tromba, per così dire — del profeta Amos contro l'idolatria[15], richiamano l'uno parole evangeliche sull'abbandono di tutto per Gesù[16], e l'altro la terminologia di Agostino, per la quale «idolatria» vale per ogni attaccamento al mondo[17], contrario a quanto insegna l'«umiltà» di Cristo[18]. Queste due pitture son dunque già partecipi della tradizione dell'«evangelismo» napoletano[19] che, per recuperare

la persona di Gesù oltre la teologia formale, tornava al Vangelo e alle lettere degli Apostoli, con lo spirito caloroso di Agostino. A questo evangelismo si riferisce la traccia di pensiero su cui il Ribera va variamente immaginando per tutta la vita, con più ricerca fin verso i suoi quarantacinque, e dopo con più definizione, e infine contemplando. La filosofia che considera intellettivamente idee, numeri, princìpi etici, ha il merito di staccare dal mondo[20], ma è priva dell'incarnazione[21], della pietà e dell'amore di Gesù[22], nonché della semplice fede. Cristo si disse mite e umile di cuore, e ci invitò ad imitarlo[23]. Mite, morì per degli immeritevoli[24]; umile, scese nella carne, e fra gli uomini fu

169

3) Ribera, «San Sebastiano curato». Leningrado, Ermitage.

povero, vergine, giudicato, condannato a morte vergognosa[25]; insegna dunque il cuore disarmato e valori inversi a quelli del mondo: se l'anima immortale si attaccherà al perituro come un idolatra al suo idolo[26], necessariamente sarà abbandonata e disperata[27]; lui invece le offre il conforto, la pace di una contemplazione senza fine[28].

Soffermandoci, ci accorgiamo che queste idee agostiniane su tre versetti di Matteo (11, 28-30) dipendono dalla concentrata e ripetuta lettura di non molte pagine: il *De vera religione*, le *Confessioni*, passi del *De libero arbitrio* e del *De ordine*. L'immaginazione però fu talvolta nutrita cercando con gli indici generali manifestazioni di concetti riportati, o leggendo San Gerolamo, o maestri antichi, come il Cicerone delle *Tusculanae* e del *De finibus*, l'Ovidio delle *Metamorfosi*. Con queste pagine dunque nascevan le immagini.

Secondo quella traccia, i *Filosofi* son solo uno dei termini di un discorso comparativo, e quindi impongono una contestualità ideale nel Ribera e in un nucleo di destinatari consapevoli[29]. La speculazione intellettiva, che essi rappresentano, è priva dell'umanità del Verbo: anche se il Ribera li dipinge non superbi come li dice Agostino[30] bensì stracciati — traendo dallo stesso Agostino, da Gerolamo e da Cicerone[31] che trascurarono i beni

170

4) Ribera, «San Rocco». Madrid, Prado.

5) Ribera, «San Matteo» (?). Madrid, Prado.

172

6) Ribera, «San Giacomo Maggiore». Madrid, Prado.

e che Democrito si cavò gli occhi per ridurre le esterne distrazioni —, essi furono dunque privi di tanto! Nelle pagine di Matteo, Pietro, Paolo e Agostino care al Ribera si leggono delle frasi sulla grandezza e la bontà di Cristo, che si confrontano con emozione con altre loro sulla sua mitezza e umiltà nel martirio: soprattutto ad esser consapevoli col Molina che era la sua volontà umana ad impedire una difesa onnipotente. «Ogni sospiro aneli al Cristo: lui solo sia desiderato, il più bello fra tutti, che amò noi deformi»[32]; non fu geloso della sua divinità, ed umilmente si spogliò ed obbedì[33]; innocente nelle mani degli ingiusti, offeso non offendeva, tormentato non minacciava[34]; eppure ebbe anche «sembiante pietoso» e «chiamò 'Venite a me, voi che soffrite'»[35]. «Gli ammaestramenti della sua debolezza»[36].

Con tale complessità di pensieri, come verso una persona conosciuta — e quale persona! —, le immagini di Cristo: la figura alta e rara nella *Crocifissione*, con vicino quel pianto silenzioso; la figura mite, nuda e maneggiata di Cogolludo; quella grande e snella ma ormai senza forza, della *Pietà* Thyssen [Fig. 2].

Con i suoi sprofondamenti nel concreto e nel semplice oltre la dottrina e l'abilità, intenderemo come il Ribera presenti la fede proprio col sangue di Cristo, incompreso dagli idolatri durante la *Messa di San Donato*[37], e col cuore ingenuo di *Zaccaria* e di *Giuseppe*[38]: Giuseppe falegname, come esprime intensamente il fanciullo alzando il paniere dei bruni attrezzi, il quale credette che proprio quel fanciullo era il messia, accettando sproporzioni troppo difficili per «i sapienti e gli accorti»[39].

L'imitazione di Cristo, poi, il Ribera la assunse sul 1632 per quattro Santi che ne sono autorità: *Matteo*, che solo fra gli evangelisti riporta la frase di Gesù «discite a me, quia mitis sum et humilis corde, et invenietis requiem animabus vestris»[40]; *Pietro* e *Paolo* per esortazioni cui abbiamo alluso[41]; e *Rocco* per aver esultato all'imitazione nel dolore della carne[42].

«Discite a me, quia mitis sum [...]»: in una città dove con la teologia si faceva morire, dipinse *San Simone* [Fig. 9] ricordando dalla leggenda che egli disse e ridisse di esser stato mandato ad assolvere non a perdere i dannosi e gli infedeli, e che lo provò scegliendo di piuttosto offrir la carne sua ai ferri del tormento[43].

«[...] et humilis corde, [...]»: imitare Cristo nell'umiltà significa per Agostino invertire i desideri del mondo[44], ma ancora una volta ne toccheremo il valore in questo contesto se andremo al cuore del vissuto: oltre dunque le nozioni e le parole sull'abnegazione degli Apostoli e dei martiri, soprattutto di *Andrea*[45], e il collegamento forse sostenuto dai Certosini fra gli Apostoli e gli eremiti antichi e moderni[46], il peso umano delle rinunce e dei dolori. Il detto improvviso di Pietro a Gesù, «ecco, noi abbiamo lasciato tutto e ti abbiamo seguito», e Gesù che concreta, consapevole: casa o fratelli o sorelle o padre o madre o moglie o figli o campi, per me[47]. Il cuore e la grazia di Rocco

[Fig. 4], «Dolcissimo Gesù, anche se prima mi stimavi tuo servo, ora che mi doni parte dei tuoi tormenti e me ne fai degno, capisco che ti sono caro e giocondo»[48], divengon più intensi per il pensiero della peste che lui ha dentro di sé.

«[...] et invenietis requiem animabus vestris». Se il peccato è non imitare Cristo e desiderare ciò che lui trascurò, e dunque, come idolatri, fissare l'anima immortale su cose periture, quando queste cose per loro natura passeranno l'anima resterà in un dolore senza speranza: Cristo invece a chi lo imita nella mitezza e nell'umiltà offre la sua pace, una contemplazione senza fine. Insieme allo stesso *Cristo dolente* [Fig. 7] che contempla, ecco allora *San Giacomo*, primo apostolo martire, col collo e la spalla già scoperti per la spada[49]; e *Giacobbe* angariato a sorvegliare il gregge di Labano poiché «servì sette anni per Rachele», e poi altri sette, ma «gli sembrarono pochi giorni di fronte alla grandezza del suo amore»[50], Rachele significando la speranza del gaudio eterno nella contemplazione di Dio e della verità[51]; ed ecco infine il *Cieco* [Fig. 10] con la scritta di speranza per il giorno in cui sarà donata contemplazione piena e senza fine anche agli occhi della carne, «Dies illa, dies illa»[52]. Il pittore sa per esperienza che, in tanta astrazione dello spirito, le membra e quanto ci circonda restano dimenticati: così la canna nella mano di Gesù, il suo petto pur robusto, la bocca smorta; e nel San Giacomo, ormai il rotolo nella mano obliosa, della lettera sulle opere, la rilasciata persona aitante con la spalla scoperta, i capelli confusi; e nel *Giacobbe* e nel *Cieco*, la composizione disgregata, col gregge o il mesto fanciullo che prendono in silenzio luogo a sé.

Ma il Ribera, con quei suoi fondamenti, non solo parla di imitazione altrui della mitezza e dell'umiltà di Cristo, ma anche la pratica nel profondo della sua arte: giacché la fede a parole, lo sapeva da San Giacomo e dal Molina, è come morta.

Per arrivare a dipingere nei quadri della Passione quel povero agnello, aveva cercato «gli ammaestramenti della sua debolezza»[53].

Mite, con Agostino salva la bellezza creata, dall'oscuramento mistico dell'immagine[54]; e quella del corpo umano dal ribrezzo di predicatori che vi indicavano solo repugnanti immondizie[55]. La bellezza creata è un raggio, sia pur lontano, di quella divina, e un dono provvidenziale[56]: come negare che essa sia innocente e dolce? Di più, niente è brutto nel creato, essendo comunque un raggio divino l'esistenza e la forma, che restano ancor nella degradazione[57]. Così mite, filtra anche Agostino delle sue durezze paoline, e non attribuisce a Cristo volontà di scacciare[58], non accusa di superbia i filosofi, non fa riferimenti personali per i peccati. Dei peccati, lui tratta solo in forma indiretta, mitologica e simbolica, perché è lucido nel veder l'insidia, ma pietoso verso gli uomini. L'insidia del bere[59], lenta[60] e nascosta[61] come quella di altri vizi, lui la esprime con un *Sileno ebbro* mentre Agostino la riferiva direttamente alla gioventù di sua

7) Ribera, «Ecce Homo». Leningrado, Ermitage.

madre[62]. E un commento agostiniano sulla vanità degli attaccamenti terreni, lui lo rispecchia con la descrizione ovidiana dei *Giganti* agli Inferi e delle loro pene vanamente replicate[63].

Umile, poi, non preferisce, come fa il mondo, le opere più costruite e formali di Sant'Agostino, ma quelle più piane e commosse. E così con le persone che raffigura non ha preoccupazioni di decoro formale o sociale, né teme somiglianze notorie: non le fa posare composte come volevano i trattatisti, e talvolta son nude ed esibite; i Santi che gli son più cari li dice belli, guardando per l'*Apostolato* il castano diverso fra capelli e barba di *Matteo*[64] [Fig. 5], e il pelo nero che affila il volto e adombra la purezza del collo di *Giacomo* [Fig. 6]; e così rendendo in un *San Rocco* [Fig. 4] l'umidità degli occhi neri e i riflessi del sudore sul volto. Poiché dall'idolatria, il distacco dev'essere interiore[65]: e come con la nudità innocente perché martirizzata e svenuta di Sebastiano, rifiuta indiscutibilmente l'impurità e la miseria di fissarlo senza trascorrere a valori spirituali e divini, così nei volti l'attenzione ascende agli sguardi gravi e commoventi, al merito, al dono, al principio di tutto.

E la stessa umiltà, cioè lo stesso ampio distacco dal mondo sull'esempio di Cristo, può trarre motivo di contemplazione e di conforto considerando insieme alla bellezza creata ciò che il mondo considera brutto: giacché esso, a parte il riscatto morale, pur nel corpo riflette la divinità con l'esistenza, con la forma, e con l'armonia cui contribuisce[66].

Sul contributo all'armonia universale, dei corpi che il mondo considera brutti, e di cui esso dice «non dovrebbero esserci» o «dovrebbero essere come questi altri»[67], Agostino era palmare, soprattutto per un pittore spesso tenebroso, dicendo «come il colore nero in una pittura diviene bello in rapporto con il tutto, così la divina provvidenza immutabile offre un bello spettacolo nell'insieme»[68]. Ed ecco dunque che i corpi che il Ribera «dice» totalmente, siano maceri ed irsuti o bellissimi, in questo spirito agostiniano non portano oltranza realistica né contrapposizione, cioè applicazioni del pensiero al particolare, ma sono gradi di un'armonia ammirata superando umilmente le ragioni del mondo, e che dà conforto e pace. Così, alle interpretazioni di bellezza e «bruttezza» nel Ribera secondo impressioni scoordinate, si potrà, volendo, sostituirne un'altra secondo queste parole di Agostino: «Tutti, secondo i rispettivi compiti e fini, sono ordinati alla bellezza dell'universo, in modo che piace moltissimo, se considerato con il tutto, quel che dà orrore se preso in sé. [...] Per contro è brutto di per sé il nostro errore, che ci fa aderire ad una parte sola del mondo»[69].

Nello stesso spirito di umile superamento del particolare per aver pace e consolazione, lo spirito del Ribera trascende anche le forme stilistiche, che potevan valere per troppo bassi raggiungimenti e successi, non fissandosi né sulla ricchezza bella alla Vouet né sulla seta reniana né sulla compattezza ottenebrata alla Battistello: giacché, se «per molti l'unico scopo è l'umano diletto, e non vogliono tendere verso i princìpi più alti [...], io non cesserò di ricordare all'uomo, che ha un occhio interiore e vede nell'invisibile, perché tali cose piacciano, in modo che osi essere giudice anche dell'umano diletto. Così si pone sopra di esso, e non ne viene dominato»[70].

La concretezza che vale per questo pittore, sembra dunque essere altrove, nell'insegnamento di Agostino quando dice: «eppure amo una sorta di luce e voce e odore e cibo e amplesso nell'amare il mio Dio: la luce, la voce, l'odore, l'amplesso dell'uomo interiore che è in me»[71].

∗ ∗ ∗

Dal 1635 ai primi anni Quaranta il Ribera cinquantenne rimedita princìpi già espressi su l'imitazione e il conforto di Cristo, ma li esprime con più nuda chiarezza, spesso con temi nuovi per lui e per tutti. In tale riconsiderazione di ciò cui si è dedicata una vita, ha molta importanza l'arte. *Sant'Agostino* è figurato nella dottrina e nell'ispirazione.

In questo tempo figura *eremiti* vecchi e molto selvatici; insieme ad altri in cui la lucidità dell'abnegazione innalza la gioventù a nitore adamantino o la snoda dolcemente; e insieme anche alla bellezza di *Sebastiani* [Figg. 8, 11, 12] e di *paesaggi* (1639)[72]; continuando a pensare che l'esistenza e la forma sono comunque doni provvidenziali, e in un'ammirevole gradazione armonica.

Con i gradi alti di questo splendore è ora più magnanimo: la bellezza umana dunque, non solo è innocente come nella nudità d'un martire estatico o svenuto: ma nelle sue forme e pose supreme l'artista esalta quanto traluce della matematica purissima[73], più che il suo grado infimo di bene[74]. Dono dolce dell'amore di Dio per noi, come la natura che circonda meravigliosa i ritiri secondo tradizione poetica — a Napoli quindi pastorali e piscatorî — dell'umanista cristiano[75]. Lascia implicito nel contesto o, chissà, vela con la mutevolezza della luna o di nubi ventilate e trascoloranti, il pensiero che quanto nella bellezza è terreno, per sua natura ci lascerà[76].

Dell'amorosa gratitudine per la dolcezza della Provvidenza si nutre ancora l'imitazione di Cristo nelle opere, secondo l'autorità dei *Santi Pietro e Paolo*, di nuovo raffigurati in due quadri gemelli, nel 1637. L'umiltà è ora figurata con la persona di *Giacobbe dormente per terra* (1639), prefigurazione secondo Agostino di «Christus jacens humiliter»[77]: così che, parimenti guidati da Agostino, potremo vedere questo significato anche nel *Battesimo* (1643) che Cristo volle ricevere da un uomo[78], nonché, insieme ad altri significati, nella *Pietà*.

Disarmandosi lo spirito dalle strutture del mondo, nel *Giacobbe* la grandezza e la rigidezza del rettangolo dipinto si sciolgono nell'abbandono del personaggio: che, essendo spiritualmente lontano dal mondo, è caro all'artista: le due linee

8) Copia da Ribera, «San Sebastiano». Le Havre, Musée des Beaux-Arts.

9) Ribera, «San Simone». Madrid, Prado.

10) Ribera, «Cieco». Oberlin College, Allen Memorial Art Museum (R. T. Miller, Jr. Fund, 55.9).

11) Copia (?) da Ribera, «San Paolo Eremita». Aix-en-Provence, Musée Granet.

12) Ribera, «San Sebastiano». Già Berlino, Kaiser-Friedrich-Museum.

13) Ribera, «Venere e Adone». Roma, Galleria Nazionale d'Arte Antica (Foto: I.C.C.D., Roma, G40478).

innocenti delle ciglia abbassate, e in quella testa barbuta e giovane si lascian guardare dei rosati che ci ricordano il ciclamino od altro (la pittura alla Van Dyck vola intorno con bruni lievi, o con vapori d'oro che anche corrono a far trasparire l'azzurro). E, nel *Battesimo*, uno degli infiniti doni della Provvidenza è anche il paesaggio serotino in cui Cristo si è ora inginocchiato: valle fresca alla base dell'immenso che si va tacitamente strappando sull'azzurro.

Il merito di chi imita l'umiltà di Cristo è nella praticata abnegazione. In questo tempo il Ribera la figura più volte con *San Giovannino* che, nelle rinunce del deserto, ha presso di sé l'umi-

le agnello di Dio[79]; una volta, in un gruppo di quattro dipinti, con due *Sante eremite* e il martire *Bartolomeo*: giacché, sotto quei princìpi, il pensiero unisce gli eremiti ai martiri come *Lucia*[80] (1637), *Cristoforo*[81] (1637), *Filippo*[82] (1639), *Agnese*[83] (1641), i quali non solo con l'etimo del nome o con le parole secondo la *Leggenda aurea*, ma imitando Cristo nel sacrificio, provarono umiltà, mitezza da agnello, e fede.

Mentre San Filippo è tirato su una croce al pari di Cristo, nell'immagine di un corpo stanco, di varie braccia alzate scure o senili, della testa già calva di un giovane, e di due soldati che mormorano, sotto quel cielo mosso di nuvole marine brilla

14) Ribera, «Apollo e Marsia». Napoli, Museo di San Martino (Foto: Sopr. ai Beni Artistici, Napoli).

all'improvviso più alto il riflesso della divina armonia.

E se il peccato è un attaccamento esclusivo dello spirito alle cose, esso contraddice all'umiltà di Cristo, ed è, come dicemmo, una forma di idolatria. Il Ribera ne cerca e ne illumina con rigore anche la forma più insidiosa: quella del diabolico buon senso che, come nella *Tentazione di San Francesco*[84], insinua con volto angelico che «solo il mezzo è quel che piace a Dio» e quindi induce a temperare la devozione con i conforti del mondo[85]. Ma poi questo rigore di princìpi, ai suoi simili lo applica con mitezza, ancor più in questa maturità rifiutando di usar l'arte a ludibrio dei peccatori. Tale mitezza che ha già filtrato

durezze di Agostino, imita ancora una volta il mite Gesù del vangelo di Matteo, e non si figura che le sofferenze da uomo lo abbiano reso giudice terribile[86]: nella *Trinità*, brividi replicatissimi, splendori sdruccioli, ramificate saette, sul gran mantello divino: ma tutto questo, sopra al nuovo pallore di Gesù riverso, povero agnello. Gerolamo insegna chiaramente che le sventure di questo mondo, come quelle del vecchio *Isacco* (1637) insieme cieco e ingannato, sono segni non dell'ira di Dio, bensì del suo caldo amore, simile a quello di chi ammaestra e corregge solo i giovani amati e d'ingegno ardente[87]. Sull'esempio di Cristo dunque, la mitezza verso i peccatori induce il Ribera a trattar del peccato con figure simboliche: come nella *Vittoria della Fede sull'Idolatria* (1636) secondo la *Psychomachia* di Prudenzio[88], e nella *Mano* (1635) che, durante il convito idolatra di Baldassare, apparve ad avvisare che quel mondo sarebbe presto finito[89]. Poi (1642) sommando nello *Zoppo* una menomazione simbolo del peccato secondo esegesi agostiniane[90], e l'invito, scritto sul biglietto che lui regge, all'amor di Dio e alla carità. Giacché l'uomo che vive secondo il vangelo, non solo sarà mite verso i peccatori ma, come Agostino, avrà compassione per la pena insita nel loro stato a causa di quel contrasto tra la fissità passionale sulle creature e il loro necessario fluire e scomparire[91].

Con maestosa allegoria, dunque, desunta da un rilievo classico[92], i piaceri del vino e dell'amore nei quali è immerso un giovane ancor forte sono, con la presenza di maschere, dichiarati fallaci perché «non durano né soddisfano, ma tormentano soltanto. Poiché quando la bella vicenda temporale ha compiuto il suo corso, l'immagine desiderata abbandona il suo amatore, si allontana, tormentandolo, dai suoi sensi», come il pittore ha letto nel *De vera religione*[93]: pensieri che in uno dei suoi momenti più elevati (1637) collegherà ad altri deposti da Ovidio nelle *Metamorfosi*. Venere immortale [Fig. 13], presa dalla bellezza di un uomo, lo preferì al cielo, e dal cielo si astenne[94]. Quella bellezza era innocente, ma per sua natura ad un momento la abbandonò. La testa pallida e bruna di Adone sulla terra e sul rosso. Pietà e non giudizio, allora, per un'amante immortale, l'anima, che già soffre e grida per quanto era insito in quella disparità[95]. E anche se l'amore di una moglie è lecito, e lei può dunque esser raffigurata più da vicino con un tipo moderno — come nel quadro oggi a Bayonne (1638) —, quando il suo amore è preposto al Cielo, per la natura delle cose anche lei resterà priva di tutto, e disperata. «Gli amori terreni, anche se il matrimonio non li fa condannare, saranno bruciati dal fuoco del tormento: che è il fuoco della privazione, e delle disgrazie che portano via tutto»[96].

In questi anni, somma chiarezza si applica anche a pensieri cui il Ribera dà chiaramente figura per la prima volta. Meglio che la fede sapiente è l'amore disarmato per l'umiltà di Cristo, come quello di *Sant'Antonio di Padova* raffigurato (1636) non come dottore qual era, bensì come amatore del Bambino, al quale ha dato abbracci e parole d'affetto[97]. E con un pathos da *Regola dell'Ordine di Gesù*[98] (che il Ribera figurò intorno al 1643) si aggiunge un'altra forma di abnegazione nel concreto: nella purezza del religioso — espressa con *San Francesco* cui l'angelo mostra per riferimento un'ampolla limpida[99] o nella lista dei sette privilegi indica quello della purezza[100] —, il sacrificio degli impulsi maschili, col *Gesuita* (1638) ove il leone è simbolo appunto dell'austera castità[101].

Questa intelligenza chiara fino in fondo la applicò anche, nella visione della sua vita, ai concetti sull'arte.

Le immagini, e le immagini sacre, celano il pericolo dell'idolatria[102], e perciò l'artista deve trascenderle per visioni spirituali come quella di *San Luca*[103] che rappresenta la Madonna come la vedono i suoi occhi interiori, e non quelli della sua carne. Perfino un filosofo antico come *Diogene* (1637), che cercava l'uomo, insegna che per conoscerlo non basta vedere[104]: anche se in questi anni di maturità magnanima e di amore per la Provvidenza l'artista non piega la sua pittura a disprezzare neanche i *Sensi*, ed anzi con Agostino ne riconosce l'innocenza. «L'errore non ha origine dalle cose […] né dalla fallacia dei sensi, i quali, impressionati secondo la natura del corpo, non fanno altro che trasmettere queste impressioni all'anima che li governa»[105]. In una seconda serie (1637) raffigurandoli dunque con persone degne di pietà, e non spregevoli come invece nella serie romana e cappuccina. Ora l'*Odorato* è un giovane servo bruno guardato mentre porta un vaso di fiori, struggente nella sua ignoranza; e il *Gusto* ha un'espressione sciocca ed allegra come quella dello *Zoppo* che ci ha invitato all'amor di Dio. E anche le arti, con Agostino, sono un dono della Provvidenza, talvolta un riflesso ispirato dell'assoluto[106]: come ci dice il *Musico* (1638), il quale, con il bastone per battere il tempo e il foglio delle note, richiama scritti di Agostino su metrica e sillabe, che distinguono fra numeri puri — quei numeri puri che, sempre secondo Agostino, sono l'alta immagine esemplare che traspare nell'universo per il *Cosmografo*[107] —, fra numeri puri e numeri sensibili[108]: anche questi, lui dunque riconosce, dono della Provvidenza, e senza colpa nessuna giacché il male, assurdo e doloroso, non è qui ma dentro a chi pretende di tenere una sillaba e così, non curandosi della forma ideale del carme, ne arresta lo svolgimento[109].

Il biondo Apollo [Fig. 14], col bel volto immutabile «d'edera e lauro eterno coronato»[110] ... nudo nel golfo del mantello sontuosamente ventilato con colori di rose sul cielo d'oro e rame splendenti, tormenta *Marsia* (1637), e questi «'a! piget, a! non est', clamabat, 'tibia tanti'»[111]: vedendo finalmente, nel dolore altissimo, che la musica terrena, per esistere deve per forza trascorrere e morire, e che sempre soffrirà chi si ferma ad essa invece di ascendere all'immota armonia assoluta[112].

Come in tutta la vita, anche nel campo dell'arte lo spirito non può fermarsi. I modelli naturali — anche proprio dei quadri con Marsia —, estranei che si allontaneranno, accertano nella vita che la bellezza è un dono ed è incolpabile, ma passa, e l'artista deve fare di più, lui deve svolgere un progetto interiore di crescente estensione: così come il musico si impedisce di fermare le sillabe, e il canto si svolge, una strofa dopo l'altra, verso un grande carme multiforme[113].

C'è movimento visibile nella forma vandyckiana — composizioni e trascolorazioni ventilate —, ma un altro movimento, che non si vede, supera questa forma ed altre che nello stesso tempo sono invece pensose e lente o aspre: quello dello spirito, che non si ferma a nessuna e sale ben oltre, a contemplare la Provvi-

15) Ribera, «Santa Caterina d'Alessandria». New York, Metropolitan Museum of Art (Samuel D. Lee Fund, 1934, 34.73).

denza che le dona, l'armonia universale, l'origine celeste[114].

Il vigore, in questo movimento invisibile cederà, nei successivi, ultimi anni della vita, conclusa nel 1652, a una quieta continuità, a composizioni che l'occhio interiore riconosce solenni oltre la differenza fra ori, velli da Maestro degli Annunci, una prospettiva silente da Codazzi.

All'entrata c'è un fermo «humiliandus omnis homo Christo», figurato con la *testa mozzata* dell'uomo più grande pur secondo l'ordine spirituale incomprensibile al mondo[115]. Ma il giogo di Cristo è soave poiché premia con la cresciuta contemplazione, in sovrumana pace, di significati vissuti tante volte. *Santa Caterina* [Fig. 15] dà al Bambino Gesù un bacio spoglio della sua leggendaria sapienza e di amori terreni[116], comparato nel quadro all'offerta di una rosa aperta. La rosa è semplice come il cuore di chi adora l'assoluto e l'atteso nell'inerme: *Simeone*, che chiede si concluda così in pace la sua vita[117], *Pastori*. Per l'*Eucarestia* gli Apostoli «vedono», mentre Giovanni ad occhi chiusi, le labbra unite e le dita al petto si smarrisce pensando a tanta comunione col maestro, anche col suo corpo, appena inghiottito. Un *Sebastiano*, scabroso per molti, ha provato la sua sincerità, è innocente nell'armonia e nello sguardo divino che ora lo avvolge di dolcezza. La vecchiaia di *eremiti*, è anch'essa nella pace dell'armonia. Tutto il resto, ormai silenzioso.

Per questo saggio mi sono molto appoggiato agli apparati di N. Spinosa in *L'opera completa del Ribera* (presentazione di A. E. Pérez Sánchez; Milano, Rizzoli, 1978): ad essi rimando anche il mio lettore, invitandolo a tener conto degli aggiornamenti proposti dallo stesso Spinosa («Un San Francesco inedito nel palazzo del Pardo e alcune considerazioni sul catalogo dei dipinti del Ribera», *Scritti di storia dell'arte in onore di Federico Zeri*, Milano, 1984, pp. 597-8, n. 5), e a considerare scambiate le illustrazioni dei nr. 163 e 164. Per gli incrementi dei quali ho tenuto conto, apro note particolari all'occasione.

[1] Per la storia di quest'opera vedi, oltre al nr. 1 del catalogo Spinosa (*op. cit.*, 1978), M. Cordaro, «Sull'attività del Ribera giovane a Parma», *Storia dell'arte*, 1980, p. 323ss.

[2] G. Mancini, *Considerazioni sulla pittura*, ed. A. Marucchi, con il commento di L. Salerno, Roma, 1956-57, I, p. 249ss. Per la questione dei *Sensi* dipinti a Roma, vedi Spinosa, cat., *op. cit.*, 1978, pp. 91-2, ma considera anche i posteriori dubbi sull'autografia del *Tatto* (N. Ayala Mallory, «Ribera, notas críticas», *Goya* 175-176, 1983, p. 58; Spinosa, *op. cit.*, 1984) e la pubblicazione dell'originale dell'*Odorato* (vedi ad esempio *Important Old Master Paintings and Discoveries of the Past Year*, cat. della mostra presso Piero Corsini, New York, 1986, nr. 19).

[3] Benoît de Canfeld (Benedictus a Canfeld), *Regula perfectionis*, Parisiis, 1610: I, 17; III, 16ss. e particolarmente III, 20 (pp. 88v-89v; 237v ss. e particolarmente 272v). Nella traduzione italiana di fra Modesto Romano: «compir ogni giorno un certo e determinato numero di mortificazioni e rinunziazioni [...] o dai sensi del corpo o dalle passioni dell'anima. Dai sensi del corpo, cioè dalla vista, udito, odorato, dal gusto e dal tatto facendo o patendo alcuna cosa ingrata e disgustevole ad essi»; «accettar quelle cose che repugnano a' suoi sensi, cioè che sono dispiacevoli alla vista, fastidiose all'udito, ingrate all'odorato, amare al gusto, ed aspre al tatto»; «io sono di questo parere (salvo sempre ogni meglior giudizio) che l'altissima, sublimissima, e perfettissima contemplazione sia quella che si fa intorno alla passione del nostro Signor Giesù Cristo, e gratissima alla Maestà sua» etc.

[4] J. Chenault, «Ribera in Roman Archives», *The Burlington Magazine*, 1969, p. 561.

[5] Cicerone, *Tusculanae disputationes*, 5, 114.

[6] Gerolamo, *ep. 76*.

[7] Sulpicio Severo, «De vita Beati Martini», 3, *Patrologia Latina*, 20, col. 162.

[8] Per le notizie sulla gioventù del Ribera alle quali si allude in questo discorso, vedi Mancini, *op. cit.*

[9] Un accostamento del giovane Ribera a Valentin è già stato proposto da F. Bologna («A proposito dei 'Ribera' del Museo di Bruxelles», *Musées Royaux des Beaux-Arts — Bulletin*, 1952, pp. 48, 50).

[10] Pietro, *II ep.*, 3, 13-15; Paolo, *ad Romanos*, 2, 4-8; Giacomo, *ep. catholica*: 1, 27; 2, 14-26. L'attribuzione al Maggiore dell'*epistola di San Giacomo* è, oltre che in Dante (*Paradiso*, XXV, vv. 76-77), nella tradizione spagnola.

[11] Matteo, 26, 53-54; Paolo, *ad Romanos*, 5, 6-9.

[12] Jacopo da Varagine (Jacobus a Voragine), *Legenda Aurea*, ed. Th. Graesse, Dresdae et Lipsiae, 1846, p. 108ss. Il seguito di questo saggio presenterà frequenti ricorsi necessari alla *Leggenda aurea*.

[13] Jacopo da Varagine, *op. cit.*, p. 540.

[14] L'orazione di San Pietro è evidentemente «separata», solitaria, nella incisione corrispondente, pubblicata da W. Vitzthum («Disegni inediti di Ribera», *Arte illustrata*, 37/38, 1971, p. 76) e ripr. da N. Spinosa (cat., *op. cit.*, 1978, nr. 22. 2).

[15] Il tema, assai frequente nell'opera del Ribera, è sempre detto «San Gerolamo e l'angelo con la tromba del Giudizio»: anche da J. Brown (*Jusepe de Ribera — Prints and Drawings*, cat. della mostra, Princeton e Cambridge Mass., 1973, p. 41), che pure (dichiarando di dipendere da J. Hand) cita fra altri un testo che permette la soluzione, cioè la *Regula Monachorum ex scriptis Hieronymi per Lupum de Olmeto collecta*: qui (cap. 23; *Patrologia Latina*, 30, col. 375) si trova infatti: «sive leges, sive dormies, sive scribes, sive vigilabis, Amos tibi semper buccina in auribus sonet»: non si tratta quindi della tromba del Giudizio, bensì di quella di Amos, ovviamente come la interpreta lo stesso Gerolamo, cioè come alta ammonizione contro l'idolatria («Verba itaque Amos, quo tempore populus Israel avulsus erat a Domino, et aureis vitulis serviebat, sive avulsus a regno stirpis David, clara voce cecinerunt instar clangentis tubae, quae interpretatur Thecue»: Gerolamo, «Com-

mentarii in Amos prophetam», *Patrologia Latina*, 25, col. 992).

[16] Matteo, 19, 21-30.

[17] Agostino, *De vera religione*, 10, 18-19.

[18] Agostino, *De vera religione*, 16, 31.

[19] Sull«'evangelismo» cinquecentesco napoletano, in relazione al nostro argomento, vedi H. Jedin, *Girolamo Seripando* etc., Würzburg, 1937: I, I, 6 (p. 132ss.); II, p. 239; II, VII, 2 (p. 268ss.).

[20] Agostino, *Confessioni*, 7, 9, 13ss.; Agostino, *De libero arbitrio*: 2, 8, 20; 2, 11, 31.

[21] Agostino, *Confessioni*, 7, 9, 14.

[22] Agostino, *Confessioni*, 7, 21, 27.

[23] Matteo, 11, 29. Agostino, *Confessioni*, 7, 9, 14.

[24] Vedi, ad esempio, il ricordo di Paolo, *ad Romanos*, 5, in Agostino, *Confessioni*, 7, 9, 14.

[25] Agostino, *De vera religione*, 16, 31.

[26] Agostino, *De vera religione*, 37, 68.

[27] Agostino, *De vera religione*: da 11, 21 a 12, 23; da 19, 37 a 23, 44.

[28] Matteo, 11, 29; Agostino, *De vera religione*, 35, 65.

[29] In un saggio di V. Pacelli («Processo tra Ribera e un committente», *Napoli nobilissima*, 1979, p. 28ss.) vediamo che da un ambiente diverso rispetto a quello del Ribera gli si poteva chiedere un'opera con riferimenti precisi ad altre sue precedenti: possiamo dunque pensare che le opere eseguite per committenti consapevoli dei significati costituissero un riferimento per richieste accettabili anche se esteriori.

[30] Agostino, *De vera religione*, da 4, 6 a 5, 8.

[31] Agostino, *De libero arbitrio*, 2, 11, 31; Gerolamo, *ep. 76*; Cicerone, *Tusculanae disputationes*, 5, 114-115, e *De finibus*, 5, 87.

[32] Agostino, *in Joannis ev.*, 10, 13 (traduz. di E. Gandolfo).

[33] Paolo, *ad Philippenses*, 2, 3-11.

[34] Pietro, *I ep.*, 2, 19-24.

[35] Agostino, *Confessioni*, 7, 21, 27 (con citaz. da Matteo, 11, 28).

[36] Agostino, *Confessioni*, 7, 18, 24 (traduz. di C. Carena).

[37] Jacopo da Varagine, *op. cit.*, p. 485.

[38] G. Seripando, *Prediche sopra il simbolo de gli Apostoli* etc., Venezia, 1567, pp. 97v-98v.

[39] Matteo, 11, 25. Vedilo commentato da Agostino, in *Confessioni*, 7, 21, 27.

[40] Matteo, 11, 29.

[41] Vedi le n. 33 e 34.

[42] F. Diedo, *Legenda Beati Rochi* (incunabolo consultato presso la Biblioteca Statale di Lucca), [p. 5r]. In *Acta Sanctorum*, agosto, III, p. 403, par. 18.

[43] Jacopo da Varagine, *op. cit.*, pp. 708-710.

[44] Vedi la n. 18.

[45] Jacopo da Varagine, *op. cit.*, p. 16ss.

[46] Vedi, ad esempio, Franciscus a Puteo, vita di San Bruno (Basilea, c. 1515), in *Patrologia Latina*, 152, col. 522.

[47] Matteo, 19, 27 e 29.

[48] Vedi la n. 42.

[49] *Atti degli Apostoli*, 12, 1-2. Jacopo da Varagine, *op. cit.*, p. 422.

[50] *Genesi*, 29, 20.

[51] Agostino, *Contra Faustum*, 22, 52.

[52] Agostino, *De vera religione*, 12, 25.

[53] Agostino, *Confessioni*, 7, 18, 24 (traduz. cit.).

[54] Vedi, ad esempio, Juan de la Cruz, *Subida del Monte Carmelo*, III, 34-36.

[55] Vedi, ad esempio, Luigi di Granata, *Devotissime meditazioni per i giorni della settimana*, in idem, *Tutte l'opere*, Venezia, 1619, p. 111.

[56] Agostino, *De vera religione*: 11, 21; 20, 40; 21, 41; 29, 52; 33, 61; 36, 67; 40, 74-75; 41, 77. Agostino, *Confessioni*, 10, 34, 51.

Sull'innocenza della bellezza, vedi anche *De civitate Dei*, 12, 8 («nec luxuria est vitium pulcrorum suaviumque corporum [...]»).

[57] Agostino, *De vera religione*: 11, 21; 18, 35-36; 19, 37; 20, 40. Agostino, *Confessioni*, 7, 11, 17.

[58] Agostino, *in Joannis ev.*: 25, 16; 25, 18.

[59] Nel simbolo del serpente, secondo G. C. Capaccio, *Delle imprese*, Napoli, 1592, II, p. 58v («si servirono del serpente alcuni per mostrar l'ebrietà, per ciò ch'è incontinente questo animale del vino»).

[60] Nel simbolo della testuggine, secondo F. Picinelli, *Mondo simbolico*, Milano, 1654, 6, 47, 186 («il Demonio con esso noi si porta da testuggine, poiché non ci s'avventa addosso con la veemenza d'un fulmine, ma passo passo e gradatamente nelle sue malvage persuasive avanzandosi, non mai si riposa finché non arrivi ove disegna»).

[61] Nel simbolo della conchiglia, secondo Picinelli, *op. cit.*, 6, 15.

[62] Agostino, *Confessioni*, 9,8,18: «si era insinuato in mia madre il gusto del vino. [...] Così, aggiungendo ogni giorno un piccolo sorso al primo, come è vero che 'a trascurare le piccole cose si finisce col cadere' (*Eccl.*, 19, 1), sprofondò in quel vezzo [...]. Ma quale rimedio poteva darsi contro una malattia occulta, se non la vigile presenza su di noi della tua medicina, Signore?» (traduz. cit.).

[63] Ovidio, *Metamorfosi*, IV, vv. 456-463. Cfr. Agostino, *De vera religione*, 20, 40.

[64] Mi riferisco al dipinto che nel catalogo del Prado porta il nr. 1074, e nel catalogo di Spinosa il nr. 54. In ambedue i testi l'opera è intitolata «San Paolo», in forza della barba allungata e della spada; ma in un *Apostolato* San Paolo sarebbe aggiunto, e invece Matteo, uno dei dodici, non può mancare: perciò, fino a che non venga scoperto un altro dipinto dell'Apostolato, con San Matteo, dobbiamo credere che il nr. 1074 raffiguri questo santo, poiché la spada fu strumento del martirio suo come di quello di San Paolo.

[65] Agostino, *sermo 62*, 17.

[66] Agostino, *De vera religione*, 39, 72; Agostino, *Confessioni*, 7, 13, 19.

[67] Agostino, *De libero arbitrio*, 3, 9, 24 (traduz. di D. Gentili). Vedi anche *Confessioni*, 7, 13, 19.

[68] Agostino, *De vera religione*, 40, 76 (traduz. di M. Vannini).

[69] *Ibidem*. Vedi anche *Confessioni*, da 7, 13, 19 a 7, 14, 20.

[70] Agostino, *De vera religione*, 32, 59 (traduz. cit.). Vedi anche 32, 60.

[71] Agostino, *Confessioni*, 10, 6, 8 (traduz. cit.).

[72] I due paesaggi del Ribera (collezione dei Duchi d'Alba) sono stati pubblicati da A. E. Pérez Sánchez in *Civiltà del Seicento a Napoli*, cat. della mostra (Napoli, 1984), pp. 416-417.

[73] Agostino, *De vera religione*: da 30, 56 a 31, 57.

[74] Agostino, *De vera religione*: 21, 41; 34, 63; 40, 74-75.

[75] Per i ritiri dell'umanista cristiano, nelle forme della tradizione poetica, ricorda la *Vida solitaria* di un altro seguace spagnolo di Sant'Agostino, fray Luis de León.

[76] Agostino, *De vera religione*, 35, 65.

[77] Agostino, *sermo 122*, 2.

[78] Agostino, *in Joannis ev.*: 4, 14; 5, 3-5; 13, 7.

[79] Agostino, *in Joannis ev.*, 7, 5.

[80] Jacopo da Varagine, *op. cit.*, p. 31.

[81] Jacopo da Varagine, *op. cit.*, p. 430.

[82] Jacopo da Varagine, *op. cit.*, p. 292.

[83] Jacopo da Varagine, *op. cit.*, pp. 113, 114.

[84] La prima versione nota è stata pubblicata da Spinosa (*op. cit.*, 1984). Una seconda versione (1642, oggi a Dresda) è pendant di una *Liberazione di San Pietro* per il collegamento che trovi illustrato in Marco da Lisbona, *Croniche degli ordini instituiti dal P. S. Francesco* (1557), Venezia, 1598-1599, I, I, p. 165 (vedi n. 99).

[85] Marco da Lisbona, *op. cit.*, I, I, p. 164 (vedi n. 99).

[86] Vedi invece Agostino, *in psal. 85*, 21: «Transeat tempus patientiae, veniat tempus judicii»: «ille resurgens, et in terram ipse veniet judicaturus; ipse videbitur terribilis, qui visus est contemtibilis».

[87] Gerolamo, *ep. 68*, 1.

[88] Prudenzio, *Psychomachia*, vv. 1-37. Devo ad Antonio La Penna la soluzione, con il rimando a questo testo, dell'iconografia del così detto *Duello fra donne* del Prado: lo ringrazio molto cordialmente.

[89] *Libro di Daniele*, 5: 1-5, 25-28, 30-31.

[90] Agostino, *sermo 5*, 8; Agostino, *in psal. 44*, 20.

[91] Agostino, *De vera religione*: da 11, 21 a 12, 23; da 19, 37 a 23, 44.

[92] D. Fitz Darby, «In the Train of a Vagrant Silenus», *Art in America*, 1943, p. 140ss.

[93] Agostino, *De vera religione*, 20, 40 (traduz. cit.).

[94] Ovidio, *Metamorfosi*, X, vv. 503ss.; vedi particolarmente i vv. 529 («capta viri forma») e 532 («abstinet et caelo: caelo praefertur Adonis»).

[95] Vedi particolarmente Agostino, *De vera religione*, 11, 22.

[96] Agostino, *De civitate Dei*, 21, 26, 2. Vedi anche Paolo, *I ad Corinthios*, 7, 28.

[97] L. Wadding, *Annales Minorum*, II, col. 261-262, XVI.

[98] Vedi *Ignatii Loiolae vita postremo recognita*, Florentiae, 1588, cap. IX.

[99] Marco da Lisbona, *op. cit.*, I, I, pp. 74-75. Devo alla cortesia del p. Jérôme Poulenc per il tramite del p. Samuele Olivieri l'indicazione delle *Croniche* di Marco da Lisbona come fonte per l'iconografia del San Francesco cui un angelo mostra un'ampolla d'acqua limpida. Son poi ricorso a questo testo nello studio di altre opere del Ribera relative a San Francesco (vedi le n. 84, 85, 100).

[100] Nella copia oggi al Museu Nacional de Arte Antiga di Lisbona (cat. Spinosa, *op. cit.*, 1978, nr. 300), dove l'angelo indica nella lista dei privilegi per i Frati Minori si legge: «Quod fratres mortis tempore tali-ter purgati et mundi ex hac vita migrabunt quod Purgatorii pene nequaquam eos prepedient quia eorum [...] cilissime transvolent ad [...] eternam». E' questo il terzo privilegio (cfr. Marco da Lisbona, *op. cit.*, I, I, p. 134; vedi n. 99).

[101] Picinelli, *op. cit.*, 5, 26, 336.

[102] Agostino, *De vera religione*, 55, 108.

[103] Mi riferisco al dipinto che A. E. Pérez Sánchez ha pubblicato come copia dal Ribera («El 'San Lucas pintando a la Virgen' de Ribera», *Ars auro prior — Studia Joanni Bialostocki sexagenario dicata*, Warszawa, 1981, p. 403ss.).

[104] Diogene Laerzio, *Vite dei filosofi*: 6, 2, 30; 6, 2, 41.

[105] Agostino, *De vera religione*, 36, 67 (traduz. cit.); vedi anche nella stessa opera, 33, 62.

[106] Agostino, *Confessioni*, 10, 34, 53.

[107] Agostino, *De libero arbitrio*: 2, 16, 42; 3, 9, 28. Agostino, *De ordine*, 2, 14, 42.

[108] Vedi ad esempio Agostino, *De ordine*, 2, 14, 41.

[109] Agostino, *De vera religione*, 22, 42-43.

[110] Mitologia e forma classiche sono frequenti nella poesia dell'agostiniano Luis de León, del quale qui traduco un verso di *Vida solitaria* («de yedra y lauro eterno coronado»).

[111] Ovidio, *Metamorfosi*, VI, v. 386. Per l'intero mito di Marsia, vedi i vv. 382-400.

[112] Agostino, *De vera religione*, 22, 42.

[113] Agostino, *De vera religione*, 22, 42-43.

[114] Agostino, *De vera religione*, 32, 59-60.

[115] Secondo lo stesso Cristo, Giovanni Battista fu il più grande degli uomini (Matteo, 11, 11): eppure, mentre Cristo fu innalzato sulla croce, egli fu ridotto del capo, perché «humiliandus erat omnis homo Christo» (Agostino: *sermo 287*, 3, 4; *sermo 289*, 3 e 5).

[116] Jacopo da Varagine, *op. cit.*, p. 789ss.

[117] Luca, 2, 25-35.

MARCIN FABIAŃSKI

The Cremonese Ceiling Examined in Its Original *Studiolo* Setting

The painted decoration with the Muses now housed in the Victoria and Albert Museum [Figs. 1, 2][1] was transferred from the octagonal umbrella vault that covered a small square chamber on the ground floor of the ex-Casa Maffi of the Monastery della Colomba in Cremona, 6 Via Belvedere. The house belonged to a prior of the Austin Friars, well known for their intellectual interests.[2] Extant sources do not specify the architect, nor do they describe the decoration. Marcantonio Michiel says that this ''round chamber with the vault that represents our celestial hemisphere was adorned and divided by'' the same person, as one may guess.[3] According to G. Grasselli, active at the beginning of the nineteenth century, there was also the now-lost *Adoration of the Child*, ascribed to the same artist who decorated the vault.[4] In G. B. Cavalcaselle's drawing, made in 1869 [Fig. 3], we see also a small window in the room.[5] After 1884 the fresco decoration was detached from its setting, probably by an art dealer called Bardini, and bought in Florence by the South Kensington Museum five years later,[6] where it has remained ever since, away from its original environment and thereby more difficult to discuss. As may be inferred from the drawing, the central section of the painting was erroneously recomposed in the museum: it was rotated by some 150°, which has not until now been noticed.

In spite of its interesting iconography and comparatively high artistic quality, the fresco has not been adequately discussed, and there are only several occasional hints and one short paper about it in the literature. Crowe and Cavalcaselle,

the authors of the first formal evaluation, ascribed the work to a painter influenced by Mantegna and by the Ferrarese school of about 1500.[7] These conclusions were generally accepted, yet art historians advanced various attributions.[8] Moreover L. Kauffmann and F. Zeri observed some artistic and compositional differences of the central part of the fresco in comparison to its other sections; hence the latter author supposed that it was repainted.[9] Recently the decoration was convincingly connected with Alessandro Pampurino by Mina Gregori, who did not mention, however, if the central section was original.[10]

Iconographically, the painted *oculus* with people leaning out is rightly associated with the famous Mantegna fresco in Mantua.[11] The figures of Apollo and the Muses were inspired by the so-called *Tarots of Mantegna*, made in fact by an anonymous Ferrarese master about 1465.[12] E. Schröter set the decoration against the background of a broad iconographic tradition, derived from Martianus Capella's description of the Muses. She also pointed out that Calliope had been singled out under the influence of Macrobius, whose idea was propagated by Ficino.[13] However, she discussed neither the figures in the *oculus*, nor the Roman busts,[14] nor the grotesquerie of the dome. Hence the iconography of the whole decoration still awaits thorough research.

Nobody has traced the genesis of the architecture of the room, if we choose not to count the remarks of Schröter, which are superficial in this respect. The German scholar related the shape of the vault to some ancient examples and compared it

1) Alessandro Pampurino (?), Vault frescoes from the Casa Maffi, Cremona. London, Victoria and Albert Museum, inv. no. 428-1889. ⌀ 4.27 m (photo: museum).

2) Alessandro Pampurino (?), Vault frescoes from the Casa Maffi, Cremona. London, Victoria and Albert Museum, inv. no. 428-1889. ⌀ 4.27 m (photo: museum).

190

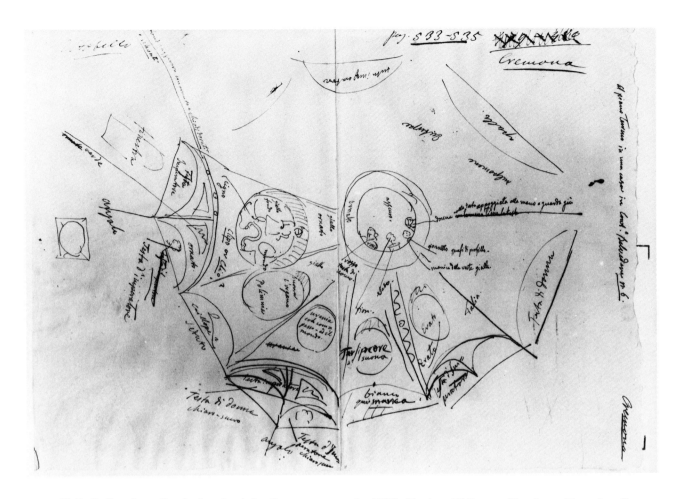

3) G. B. Cavalcaselle, A sketch of the Cremonese vault, 1869. Venice, Biblioteca Marciana, *Taccuino di G. B. Cavalcaselle*, fol. 10 (photo: biblioteca).

to that of the Chigi Chapel by Raphael.[15] Nor have the functions of the hall been explained, which might be done, owing to the lack of written sources about the patron, only after the aforementioned questions are solved.

Thus it is neither known how the room originally looked, nor if all the sections of the decoration are original, what role was played in the programme by other parts of the painting, apart from the Muses, and finally, why this ''round chamber'' with the Muses was covered by a dome, or, in Michiel's words, ''the vault that represents our celestial hemisphere.''

$$* * *$$

Originally the dome vaulted a small square room belonging to a priest. As the house it was in no longer exists and we do not possess any contemporary descriptions, except Michiel's

hint and nineteenth-century sources,[16] all we can do is to guess at the layout of the room with the help of comparable structures.

In the corners of the square room, four halves of a groin vault playing the role of pendentives are set under the actual octagonal vault in the form of an umbrella, every second spandrel of which is wider. The halves of a groin vault are supported by a semicircular squinch, ca. 1.3 m in diameter. The spandrels sustained by these squinches, however, are even wider, so their extreme parts embrace the squinches and merge with the walls of the room directly.

All four remaining spandrels, wider than the aformentioned ones, rest directly on the chamber walls, closing them with arches, each ca. 1.9 m in diameter (thus about one third larger than the diameter of the squinches, whereby one of them

191

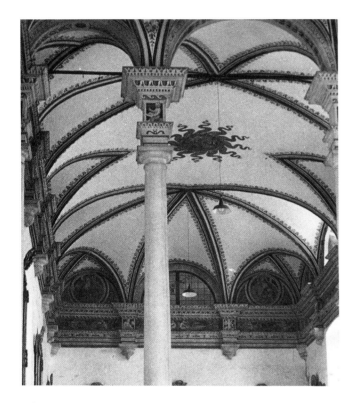

4) Certosa di Pavia, Grand Refectory vault
(photo: M. Fabiański).

5) Milan, Vault of the chancel of S. Maria delle Grazie by
Bramante, after 1490 (photo: M. Fabiański).

contains an open arch, probably closing the original entrance.

A peculiarity of the umbrella is that its groins vanish in a certain place, above which the spandrels merge with each other in such a way that the central part of the vault is smooth.

So far, it has not been determined whether the construction in question was typical or exceptional. We know that umbrella vaults were built in antiquity, but generally they were put over circular or polygonal halls, and if these were rectangular pendentives were inserted.[17] In modern times umbrellas were constructed by Brunelleschi[18] and, later, by other architects such as Bramante.[19]

The motif of halves of a groin vault occurred in the Florentine school as early as the end of the fourteenth century.[20] In Brunelleschi's architecture, for instance, they play the role of pendentives and a layout of a vault with such supports was included in the treatise of Francesco di Giorgio Martini (Cod. Tor. Sal., fol. 22r).

We can be sure, therefore, that both motifs — that of an umbrella and that of halves of a groin vault in place of pendentives — were fairly widespread in Italy in the last quarter of the Quattrocento. By that time they had been combined in Lombardy. One may think of such examples as semi-umbrellas closing the shorter sides of rectangular rooms, such as the refectories of the Milanese churches S. Maria della Pace,[21] S. Maria delle Grazie, built by Bramante in the last decade of the century, and that of the Certosa di Pavia, ca. 1500 [Fig. 4].[22]

The oldest known example of a full octagonal umbrella over a square room, with halves of a groin vault instead of pendentives, is the vault in the chancel of S. Maria delle Grazie, designed by Bramante after 1490 [Fig. 5]. One can also add the dodecagonal vault in the oratory S. Maria alla Fontana (after 1508),[23] the umbrella in the chapel S. Giuseppe in S. Maria della Pace (ca. 1520)[24] and the other one in the Casa degli Atellani, after 1521 [Fig. 6].[25] Apart from the construction in Cremona, all the other works of this kind from the beginning of the Cinquecento are in Milan and differ from the former: the groins separating the spandrels can be seen in every part of the vault,

6) Milan, Casa degli Atellani, Vault in the Sala dello Zodiaco, after 1521. From *Storia di Milano*.

hence also in its centre; and all the umbrellas except the one in the chancel of S. Maria delle Grazie are regular polygons with spandrels of equal width. This solution is the simplest, and, if we consider the number of such vaults, it was the most common one. Another simple, but otherwise exceptional construction is that by Bramante in the choir of S. Maria delle Grazie [Fig. 5]. The radical diversification of the width of its spandrels results from the equal size that was assumed for all twelve lunettes. Consequently, the size of the squinches closing the halves of a groin vault increased in comparison to the diameters of the four remaining lunettes. Obviously the width of the spandrels above the squinches was enlarged by the same proportion.

In summary, the vault in Cremona is exceptional thanks to two traits: the groins vanish towards its centre, where a homogeneous surface is created, and the four spandrels of the vault above the axes of the room walls are widened at the cost of the remaining parts of the umbrella.

The reason for reducing the size of the latter could be the need for a doorway as wide as 1.9 m. It is, however, doubtful if so wide an entrance to this small chamber was necessary. Suffice it to say that in the Gubbio *studiolo*, which is of comparable size, the portal was only 0.975 m wide.[26] The need for a wide opening does not account for the fact that the halves of a groin vault were reduced even more and they do not support, contrary to similar constructions, the whole spandrel

above each of them, but its middle part only. We may surmise, therefore, that the architect in Cremona did not want to enlarge the entrance and the diameter of the main lunettes but aimed at reducing the size of the other ones. Only now can we tell why the squinch formed by each half of a groin vault is smaller than the width of the spandrel above: we see that the designer did his best to have the smallest possible lunettes in the corners of the room but tried to keep the actual vault as regular as possible.

We do not know the original number of doors and windows. The only other umbrella of the type of the vault in question to be found in a secular building (the Casa degli Atellani in Milan) vaulted the square Sala dello Zodiaco [Fig. 6], which originally had only one entrance and no window at all.[27] Other irregular openings there were made later. We may remark that the small window in Cavalcaselle's drawing [Fig. 3] is situated asymmetrically under the lunette to the left of the doorway, which might indicate either that it was added, or that there was the second window to the right of the doorway, not marked by Cavalcaselle. Anyway, the Cremonese room, like that in Milan, was most probably isolated. This conjecture is made more plausible if we notice that under the reconstructed umbrella there is only one open arch, whereas the other respective places are filled with lunettes. However, there is a slight possibility that originally there were two large openings in front of each other because the lunette facing the actual entrance is devoid of any decoration.

***

The painted decoration of all the smaller and two larger lunettes and that of the whole vault has luckily survived up to the present day. It is divided into geometrical fields closely following the structure of the vault.

All the lunettes are adorned with foreshortened images of shallow niches closed by painted archivolts. The eight smaller lunettes contain profile busts gazing in pairs at one another, the two larger ones, the figures of Apollo and Calliope, while the spot in front of the entrance is empty.

The decoration of the umbrella is divided into fields resembling trapezia and corresponding to the parts of the spandrels separated by distinct groins, and, in the middle smooth area, into a *tondo* [Figs. 1, 2]. Each of the quadrilaterals is surrounded by ornamental borders with the motif of palmettes, hemmed with depicted frames. An illusionistic image of a round shallow recess, surrounded by a cornice and containing a figure of a Muse, is inscribed in each of the trapezoids. The rest of the quadrilaterals is adorned with grotesquerie. The *tondo* in the middle of the vault [Fig. 40] is framed with a Moresque border. It accomodates an image of

7) **Scribonia and Galba (?) or Titus (?). Detail of Fig. 1 (photo: museum).**

an *oculus* with three persons leaning out from behind a parapet.

The whole decoration, in subdued greyish-brown hues, is almost monochrome. The exceptions are blue backgrounds in the two large lunettes and especially the scene in the *oculus*, painted in relatively lively and natural colours. The architectural elements are consequently depicted as if they were lighted from one source. Only the parapet of the *oculus* is represented as though the rays were emitted from another place, and their direction differs from that of the others by ca. 150°. This discrepancy, however, is caused by the faulty reconstruction of the vault in the museum.

The smaller lunettes are embellished with eight classical profiles made up as an imitation of bas-relief. A review of these images will start clockwise from the left-hand pair facing the doorway [Fig. 7]

The woman's head depicted on the left-hand lunette has a peculiar hair style. Slightly undulating hair adheres to the crown of the head, whereas below the hair is entwined into three thick braids in the form of rolls, forming a small pointed lump above the atlas. A similar hair style recurs only on antique coins portraying Scribonia, Augustus' second wife [Figs. 8, 9],[28] so there can be little doubt who the sitter was.

It is difficult to identify the profile of a stout man with knitted brows, hooked nose, projecting chin and Adam's apple. The conventional treatment of the features, also to be seen in the other parts of the cycle, prevents our jumping to farfetched conclusions. The profile shares some of its general

characteristics with the one discussed at the end of this review. In both cases there might be simulacra of Galba [Figs. 10, 11][29] or Titus [Figs. 12, 13].[30]

It is not easy, either, to tell who is represented in the following pair on the left-side lunette [Fig. 14]. The head belongs to a fleshy man with a double chin, slightly hooked nose and he is wearing a *corona radiata* on his curly hair. This picture displays some affinities with certain images of Trajan [Fig. 15].[31]

His partner is a man with a long, straight nose, distinct chin and undulating hair, embellished with a *corona radiata*. These traits resemble portraits of Augustus [Figs. 16, 17],[32] whose likeness it possibly is.

The head of an obese man in the next pair of lunettes [Fig. 18] stands out, thanks to the curly hair, forming a so-called diadem above the forehead and crowned with a laurel wreath. Conventional though his features are, one can be sure it is Nero [Figs. 19-21].[33]

Some doubts arise, however, when one looks at the accompanying bust of a woman with a long neck, who is wearing a round bonnet fringed with a roll from which curls escape. This image shows a similarity to a drawing of a coin showing Agrippina, Nero's mother [Fig. 22]. In the sixteenth century another coin was known, representing Nero and Agrippina in front of each other, but it was depicted in a quite different way.[34]

In the fourth corner of the room there are two male heads

8) Scribonia. After Fulvio.

10) Galba. After Fulvio.

9) Scribonia. After Vico.

11) Galba. After Vico.

12) Titus, medallion by G. A. Amadeo on the façade of the Certosa di Pavia, last quarter of the fifteenth centruy (photo: M. Fabiański).

13) Titus. After Vico.

with curly hair crowned with laurel wreaths [Fig. 23]. The profile on the left, with knitted eyebrows, straight pointed nose and beard, corresponds to images of Lucius Verus [Figs. 24, 25].[35] His partner resembles the first profile noted above, hence it might be Galba or Titus.[36]

As has been demostrated, the heads below the squinches were inspired either by Roman coins, or by related drawings, and most of them, their conventional stylization notwithstanding, display details of clothing or hair style of the sitter. In comparison with their models, the painted profiles stand out owing to their long hair depicted as an ornament (e.g., "Augustus", "Agrippina", "Galba"), sharp folds ("Agrippina", Scribonia) and a peculiar structure of the auricles consisting of three distinct parts: a pointed and lightly concave upper section, the medium one with a rounded edge and an oval lobe.

The figures of Apollo and Calliope below the larger spandrels, as well as those of the other Muses in the circular niches painted on the umbrella, derive from the so-called *Tarots of Mantegna*. Hence are the attributes of the respective Muses and Apollo, and a disc, common to all of them except Urania, who has a globe instead, and Calliope, left without this symbol. The figures in the *tondi*, beginning clockwise from the one above Scribonia, represent: Urania [Fig. 35], Terpsichore, Erato [Figs. 26-28], Thalia, Melpomene [Figs. 29-31], Euterpe, Clio [Figs. 32-34] and Polyhymnia [Figs. 35, 36]. The series is completed by Calliope [Fig. 37], depicted on the larger

lunette to the left of the doorway, and, in front of it, Apollo [Figs. 38, 39].

All the Muses are barefoot; only Calliope wears sandals. A singular trait of the figures is their apparent bulk and chiaroscuro combined with distinct outlines, which gives them a graphic character to the same degree as in the *Tarots*. The painter followed neither the details, nor the style of the engravings. Generally he demonstrated a good command of human anatomy and the ability to render a moving body, abundant, wind-blown hair and billowing robes with plentiful folds. In the cases of Melpomene, Erato, Euterpe and Calliope, the robe is cut in two and joined by a button, uncovers a leg and, parted by a sudden gust, creates picturesque forms which might make one think even of the lavish folds of some late-Gothic figures in Northern European art.

The remaining surface of the vault trapezoids is adorned with grotesquerie containing such motifs as busts of women, bulls and Pegasusses with twining acanthus, as well as candelabra, pairs of *amorini* riding floral hybrids and cornucopia. The decoration, however, is dominated by a classical floral ornament and with its motifs resembles the "archaeologizing" grotesquerie from Pinturicchio's workshop.[37] The way of depicting the ornament is closely related to the figurative sections of the decoration: their forms, having a relief-like quality, are at the same time linear and prove that the painter was a good student of anatomy. Although the models of the ornaments, probably graphical, have not been found yet, it may

196

14. Trajan (?) and Augustus (?). Detail of Fig. 1 (photo: museum).

15) Trajan. After Goltz.

16) Augustus, medallion by G. A. Amadeo on the façade of the
Certosa di Pavia, last quarter of the fifteenth century
(photo: M. Fabiański).

17) Augustus. After Fulvio.

18) Nero and Agrippina (?). Detail of Fig. 2 (photo: museum).

19) Nero, medallion by G. A. Amadeo on the façade of the
Certosa di Pavia, last quarter of the fifteenth cetury
(photo: M. Fabiański).

20) Nero, façade frieze of the Palazzo Fodri, Cremona,
ca. 1490 (photo: M. Fabiański).

NERO IMPERATOR.   XLVII

Domitii Neronis & Agrippinæ Au/
gustę filius primus Claudiæ familiæ
p adoptione uictrico Claudio postea
penitentem infertus Trimulus, n.pa-
trem amiferat apud amitam Lepidã
nutritus fub faltatore Tomfore & cy
tharedo pedagogis uitata femper iu/
bente Matre Philophia Aurigandi &
fcena agendi studiofus Incendiarius

21) Nero. After Fulvio.

198

22) Agrippina, Nero's mother. After Fulvio.

be surmised, in an analogy with the busts and Muses, that the artist used these paradigms rather liberally and left a strong stylistic imprint of his own.

The *oculus* depicted in the middle of the umbrella [Fig. 40] contains a parapet formed by two cornices encircling an opening. From behind the upper cornice a man, woman and an adolescent lean out, seen against the background of a blue sky with a cloud. The scene, completed by a flowerpot with a flowerless carnation,[38] is painted in comparatively lively, natural hues, contrasting with the remainder of the decoration and, unlike it, suggesting that it is not merely an architectural ornament, but a depiction of a real scene.

The elderly balding man leans on his right palm, depicted in a very incongruous way, incompatible with the style of the other parts of the figure. Being painted in a softer way, probably later, the hand contrasts with the sharp linear face. The ear is equally sharp, with an acute upper part and a distinct lobe. The woman and adolescent appearing on the other side of the opening have brown hair, presumably repainted.[39] The lady supports her head with her palm, whereas the boy, seen in profile, turns his head towards her.

The scene derives from the fresco painted by Mantegna in the Camera Picta in Mantua between 1465 and 1474 [Fig. 41]. The Cremonese *oculus* corresponds to it not only in its general design and the contrast with the other parts of the vault decoration, but also in some details. The lemon tree in the tub in Mantua was replaced by the carnation in Cremona, whereas the pair of ladies was supplanted by the woman and boy. The differences consist in the introduction of the elderly man and the lack of *putti*, peacock and most of the figures. Moreover, the style of the Cremonese fresco is inferior to that of its archetype.

The figures and the flowerpot are depicted as if they were parts of vertical pictures, later hung horizontally (*quadri riportati*). In effect, the illusion aimed at by the artist was completely destroyed.

On the whole, however, the painter was acquainted with some principles of illusionistic painting, best carried out in the *tondi* with the Muses and in the archivolts, worst, in the figures in the *oculus*. This artistic current, inaugurated in Padua in Mantegna's circle, spread also to Lombardy towards the end of the fifteenth century.[40] The style of the three-dimensional, yet linear figures could have been derived from the same artist as well. The peculiar shape of the auricles of the ancient profiles and of the man in the *oculus* may arguably be connected with the Ferrarese school, in particular with Cosmè Tura and Francesco Cossa,[41] whereas Northern European art, presumably through the medium of Venice, was the source of the graphical and decorative character of the scenes, especially of the sharp folds of the Muses and some of the busts. All these features are independent of the iconographic models of the scenes, so they should be attributed to the brush of the painter, probably Alessandro Pampurino, ca. 1500. They also suggest that the whole decoration has not been essentially repainted, and, therefore, that it conserves its primitive iconographic programme. The only lost, probably original, part of the decoration we know about is the *Adoration of the Child*, mentioned by Grasselli.

Some further conclusions may be reached after our scrutiny of the frescoes and their connections with the architecture. Only now do we know the reason for making the apex of the vault smooth by eliminating the groins: solely on such a surface could the illusionistic *oculus* be painted. The twofold sizes of the lunettes were, as it seems now, stimulated by the necessity that the ancient profiles be accommodated in small rather than large fields. And the monochromatic character of all the parts of the decoration apart from that in the parapet of the *oculus*, ill-placed in the museum, corresponds to the actual light falling through the doorway. Thus our conjecture that the room had initially only one large opening is corroborated, though one cannot exclude the existence of one or two windows on the either side of the doorway.[42]

Our deductions, drawn from formal analysis, allow us to state that at least the general programme of the painted

23) Lucius Verus and Galba (?) or Titus (?). Detail of Fig. 2 (photo: museum).

24) Lucius Verus. After Fulvio.

25) Lucius Verus. After Goltz.

decoration was known when the vault was being built and the architect was therefore compelled to submit an individual design which was a modified version of the popular type of umbrella vault. The painter's fairly faithful following of various models leads to the conclusion that these were likely to have been indicated by the author of the iconographic programme who also influenced the choice of architectural solutions, thus controlling the whole enterprise. Michiel's hint about adorning and dividing the chamber, quoted at the beginning of this paper, also suggests that the architectural divisions were

26) Terpsichore and Erato. Detail of Fig. 1 (photo: museum).

TERPSICORE · XIII ·

27) Terpsichore. From the *Tarocchi*. After Hind.

ERATO · XIIII

28) Erato. From the *Tarocchi*. After Hind.

29) Thalia and Melpomene. Detail of Figs. 1-2 (photo: museum).

30) Thalia. From the *Tarocchi*. After Hind.

31) Melpomene. From the *Tarocchi*. After Hind.

32) Euterpe and Clio. Detail of Fig. 2 (photo: museum).

33) Euterpe. From the *Tarocchi*. After Hind.

34) Clio. From the *Tarocchi*. After Hind.

35) Polyhymnia and Urania. Detail of Fig. 1 (photo: museum).

36) Polyhymnia. From the *Tarocchi*. After Hind.

subordinated to its decoration. However, we are not able to say why the patron and architect chose just a ''vault that represents our celestial hemisphere'', or a dome. This problem can be solved only when the meaning of the iconographic programme has been discussed.

✳✳✳

The eight ancient profiles do not represent the first eight Caesars, but several ruling during the first and second centuries, Augustus' second wife, Scribonia, and, perhaps, Agrippina, Nero's mother. Their likenesses make one think that an educated man in sixteenth-century Italy could identify at least some of them, despite the fact that they are not named. The selection of the personalities represented, however, proves that the author did not want to create an oderly sequence of historical dignitaries, such as the one in Mantua. The question arises if these busts had any meaning at all?[43] The intellectual bias of the Cremonese Austin friars, one of whom was the patron, would suggest an affirmative answer.

The motif of Roman Caesars was reintroduced to literature and art by Petrarch, who recognized these politicians as epitomes of good rulers and commanders.[44] His work *De viris illustribus* influenced the programme of the decoration of the

204

37) Calliope. Detail of Fig. 2 (photo: museum).

Sala Virorum Illustrium in Padua, expressing the idea of *Virtus Romana*.[45] From then on the interest in Roman coins began to increase.[46] Images of Roman Caesars were interpreted in a moral way, and in the Palazzo Pubblico in Siena they were even labelled as the quintessence of virtue.[47] Probably ethical meaning is to be found in Mantegna's emperor's cycle in the Camera Picta.[48] A moralizing interpretation of the Caesars' series spread to Lombardy after most of Petrarch's works, *De viris illustribus* included, were transferred to Pavia in 1388.[49] Thenceforth this town became a centre of research on ancient Rome, and the interest in emperors' images on coins radiated to the whole province. Numerous profiles of Caesars on Lombard church façades [e.g., Figs. 12, 16, 19] and in some palaces [e.g., Fig. 20] prove that there were large collections of coins, and, perhaps, that artists possessed good drawings or prints. Books issued slightly later indicate that the Caesar's mothers and wives were also highly regarded. The works of this kind, as well as Suetonius' *Lives*, stressed the moral values of the personalities discussed and depicted, conceived as epitomes of virtue.[50] It may be said, therefore, that generally the emperor's cycle was a counterpart of that of famous men, which was traditionally didactic and was often juxtaposed with (or took the place of) that of personifications of virtues.[51] In the fifteenth century, Poggio recommended the images of famous men for libraries and the like, as a source of inspiration.[52] Let us also remember that emperors' simulacra were placed in *studioli* just because of the ethical significance attributed to them.[53]

This moralizing interpretation of the eight profiles in Cremona, in accordance with current trends, makes the casual chronological arrangement of the sitters unimportant. Augustus, Galba, Titus, Trajan and Lucius Verus, as well as their mothers and wives, were considered to epitomize virtues.[54]

In his *Dialogue on the History of Poets*, first edited in 1544, L. G. Gyraldus, who at the beginning of the sixteenth century was active in Northern Italy,[55] began poetic history with an encomium of a few Caesars' gifts and achievements in this field. Following ancient texts he praised Augustus, Nero, Titus and Lucius Verus,[56] who are supposedly represented in Cremona. These profiles may thus have been recognized as images of persons steeped in the art of poetry. The Caesars in the room could thus have been meant to stand for virtues, and some of them may possibly have been identified as persons

205

38) Apollo. Detail of Fig. 1 (photo: museum).

39) Apollo. From the *Tarocchi*. After Hind.

who excelled in poetry.

The Muses on the vault, not named either, but easily identifiable, are arranged in the sequence of the *Tarots of Mantegna*, derived from the *Fable on the Nine Muses* by Fulgentius. The only discrepancy is that Polyhymnia was displaced from the fourth position, between Erato and Thalia, to the eighth, after Clio.[57] The other basic paradigm of the *Tarots* and Cremonese medallions stems from the concept of the Muses as celestial spheres, deriving ultimately from Capella and Macrobius. Consequently the Muses were endowed with discs.

It is common knowledge that Fulgentius' Muses stood for science and learning, and that his concept greatly influenced the literature of the Middle Ages, and also especially that of the modern era. As the motif of the Muses playing musical instruments connected with celestial spheres and transmitting the light of Divine inspiration was very popular in the Renaissance,[58] the goddesses in question may have been of intellectual import. Such was the significance of the Muses in Filarete's Palace of Virtue, and the goddesses were often represented in Italian libraries in the second half of the fifteenth century.[59] The *Tarot* series and that in Cremona could thus be interpreted as a symbol of the liberal arts or an encyclopedia of human knowledge.

The grotesquerie completing the decoration could be a supplement to the content of its figurative parts.[60] In Benvenuto Cellini's opinion, grotesques were especially

206

40) *Oculus*. Detail of Figs. 1-2 (photo: museum).

appropriate for "chambers, baths, *studies*, halls, and other places of the like nature,"[61] while Giovanni B. Armenini recommended the ornament for "loggias, *libraries*, gardens, bedrooms, courts, stairs, baths, conservatories, hallways and every type of small room."[62] Both authors thus agree that such decoration was suitable for rooms devoted to scientific and literary occupations which were connected with the Muses and virtues.[63] Accordingly, we should explain a statement by Pirro Ligorio, who writes that "the ancients (...) so linked grotesque figures [with] the things of heroes and of the Muses."[64] Ligorio continues that the Muses, Mnemosyne, Apollo, Athena and Hercules depicted among grotesques stood for the human craving "for immortal pleasures of the best cognizance (...) of the supreme creator who has made heaven and earth so various in its concepts."[65] This author confirms thus indirectly that the Muses' images in the Cremonese ceiling ought to have been connected with intellectual endeavours. The association of the goddesses with the grotesquerie results probably from the fact

41) Andrea Mantegna, Decoration of the vault in the Camera Picta, Mantua, fragment (photo: M. Fabiański).

that it was only in "grottoes" that Renaissance artists discovered Roman ornaments of that kind, so rooms with grotesques made them think of caves, and caves were considered as natural abodes of the Muses, patronesses of studies.[66] Hence the Cremonese chamber may have been referred ot as a "grotto-*musaeum*": it resembled a cave, thanks to its ornament.

If the decoration of this interior corresponded to its function, then we are entitled to assume that it served some of the same purposes as later Giovio's *musaeum* in Como, which was embellished with images of the playing Muses. The latter room was a place of solitary studies and literary activites, such as poetic declamations and chamber concerts.[67] Even the modest size of the Cremonese hall (ca. 18.5 m²) would not exclude such occupations,[68] though meditations and learned conversations seem to have been more probable in this case. The Augustinian monk in Cremona may thus have had a *studiolo* in his house.

The motif of an *oculus* could have been introduced to make the vault more *all'antica*, which would agree with the trend observed in the other parts of the decoration. But why in so important a place did the artist paint three persons and a carnation that apparently do not have anything to do with the Muses and emperors? Did it result from his liberal artistic imagination, or was it a kind of pictorial joke? The latter seems rather unlikely because the remainder of the paintings belongs to a consistent iconographic scheme, and, what is perhaps more important, the scene in the *oculus* must have been very important for the patron as he even decided to have the architectural design modified. The idea of individualizing this section, as in the Camera Picta in Mantua, with natural colours could have resulted from the need to make it contrast with the rest of the paintings — an architectural chiaroscuro decoration, romanizing, monochrome and carrying a universal message. Mantegna used one colour only in the ornamental part of the vault with the fictive reliefs and medallions of emperors, i.e., the section which is an architectural ornament and presumably expresses general concepts.[70] All the historical scenes on the walls and the one in the *oculus* are polychrome. Did the author from Cremona aim at marking the *oculus* containing a historical view out of the monochrome architectural ornaments of that Muses' grotto, as the room might be called? If so, the scene could depict the patron's contemporaries peeping through the opening to admire the interior of the *musaeum*.

Recently G. Mulazzani put forward an interpretation of Mantegna's *oculus* based on Plinius' *Panegyricus Traiani*.[71] The ancient writer praises Trajan's virtues, partially known in public, and advises that it is better for the emperor to be able to "peep inside" even the most secluded crannies of the palace to appreciate the virtues buried there.[72] If we accept Mulazzani's conclusions, then the people gazing into the Cremona room through the hole could admire the virtue of knowledge represented by the Muses and that of the emperors.[73] Although this explanation is better founded by the overall programme of the Cremonese decoration than by what we know about the Camera Picta, the ancient text is so equivocal that one cannot but be cautious.

R. Signorini justly criticized Mulazzani's dubious interpretation, but his explication, based on a text by Lucian of Samos,[74] is forced as well. Neither do the quoted fragments correspond exactly to the five persons depicted behind the aprapet, nor do they account for the other elements represented in the opening. Thus what we know about the Mantegna *oculus* does not help us to understand the Cremonese one.

The *Adoration of the Child*, which presumably constituted an original part of the decoration, could well have served as a background for learned conversations led by its ecclesiastical owner, in the same way as religious scenes in Cornaro's *Odeion* in Padua corresponded to its possessor's occupation.

Although we cannot be sure what the exact role of the scene in the *oculus* in its context, there can be little doubt that the room was conceived as was a domed *studiolo-musaeum*. Ca. sixty years after the room was decorated Pirro Ligorio wrote that *musaea* as temples, or places dedicated to the Muses, such as the one in the Villa Hadriana, "had been round so as to represent memories of the things which chime and rotate in the manner of heavens."[75] Elsewhere he explained that Mnemosyne, the mother of the nine Muses, is "the Memory of all the fine sciences, named after the Muses,"[76] so his "memories of the things which chime" in the *musaea* can be identified with the Muses themselves. In this way the author's interpretation accounts for Michiel's words that the Cremonese vault "represents our celestial hemisphere." This neo-Platonic simile of the Muses and heavenly spheres gave rise to the form of the domed *musaeum* designed in the 1460's by Filarete.[77] And it was just this treatise, at the end of the fifteenth century well known in Milanese artistic circles the Cremonese author was so close to, that could have influenced the choice of the architectural type of the room. It has been demonstated that the architectural shape of the Cremonese vault was chosen very carefully to correspond to the paintings, so it ought to have had a symbolic meaning as well. In his *musaea* Filarete featured personifications of the liberal arts, as well as portraits of some outstanding personalities who excelled in the disciplines, whereas in the Cremonese hall the former were superseded by the Muses and the latter by some emperors and ancient women. In effect, the iconography of the locale refers to Roman antiquity, as does the architecture of the room. The conjectural function of the hall, an "antique" place for studies, learned conversations and, possibly, concerts, is a novelty: the room is one of the earliest examples of humanist halls in clergy-owned houses.[78]

* I should like to express my gratitude to the many persons and institutions who enabled me to complete this study, above all to Professor Adam Matkiewicz, Uniwersytet Jagielloński, Crocow; Professor Karolina Lanckorońska, Rome, and also to Mr. Robert Anderson, London, and Mr. Enrico Dal Pozzolo, Padua-Venice; as well as to the Università di Padova and the Uniwersytet Jagielloński.

[1] Inv. no. 428-1889. Cf. C. M. Kauffmann, *Victoria and Albert Museum. Catalogue of Foreign Paintings I*, London, 1973, pp. 8-9, no. 7.

[2] In 1499 an agreement about the fusion of the convents of S. Colomba and S. Monica was signed in this building, cf. Un topo d'archivio [C. Bonetti], "L'unione dei conventi di Santa Monica e Santa Columba (1497-1544) I", in *La Provincia*, 25 July 1911. It is also known that S. Monica was a monastery of Austin Nuns, cf. G. De Vecchi, *Brevi cenni storici sulle chiese di Cremona*, Cremona, 1907, p. 143. — M. Michiel (*Notizia d'opera di disegno*, ed G. Frizzoni, Bologna, 1884, p. 92) refers to the building as the "casa del Prior di S. Antonio" and the Cremonese church S. Antonio Abbate belonged to the Augustinians in the early sixteenth century (De Vecchi, *op. cit.*, p. 43.. — A. Cavalcabò, *Le vicende dei nomi delle contrade di Cremona*, Cremona, 1933, p. 110, no. 187). — Cf. also M. G[regori], "Alessandro Pampurino", in: *I Campi e la cultura artistica cremonese*

del Cinquecento, Milan, 1985, p. 43. — For intellctual interests of the Austin Friars cf. D. G., "La biblioteca agostiniana di Cremona alla fine del secolo XVI", in *Analecta Augustiniana*, 24, 1961, pp. 313-330.

[3] Michiel, *op. cit.*, p. 93: "El camerin rotondo con la volta che rappresenta el nostro hemispherio celeste, fu ornato e compartito da". Unfortunately the rest of the text is now lost.

[4] G. Grasselli, *Abecedario biografico dei pittori, scultori ed architetti cremonesi*, Cremona, 1984, p. 42 (first ed. 1827). — I am indebted to Professor Mina Gregori for having drawn my attention to this text.

[5] The drawing was rediscovered and first published (in part) by G. Merlo, "I disegni di Giovanni Battista Cavalcaselle", in: *I Campi*, as in n. 2, p. 454.

[6] G[regori], as in n. 2, *loc. cit.*

[7] J. A. Crowe and G. B. Cavalcaselle, *A History of Painting in North Italy*, London, 1871, vol. 2, pp. 441 and 451; second ed., London, 1912, vol. 3, pp. 332-336.

[8] For older literature cf., e. g., F. Bologna, "The Cremonese Ceiling from Via Belvedere", in *The Burlington Magazine*, 106, 1954, pp. 167-171, and Kauffmann, as in n. 1, *loc. cit.* Both ascribed the fresco to Antonio della Corna. — F. Zeri (in his review of Kauffmann's Catalogue in *Antologia di belle arti*, 2, 1978, nos. 7-8, p. 319) criticised Kauffmann's attribution. — Recently V. Rastelli (*La "Vera storia" di Palazzo Fodri*, Cremona, 1982, p. 192) expressed serious doubts concerning the former attributions, whereas M. Tanzi ("Decorazione pittorica dell'atrio", *ibidem*, pp. 182-183, and *idem*, "Novità e revisione per Altobello Melone e Gianfrancesco Bembo", in *Ricerche di storia dell'arte*, 17, 1982, p. 55. 4) ascribed the fresco to Bramantino.

[9] Kauffmann (as in n. 1, *loc. cit.*) wrote that "in that case the earthly, realistic spectators above seem incongruous." — Zeri (as in n. 8, *loc. cit.*).

[10] G[regori], as in n. 2, pp. 43-44. Her deductions find additional corroboration in that the ears in the fresco are of the similar shape to the ones in Pampurino's St. Nicholas, Anthony and Jerome in S. Michele in Cremona. However, M. Bona Castellotti ("I Campi", in *Arte Cristiana*, 73, 1985, no. 711, p. 429) has doubted if these saints were actually painted by Pampurino.

[11] Crowe and Cavalcaselle, as in n. 7, *loc. cit.* Bologna, as in n. 8, *loc. cit.* Kauffmann, as in n. 1, *loc. cit.*

[12] A. Hind, *Early Italian Engraving*, vol. 1, London-New York, 1938, p. 232. J. Seznec, *La survivance des dieux antiques* (Studies of the Warburg Institute, vol. 11), London, 1940, p. 174. Bologna, as in n. 8, p. 167. Kauffmann, as in n. 1, p. 9. G[regori], as in n. 2, *loc. cit.*

[13] E. Schröter, *Die Ikonographie des Themas Parnass vor Raphael* (Studien zur Kunstgeschichte, Bd. 6), Hildesheim-New York, 1977, pp. 365 ff.

[14] Only Crowe and Cavalcaselle (as in n. 7, *loc. cit.*) and Bologna (as in n. 8, p. 168) mention the profiles, but in most general terms.

[15] Schröter, as in n. 13, pp. 382 ff.

[16] Cf. n. 4 and 5. However, one cannot infer from these sources that initially the *Adoration* decorated the room, or that the small window was there.

[17] Cf. F. Rakob, "Litus Beatae Veneris Aureum", in *Mitteilungen des Deutschen Archäologischen Institutes, Römische Abteilung*, 68, 1961, pp. 131-144. J. J. Rasch, "Die Kuppel in der römischen Architektur", in *Architectura*, 15, 1985, pp. 117-139, esp. 130-133.

[18] M. Horster, "Brunelleschi und Alberti in ihrer Stellung zur römischen Antike", in *Mitteilungen des Kunsthistorischen Institutes in Florenz*, 17, 1973, pp. 34 ff.

[19] Cf. A. Bruschi, *Bramante*, London, 1977, p. 46.

[20] G. Marchini, "Il Palazzo Datini a Prato", in *Bolletino d'arte*, 46, 1961, pp. 212-218.

[21] F. Malaguzzi Valeri (*La corte di Lodovico il Moro*, vol. 2, Milan, 1915, pp. 207-208) dates the vault to the last decade of the fifteenth century. F. Manzini (*Affreschi lombardi del Quattrocento*, Milan, 1965, pp. 498-500, tav. 316) credits C. Cesariano with general architectural supervision. Cf. also S. Gatti, "L'attività milanese del Cesariano dal 1512-13 als 1529", in *Arte lombarda*, no. 15, 1971, p. 226.

[22] Other Milanese examples of such a construction include numerous rooms in the Castello Sforzesco and in the Rocchetta. Cf. Malaguzzi Valeri, as in n. 21, vol. 1, Milan, 1913, pp. 332, 335, 338, 340, 341, 347. — Also the sacristy of S. Maria della Passione, and, elsewhere, rooms in S. Vittore di Meda, S. Magno di Legnano, and S. Abbondio in Cremona; the refectory of S. Agostino in Crema, the interior of the main gate in the Certosa di Pavia and C. Cesariano's sacristy of S. Giovanni Evangelista in Parma.

[23] Cf. A. Rovetta, "Nuove ricerche per S. Maria alla Fontana in Milano", in *Arte lombarda*, no. 62, 1982, pp. 141-150.

[24] A. Venturi, *Storia dell'arte italiana*, vol. 9 pt. 2, Milan, 1926, pp. 746-747.

[25] The part of the house with the hall was constructed after 1521 and rebuilt in the early nineteenth century and again in 1921. Cf. *Storia di Milano*, vol. 8, Milan, 1957, p. 326. P. Portaluppi, *La casa de gli* [!] *Atellani in Milano*, Milan, 1922, pp. 23 and 35. G. C. Bascapé, *I palazzi della vecchia Milano*, Milan, 1977, p. 160.

[26] Cf. L. Cheles, *The Studiolo of Urbino*, Wiesbaden, 1986, fig. 70.

[27] During the 1921 restoration the question of the original lighting and that of the initial function of the room were not cleared. Cf. Protaluppi, as in n. 25, *loc. cit.*

[28] Cf. e. g. A. Fulvio, *Illustrium imagines ...*, Rome, 1517, fol. 25.

[29] Cf. the reproductions in: H. Mattingly, *Coins of the Roman Empire in the British Museum*, London, 1976 (henceforth quoted as CRE), vol. I, pl. 55/17-18. Fulvio, *op. cit.*, fol. LI. *Chronicum Abbatis Urspurgensis ...*, Antwerp, 1557, pl. LXIII. H. Goltz, *Vivae omnium fere imperatorum imagines*, Antwerp, 1557, pl. VII.

[30] For Titus see *Chronicum ...*, as in n. 29, pl. LXV, Goltz, as in n. 29, pl. XI. — For Amadeo's medallions in the Certosa di Pavia (figs. 12, 16 and 19) cf. C. R. Morscheck jr., *The Relief Sculptures of the Certosa di Pavia, 1473-1499*, New York-London, 1978, pp. 236-252. — However, it might also be a stylized representation of Vespasian. Cf. H. Mattingly, *Roman Coins*, London, 1965 (henceforth quoted as *RC*), pls. XXXIV, 5-7; XLIII, 9.

[31] Try as I might, I could not find any close model. Perhaps the simulacrum was based on the coin with Trajan (*CRE*, vol. 4, pl. 25/7, no. 720; *RC*, pl. XXVIII, 12 and 13), or, less probably, the one with Augustus (*RC*, pl. XXVI, 6, and E. Vico, *Omnium Caesarum verissimae imagines ex antiquis numismatis desumptae*, n. p., 1554, fol. 6. *Chronicum*, as in n. 29, p. XLV). The head could also be interpreted as an image of Nerva (*RC*, pl. XXIX, 4).

[32] *CRE*, vol. 1, pl. 25/10, 11 and 14 — nos. 141, 143 and 149; pl. 30/7 and 8 — nos. 88 and 89; pl. XLIX, 2. Morscheck, as in n. 30, *loc. cit.* Fulvio, as in n. 29, fol. XXIIv. S. Erizzo, *Discorso sopra le medaglie de gli antichi*, Venice *s. a.*, p. 3.

[33] *CRE*, vol. 1, pl. 42/7, no. 164; pl. 43/9, no. 209. *RC*, pl. XXXIII, 14. — Morscheck, as in n. 30, *loc. cit.* — For Fundulo's façade frieze in the Palazzo Fodri, e. g., L. Cambelli, *L'arte della terracotta a Cremona nella seconda metà del Quattrocento*, Cremona, 1969, pp. 10-11.

[34] E. Vico, *Le imagini delle donne auguste ...*, in Vinegia [Venice], 1557, p. 103.

[35] Fulvio, as in n. 29, fol. LXXVIIIv. Erizzo, as in n. 32, p. 339. — To a smaller degree the profile resembles some images of Septimius Severus (*RC*, pl. XXXV, 11).

[36] Cf. notes 29 and 30.

[37] E. g., the frescoes in the Baglioni chapel in S. Maria Maggiore in Spello, 1501, decoration of the vault of the Basso della Rovere chapel in S. Maria del Popolo, Rome, before 1500, and that of the vault of a hall in the Palazzo Giuliano della Rovere, Rome, all of them by Pinturicchio; as well as the grotesques in the Asolani castle, Minerbio, by A. Aspertini. Cf. N. Dacos, *La découverte de la Domus Aurea et la formation des grotesques à la Renaissance* (Studies of the Warburg Institute, vol. 31), London-Leyden, 1969, pp. 68 ff. and 83.

[38] I am indebted to Dr. Jan Rafiński, Uniwersytet Jagielloński, Cracow, for identifying the family (*Canophylaceae*).

[39] The presumption is based on the facts that 1) the colour is less saturated near the fringe of the patch and 2) it reflects light at another angle than the other parts of the fresco.

[40] Cf. M. Dalai Emiliani, ''Per la prospettiva 'padovana': Foppa rivisitato'', in *Arte lombarda* 16, 1971, p. 135, n. 64. G. Scotti, ''Alcuni ipotesi di lettura per gli affreschi della Capella Portinari alla luce degli scritti di s. Antonio vescovo di Firenze'', in *Arte lombarda* no. 64, 1983, p. 76.

[41] The auricles painted by C. Tura, however, are not pointed in the upper part. Cf. I. Lermolieff, *Die Werke italienischer Meister in den Galerien von München, Dresden und Berlin*, Leipzig, 1880, p. 277.

[42] C. Cennini (*Il libro dell'arte*, ed. D. V. Thompson, New Haven, Conn., 1932, cap. 8, p. 5) recommended artists paint light according to its actual direction. Cf. M. Baxandall, *Painting and Experience in Fifteenth Century Italy*, Oxford-New York, 1984, p. 121.

[43] C. L. Joost Gaugier (''The History of Visual Theme as Culture and Experience of an Urban Center I'', in *Antichità viva*, 22, 1983, no. 4, p. 13) denies any conceptual significance to the cycle of emperors in the Casa Petrocca in Brescia, ca. 1500, because the portraits were not named.

[44] Cf. P. de Nolhac, ''Le 'De viris illustribus' de Patrarque'', in *Notices et extraits des manuscrits de la Bibliothèque Nationale et autres bibliothèques*, 34, 1891, pp. 61-148.

[45] Cf. T. E. Mommsen, ''Petrarch and the Decoration of the Sala Virorum Illustrium in Padua'', in *Art Bulletin*, 34, 1952, pp. 95-105. A. Schmitt, ''Zur Wiedererlebung der Antike im Trecento'', in *Mitteilungen des Kunsthistorischen Institutes in Florenz*, 18, 1974, pp. 167-173.

[46] Cf. A. Magnaguti, ''Il Petrarca numismatico'', in *Rivista italiana di numismatica*, 20, 1907, pp. 155-157. R. Weiss, *The Renaissance Discovery of Classical Antiquity*, Oxford, 1969, p. 37.

[47] N. Rubinstein, ''Political Ideas in Siene Art'', in *Journal of the Warburg and Courtauld Institutes*, 21, 1958, pp. 179-207. — Cf. also C. L. Joost Gaugier, ''A Rediscovered Series of Uomoni Famosi from Quattrocento Venice'', in *Art Bulletin*, 68, 1976, no. 2, p. 187.

[48] Schmitt, as in n. 45, p. 211. — Joost Gaugier (as in n. 47, p. 188) suggested that Mantegna had been influenced by the now-lost cycle of famous men painted by Uccello in the Casa Vitalini, Padua, in the forties. R. Lightbown (Mantegna, Oxford, 1986, p. 112) maintains that Mantegna's emperors may have had dynastic significance, whereas A. Martindale (''The Middle Age of Andrea Mantegna'', in *Journal of the Royal Society of Arts*, 127, 1978, pp. 631-633 and 641-642) doubts whether there is any point in interpreting the iconography of the Camera.

[49] In 1426 Petrarch's manuscript was catalogued in Pavia (Nolhac, as in n. 44, p. 73). — For the role of Pavia cf. also S. Bandera, ''Persistenze tardogotiche a Cremona'', in *Paragone*, 28, 1977, no. 323, p. 37.

[50] P. O. Rave, ''Paolo Giovio und die Bildnisvitenbücher des Humanismus'', in *Jahrbuch der Berliner Museen*, 1, 1959, p. 136.

R. J. Dingley, ''Marvell and the Twelve Caesars'', in *Journal of the Warburg and Courtauld Institutes*, 45, 1982, p. 245.

[51] Numerous medieval examples are discussed by J. Kronjäger, *Berühmte Griechen und Römer als Begleiter der Musen und der Artes Liberales in Bildzyklen des 2. bis 14. Jahrhunderts*, Marburg/Lahn, 1973, passim, esp. pp. 83 ff.

[52] Poggio, ''De nobilitate liber'', in: *idem, Opera omnia*, ed. R. Furini, Turin, 1964, vol. 1, pp. 65 and 123. These fragments were discussed by C. L. Joost Gaugier, ''Poggio and Visual Tradition'', in *Artibus et Historiae*, 12, 1985, pp. 58-59.

[53] Cf. W. Liebenwein, *Studiolo* (Frankfurter Forschungen zur Kunst, Bd. 6), Berlin, 1977, p. 70 ff.

[54] Cf., e. g., Dio Cassius, *Historiarum romanarum* ..., ed. F. G. Sturzius, Lipsiae [Leipzig], 1824, vol. 4, lib. XLIV, 2 (Galba) and LXVIII, 4 (Trajan). Benvenuto de Rambaldis, *Liber Augustalis*, in: F. Petrarca, *Opera omnia*, Basileae [Basel], 1554, pp. 575 (Augustus), 576 (Titus), 577 (Trajan and Venus). — For women, cf. Andreae de Acciardis de Florenticae *Comitissae*, Bern, 1559, unpaginated: ''Et si extollendi sunt homines dum concesso sibi robore magna facerint, quanto amplius mulieres (quibus fere omnibus a natura rerum mollices insita, et corpus debole ac tardum ingenium datum est) si virilem evaserint animum, ac ingenio celebri, ac virtute conspicua audeant atque perficiant dificillima vires extollendae sunt.'' Cf. also Joost Gaugier, as in n. 43, p. 12.

[55] Cf. E. Panofsky, *The Iconography of Corregio's Camera di San Paolo* (Studies of the Warburg Institute, vol. 21), London, 1961, pp. 31-35.

[56] L. G. Gyraldus. ''De historia poetarum ...'', in: *idem, Opera omnia*, Lugduni Batavorum [Leyden], 1696, vol. 2, cols. 269-270: ''Augustus, qui, licet Tranquillus dicat quod summatim poëticam attingit, et plane poëmatum non imperatum fuisse, librum tamen hexametris versibus editum reliquit, cuius argumentum et titulus, Sicilia (...) Recitantes quoque Augustus benigne et patienter audivit, nec tantum carmina et historias, sed et orationes et dialogis componi tamen aliqui de se.'' Col. 272: ''At Nero egregiè poëtice facultati operam dedit.'' Col. 273: ''Titus (...) in utraque lingua usque adeo facundus, ut causas altine ageret et tragoedias Graece componeret.'' Col. 277: ''L. Verus Antonius (...) carminum et maxime tragicorum studiosus fuit (...) melioque orator factus est quam poëta.''

[57] It was noticed by Schröter, as in n. 13, p. 382. Here are the sequence and numbers of the *Tarots*: Calliope — 11, Urania — 12, Terpsichore — 13, Erato — 14, Polyhymnia — 15, Thalia — 16, Melpomene — 17, Euterpe — 18, Clio — 19, Apollo — 20.

[58] Cf. Schröter, as in n. 13, pp. 365 ff.

[59] For Filarete cf. my forthcoming paper ''Musaea in Filarete's Trattato, in *Biuletyn Historii Sztuki*, 48, 1986. For libraries, Liebenwein, as in n. 53, *loc. cit.*

[60] For a general significance of grotesquerie, cf., e. g., C.G. Harpham, *On the Grotesque*, Princeton, N. J., 1982, p. 39. — Cf. also C. Ossola, *Autunno del Rinascimento* (Biblioteca di lettere italiane, vol. 9), Florence, 1971, pp. 184 ff.

[61] My italics. B. Cellini, *The Autobiography* [Reading, Pa., 1936], Chapter VI, p. 53.

[63] My italics. G. B. Armenini, *On the True Percepts of the Art of Painting*, ed E. J. Olszewski, n. p., 1977, p. 264 (bk. III, chapter XII).

[63] The clearest expression of this concept is to be found in B. Taegio, *Il liceo ... libro secondo*, In Melano [Milan], 1571, fol. 50v: ''per le muse altro non s'intende che le scienze, e lodevoli discipline.''

[64] My translation. P. Ligorio, *Libro VII dell'antichità*, Vatican Library, Cod. Ottob. Lat. 3368, fol. 119v: ''Gli antichi (...) cosi havevano ligati di figure grottesche, le cose delli heroi e delle Muse.'' The quotation was also published by Dacos, as in n. 37, p. 161

[65] My translation. *Ibidem*, fol. 126r: "Le buone Muse (...) la madre Mnemosine, Apollo, Pallade, Hercole, Tutte vi furono dipinte, per significare l'opere et gli giorni felici di coloro che sono dediti alle cose megliori, et conducono l'huomo all'immortali piaceri dell'optimo conoscimento, all'altra et profonda cogitazione in vedere con gli occhi dell'inteletto quanto sia meraviglioso il summo opifice, che ha fatto i cieli, et la terra tanto varia delli suoi concetti."

[66] Cf., e. g., G. Boccaccio, *L'Amato*, ed. Bruscoli, 1840, p. 48. — Ligorio, *Libro I* (Cod. Ottob. Lat. 3364), s. v. antro. — Schröter, as in n. 13, p. 284. — N. Miller, *Heavenly Caves*, Boston-London-Sydney, 1982, *passim*.

[67] For Giovio's *Musaeo*, e. g., Z. Waźbiński, *Musaeum Paola Giovia w Como*", in *Acta Universitatis Nicolai Copernici. Nauki humanistyczno-spoleczne fasc. 99: Zabytkoznawstwo i Konserwatorstwo*, 8, 1979, pp. 115-144. — R. P[avoni], "Il museo", in: *Collezioni Giovio*, Como, 1983, p. 15.

[68] Concerts were also held in the octagonal hall (ca. 30 m²) in Cornaro's *Odeion* in Padua.

[69] For jokes cf. Martindale, as in n. 48, pp. 632-633. Lightbown, as in n. 48, p. 102.

[70] Cf. C. Elam, "The Camera Picta", in D. Chambers and J. Martinean eds., *Splendors of the Gonzaga*, London, 1981, p. 120.

[71] G. Mulazzani, "La fonte letteraria del 'Camera degli Sposi' di Mantegna", in *Arte lombarda*, no. 50, 1978, pp. 36-40. *Idem*, "Considerazioni sulla costruzione spaziale della 'Camera degli Sposi' alla luce dell'identificazione della sua fonte letteraria", in: *La prospettiva rinascimentale*, Florence, 1980, pp. 177-182.

[72] Plinius Caecilus II, "Panegiricus Traiani", in: *idem, Epistulae*, ed. W. Borkowski, Wroclaw, 1837, vol. 3, 83, 1-2: "Habet hoc primum magna fortuna, quod nihil occultum, nihil tectum esse patitur; principum vero non domus modo, sed cubicula ipsa intimosque secessus recludit omniaque arcana nascenda famae proponit atque explicat. Sed tibi, Caesar, nihil accomodantium fuerit ad gloriam quam poenitus inspici. Sunt quidem praeclara quae in publicum profers, sed non minora ea quae limine tenes."

[73] Cf. *ibidem*, 47 and 49.

[74] R. Signorini, *Opus hoc tenue. La camera Dipinta di Andrea Mantegna*, Mantua, 1985, pp. 228 ff., esp. 240-241.

[75] My translation and italics. Ligorio, *Libro XII*, Cod. Ottob. Lat. 3371, fol. 187v: "Musaea, Musaeum, era detto ogni luogo dedicato alle Muse (...) Et Museo anchora si diceva il Tempio delle Muse che si edificava come quelli delle Academie (...) Nella Villa Hadriana Tiburtina nel luogo della sua Academia, i quali tempii *erano rotondi per rappresentare le memorie delle cose che consonano et a guisa de cieli si rivolgono* et inchinato alle cose presente alla consonantia, delli tempi passati e preteriti et delle futuri, et consonantemente conciliati rappresentati nell'intelletto."

[76] My translation. *Ibidem*, fol. 163v: "Mnemosyne, è il nome della matre delle nove Muse (...) cioe Memoria di tutte le belle scientie nominate dalle Muse."

[77] Cf. Fabiański, as in n. 59.

[78] Another early example of such a room is Cornaro's *Odeion* in Padua, ca. 1530.

Summary:

VIVIAN B. MANN

"New" Examples of Jewish Ceremonial Art from Medieval Ashkenaz

Earlier literature on Jewish ceremonial art from medieval Ashkenaz (the Jewish community of Northern France and the Rhineland and areas under its influence) encompassed only a small number of extant objects from that period. These can be divided into two groups: those that are uniquely Jewish in form, and those that represent an adaptation of types in general use. The present study enlarges the corpus by integrating material published in general sources or recently discovered in treasure troves. Some of these works had not been previously identified as Judaica, for example, the double cups known as *Doppelkopf* or *Doppelscheuer*. The popularity of this last form among Ashkenazi Jews is indicated by numerous representations of the type in illuminated Hebrew manuscripts, and can be understood in the context of German customs and the evolution of the Jewish marriage ceremony during the High Middle Ages.

JOSEPH GUTMANN

The Dura Europos Synagogue Paintings and their Influence on Later Christian and Jewish Art

The amazing discovery of the Dura Europos synagogue, accurately dated 245 A.D., has raised many scholarly questions. Some scholars, for instance, armed with the presumptive stern injunction of the Second Commandment, were utterly shocked by this archaeological find, and have had to revise their preconceived theories. Another major scholarly debate is whether the Dura synagogue paintings exerted an influence on later Christian and Jewish art. According to some scholars, there exist definite iconographic parallels between the Dura synagogue depictions and medieval Spanish, Byzantine and Jewish art. This paper examines the iconographic features found in the biblical illustrations of the Dura synagogue and in later medieval art and comes to the conclusion that no concrete and indisputable connection can be established.

COLIN EISLER

Power to Europe's Chosen Peoples.
A New Maccabean Page for Louis XIV by Liévin Cruyl

In his discussion of two previously unknown drawings by Liévin Cruyl, the author points out the significant identification of Europe's rulers and their states with Israel. Cruyl's page for Louis XIV draws upon renderings of reconstructions of the Temple of Solomon, and it was that building which provided the point of departure for many of the leading palaces — the Escorial and the Louvre, among others. Not only did the identification of the monarchy with the Tree of Jesse — the ancestors of Christ, placing them among the descendants of David — justify its rule, such association was also made by the new mercantile republics. Venice and the North Netherlands, both perpetually rescued from and by the sea, associated their profitable economy with that of the Jews, whose way of life was freed from the communism so fundamental to the tenets of early Christianity.

RALF BUSCH

Constantin Uhde as a Synagogue Architect

The Brunswick architect Constantin Uhde (1836-1905) erected the Brunswick synagogue and fellowship house in 1873/74. These structures are influenced a great deal by the Romanesque style. Following a visit to Spain in 1888, he integrates elements of Moorish style into his Wolfenbüttel synagogue. These come even stronger to fore in his planned Dortmund synagogue, 1896 (never built), in order to "point out the Oriental origin of the people and the symbolism of their religion." The Gentile Uhde sensitively identifies with an imaginary "national" style and historicizes in a time where elsewhere "new architecture" was attempting to find more modern style forms.

GABRIELLE SED-RAJNA

Miriam's Dance

Biblical illustration in Late Antiquity was characterized by illustrating the text episode by episode, as well as by embellishing the narration with elements rooted in Jewish legend. Such detailed illustration is known to us today from Christian landmarks and manuscripts. These traditions were passed on in a way difficult to trace, and survived until the

Middle Ages. Some of these elements also appear in the four-teenth-century Haggadot Biblical cycles in Spain. However, a comparison image by image between the Haggadot cycles and those on the Christian landmarks shows that it could not possibly have been the Christian that served as a model for the Jewish ones. The Haggadot Biblical illustrations probably derive from traditions originating in Jewish *milieux* around the year 200, and these were transmitted through Jewish communities, perhaps in Southern Italy or North Africa, to the artists of the Iberian peninsula in the fourteenth century. It is probably through a parallel line of transmission that certain elements of this tradition came down to the Christian artists whose works permit a partial reconstruction of the original ancient tradition.

fundamentally varied. Especially difficult for them was the portrayal of the five wise men of Bne Braq, who debated the Exodus until morning. The prototype for this scene was Merian's portrayal of the banquet given by Joseph in Egypt for his brothers. But the number of persons seated at the table did not fit at all. The scribes and painters mostly reduced the number, but only rarely did they succeed in reducing the number to five. Further details were conducive to adapting the scene to the text of the Haggadah: the fact that it is morning; the presence of a bookshelf, defining those seated at the table as scholars. In contrast to the German-Ashkenaz scribes and painters, those in Italy were influenced by the Venetian prints of 1599 and 1609, which were also occasionally used by German-Ashkenaz illuminators.

ZIVA AMISHAI-MAISELS
The Iconographic Use of Abstraction in Jankel Adler's Late Works

The fluctuation of Jankel Adler's style during World War II between abstraction and figuration has been explained until now in purely stylistic terms. In this article, the reasons for this development are seen to derive from Adler's war-time experiences and from his attempts to deal with the Holocaust in his art. The development of this reaction is traced from *Girl with Rocking Toy*, of 1941, through the major works of 1943, *Destruction*, *Beginning of a Revolt*, and *No Man's Land*, in all of which the stylistic fragmentation of the figure is shown to have a distinct iconographic meaning. This is equally true of Adler's enigmatic *Treblinka*, of 1948, whose pictorial and stylistic sources are explored. In the final analysis, Adler's use of abstraction is shown to result from his need to express a current, frightening reality from a safe distance.

URSULA SCHUBERT
The Rabbinical Conception of the Showbread Table and the San Isidoro de Leon Bible, 960 A.D. (Real Colegiata, cod. 2, fol. 50r)

In contrast to the portrayal of the showbreads in two rows next to each other in the Codex Amiatinus (Northumbria, seventh century), in the Spanish Hebraic manuscripts of the Late Middle Ages the showbreads are arranged on the table in two rows on top of each other. The portrayal was not supplied by the corresponding chapters in Exodus and Leviticus, but instead, above all, by the pertinent considerations of the rabbinical scholars in the Mischna, Menahot XI. A completely unexpected parallel to the portrayal of the showbreads arranged on top of each other on the showbread table is found in the San Isidoro de Leon Bible, 960 A.D., and in both extant copies of this manuscript of 1162 A.D. and the beginning of the thirteenth century, respectively. The high priest Aaron, shown together with sacred objects within the holy tabernacle, is surprisingly portrayed in the garb of a high priest in the same context in both the Dura Europos Synagogue (mid-third century A.D.) and the *Regensburg Pentateuch* (Bavaria, ca. 1300). In addition, in the latter the showbread table has the same misleading appearance as in the Christian Bible of 960, in which it is designated as "labrum" and is therefore undoubtedly misunderstood. Such "misunderstandings," together with the unusual position of the showbreads on the table, for which only rabbinical scriptures could be the source, support the belief that the suspected fifth-century prototype for the Bible of 960, at least for the portrayal of fol. 50r, was based on a late classical Bible illumination of Jewish origin.

KURT SCHUBERT
The Wise Men of Bne Braq in Haggadah Illuminated Manuscripts of the Eighteenth Century

The iconography of the Amsterdam *Pesach Haggadah* (print 1695; 1712) is influenced by Mathaeus Merian's *Icones Biblicae*. Its "ideator" was a Christian who converted to Judaism in Amsterdam. The German-Ashkenaz scribes and painters of the eighteenth century repeatedly followed the prototypes of the Amsterdam editions of prints, which they for the most part only slightly, but also at times more

PHILIPP P. FEHL
The *Stadttempel* of the Jews of Vienna: Childhood Memories and History

This essay attempts to bring to life the architecture of Vienna's oldest synagogue, the classicistic *Stadttempel* by Joseph Kornhäusel, in terms of the tradition of the worship and spiritual hopes for the sake of which it was founded. The author's childhood was lived, to some extent, under the shelter of this tradition. He draws on his memories to find access to his interpretation of historical data connected with the foundation of the *Tempel* and to explore the interconnection of the style of the *Tempel*'s architecture and the religious function of the building. The duties and problems of an author's personal involvement in the writing of history, and especially the history of art, are a major concern.

Added to the essay are a transcription of the first by-laws of the *Stadttempel* and Isaac Noah Mannheimer's (the *Tempel*'s first spiritual leader's) preface to the collection of his chancel orations in which he expounds the *Tempel*'s founders' purposes and hopes in an appropriately lofty style, which may be compared to the elevated language of the *Tempel*'s architecture.

MOSHE BARASCH
Reflection on Tombstones: Childhood Memories

The article is devoted to the images found on some of the mid-eighteenth- to nineteenth- century tombstones in the Jewish cemetery of Czernowitz, the author's hometown. As tombstones are a product of an essentially social art, the social conditions in which the tombstones were produced are examined. In particular, the author illustrates who the carvers were and how they were trained. Then the artistic treatment of the tombstones is discussed. Especially the script and the decorative motifs are the subject of closer scrutiny. The writer concludes that an interpretation of the tombstones holds the key to an understanding of the complex and rich community life of an irrevocably lost culture, which has yet to receive the attention it deserves.

JOSEPH MANCA
Renaissance Theater and Hebraic Ritual in Ercole de' Roberti's *Gathering of Manna*

The setting of Ercole de' Roberti's *Gathering of Manna* forcibly recalls the staging used for secular plays produced in Ferrara at the end of the Quattrocento. This reflection of theater design in a painting is more than an empty, formal borrowing, for it can be shown that the theatricality of the picture probably reflects several arguments put forth by L. B. Alberti and Pellegrino Prisciano, who connect the origins of theater with primitive religious celebrations and, more specifically, with the events that surrounded the original Gathering of Manna. Furthermore, the theatricality of the picture, along with other aspects of the *Gathering of Manna*, turns out to serve as flattery of Duke Ercole I d'Este, having as its aim a subtle comparison of the Duke with Moses.

JACK WASSERMANN
Observations on Two Statues in the Museo dell'Opera del Duomo and the Porta della Mandorla in Florence

In opposition to current belief, two early Quattrocento statues in the Museo dell'Opera, Florence, assumed to represent an *Annunciation*, are shown not to have been executed for the lunette of the Porta della Mandorla. Close examination of the physical structures of the statues, the principal method used for this demonstration, reveals that they were designed to be viewed more panoramically, even especially in the case of the angel, than a two-dimensionally disposed lunette would allow, and that they do not form a narrative group at all. The study proceeds to develop the minimum requirements the original sites of the statues must have had, and it concludes with speculations on the character and fate of the missing *Annunciation* group that did occupy the lunette of the Porta della Mandorla beginning in 1414.

CARLO DEL BRAVO
Ribera's Concept of Harmony

The young Ribera seems to have had some relationship to Bernardo Strozzi and the Capuchin Fathers.

However, the dominant iconology in Ribera's works seems to come from the tradition of local "evangelism," as in Luis de Molina, with a focus on the imitation of Christ in mildness and humility, and with the main sources being St. Matthew and St. Augustine.

By reconstructing this coherent iconology, Ribera's images of physical decay are not to be considered apart from those of beauty, in accordance with the Augustinian assertion of the relative beauty of all creation since it derives its existence and form from God, nor from the assertion of a higher universal harmony, where all things fit into their proper place. What we see as ugly comes, if anything, from limiting our attention to what is particular.

MARCIN FABIAŃSKI
The Cremonese Ceiling Examined in its Original *Studiolo* Setting

The paper discusses the problem of the original shape and meaning of the vault fresco painted for a prior's house in Cremona, probably by Alessandro Pampurino ca. 1500, but now kept in London. The design of this umbrella dome seems to have been modified in view of the prospective decoration: smaller lunettes do justice to profiles of Caesars and the smooth apex enhances pictorial illusionism of the *oculus* both modifications suggest that the whole enterprise was directed by one person. The chamber the vault belonged to was relatively secluded. The images of Caesars (some could be identified), the Muses and grotesquerie may well have been connected with its function as a place of solitary studies and literary activities (*studiolo-musaeum*), whereas the meaning of the painted *oculus* remains obscure.

Résumés:

VIVIAN B. MANN
"Nouveaux" exemples de l'art cérémoniel des Ashkénazes au Moyen-Âge

La littérature ancienne concernant l'art cérémoniel du Moyen-Âge des Ashkénazes — colonies juives dans le nord de la France et en Allemagne, en particulier en Rhénanie — traite seulement d'un petit nombre d'objets de cette époque. On di-stingue deux groupes d'objets, les uns destinés au seul usage juif d'après leur forme, les autres de type usuel commun.

La présente étude élargit cette collection en y ajoutant du matériel publié dans des écrits de source générale ou des objets découverts récemment comme trésors "Sans maître".

Quelques uns de ces objets n'avaient pas été identifiés jusqu'ici comme judaïques, par exemple les coupes doubles connues sous le nom de "tête double" (*Doppelkopf*) ou "grange double" (*Doppelscheuer*). Ce type était très apprécié des Ashkénazes comme le montrent de fréquentes représentations dans des manuscrits enluminés. On le comprend en se rapportant aux coutumes allemandes et au développement du cérémonial du mariage juif pendant le Moyen-Âge.

JOSEPH GUTMANN
Les peintures de la synagogue de Dura Europos et leur influence sur l'art chrétien et juif de l'époque suivante

La découverte surprenante de la synagogue de Dura Europos a posé de nouvelles questions à résoudre. Quelques chercheurs — en particulier ceux pour lesquels le deuxième commandement faisait toujours absolument loi — ont dû réviser leurs théories sous l'influence des découvertes archéologiques.

Un autre point litigieux est la question de savoir s'il est possible de prouver l'influence des peintures de Dura Europos sur l'art chrétien et juif de l'époque suivante. Certains sont d'avis qu'on peut établir clairement des parallèles iconographiques avec l'art du Moyen-Âge espagnol, byzantin et juif. La présente étude considère par contre comme non prouvée l'influence des peintures bibliques de Dura Europos sur celle de l'art moyenâgeux après les avoir comparées.

COLIN EISLER
Pouvoir pour les peuples élus d'Europe. Nouveau feuillet sur l'histoire des Maccabées pour Louis XIV par Liévin Cruyl

Dans son commentaire de deux dessins autrefois inconnus de Liévin Cruyl, l'auteur souligne l'identification significative des souverains européens et de leurs états à l'ancien Israël. Le feuillet de Cruyl pour Louis XIV montre une reconstruction du temple de Salomon, édifice qui a servi de modèle à l'Escorial et au Louvre. Non seulement la monarchie a cherché à légitimer sa position en s'identifiant à l'arbre de Jessé — les ancêtres du Christ et les descendants du roi David — mais aussi les jeunes républiques commerçantes ont établi de telles associations: Venise et les Pays-Bas ont ainsi comparé leur vie économique orientée vers la prospérité à celle des Juifs qui n'était limitée ni par des interdits et restrictions contraires aux bénéfices ni par le postulat d'une communauté de biens tel qu'il est compris dans certains dogmes du christianisme primitif.

RALF BUSCH
Constantin Uhde comme architecte de synagogue

L'architecte de Braunschweig Constantin Uhde (1836-1905) a construit en 1873/74 la synagogue de Braunschweig et la mairie. Ces édifices sont essentiellement imprégnés de style roman. Après un voyage en Espagne en 1888 il mêle des éléments de style mauresque à la construction de la synagogue de Wolfenbüttel. Ces éléments se retrouvent de façon plus renforcée dans la maquette d'une synagogue à Dortmund qui ne sera pas édifiée: "il voulait montrer l'origine orientale du peuple et la symbolique de sa religion." Uhde, qui n'est pas juif, recrée ainsi un style "national" en épousant les sentiments d'un peuple et en historisant à une époque où l'on commençait ailleurs dans la "nouvelle architecture" à chercher d'autres formes de style plus adaptées à l'époque.

GABRIELLE SED-RAJNA
La danse de Miryam

L'imagerie biblique de l'Antiquité tardive se caractérise par une illustration du texte épisode par épisode, ainsi que l'enrichissement du récit par des éléments puisés dans la légende juive. Cette illustration spécifique est connue aujourd'hui grâce à des monuments et manuscrits chrétiens. Par une transmission dont les voies sont difficiles à tracer, ces traditions ont survécu jusqu'au Moyen-Âge. Certains éléments en apparaissent également dans les cycles bibliques des Haggadot exécutés en Espagne au XIVe siècle. Toutefois, une comparaison image par image entre les cycles des Haggadot et ceux des monuments chrétiens montre que ces derniers ne peuvent pas être considérés comme ayant servi de modèles aux peintres juifs. Les images bibliques des Haggadot dérivent probablement d'une tradition créée en milieux juifs vers l'an 200 et transmise, peut-être via les communautés juives d'Italie du Sud ou d'Afrique du Nord, jusqu'aux artistes de la péninsule ibérique du XIVe siècle. C'est probablement grâce à une filière de transmission parallèle que certains éléments de cette tradition sont parvenus aux artistes chrétiens dont les oeuvres permettent de reconstituer partiellement l'antique tradition.

ZIVA AMISHAI-MAISELS
L'abstraction comme fonction iconographique dans l'oeuvre tardive de Jankel Adler

Les hésitations de Jankel Adler entre l'abstraction et la figuration ont été jusqu'à présent toujours interprétées à l'aide de concepts stylistiques.

Le présent travail montre que son expérience de la guerre et la tentative de surmonter celle de l'holocauste au moyen de l'art sont à l'origine de son évolution. En montrant les différentes phases de cette évolution, de *La petite fille à la balançoire* (1941) aux oeuvres centrales de 1943 (*Destruction*, *Début de l'insurrection*, *No Man's Land*), on démontre l'importance de la signification iconographique de la dissolution de la forme qui caractérise toutes ces oeuvres. C'est valable également pour le tableau d'Adler *Treblinka* (1948) qui pose de nombreuses énigmes et dont on explore encore les sources thématiques et stylistiques. L'analyse montre que l'utilisation de l'abstraction naissait du besoin d'Adler de se distancier d'une réalité présente et épouvantable pour pouvoir l'exprimer.

KURT SCHUBERT
Les sages de Bne Braq dans l'illustration des Haggada du 18e siècle

L'iconographie des *Pesach Haggada* d'Amsterdam (imprimés en 1695, 1712) est influencée par les *Icones Biblicae* de Mathaeus Merian. Le responsable en est un Chrétien qui s'est converti au Judaïsme à Amsterdam. Les copistes et les peintres du 18e siècle de la région ashkénaze allemande s'en tenaient en général aux modèles des éditions d'Amsterdam qu'ils variaient souvent un peu seulement mais parfois aussi plus fortement. Leur principale difficulté résidait dans la représentation des 5 sages de Bne Braq qui discutent jusqu'au matin de la sortie d'Egypte. Pour cette scène, ils s'inspiraient de la représentation de Merian du repas offert par Joseph à ses frères en Egypte. Cependant, cette représentation ne convenait pas avec le nombre des personnes assises à la table. La plupart du temps, ils réduisaient ce nombre, mais ce n'est que rarement qu'ils parvenaient à le réduire à cinq personnes. Quelques détails offraient à certains d'entre eux la possibilité d'adapter la scène aux textes des Haggada: bougies consumées, élèves attendant dans ou derrière la porte, ce qui suggère l'heure matinale, étagère à livres servant à identifier les hôtes comme savants. Contrairement aux copistes et aux peintres ashkénazes allemands, les Italiens étaient influencés par les éditions vénitiennes de 1599 et 1609, qui étaient utilisées de temps à autre également par les illustrateurs ashkénazes allemands.

URSULA SCHUBERT
La représentation rabbinique de la table aux pains d'oblation et la bible de St. Isidore de Leon, a. d. 960 (Real Colegiata, cod. 2, fol. 50)

Au contraire de la représentation des pains d'oblation dans le Codex Amiatinus (Northumbrie, 7e siècle) en deux rangées l'une à côté de l'autre, les manuscrits hébraïques de la fin du Moyen-Âge en Espagne les représentent en deux rangées l'une au-dessus de l'autre.

Ce n'est pas sur les chapitres correspondants de l'Exode et du Lévitique qu'ils s'appuyaient, mais sur les textes relatant les réflexions des savants rabbiniques dans la Mischna, Menahot XI. On trouve un parallèle tout à fait inattendu à cette représentation des pains d'oblation les uns au-dessus des autres dans la bible de St. Isidore de Leon a.d. 960 et les deux copies conservées de ce manuscrit de 1162 et du début du 13e siècle. Le grand prêtre Aaron y est représenté à l'intérieur du sanctuaire avec tous les objets du culte et en grande tenue de prêtre. Il est étonnant de constater qu'il l'est de la même façon aussi bien dans la synagogue de Dura Europos (milieu du 3e siècle ap. J.C.) que dans le *Pentateuque de Regensburg* (Bavière, vers 1300). Dans ce dernier, la table aux pains d'oblation est de plus également représentée de le même façon trompeuse que dans la bible chrétienne de 960 où elle est désignée comme ''labrum'', et ainsi sans aucun doute mal interprétée. De tels ''malentendus'' ajoutés à l'entassement des pains d'oblation sur la table — dont on ne trouve l'origine que dans le manuscrit rabbinique — laissent supposer que l'on a utilisé une illustration de la bible de l'antiquité tardive de provenance juive pour le modèle du 5e siècle — du moins pour le folio 50r — ce que l'on supposait déjà pour la bible de 960.

PHILIPP P. FEHL
Le *Temple de la Cité* des Juifs à Vienne: souvenirs d'enfance et histoire

L'article essaie de redonner vie à l'architecture de la plus ancienne synagogue viennoise, le Temple de la cité néoclassique de Josef Kornhäusel, à la lumière de l'office traditionnel et des espérances spirituelles de ses fondateurs. L'auteur a passé sa jeunesse au sein de cette tradition. Il recherche dans ses souvenirs pour retrouver les dates historiques liées à la fondation du temple et la relation entre le style de son architecture et sa fonction religieuse. Les devoirs et les problèmes que trouve un auteur impliqué personnellement en écrivant l'histoire, surtout l'histoire de l'art, sont particulèrement importants et significatifs.

En annexe de cette étude se trouvent les premiers statuts du temple et la préface d'Isaac Noah Mannheimer à une collection de ses sermons dans lesquels il explique les intentions et les espoirs des fondateurs du temple — dans un style noble similaire à l'architecture du temple.

MOSHE BARASCH
Réflexions sur des pierres tombales: souvenirs d'enfance

L'article est consacré à l'art ornemental de quelques tombes des 18e et 19e siècles au cimetière juif de Czernowitz, ville natale de l'auteur.

Comme les pierres tombales sont le produit d'un art orienté socialement, il faut considérer de plus près les circonstances dans lesquelles elles ont été faites. L'auteur parvient en particulier à identifier certains tailleurs de pierre et à reconstituer leur formation. Il commente la forme artistique des tombes en s'attachant surtout aux inscriptions et au décor.

L'auteur conclut que c'est dans l'interprétation de ces pierres tombales que se trouve la clé de la compréhension de la vie complexe et variée d'une communauté qui était imprégnée d'une culture irrémédiablement perdue, et qui est digne d'être honorée.

JOSEPH MANCA
Le théâtre de la Renaissance et le rituel hébraïque dans *Le ramassage de la Manne* de Ercole de' Roberti

Les décors dans le tableau de Ercole de' Roberti *Le ramassage de la Manne* rappellent clairement ceux d'une scène de théâtre, comme celles utilisés à Ferrare dans les représentations profanes à la fin du Quattrocento.

Mais cette reproduction d'un décor de théâtre n'est pas un emprunt formel et gratuit; le caractère théâtral du tableau reflète probablement les arguments de L. B. Alberti et Pellegrino Prisciano qui voient l'origine du théâtre dans les premières fêtes religieuses et plus précisément dans les événements qui entouraient le ramassage de la Manne. En plus d'autres aspects, le côté théâtral du tableau sert à flatter le Duc d'Este car il contient une subtile comparaison entre le Duc et Moïse.

JACK WASSERMANN
Remarques sur deux statues du ''Museo dell'Opera del Duomo'' et sur la ''Porta della Mandorla'' à Florence

Contrairement à l'opinion courante, il est démontré que deux statues de la première partie du Quattrocento au Museo dell'Opera à Florence réprésentent apparemment une Annonciation, n'ont pas été exécutées pour la lunette de la ''Porta della Mandorla''. La méthode principale utilisée pour cette démonstration — l'analyse exacte des structures physiques des statues — montre que ces statues, surtout dans le cas de l'ange, ont été faites pour être vues sous un angle plus panoramique que ne le permettrait la lunette dont la disposition est à deux dimensions. De plus, elles ne forment en aucun cas un groupe narratif.

L'étude révèle ensuite les conditions minimales que devaient remplir les places d'origine des statues et elle se termine par des suppositions sur le caractère et la destinée du groupe de l'Annonciation disparu qui devait orner la lunette de la ''Porta della Mandorla'' au début de 1414.

CARLO DEL BRAVO
La conception de l'harmonie de Ribera

Le jeune Ribera a certainement eu des contacts avec Bernardo Strozzi et les Capucins.

L'iconologie dominante dans l'oeuvre de Ribera semble s'inspirer de la tradition d'«évangelismes» locaux, comme chez Luis de Molina: le thème central en est le Christ humble et clément. Cette façon de le représenter trouve ses principales sources dans l'Evangile selon Saint Matthieu et dans les écrits de Saint Augustin.

Tout en reconstituant ce contexte iconologique, il ne faut pas opposer les tableaux de Ribera où il illustre la déchéance physique à ceux où il montre la beauté. Il ne faut pas oublier la phrase augustienne sur la beauté de la Création considérée dans son ensemble comme oeuvre de Dieu. Tout se trouve à une place prédestinée et s'insère dans l'harmonie supérieure de l'univers. Si nous trouvons quelque chose d'horrible, ce n'est que le résultat de notre vision partielle et limitée qui se concentre seulement sur le détail et ne nous permet pas de concevoir tout l'ensemble.

MARCIN FABIAŃSKI
La coupole de Crémone, examinée dans son milieu de *studiolo* d'origine

L'article traite du problème de l'aspect d'origine et de la signification de la fresque de la voûte probablement peinte vers 1500 par Alessandro Pampurino pour la maison d'un prieur de Crémone, et actuellement conservée à Londres. L'exécution de cette coupole semble avoir été modifiée en considération de

l'ornementation future: de plus petites lunettes sont adaptées aux profils des Césars et une cîme floue augmente l'illusion figurative de l'*oculus*, ce qui suggère que tous les travaux ont voûte été dirigés par une seule personne. La salle où se trouvait la voûte était relativement close. La reproduction des Césars — dont certains out pu être identifiés — les muses et le côté grotesque pouvaient faire conclure à la fonction de cette pièce en tant que lieu d'études solitaires et d'activités littéraires (*studiolo-musaeum*) bien que la signification de l'*oculus* peint ne soit pas encore claire.

Zusammenfassungen:

VIVIAN B. MANN
''Neue'' Beispiele mittelalterlicher aschkenazischer Zeremonialkunst

Die frühere Literatur zur jüdischen Zeremonialkunst im mittelalterlichen Aschkenaz, dem jüdischen Siedlungsgebiet in Nordfrankreich und Deutschland, insbesonders dem Rheinland, behandelt nur eine kleine Anzahl noch vorhandener Gegenstände aus dieser Epoche. Man unterscheidet 2 Gruppen: Gegenstände, die sich durch ihre Form als ausschließlich für den jüdischen Gebrauch bestimmt erweisen, und solche, die eine Adaptation allgemein gebräuchlicher Typen darstellen. Die vorliegende Arbeit erweitert diese Sammlung indem sie ihr Material hinzufügt, das in allgemeinen Quellen publiziert oder erst kürzlich als herrenlose Schätze gefunden wurde. Einige dieser Objekte waren bisher nicht als Judaica identifiziert worden, wie beispielsweise die als ''Doppelkopf'' oder ''Doppelscheuer'' bekannten Doppelbecher. Dieser Typus war bei den aschkenazischen Juden sehr beliebt, wie auch häufige Darstellungen in hebräischen illuminierten Handschriften beweisen. Dies wird im Zusammenhang mit deutschem Brauchtum und der Herausbildung des jüdischen Hochzeitszeremoniells während des Mittelalters verständlich.

JOSEPH GUTMANN
Die Malereien der Synagoge von Dura Europos und ihr Einfluß auf die christliche und jüdische Kunst späterer Zeit

Die überraschende Entdeckung der Synagoge von Dura Europos hat die Wissenschaft mit neuen Fragen konfrontiert. Einige Forscher, vor allem jene, für die bis zu diesem Zeitpunkt die absolute Verbindlichkeit des 2. Gebotes gegolten hatte, mußten unter dem Eindruck der archäologischen Funde ihre Theorien einer Revision unterziehen. Einen weiteren Streitpunkt bildete die Frage, ob sich aus den Malereien von Dura Europos ein Einfluß auf die christliche und jüdische Kunst späterer Zeit feststellen läßt. Manche Forscher vertreten die Ansicht, daß sich eindeutig ikonographische Parallelen zu der spanischen, byzantinischen und jüdischen Kunst des Mittelalters herstellen lassen, während die vorliegende Arbeit, nach einem Vergleich der biblischen Darstellungen von Dura Europos mit jenen mittelalterlicher Kunst, eine unbestreitbare Einflußnahme ersterer auf letztere, als nicht erwiesen ansieht.

COLIN EISLER
Macht für Europas auserwählte Völker. Ein neues Blatt zur Makkabäergeschichte für Ludwig XIV. von Liévin Cruyl

In seiner Besprechung zweier früher unbekannter Zeichnungen Liévin Cruyls betont der Autor die bezeichnende Identifikation europäischer Herrscher und ihrer Staaten mit dem alten Israel. Cruyls Blatt für Ludwig XIV. zeigt eine Rekonstruktion des salomonischen Tempels, des Gebäudes, das für viele Palastbauten — so der Escorial und der Louvre — Vorbild war. Nicht nur die Monarchie rechtfertigte ihre Position indem sie sich mit dem Baum Jesse — den Ahnen Christi und Nachkommen König Davids — identifizierte; solche Assoziationen wurden auch von den jungen Handelsrepubliken hergestellt. Venedig und die Niederlande assoziierten ihr auf Prosperität ausgerichtetes Wirtschaftsleben mit dem der Juden, das weder von gewinnfeindlichen Verboten und Restriktionen noch vom Postulat noch Gütergemeinschaft, wie es in manchen frühchristlichen Glaubenssätzen enthalten ist, eingeengt wurde.

RALF BUSCH
Constantin Uhde als Synagogenarchitekt

Der Braunschweiger Architekt Constantin Uhde (1836-1905) hat 1873/74 die Braunschweiger Synagoge und das Gemeindehaus errichtet. Diese Gebäude sind überwiegend durch den romanischen Stil geprägt. Nach einem Besuch in Spanien 1888 läßt er in die von ihm errichtete Synagoge in Wol-

fenbüttel maurische Stilelemente einfließen. Diese verstärkt er 1896 in einem nicht ausgeführten Entwurf für eine Synagoge in Dortmund, um "auf den orientalischen Ursprung des Volkes und der Symbolik seiner Religion" hinzuweisen. Der Nichtjude Uhde empfindet damit einen gedachten "nationalen" Stil nach, einfühlend und historisierend in einer Zeit, als sich andernorts "neues Bauen" anschickte, nach zeitgemäßeren Stilformen zu suchen.

GABRIELLE SED-RAJNA
Der Tanz der Miriam

Die biblischen Bilderzyklen der Spätantike sind durch eine episodenweise Illustration des — um Elemente aus der jüdischen Legendenwelt bereicherten — Bibeltextes gekennzeichnet. Diese spezifische Illustration ist heute durch Monumente und Manuskripte, die aus der christlichen Kunst stammen, bekannt. Auf Wegen, deren Spuren sich nur schwer verfolgen lassen, weitergegeben, hat diese Bildtradition bis ins Mittelalter überlebt. Einige Elemente finden sich ebenfalls in den spanischen Haggadot des 14. Jahrhunderts. Ein Vergleich der Bibelzyklen der Haggadot mit jenen aus der christlichen Kunst beweist, daß letztere auf keinen Fall jüdischen Künstlern als Vorlage gedient haben können. Die biblischen Darstellung entstammen aller Wahrscheinlichkeit nach einer in jüdischen Kreisen um das Jahr 200 entstandenen Tradition, die, vielleicht über die jüdischen Gemeinden Süditaliens und Nordafrikas, im 14. Jahrhundert die Künstler der Iberischen Halbinsel erreichte. Es ist anzunehmen, daß, auf einem parallel dazu verlaufenden Übertragungsweg, einige Elemente dieser Tradition zu christlichen Künstler gelangten, deren Werke eine teilweise Rekonstruktion der antiken Tradition ermöglichen.

ZIVA AMISHAI-MAISELS
Abstraktion als ikonographische Funktion in Jankel Adlers Spätwerk

Jankel Adlers Schwanken zwischen Abstraktion und Figuration wurde bisher ausschließlich mit Hilfe stilistischer Begriffe erklärt. Die vorliegende Arbeit zeigt, daß Adlers Erfahrung des Krieges und sein Versuch, den Holocaust mit künstlerischen Mitteln zu bewältigen, die Ursache dieser Entwicklung sind. An Hand der Stationen dieser Entwicklung, die vom *Mädchen mit Schaukelspiel* (1941) zu den Hauptwerken des Jahres 1943 (*Zerstörung*, *Beginn des Aufruhrs*, *Niemandsland*) führt, wird gezeigt, wie der stilistischen Auflösung der Gestalt, die alle diese Werke kennzeichnet, ikonographische Bedeutung zukommt. Das gilt auch für Adlers Gemälde *Treblinka* (1948), das viele Rätsel aufgibt und dessen thematische und stilistische Quellen erforscht werden. Die Analyse zeigt, daß Adlers Verwendung der Abstraktion seinem Bedürfnis entsprang, einer gegenwärtigen und erschreckenden Realität aus sicherer Distanz Ausdruck zu verleihen.

KURT SCHUBERT
Die Weisen von Bne Braq in der Haggadaillustration des 18. Jahrhunderts

Die Ikonographie der Amsterdamer *Pesach Haggada* (Druck 1695; 1712) ist beeinflußt von Mathaeus Merians *Icones Biblicae*. Dafür verantwortlich war ein Christ, der in Amsterdam zum Judentum konvertierte. Die jüdischen Schreiber und Maler des 18. Jahrhunderts im deutsch-aschkenasischen Raum hielten sich vielfach an die Vorlagen der Amsterdamer Druckausgaben, die sie oft nur leicht, bisweilen aber auch stärker, variierten. Besonders schwer war es für sie bei der Darstellung der 5 Weisen von Bne Braq, die bis zum Morgen über den Auszug aus Ägypten diskutierten. Für diese Szene war die Vorlage Merians Darstellung vom Gastmahl, das Joseph seinen Brüdern in Ägypten gab. Das paßte aber ganz und gar nicht zu der Anzahl der bei Tisch Sitzenden. Meistens reduzierten die Schreiber und Maler die Anzahl, aber nur selten gelang ihnen die Reduzierung auf fünf Personen. Weitere Einzelheiten boten einigen von ihnen die Möglichkeit, die Szene an den Text der Haggada anzupassen: Heruntergebrannte Kerzen; Schüler in oder vor der Tür, die auf die morgendliche Stunde hinweisen; Bücherregal, um die bei Tisch Sitzenden als Gelehrte zu definieren. Im Gegensatz zu den deutsch-aschkenasischen Schreibern und Malern waren die italienischen von den venezianischen Drucken von 1599 und 1609 beeinflußt, die fallweise auch von den deutsch-aschkenasischen Illustratoren benützt wurden.

URSULA SCHUBERT
Die rabbinische Vorstellung von Schaubrottisch und die Bibel von S. Isidoro de Leon, a. d. 960 (Real Colegiata, cod. 2, fol. 50)

Im Gegensatz zur Darstellung der Schaubrote im *Codex Amiatinus* (Northumbrien, 7. Jh.) in zwei Reihen nebeneinander wurden in hebräischen Handschriften des Spätmittelalters in Spanien die Schaubrote auf dem Schaubrottisch in zwei Reihen übereinander angeordnet. Die Textgrundlage für eine solche Darstellungsweise boten aber nicht die entsprechenden Kapitel in Exodus und Leviticus sondern vor allem die diesbezüglichen Überlegungen der rabbinischen Gelehrten in der Mischna, Menahot XI. Eine völlig unerwartete Parallele zur Darstellung der auf dem Schaubrottisch übereinander angeordneten Schaubrote findet sich in der Bibel von S. Isidoro de Leon a.d. 960 und den beiden erhaltenen Kopien dieser Handschrift von 1162 und Anfang 13. Jh. Der in diesen Handschriften zusammen mit den Kultgegenständen innerhalb des Heiligtums wiedergegebene Hohepriester Aaron ist überraschenderweise im selben Zusammenhang sowohl in der Synagoge von Dura Europos (Mitte 3. Jh. n. Chr.) als auch im *Regensburger Pentateuch* (Bayern, um 1300) ebenfalls in hohepriesterlicher Kleidung dargestellt. In der zuletzt erwähnten Handschrift hat außerdem der Schaubrottisch dasselbe irreführende Aussehen wie in der christlichen Bibel von 960, wo er als ''labrum'' bezeichnet und daher zweifelsfrei mißverstanden ist. Solche ''Mißverständnisse'' zusammen mit der ungewöhnlichen Übereinanderstapelung der Schaubrote über dem Tisch, wofür nur das rabbinische Schrifttum die Voraussetzung bot, legen die Vermutung nahe, daß für die — für die Bibel von 960 vermutete — Vorlage aus dem 5. Jh. zumindest für die Darstellung fol. 50r eine spätantike Bibelillustration jüdischer Provenienz herangezogen wurde.

PHILIPP P. FEHL
Der Stadttempel der Juden zu Wien: Kindheitserinnerungen und Geschichte

Der Artikel ist ein Versuch, die Architektur der ältesten Wiener Synagoge, des klassizistischen Stadttempels von Josef Kornhäusel zu verlebendigen, und zwar im Lichte des traditionellen Gottesdienstes und der spirituellen Hoffnungen der Tempelgründer. Der Autor verbrachte seine Jugend zu einem gewissen Maße im Schutze dieser Tradition. Er sucht in seiner Erinnerung um Zugang zu finden zu den mit der Gründung des Tempels verbundenen historischen Daten, und um den Zusammenhang zwischen dem Stil der Tempelarchitektur und der religiösen Funktion des Gebäudes zu untersuchen. Die Aufgaben und Probleme eines persönlich involvierten Autors bei der Geschichtsschreibung, insbesondere der Kunstgeschichtsschreibung sind von besonderer Bedeutung.

Im Anhang zu der Studie befinden sich die ersten Statuten des Stadttempels und Isaak Noah Mannheimers Vorwort zu einer Sammlung seiner Kanzelreden, in welchen er, in einem der Tempelarchitektur vergleichbaren erhabenen Stil, die Absichten und Hoffnungen der Tempelgründer erläutert.

MOSHE BARASCH
Überlegungen zu Grabsteinen: Kindheitserinnerungen

Der Artikel ist der Ornamentik einiger Grabsteine des 18./19. Jahrhunderts auf dem jüdischen Friedhof von Czernowitz, der Geburtsstadt des Autors, gewidmet. Da Grabsteine das Produkt einer sozial orientierten Kunst sind, werden die Verhältnisse, unter denen sie entstanden sind, einer näherer Betrachtung unterzogen; im besonderen gelingt es dem Autor einzelne Steinmetze zu identifizieren und ihre Ausbildung zu rekonstruieren. Die künstlerische Ausgestaltung der Grabsteine wird besprochen, wobei besonderes Interesse der Inschrift und dem Dekor gilt.

Der Autor kommt zum dem Schluß, daß in der Deutung dieser Grabsteine der Schlüssel zu Verständnis für das komplexe und vielfältige Leben eines Gemeinwesens liegt, das eingebettet war in eine unwiederbringlich verlorene Kultur, welcher noch die ihr gebührende Würdigung zuteil werden soll.

JOSEPH MANCA
Renaissancetheater und hebräisches Ritual in Ercole de' Robertis *Die Mannalese*

Die Szenerie von Ercole de' Robertis Gemälde *Die Mannalese* erinnert eindeutig an ein Bühnenbild, wie es für weltliche Aufführungen in Ferrara zu Ende des Quattrocento üblich war. Bei dieser Wiedergabe einer Theaterszenerie handelt es sich aber um mehr als um eine sinnlose, formale Anleihe; es erweist sich, daß der theatralische Charakter des Gemäldes aller Warscheinlichkeit nach eine Wiedergabe der Argumente L. B. Albertis und Pellegrino Priscianos ist, die den Ursprung des Theaters auf primitive religiöse Feiern und spezifischer, auf die Ereignisse, die die Mannalese begleiteten, zurückführen. Neben anderen Aspekten dient die Theatralik des Gemäldes dazu, Herzog Ercole d'Este zu schmeicheln, indem feinsinnig der Vergleich zwischen dem Herzog und Moses gezogen wird.

JACK WASSERMANN
Bemerkungen zu zwei Statuen im Museo dell'Opera del Duomo und zur Porta della Mandorla in Florenz

Im Gegensatz zu einer weitverbreiteten Meinung wird nachgewiesen, daß zwei aus dem frühen Quattrocento stammende Statuen im Museo dell'Opera in Florenz, die anscheinend eine Verkündigung darstellen, nicht für die Lünette der Porta della Mandorla angefertigt worden waren. Die für diese Darlegung angewendete Hauptmethode, die genaue Überprüfung der physikalischen Strukturen der Statuen, zeigt, daß diese, insbesondere die Statue des Engels, mehr für eine übersichtlichere Betrachtung gedacht waren, als die zweidimensional angeordnete Lünette es zulassen würde, und daß sie in keinem Fall eine narrative Gruppe bilden. Im folgenden enthüllt der Aufsatz die Minimalbedingungen, die von den ursprünglichen Aufstellungs-

orten der Statuen zu erfüllen waren, und er schließt mit Vermutungen über den Charakter und das Schicksal der verschollenen Verkündigungs-Gruppe, die sich in der Lünette der Porta della Mandorla anfangs 1414 befunden hatte.

CARLO DEL BRAVO
Riberas harmonisches Konzept

Der junge Ribera hat wahrscheinlich Kontakte zu Bernardo Strozzi und den Kapuzinern gehabt.

Die dominante Ikonologie in Riberas Werk scheint sich von einer Tradition lokaler ''Evangelismen'', wie bei Luis de Molina, herzuleiten, mit der Darstellung des milden und demütigen Christus als thematischem Schwerpunkt; eine Betrachtungsweise für die das Matthäusevangelium und die Schriften des hl. Augustinus die Hauptquellen bilden.

Bei der Herstellung dieses ikonologischen Zusammenhanges darf man Riberas Bilder in denen er physischen Verfall veranschaulicht, nicht gegensätzlich zu jenen sehen, die das Schöne darstellen; eingedenk des Augustinischen Satzes von der Schönheit der Schöpfung in ihrer Gesamtheit, da sie ein Werk Gottes ist. Alles steht an seinem vorbestimmten Platz und fügt sich in die höhere Harmonie des Universums ein. Erscheint uns etwas als häßlich, so ist das nur ein Resultat unserer beschränkten Sichtweise, die sich auf das Einzelne konzentriert und dabei das Ganze übersieht.

MARCIN FABIAŃSKI
Das Cremoneser Gewölbefresko im Kontext seiner ursprünglichen Studiolo-Umgebung

Der Aufsatz beschäftigt sich mit dem Problem des ursprünglichen Aussehens und der Bedeutung des Gewölbefreskos, das vermutlich von Alessandro Pampurino um 1500 für das Haus eines Priors in Cremona gemalt wurde, und das sich jetzt in London befindet. Die Ausführung dieser Kuppel scheint im Hinblick auf ihre künftige Ausschmückung modifiziert worden zu sein: Kleinere Lünetten werden den Profilen der Cäsaren gerecht und ein weicher Gipfel steigert den bildlichen Illusionismus des Oculus, was vermuten läßt, daß das ganze Unternehmen von einer Person geleitet wurde. Der Raum, zu welchem das Gewölbe gehörte, war relativ abgeschlossen. Die Darstellungen der Cäsaren — einige konnten identifiziert werden —, die Musen und das Groteske entsprachen der Funktion dieses Raumes als Ort einsamer Studien und literarischer Aktivitäten (*studiolo-musaeum*), wobei die Bedeutung des gemalten Oculus unklar bleibt.

Information about the authors — nota informativa sugli autori del presente numero — über die Autoren — les auteurs:

VIVIAN B. MANN   Curator of Judaica, The Jewish Museum, New York

JOSEPH GUTMANN   Professor of Art History, Wayne State University, Department of Art and Art History, Detroit, Michigan, USA

COLIN EISLER   Professor of Art History, New York University, Institute of Fine Arts, New York

RALF BUSCH   Director of the Helms-Museum, Hamburg, West Germany

GABRIELLE SED-RAJNA   Art Historian at the Institut de Recherche et d'Histoire des Textes, Centre Felix Grat, CNRS, Paris, France

ZIVA AMISHAI-MAISELS   Professor of Art History, The Hebrew University of Jerusalem, Israel

KURT SCHUBERT   Director of the Institut für Judaistik, Universität Wien (Vienna), Austria

URSULA SCHUBERT   Art Historian, Institut für Judaistik, Universität Wien (Vienna), Austria

PHILIPP P. FEHL   Professor of Art History, University of Illinois, Champaign-Urbana, Illinois President of the International Survey of Jewish Monuments

MOSHE BARASCH   Professor of Art History, The Hebrew University of Jerusalem, Israel

JOSEPH MANCA   Art Historian, Seton Hall University

JACK WASSERMAN   Professor of Art History, Temple University, Philadelphia, USA

CARLO DEL BRAVO   Professor of Art History, University of Florence, Italy

MARCIN FABIAŃSKI   Art Historian, Jagellonian University, Cracow, Poland

Photographic sources:

artibus
et
historiae

PREVIOUS ISSUES

artibus et historiae nr 7 (IV), 1983

John Monfasani – A Description of the Sistine Chapel Under Pope Sixtus IV
Elise Goodman-Soellner – The Poetic Iconography of Veronese's Cycle of Love
Erasmus Weddigen – Zur Wiederkehr eines Unbekannten: Jacopo Tintoretto
Zygmunt Waźbiński – Adriano de Vries e la scuola di scultura in Praga. Contributo alla diffusione dell'academismo fiorentino in Europa alla fine del XVI e inizio XVII secolo
Carlo Del Bravo – Sul significato della luce nel Caravaggio e in Gianlorenzo Bernini
John F. Moffitt – «Le Roi à la ciasse»?: Kings, Christian Knights, and Van Dyck's Singular «Dismounted Equestrian-Portrait» of Charles I
William L. Barcham – The Chappella Sagredo in San Francesco della Vigna
Lubomír Konečný – Überlegungen zu einem Stilleben von Pieter Boel (Samt einigen Hypothesen zum Grafen von Arundel und W. Hollar)
Werner Hofmann – Picasso's *Guernica* in its Historical Context

artibus et historiae nr 8 (IV), 1983

David Alan Brown – Raphael's *Small Cowper Madonna and Madonna of the Meadow*: Their Technique and Leonardo Sources
Russell Panczenko – Cultura umanistica di Gentile da Fabriano
Augusto Gentili – Per Lorenzo Lotto e i suoi contesti storici: due episodi ridocumentati, tra polemica e progetto
Patrick M. de Winter – Castle and Town Residences of Philip the Bold, Duke of Burgundy (1364-1404)
Maurizio Marini – Equivoci del caravaggismo 2: A) Appunti sulla tecnica del «naturalismo» secentesco, tra Caravaggio e «Manfrediana methodus». B) Caravaggio e i suoi «doppi». Il problema delle possibili collaborazioni
Alicja Helman – The Present-Day Meaning of a Work of Art

artibus et historiae nr 9 (V), 1984

George Kubler – Les sources écrites de la cosmogonie andine
Adam S. Labuda – Wort und Bild im späten Mittelalter am Beispiel des Breslauer Barbara-Altars (1447)
W. R. Rearick – Observation on the Venetian Cinquecento in the Light of the Royal Academy Exhibition
Alessandra Ottieri – Laguna di Venezia, mare di Galilea: la *Vocazione dei figli di Zebedèo* di Marco Basaiti
Saul Levine – Michelangelo's Marble *David* and the Last Bronze *David*: the Drawings
Christoph Stöcker – Dürer, Celtis und der falsche Bischof Achatius. Zur Ikonographie von Dürer *Marter der Zehntausend*
Elizabeth Hutton Turner – Who is in the Brothel of Avignon? A case for Context
Karsten Harries – Space, Place, und Ethos: Reflections on the Ethical Function of Architecture

artibus et historiae nr 10 (V), 1984

Jan Bialostocki – A New Look at Rembrandt Iconography
Julius S. Held – A Rembrandt «Theme»
Margaret Deutsch Carroll – Rembrandt's *Aristotle*: Exemplary Beholder
Cecil Gould – Raphael's *Double Portrait* in the Louvre: an Identification for the Second Figure
Norman E. Land – On the Poetry of Giovanni Bellini's *Sacred Allegory*
Erasmus Weddigen – Jacopo Tintoretto und die Musik
Milly Heyd – Dali's *Metamorphosis of Narcissus* Reconsidered
Dieter Wuttke – Die Emigration der Kulturwissenschaftlichen Bibliothek Warburg und die Anfänge des Universitätsfaches Kunstgeschichte in Großbritannien
Mieczysław Porębski – Les avant-gardes

artibus et historiae nr 11 (VI), 1985

Carlo Del Bravo — Quadri a lume di notte. Georges de La Tour e Sant'Agostino
Józef Grabski — On Seicento Painting in Naples: Some Observations on Bernardo Cavallino, Artemisia Gentileschi and Others
Dieter Wuttke — Humanismus als integrative Kraft. Die Philosophia des deutschen «Erzhumanisten» Conrad Celtis. Eine ikonologische Studie zu programmatischer Graphik Dürers und Burgkmairs
Edward J. Olszewski — Distortions, Shadows, and Conventions in Sixteenth Century Italian Art
Jindřich Chalupecký — Marcel Duchamp: a Re-evaluation
Teresa Grzybkowska — The Pseudojapanese in «Young Poland» Art
Pietro Montani — Scritti sull'arte di S. M. Eisenstein. Nota introduttiva
S. M. Eisenstein — Scritti sull'arte. Il montaggio in pittura (su Serov, Repin e altri)

artibus et historiae nr 12 (VI), 1985

Benedict Nicolson — Orazio Gentileschi and Giovanni Antonio Sauli
Zygmunt Waźbiński — San Luca che dipinge la Madonna all'Accademia di Roma: un «pastiche» zuccariano nella maniera di Raffaello?
Judith Dundas — A Titian Enigma
Christiane L. Joost-Gaugier — Poggio and Visual Tradition: Uomini Famosi in Classical Literary Description
Carlo Del Bravo — Dal Pontormo al Bronzino
Luba Freedman — Rembrandt's Portrait of Jan Six
John F. Moffitt — Fighting Forms: The Fate of the Animals. The Occultist Origins of Franz Marc's «Farbentheorie»
Karl Clausberg — Konventionelle und individuelle Physiognomik zur Zeit Heinrichs des Löwen. Ein Beitrag zum mittelalterlichen Expressionismus-Problem
Rachel Wischnitzer — Picasso's Guernica. A Matter of Metaphor

artibus et historiae nr 13 (VII), 1986

Susan Koslow — The Curtain-Sack: A Newly Discovered Incarnation Motif in Rogier van der Weyden's Columba Annunciation
Diane Cole Ahl — Benozzo Gozzoli's Frescoes of the Life of Saint Augustine in San Gimignano: Their Meaning in Context
Augusto Gentili — Nuovi documenti e contesti per l'ultimo Carpaccio. I: L'Incontro di Gioacchino e Anna per San Francesco in Treviso
Cecil Gould — The Earliest Dated Titian?
Caterina Limentari Virdis — Italiam versus negociorum suorum causa. Osservazioni su Rubens e i suoi modelli in Italia
Maria Rzepińska — Tenebrism in Baroque Painting and Its Ideological Background
Franco Bernabei — Venezia roman(t)ica e gotica
Joyce Brodsky — Delacroix's Le Lever, Cézanne's Interior with Nude, Picasso's Les Demoiselles d'Avignon, and the Genre of the Erotic Nude
Jindřich Chalupecký — Les ready-made de Duchamp et la théorie du symbole
Roelof van Straten — Panofsky and ICONCLASS

artibus et historiae nr 14 (VII), 1986

Sarah Blake Wilk — Donatello's Dovizia as an Image of Florentine Political Propaganda
Timothy Verdon — Donatello and the Theater: Stage Space and Projected Space in the San Lorenzo Pulpits
Rona Goffen — Bellini, S. Giobbe and Altar Egos
Arthur K. Wheelock, Jr. — St. Praxedis: New Light on the Early Career of Vermeer
James Elkins — Two Conceptions of the Human Form: Bernard Siegfried Albinus and Andreas Vesalius
Alicja Kępińska — Chaos as a Value in the Mythological Background of Action Painting
Giuseppina Dal Canton — Redon e la melanconia
Philipp P. Fehl — Hermeticism and Art: Emblem and Allegory in the Work of Bernini

artibus et historiae nr 15 (VIII), 1987

artibus et historiae nr 16 (VIII), 1987